THE MONGOL CONQUESTS IN WORLD HISTORY

GLOBALITIES
Series editor: Jeremy Black

GLOBALITIES is a series which reinterprets world history in
a concise yet thoughtful way, looking at major issues over large
time-spans and political spaces; such issues can be political, ecological,
scientific, technological or intellectual. Rather than adopting a narrow
chronological or geographical approach, books in the series are
conceptual in focus yet present an array of historical data to justify
their arguments. They often involve a multi-disciplinary approach,
juxtaposing different subject-areas such as economics and religion
or literature and politics.

In the same series

China to Chinatown:
Chinese Food in the West
J.A.G. Roberts

Cinemas of the World
James Chapman

Faith and Sword:
A Short History of
Christian–Muslim Conflict
Alan G. Jamieson

Geopolitics and Globalization
in the Twentieth Century
Brian W. Blouet

The Global Financial System,
1750–2000
Larry Allen

A History of Language
Steven Roger Fischer

A History of Reading
Steven Roger Fischer

A History of Writing
Steven Roger Fischer

Landscape and History since 1500
Ian D. Whyte

Mining in World History
Martin Lynch

Monarchies 1000–2000
W. M. Spellman

Navies in Modern World History
Lawrence Sondhaus

Sovereign City:
The City-State through History
Geoffrey Parker

Why Wars Happen
Jeremy Black

THE MONGOL CONQUESTS
IN WORLD HISTORY

Timothy May

REAKTION BOOKS

For my wonderful and beautiful wife, Michaeline,
without whom I would still be writing this book

Published by Reaktion Books Ltd
33 Great Sutton Street
London EC1V 0DX, UK
www.reaktionbooks.co.uk

First published 2012

Printed and bound in Great Britain
by MPG Books Group

British Library Cataloguing in Publication Data
May, Timothy Michael.
The Mongol conquests in world history. – (Globalities)
1. Mongols – History – To 1500.
I. Title II. Series
950.2-dc22

ISBN 978 1 86189 867 8

CONTENTS

INTRODUCTION

When asked to write this book by the editor of the Globalities series, Jeremy Black, I did not hesitate, as the Mongols always seem to have at least a cameo appearance, if not a starring role, in the discussion of world history. The title of the project could easily have been changed to *The Mongol Empire Is World History* although it would look odd on the spine of a book. I can think of no period other than perhaps the past 200 years in which the world was more interconnected. The conquests of Alexander? Despite a brief foray to the Indus and the Libyan Desert, the Alexandrian world excluded much of Asia and virtually all of Africa. The Roman Empire? Largely a Mediterranean event except for the more rustic provinces to the north and a few merchants dealing with India. Perhaps the Crusades? Again, primarily a Mediterranean event, although more of Europe and North Africa was involved, but it did not impact upon China or India. The Age of Exploration is always a good place to begin, but without the Mongol Empire would Columbus have sailed? After all, he was trying to reach the Great Khan in China. In short, the Mongol Empire is the very definition of world history. True, the Mongols did not have a huge impact on Africa or the New World, but for the Eurasian landmass no event or empire had a larger impact in history. The Mongols brought military innovation, international commerce, the spread of world religions and the diffusion of technology and ideas together in one crucible – the Mongol conquests. After the dust settled, the world had irrefutably changed and could never return to the way it once was.

In the 1970s John Andrew Boyle, the great historian of the Mongol Empire, coined the term 'Mongol World Empire' – and he hit the nail on the head.[1] It is unknown if Boyle considered the Mongols through the lens of world history, but he clearly saw the Mongols as an empire that dominated the medieval world and could not be viewed in a strictly regional sense. In his preface to Boyle's *The Mongol World Empire*, Owen

Lattimore noted that in order to properly understand the place of the Mongols in world history, 'we need to bring into better balance the enormously rich and Middle Asian sources'.[2] Lattimore alludes to a basic issue of the study of the Mongol Empire – the number of languages involved in the sources often leads to examining the Mongols in a regional rather than a holistic or world perspective. At the same time one should not only consider the Mongol World Empire in a geographical but also a temporally transcendent sense. The Mongol moment is truly a pivotal and perhaps an axial era in history. In many ways it is the dividing point between the pre-modern and the modern ages.

This idea of the Mongol Empire as the dividing point, or perhaps even the beginning of modern history, is buttressed by the opinion of esteemed scholar of East Asia Arthur Waldron. In his introduction to Bertold Spuler's classic work *The Mongol Period* (1994), the middle volume of Spuler's trilogy on the history of the Muslim world, Waldron wrote:

> Where should one begin the study of modern history? The soundest answer is probably with the Mongols. The great states of Eurasia today – China, Russia, and India, as well as most of the Middle East – all were once incorporated into Mongol empires, and changed by that experience. The modern history of those states, moreover, began when the Mongol empires ended then the component parts reconstituted themselves, emerging as successor states that, although independent, nevertheless bore an unmistakable Mongol stamp. Study the Mongol empires and their gradual breakdown, then, and you have the basis for an integrated understanding of contemporary Eurasia.[3]

It is difficult to dispute Waldron's contention. Indeed, it is only by investigating the Mongol Empire and the changes that it brought to the Eurasian continent that we truly see an integrated Eurasia and indeed an integrated world. While trade routes have connected cultures and civilizations for hundreds of years, the view of the world by a particular civilization was compartmentalized. The Romans possessed a clear view of the Roman world as did the empires of Iran and the many dynasties of China of theirs, but their vision of the world outside their respective borders remained murky. Although knowledge of the outside and the Other is always elusive, with the Mongol Empire unprecedented numbers of travellers, merchants, missionaries and others criss-crossed the Eurasian landmass and even beyond. Granted, many other regions remained outside the empire, but the ramifications of the advent of the Mongol Empire created conditions and events that led not only to an integrated Eurasia but an integrated world, which, of course, is what this volume will demonstrate.

The Mongol Empire's importance in world history is most apparent in two fashions. The first is through its immense size at its peak, making it the largest contiguous empire in history – approximately 7.5 million sq km (14 million sq miles), or roughly the size of the continent of Africa. Although it became divided politically, nonetheless a considerable amount of interaction existed across Eurasia and beyond through Mongol domains, no matter how one defines them.

The second is shown by the sheer number of languages used in the sources related to the study of the Mongol Empire. Perhaps the most important are Chinese and Persian, based on the number of sources in these languages, but the sources also include Mongolian, Russian, Old Slavonic, Arabic, Latin, Old French, Japanese, Italian, Armenian, Georgian, Old Uighur, Tibetan and others. Few people can master all of these. Added to this is the problem of transliterating names from a wide variety of scripts, potentially ending up with a plethora of spellings for any given name. Take Khubilai, for instance. Qubilai, Khubilai, Kublai and Kubla have all been used, and are acceptable depending on which system of transliteration and language one uses. Most scholars have no difficulty keeping track of who is who, but a novice to the history of the Mongol Empire can easily be overwhelmed by the names. Other problems resulting from the variety of languages will be discussed later.

Yet evidence of the Mongols' importance to world history is in many ways best demonstrated by the problem of studying the Mongols – where does one begin? Indeed, where does one even place them in Asia? Certainly they were an Asian people and the bulk of the empire existed in Asia, but does Asia include the Middle East? And what of the European domains? The Mongols' importance to Europe, and by extension to world history, is aptly demonstrated by David Morgan's classic and still standard introduction to the study of the Mongols, *The Mongols* (1986). Indeed, *The Mongols* is actually a part of Blackwell's Peoples of Europe series.

When I received my first copy of this magnificent book as an undergraduate, I remember being perplexed by this odd placement. After all, a quick glance at any picture of the Mongols makes it quite clear that they were not from Europe. Although Morgan adeptly explains the reasoning for the inclusion of *The Mongols*, the simple idea that the editors of the series wanted to include the Mongols in the series indicates more than a quirky inclusion or that a Peoples of Asia series did not yet exist (although it does now). The place of *The Mongols* in the series should tell the reader that despite being quite removed from Europe the extent of the Mongol Empire greatly influenced events in Europe.

The fact of the matter is that the Mongol Empire can be examined as part of Europe, the Middle East, East Asia, central Eurasia and even south Asia. Yet in doing so students and scholars risk missing the forest for the trees. Certainly the empire's impact on each region has been immense, but ultimately the Mongol Empire was a huge continental entity. Common threads connected these regions and to ignore the fact that events in the Middle East impacted events in the European or East Asian sections leads to an underestimation of the complex reality of the empire. In short, to fully understand the Mongol Empire it must be viewed as a whole. Certainly regional perspectives are useful but until the late thirteenth century the empire was still very much a single entity in a variety of ways even if not politically.

HISTORIOGRAPHY AND PROBLEMS

As with any historical field, the historiography of the Mongol Empire has its problems. As mentioned above, the first and foremost issue is the abundant number of languages used in the primary documents. A single scholar could not hope to master all of them, although there are many scholars who know a sizeable number. Most of the earlier scholars on the Mongol Empire did not start with the notion of study of the Mongol Empire as being a part of world history.

Yet most scholars of the Mongol Empire began their careers in a different field and slowly but inexorably became Mongolists. A scholar of Islamic history may be trained in Arabic and Persian but is unlikely to learn Chinese or Russian, and a scholar of medieval China is unlikely to learn Armenian or Georgian. Their research is tied to their respective regional fields. Thus many scholars became regional specialists of a branch of the empire, usually focused on the four divisions of the post-1260 empire: the Empire of the Great Khan or Yuan Empire (being East Asia, including Mongolia and Tibet); the Chaghatayid Khanate (roughly central Asia); the Jochid or Kipchak Khanate, popularly known as the Golden Horde (from the Carpathians in the west into Kazakhstan in the east); the Ilkhanate or Persia (the Middle East from modern Turkey into Afghanistan, but excluding Greater Syria and Arabia).

While these scholars did dabble with larger concepts of connecting the empire, much of their work was hampered by lack of access to other documentary evidence due to the lack of linguistic skills. Even today scholars work with the materials in their research languages and then augment them with any available in translation from languages they do not know. Unfortunately what was translated was often fragmentary. This by no means diminishes the importance of this generation of scholars' work. Many pieces have become seminal for the study of the Mongol Empire and have led to a better understanding of the post-1260 empire than the empire at its height.

The historiography of the study of the Mongol Empire is slowly changing due to the efforts of a number of scholars. A few recent commentaries on the historiography have been published, so I will not review it here.[4] I would, however, like to bring attention to a few works by one author that have been crucial in transforming the Mongol Empire from regional studies to a more holistic approach and placing the empire in the context of world history. Thomas Allsen, arguably the greatest scholar of the Mongol Empire, successfully mastered a number of languages and has approached the empire from a more integrated perspective. His classic work *Mongol Imperialism* (1987) examined the policies of the fourth Mongol khan, Möngke (r. 1251–1259), and established how the Mongol administration tied the empire together in a coherent manner. This was followed by *Commodity and Exchange in the Mongol Empire* (1997), which demonstrated the importance of Islamic textiles in the economics and court life of the Mongol Empire. *Culture and Conquest in Mongol Eurasia* (2001) has become a standard work in classes on the Mongol Empire since it illustrates the wide variety of goods and ideas that traversed Eurasia due to Mongol influence. His many articles and other works continue to examine the empire as a complete entity and not from a regional perspective. Allsen's fourth book, *The Royal Hunt in Eurasian History* (2006), while not exclusively on the Mongol Empire, focused on hunting traditions among royal elites. Through this Allsen makes a significant contribution to our understanding of world history. Needless to say, much of the emphasis does rest on the Mongols and how they influenced other areas with their traditions and also their commonalities with other royal elites.

A second problem is the issue of Mongolia and its connection to the Mongol Empire. Historically it is connected to the history of East

Asia, yet the standard definition of East Asia, as posited by Jonathan K. Fairbank and others, includes heavy Chinese influence, particularly in terms of Confucian political theory and ethics. It is safe to say that Mongolia in all its history, even under Qing domination (1691–1911), eluded Confucian ethics and philosophy as a major influence in culture and society. Geographically it is Northeast Asia, but this is a fairly new designation and it is unclear as to what it means beyond geography. Mongolia has also been a satellite of the former Soviet Union, becoming the second communist state in history in 1921. Yet grants, think tanks and so on that are tied to studying the states of the former Soviet Union rarely include Mongolia. Although being tied economically, academically, socially, militarily and politically to the Soviet Union (and then Russia), Mongolia, for a variety of reasons, was never annexed and thus was not part of the Soviet Union. Yet at the same time it is excluded from East Asia. So where does it fit? The terms Inner Asia and central Eurasia perhaps fit it best, but these are vague geographical terms that are difficult to define coherently.

Despite all these concerns, the study of the Mongol Empire is world history and vice versa – otherwise one could argue that there would be little impetus for this book. A brief survey of some of the most well-known and used primary sources clearly demonstrates the place of the Mongol Empire in world history. Indeed, the authors of these histories seem to break from a mould of regional chronicles or histories and try to place their concerns in a larger context. Certainly many local or regional sources exist but the major sources do attempt to understand the Mongol Empire in a larger context.

A favourite source in world history classes and for the study of the Mongol Empire is *The Travels of Marco Polo*. It is safe to say that Marco Polo remains the most famous traveller in history, even if Ibn Battuta, the North African judge and traveller, covered more miles, and more people have heard of Marco Polo than have read his book. Still, the famed Venetian travelled throughout the Mongol Empire and beyond, perhaps even to Zanzibar. And even if he did not make it to the latter, he heard and saw more of the world than virtually all of his contemporaries. So fantastic were his stories that most refused to believe them and, as he lay upon his deathbed, friends and family, perhaps fearing for his soul, urged him to recant. Polo could only reply, 'I have not told half of what I saw.'[5]

Although many criticisms have been levelled at what Marco Polo did not mention, the majority of scholars read his writings with confidence that there is plenty of evidence that he did indeed go to China and beyond and that what he omits must be considered in the context of his social circles – the Mongol elite.[6] This cannot be overlooked. As Stephen Haw, Peter Jackson, Igor De Rachewiltz and David Morgan all demonstrate, Marco Polo looked at the world from the perspective of a Mongol, or at least as one of their employees. While his status was not quite as great as he hinted at in his writings, he still served the court of the Khubilai Khan and provides plenty of information that was new to Europeans from the perspective of a merchant and government functionary of the Mongol Empire.

Other European sources include a few crucial travel accounts from Franciscan monks, John of Plano Carpini and William of Rubruck. Plano Carpini was sent by Pope Innocent IV to gather intelligence on the Mongols shortly after the Mongol invasion of Poland and Hungary. Plano Carpini provides us with an insight into how terrifying the Mongols truly were to those outside the empire, a view of the world from a rather parochial monk – this being his first venture beyond Western Christendom. William of Rubruck arrived at Karakorum during the reign of Möngke Khan. While this also provides a snapshot of the world beyond Christendom, William of Rubruck almost joyfully embraces the experience and tries new things such as drinking *kumiss*, fermented mare's milk and the Mongol beverage of choice – which he enjoys – and also engages in religious debates.

Moving eastward, there is 'Ala al-Din Ata Malik Juvaini's aptly named *Ta'rîkh-i-Jahân-Gusha* (*The History of the World Conqueror*). Juvaini, another employee of the Mongol court, this time that of Möngke's brother, Hülegü, wrote his history in Baghdad. It includes not only histories of the Mongols up to 1256, ending with the destruction of the Ismailis, also popularly called the Assassins, but also histories of the Khwarazmian Empire and the Empire of Kara Khitai, two states absorbed by the Mongols. Having access to key members of the government as well as his father, who also served the Mongols, Juvaini gives us a vivid picture of Mongol court activities. His work is much stronger on events in the Middle East than elsewhere, but there is still a clear effort to show how policy dictated in Mongolia affected southwest Asia. Unfortunately his work stops in 1256 and politely ignores the Mongol destruction of Baghdad, where Juvaini later served as the governor.

A source completely hostile to the Mongol Empire was written by an individual who not only survived the Mongol onslaught but also wrote his work from the relative safety of the Sultanate of Delhi. As a refugee, Minhaj Siraj Juzjani wrote his history of the Mongols from the perspective of trying to make sense of the Islamic world, particularly the various Muslim dynasties. Nonetheless, a sizeable section of his work is devoted to the Mongols and the implications of their arrival. He also provides additional information on the Mongols in the appropriate section of particular Muslim dynasties that had encounters with them.

Another major work, and arguably the most important, is Fazullah Rashid al-Din's *Jami' al-Tawarikh* (*Compendium of Chronicles*). While Rashid al-Din focuses on the Mongol Empire, his intent was to compile the history of the world and include as many areas as he could. While he ultimately failed in this endeavour, we have a nuanced study of the Mongol Empire that uses long-lost sources and corroborates much of what appears in other sources as well as shedding light on them. Furthermore, it gives us glimpses into how Rashid al-Din and perhaps even the Mongol court viewed regions beyond the pale of their control, such as those of the Franks or Western Europe. This work is now available in translation by William Thackston and has altered, to some extent, how those who worked on the eastern portion of the Mongol Empire view it.

Although many other sources also exist in Persian, Arabic sources are of great importance. As the ample bibliography and research of the Mamluk historian Reuven Amitai demonstrates, those Arabic sources emanating from the Mamluk Sultanate yield rich results for the Mongol Empire. This is true not only for the Ilkhanate, the closest Mongol territory to the Mamluks, but also for other regions of the Mongol Empire including the pre-dissolution era. Of particular importance is the work of ibn Fadl Allah, an encyclopaedist who, in his *Kitab Masalik al-Absar wa Mamalik al-Amsar*, devoted a significant section to the Mongol Empire from the rise of Chinggis Khan to his own era. Other authors include Ahmad ibn 'Abd al-Wahhab al-Nuwayri, Muhammad ibn Ahmad al-Dhahabi, Baybars al-Mansuri and Ahmad ibn 'Ali al-Maqrizi. Although outsiders, the Mamluk authors provide a glimpse of the Mongol Empire from a hostile yet very engaged and knowledgeable perspective. In addition it is often clear that they not only read their peers, but also the works of authors in the Mongol Empire.

While technically not a Mamluk author, Ibn Battuta's work is invaluable. The scholar from Morocco travelled throughout much of the Islamic world, which by the fourteenth century included all of the

Mongol Empire except the territories of the Yuan Empire in East Asia. Nonetheless, Ibn Battuta even ventured there as well as territories neighbouring the Mongols such as the Mamluk Sultanate and the Sultanate of Delhi. Thus in Ibn Battuta we have the rare informant who travelled not only throughout the empire but also served in positions, usually as a *qadi* or judge, in states hostile to the Mongols. His perspective is unique and valuable. However, as with all sources, one must read Ibn Battuta with caution. As scholar Ross Dunn has demonstrated in his narrative commentary on Ibn Battuta's travels, there are times when it appears that Ibn Battuta recycled work from previous authors – a frequent occurrence in many medieval sources.

Arab authors prior to the rise of the Mamluk Sultanate also remain important sources. Ibn al-Athir, who wrote the mammoth chronicle known as the *al-Kamil fi al-Tarikh*, provides one of the most descriptive images of the Mongol invasion of the Khwarazmian Empire. Although Ibn al-Athir wrote from the safety of Mosul and acquired much of his information from refugees, much of what he wrote is similar to that of the aforementioned Juzjani, his contemporary in Delhi. Indeed, the overwhelming dread conveyed in Ibn al-Athir's work is pervasive and clearly demonstrates why the Mongols were viewed as a punishment sent by God.

While most of the sources are written by individuals working for the Mongols, refugees or observers in hostile, yet distant, states, Muhammad al-Nasawi is different. He was in the employ of the Khwarazmian government, which suffered destruction with the Mongol invasion of 1219. Thus from Nasawi we gain a rich history of the pre-invasion Khwarazmian state, the devastation of the Mongols and life as a refugee while he served as the secretary for the last Khwarazmshah, Jalal al-Din, who attempted to establish a bulwark against the Mongols in the ashes of his father's empire. Nasawi gives the reader a window to view the rise and fall of one empire while witnessing the ascension of another. At the same time the shortfalls of one who sought to stop the Mongols are revealed.

The Eastern sources are of equal importance. The lone extant Mongolian document is *The Secret History of the Mongols* (c. 1252), best translated and edited by Igor de Rachewiltz although other translations are also very useful. *The Secret History* describes the Mongol world up to the reign of Ögödei Khan (r. 1229–1241) with the majority of the work focused on Chinggis Khan. It can be a difficult text as it was written for a specific audience (the Mongol court and only the Mongol court, hence 'secret'). As a result many things are not elaborated upon as it was assumed that the reader would understand the nuances and context. The majority of the work focuses on activities in Mongolia and the details become sparse on events taking place outside Mongolia, yet give the reader a clear indication of what the Mongols thought important. Other thirteenth-century Mongolian sources such as the *Altan Debter* (Golden Book) have vanished, although parts of Mongolian sources appear in Rashid al-Din's work as well as in Chinese sources such as the *Sheng Wu Qin Zheng Lu* (The Chronicle of the Holy Warrior), which is concerned with the campaigns of Chinggis Khan.

The major Chinese source is the *Yuan Shi* or History of the Yuan Empire, compiled from Yuan records by the Ming Empire in 1369 according to rules of Chinese historiographical tradition established by the great Han historian Sima Qian. While there are pitfalls with this process, the *Yuan Shi* nonetheless offers a wealth of biographical information in addition to details of campaigns and government. The biographical information is of vast importance since most sources, excluding Rashid al-Din's *Jami' al-Tawarikh*, do not dwell on the lives of most of the figures in the Mongol government, excluding the khans. With 4,000 pages of information it is an invaluable source, particularly as the information for the first 100 years of the Mongol Empire extends beyond the Yuan Empire. Unfortunately only bits and pieces have been translated into other languages, although the majority is available in Mongolian along with other Chinese sources. Hopefully by the time this book is in print, that situation will have changed, since a full translation is now in progress. Undoubtedly it will transform how scholars approach the empire in the same way as Thackston's translation of Rashid al-Din did for non-Persian readers.

Just as the Ming compiled the *Yuan Shi*, the Mongols ordered the compilation of the histories of the empires of China that they conquered. Thus we have the *Jin Shi* and the *Song Shi*. These are more regionally focused, but taken as a whole shed light on virtually the whole of East Asia prior to the rise of the Mongols as well as on the Mongol conquest of the Jin, Song and Xi Xia empires. Other sources include the *Guang Yu Tu* (Extended Map of the Earth), *Huihui Yaofang* (Muslim Medicinal Recipes) and *Yinshan Zhengyao* (Proper and Essential Things for the Emperor's Food and Drink).

All are a synthesis of Chinese and Islamic scholarship only made possible by the Mongol Empire. The *Guang Yu Tu* compiled by Zhu Siben provides detailed geographic information throughout East Asia and then extends beyond Eurasia and as far as west Africa.[7] The *Huihui Yaofang,* in the process of being translated in Germany, is a medical encyclopedia of Islamic medicine. It is believed that the Mongols preferred Islamic medical care to other forms and that the publication of this work is evidence of the Mongol court's attempt to promote it.[8] Finally, the *Yinshan Zhengyao* is an intriguing book of recipes. As will be discussed later, it clearly demonstrated the interconnectedness of the different parts of the Mongol Empire as well as showing us what might be on the menu at the court of the khans. This work has been translated into English with copious notes and a detailed introduction.[9]

A number of other Chinese primary sources exist, but they tend to be more regionally or locally focused. The *Meng-Da Bei-Lu* (Record of the Mongols and Tatars), a travel account written by Zhao Hong, a representative from the Song court during the Mongol invasion of the Jin Empire, gives the view of an enemy of the Jin on an embassy to the Mongols who has a keen eye for the Mongol military and leaves a fascinating account of all facets of the Mongol military machine, including how they trained their horses. *Heida Shilue* (Brief Account of the Black Tatar) by Peng Daya, a Song emissary, is another travel account that tells us more about the early Mongol invasions. A third source from this period is the *Xi Yuji* (Record of a Journey to the West) by Li Zhichang, an adept of the Taoist sage Changchun. It is an account of Changchun's journey from China to Mongolia to Samarqand and Afghanistan. He made the journey after Chinggis Khan summoned him, hoping to find a secret to longevity. The account is remarkable in that not only do we have philosophical discussions with Chinggis Khan but also a unique perspective of the Mongol Empire as it formed in East Asia and Central Asia. The *Xi Yuji* was translated by Arthur Waley and remains in print.[10]

Significant strides have also been made in the secondary material. On the eastern end of the empire, James P. Delgado's highly readable book, *Khubilai Khan's Lost Fleet*, makes a useful contribution to the study of the Mongols' place in world history.[11] In addition to writing a compelling story of Khubilai Khan's attempted invasions of Japan, Vietnam and Java via the sea, he demonstrates how these events later influenced the national identities of these regions. David Bade's *Khubilai Khan and the Beautiful Princess of Tumapel* is another noteworthy contribution as it is one of the very few studies that deal directly with the Mongol invasion of Java. In addition to scholarly analysis of the actions there, Bade provides translations of several of the Indonesian sources, otherwise rather inaccessible. Ironically, Bade's book is also rather inaccessible as it was published in Mongolia, although it is in English. Bade's analysis usefully demonstrates that the Javanese sources do not focus on world conquest or destruction. Indeed, there is no mention of cities being levelled or of the usual massacres that accompany a visit from the Mongols. Rather, the Javanese sources focus on diplomacy, commerce and Khubilai's attempts to acquire princesses from the kingdoms of Indonesia. As a result, we have sources that provide a different perspective on the Mongols than those of the mainland.

While chapter One of this book provides a brief biography of Chinggis Khan, a number of useful biographies exist. Paul Ratchnevsky's *Genghis Khan: His Life and Legacy* is still probably the most authoritative and scholarly, but can prove challenging for the uninitiated. The best in terms of general accessibility, which also places Chinggis Khan as a major influence in the Islamic world, is that of Michal Biran. Ruth Dunnell's Chinggis Khan biography is also quite good, particularly for classroom use due to its concise nature. A number of other works can be found in the bibliography, but these are the three best. Biography has not been a major feature of the Mongol Empire. Indeed, beyond the dozen or so biographies of Chinggis Khan, we have Morris Rossabi's classic eponymous work on Khubilai Khan as well as his *Voyager from Xanadu* which discusses the lives of two high-ranking members of the Church of the East (the Nestorians) who travel to Europe as ambassadors. There is also Richard Gabriel's enthusiastic biography of the general Sübedei. Other biographical information tends to be fragmentary and included in other studies, such as the aforementioned work by Allsen on Möngke. Igor de Rachewiltz, perhaps the foremost authority on the Mongols as evidenced by his book *The Secret History of the Mongols*, edited *Personalities in the Mongol Empire*, which provides several short biographies of major figures within the empire ranging from Mongol generals such as Sübedei to non-Mongol administrators such as Sayyid Ajall and Yelü Chucai. Nonetheless much work needs to be done on the leadership of the Mongol Empire – both the Mongol and non-Mongol figures.

As indicated at the beginning of this section, this historigraphical study does not address all books dealing with the Mongols or that include the Mongols as an integral part of world history. These can be found in the bibliography. I have also reserved some of my comments on some works for inclusion in chapters where they will be more salient.

Chinggis Khan,
19th-century Chinese
woodcut that may have
been based on an earlier
piece. The boots and
fur-trimmed headgear
depict a more Mongol-
like appearance than
many portrayals.

THEORETICAL CONCERNS

It is easy to get swept up in 'Mongol mania' when trying to explain the
Mongol impact in world history.[12] One can fall into the trap of tying
many things to the Mongols without recognizing other factors. This
book will attempt to avoid this pitfall, but only the reader will be able
to judge the author's success. When examining the impact of the Mongol Empire, or any other state, polity or people, one must discern
whether a change would have occurred if not for a specific preceding
event. Although historians tend to look at the word 'inevitable' with
disdain, some things besides taxes and death may be so. Thus the discussion will be about things that are directly linked to the Mongols, or
what might be indirectly linked to the Mongols but occurred as a ramification of Mongol activity.

Yet even then one must be wary of drawing out indirect influences
too far. For instance, it would be easy to credit (or damn, depending

on the hyperbole of the time) the Mongol Empire for the Bolshevik Revolution. This may seem a bit far-fetched, and it is, but then Vladimir Ilyich Ulyanov Lenin did have Kalmyk ancestry. The Kalmyks were Oirat Mongols who migrated to the Volga River in 1636 after growing weary of the perpetual internecine fighting among the Oirats. The Oirat Mongols were a powerful Mongol confederation in western Mongolia that did not recognize the Chinggisid principle as the sole legitimizing influence in ruling; that is to say, they did not recognize a khan or prince from the lineage of Chinggis Khan. The Oirat took their name from one of the Forest People around Lake Baikal that submitted to Chinggis Khan in 1209, yet their leadership claimed a lineage from Toghril Ong-Khan, khan of the Kereits whom Chinggis Khan defeated.[13] With the dissolution of the Mongol Empire in 1260–5, the unity of the Chinggisid princes declined and allowed other groups to gradually assert their independence. In the fifteenth century the Oirats gradually became a major force in the area of modern western Mongolia, Kazakhstan and Xinjiang in China. Without the Mongol Empire the Chinggisids would have never come to prominence, and thus no opposition to them would have grown, and thus no Oirats. Therefore they could not have had a civil war that would cause one faction to move west to the Volga in frustration, and thus no ancestry for Lenin, and perhaps no Lenin, resulting in no Bolshevik Revolution and all that it entails. This argument, 100 years ago, would have also associated Lenin's callousness to his Mongol heritage, overlooking that every society has a mean streak, but it had been fashionable to blame all bad things in Russia on the Mongols for centuries. Indeed, alcoholism in Russia has been attributed to the Mongols by some scientists.[14]

Of course we could draw this exercise out further. With the creation of the Soviet Union we ultimately have the Mongol Empire creating the Cold War, influencing the election of John F. Kennedy and bringing about his assassination. The creation of the Soviet Union and its dominance of much of the former Mongol Empire leads us to the Soviet–Afghan War, which included the involvement of many offshoots of the Mongols such as the Uzbeks. The collapse of the Soviet Union led to the hegemony of the United States and a desire for a new 'enemy', which was found in radical Islam, leading to the Taliban, the events of 9/11 and the US invasion of Afghanistan and Iraq. Thus one could argue that the Mongols caused the tragedy of 9/11. In so doing, we could prove that history is indeed circular rather that teleological, as Mongolian troops have served in the so-called 'Coalition of the Willing' in both Afghanistan and Iraq – perhaps as a vanguard for a new

Mongol Empire if one wanted to take a conspiracy theory perspective. It is simple enough to make this case and perhaps also the case that the Mongols, with their adoption of new musical styles and the Pax Mongolica allowing new musical instruments, tastes and fashions to spread, are responsible for one of the greatest scourges of humanity – disco. With their love of drink and gold embroidered cloth or *nasij*, one could easily envision a disco ball hanging from the ceiling in Karakorum. And, indeed, one German group from the disco era not only named themselves after Chinggis Khan (Dschinggis Khan as the Germans spell it), but had a member of the band pose as Chinggis Khan as well as having two hit singles based on a Chinggis Khan theme, one of which almost carried them to Eurovision glory in 1979.[15]

The preceding paragraph is, of course, an exercise in absurdity. The point is that one may indeed link tangential events back to one event, however, to do so ignores other mitigating actions such as the First World War, European colonialism and imperialism, the success of ABBA and Donna Summer, and the unexpected creation of polyester. Indeed, the linking of Lenin to Chinggis Khan is speculation best left for discussion after a few drinks and not for serious discussion in a scholarly book, but it is exactly the type of pitfall that the author will hopefully avoid, as well as subtler ones. In essence, while I contend the Mongols have been highly influential and perhaps set the stage for the modern world, they were not the only factor.

I will, however, demonstrate that the conquests that created the Mongol Empire must be seen as a key and direct cause for monumental historical changes in world history. They served not only as a catalyst for change, but also were not a regressive force that set back progress in various parts of the world. This is a claim often made in nationalist histories, for instance the myth of the Mongol Yoke that prevented Russia from advancing at the same pace as Western Europe. The Mongol conquests have also been used as an excuse in the Middle East and China. Furthermore, many of the advances that occurred could not or would not have happened without the Mongol conquests.

The conquests served as a catalyst in many ways that will be explored throughout the chapters of this book, however they served most obviously and directly by simply altering the map of the world. More than twenty states disappeared by the end of the conquests: Xi Xia, the Jin Empire, Song Empire, Kara Khitai, Khwarazmian Empire, the Ismaili Kingdom, the Abbasid Caliphate, the Seljuks of Rum, the Ayyubid Kingdom of Damascus and Aleppo, Vladimir-Suzdal, the

Kipchak confederacy, the Kereit Khanate, the Naiman confederacy and, of course, the Tatars of Mongolia are but a sample of independent principalities, kingdoms, khanates and sultanates that vanished after the collapse of the Mongol Empire. Within a span of 50 years the map of Eurasia had irrevocably changed. Part One of this book will examine the conquests and their immediate and long-term ramifications on the political geography of Eurasia as well as provide a contextual framework for Part Two, the Chinggis Exchange.

Christopher Columbus, Heinz Guderian, the Dalai Lama, William Shakespeare and John Wayne. A seemingly diverse and unconnected list of names, yet they all have something in common. In one way or another they are intimately connected to Chinggis Khan and are thus part of what might be termed the Chinggis Exchange. Just as Columbus's 'discovery' of, or rather accidental landing in, the New World transformed multiple societies through the direct and indirect exchange of New World and Old World animals, plants, germs and culture known as the Columbian Exchange (a term coined by Alfred Crosby), the Mongol conquests and empire caused a perceivable shift in technology, ideas, culture, religion, warfare and many other areas. The Columbian Exchange is, in many ways, a carry-over of the Chinggis Exchange, yet at the same time remains quite separate. The Chinggis Exchange is not simply an extension of the syllogism of the Mongols and the Bolshevik Revolution posed above. Indeed, Part Two is an effort to avoid that syllogism, yet at the same time it is hoped that at the end it will be clear that the Mongol impact on world history is undeniable and enormous.

So why the Chinggis Exchange? Well, for one it is a bit more pithy than 'The Mongol Impact on world history', but most importantly it conveys the idea of 'The Mongol Impact on World History'. Without the rise of Chinggis Khan it is very unlikely that the Mongol Empire and its resulting impact would have happened. While it is not trendy to consider the 'Great Man' idea in scholarship, one must remain open to the idea that there are sometimes truly great men or women who dramatically transform the world or at least set history on a path that it otherwise would not have taken. While it is true that every individual is a product of his or her era and society, at times there are those who have the vision or ability to transcend it. This certainly should not be misconstrued as a view that Chinggis Khan planned the entire thing. Indeed, I am not convinced that Chinggis Khan even wanted an empire, but rather that he would have been quite content ruling Mongolia. His accomplishments, however, are what inspired others and set forces in motion that could not be reversed. Thus even after the dissolution of the Mongol Empire roughly 8.5 million sq km (14 million sq miles) were ruled by his descendants and neighbouring states had to engage in some form of relations with those descendants. For decades and even centuries after Chinggis Khan's death, his shadow loomed over his former empire and well beyond. If one considers the world prior to the Mongol Empire and the post-empire period, it is clear that it was vastly different and considerably more interconnected. While it is often said that the Mongols ushered in globalism, one should approach this with a bit more restraint. Indeed, while the Mongols set the conditions and served as facilitators, most of the Chinggis Exchange was the result of the efforts of the subjects of the Mongols and outsiders. Nonetheless, one should not discount direct Mongol action in the Chinggis Exchange, as Part Two will demonstrate.

PART ONE

THE MONGOL CONQUESTS
AS CATALYST

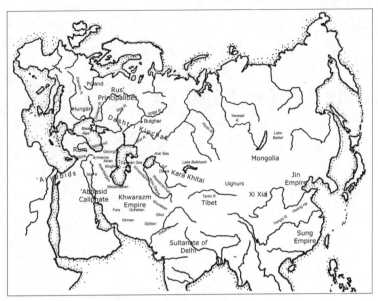

Eurasia before the Mongol Conquest.

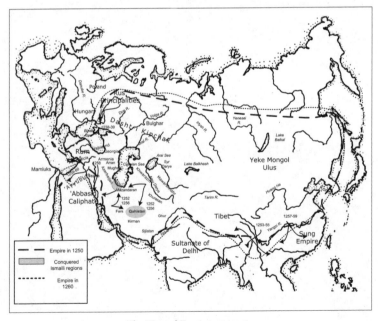

The Mongol Empire, 1250–1260.

1

THE FORMATION OF THE
MONGOL EMPIRE

The Mongol Empire founded by Chinggis Khan (also known as Genghis Khan in the West) became the largest contiguous empire in history, stretching from the Sea of Japan to the Mediterranean Sea and the Carpathian Mountains. At its peak more than one million men were under arms and enrolled in the armies of the khan, or the emperor, of the Mongol Empire. Family units provided support and logistics while wives and daughters maintained the herds and flocks that sustained the Mongols' nomadic lifestyle. The Mongol khans became determined to conquer the world and indeed, with the resources at their disposal, there was little reason why they would fail. Yet, eventually, the empire collapsed, partially under its own weight and internecine feuds. The following is a brief history of the rise of the Mongol Empire and its subsequent expansion across Asia and into Europe until it separated into four separate and smaller, yet still powerful, kingdoms.

THE RISE OF CHINGGIS KHAN

Unquestionably the most difficult stage in the rise of the Mongol Empire was the unification of Mongolia under Chinggis Khan. As his childhood included the death of his father, his own enslavement, fratricide, the kidnapping of his wife and military defeat, there was no obvious portent that Temüjin, as Chinggis Khan was known in his youth, would become the supreme power in the Mongolian steppe and, indeed, the world. Other powerful and more significant leaders and tribes existed.

Much of the chaotic nature of steppe politics and power was due to the collapse of the Liao Dynasty (907–1125). Although the Liao Dynasty is often considered, and rightfully so, a Chinese dynasty, Liao was the dynastic name of the Khitans, a Mongolian people who ruled as

Chinese emperors but also as khans over much of Mongolia, meaning the area bounded by Lake Baikal and the Siberian taiga to the north, the Greater Khingan Mountains to the east, the Altai Mountains to the west, and the steppe zone south of the Gobi Desert and north of the Ordos Loop. Liao control in the steppe not only rested on their manipulation of tribes but also in the placement of Khitan troops in the steppe, complete with 'towns' that supported the mobile garrisons with smiths, granaries and other logistical support.

The rebellion of the Jurchen tribes in Manchuria ended the Liao rule. Although remnants fled to modern Kazakhstan and Kyrgyzstan to establish the Western Liao of Kara Khitai Empire, the Jurchen supplanted the Liao in northern China with the Jin Empire (1125–1234), Jin being the dynastic name they assumed. While the Jin also attempted to maintain control in the steppe, it was less effective. Thus many former vassals of the Khitan gained their independence and struggled against each other not only to secure their freedom but also to assert their dominance over other groups as well as against the Jin's own efforts to exert influence over steppe affairs. The Mongols were but one of the groups competing for survival on the Mongolian steppes.

At the time of Temüjin's birth in 1162 the Mongols were a broken power, having suffered significant defeats by their hereditary enemies, the Tatars in eastern Mongolia, and the Jin Dynasty of northern China.[1] The ramifications of this defeat were immense, causing the Mongols to fall from being a major force in the steppe to a minor power, often requiring the support of more powerful polities against the continual menace of the Tatars. Indeed, the Tatar resurgence and the Mongol decline was part of the balancing act the Jin Empire and previous empires in China played to prevent steppe nations from becoming too powerful. Nonetheless, although the Mongols were now without a true khan, certain leaders still carried significant weight and continued the struggle against the Tatars. Yisügei Bahadur (meaning hero or brave) was one such leader among the Borjigin Mongols. An ardent enemy of the Tatars, Yisügei served as a vehicle for the changes that swept across Mongolia for the rest of the twelfth century.

Yisügei, with his wife Hö'elün, whom he gained through rather nefarious yet traditional means of kidnapping, fathered Temüjin along with three other sons and a daughter. Hö'elün, a member of the Olqunu'ut people, had been accompanying her new husband, Chiledü of the Merkit, back to his pasturelands when Yisügei and his brothers attacked. Chiledü escaped, but Yisügei abducted Hö'elün and thus she became his senior wife. She gave birth around 1162 to Temüjin, and then to Jochi-Kasar, Kachun and Temüge, and also to the youngest, a daughter named Temülün. Yisügei also married a second wife, named Ko'agchin, who gave him two sons, Bekhter and Belgütei.[2]

The children had only a brief time with their father, though. When Temüjin was eight or nine years old, Yisügei took him to find a future bride. Along their journey they encountered Dai-Sechen, a leader among the Onggirat, a Turkic people in eastern Mongolia. Dai-Sechen convinced Yisügei that his daughter, Börte, only slightly older than Temüjin, would be a good wife for him. Furthermore, and perhaps the deciding factor, Dai-Sechen prophesized greatness for the young Mongol lad, saying:

> This son of yours is a boy
> Who has fire in his eyes,
> Who has light in his face.[3]

Dai-Sechen told Yisügei of a dream he had the previous night about a white gyrfalcon clutching the sun and the moon, which flew to Dai-Sechen. The Onggirat chieftain interpreted the dream as Temüjin being the gyrfalcon, and by clutching the sun and moon it was obvious he would rule the world.[4]

Yisügei accepted this auspicious omen and left his son with the Onggirat before returning to the Borjigin Mongols. On his way home Yisügei stopped at a camp to rest and eat. Among the steppe nomads there was, and still is, the custom that one is obliged to grant hospitality if someone comes to one's camp seeking food or shelter. This was typical behaviour and both reciprocal and crucial to survival in the harsh environment of the steppe. Unfortunately for Yisügei, the particular camp he visited was that of some Tatars. Despite the enmity of the Mongols and Tatars, during a non-hostile visit the Tatars were obligated to accept and tend to their visitor's needs. Nonetheless, the Tatars recognized the Mongol chieftain and poisoned his food and drink. Thus by the time Yisügei reached his home he was near death. His last request was that Temüjin should be brought home, although he died, in the early 1170s, before Temüjin arrived.

The death of Yisügei carried grave ramifications for the Mongols. As Yisügei had been the leader of the Borjigin Mongols, one of the major divisions among the Mongols, the Borjigin were now leaderless. Although Temüjin had returned, no one accepted the leadership of a ten-year-old boy or his slightly older half-brothers. Thus most of the clans that had followed Yisügei flocked to the Tayichiut, the other major division; other clans found leadership and protection elsewhere. Thus Temüjin's family became impoverished and was forced into a sub-sistence-based life; without the leadership of his mother, Hö'elün, they all probably would have died.

It was during this period of ostracism that Temüjin and his elder half-brother Bekhter became embroiled in a contest of power. Despite their precarious existence, Bekhter hoarded food and stole a fish and a bird that Temüjin and his brother Jochi-Kasar caught. By keeping the food Bekhter ensured his own survival, but not that of his brothers. This led Temüjin, with the assistance of Jochi-Kasar, to murder Bekhter. The quarrel, however, was ultimately over power.[5] Although Temüjin was the eldest son of the senior wife, Hö'elün, and thus most likely to be the leader when he obtained his majority (at the age of fifteen), Bekhter was a few years older. Obtaining his majority first he would not want to be of inferior rank to his younger half-brother. Bekhter could also assume leadership by Levirate marriage. A common tradition among the nomads was that the sons or brothers of a man could marry his wives, excluding their own mother. Thus it was feasible that Bekhter could marry Hö'elün, becoming Temüjin's father and effectively his lord. Temüjin's murder of his brother, in all likelihood, had more to do with this threat than with the theft of a fish and a small bird.

While Temüjin successfully staved off a threat to his primacy among his family, it triggered a reaction among the other Mongols. This murder violated nomadic custom and although Temüjin's family was no longer a major factor in steppe politics it still demanded atten-tion. As a result the Tayichiut raided Temüjin's camp. While Temüjin and his brothers avoided capture for several days, ultimately the Tayichiut captured Temüjin and brought him to their camp where he was kept captive, possibly for a few years.[6]

Temüjin eventually escaped and through a few adventures gradu-ally established himself as a leader with a small but loyal following out-side his family. It was during this period that he claimed his bride from Dai-Sechen in the early 1180s. In addition to marrying Börte, he used a gift Hö'elün received from Chotan, Börte's mother, to develop a client relationship with the powerful leader of the Kereits, Toghril Ong-Khan.[7] Toghril, as ruler of the Kereits, dominated central Mongolia in the river basin of the Selenge, Orkhon and Tula rivers. Temüjin demonstrated a flair for politics by using his father's ties to Toghril to gain his patronage, and as Hö'elün allowed him to invest her wealth into alliances. Yisügei had, on more than one occasion, assisted Toghril in gaining or regaining his throne. Furthermore, the two had been blood-brothers, or *anda*, and it was on this claim that Temüjin now called. However, his success would not last.

Less than a year after gaining his bride and the protection of the powerful khan of the Kereit, the Merkits avenged the abduction of Hö'elün by raiding Temüjin's camp. As Temüjin and the others fled, uncertain of who was attacking them, Börte was inadvertently left behind in the confusion and carried off by the Merkit. Temüjin then turned to Toghril for assistance. Although Temüjin, in the grand scheme of things, was a minor figure in Toghril's hierarchy, Toghril agreed to assist him. Toghril probably based his decision more on potential rewards in terms of plunder than loyalty to a new and rather insignificant servitor. Toghril called upon Jamuqa, another Mongol, to join in the campaign. Jamuqa was not only a client of Toghril but also his war chief or leader, as well as the *anda* of Temüjin. Jamuqa, earlier in his life, had also been a victim of the predations of the Merkit and thus also had an axe to grind with them.[8] The subsequent attack on the Merkit was tremendously successful, not only regaining Börte, but also seriously disrupting and weakening the Merkit.

Yet there were some unforeseen consequences. One was that by the time Börte had been rescued, several months had passed. On the return journey she gave birth to a son, named Jochi. The name Jochi means 'guest' and was probably chosen as Jochi appears not to have been the son of Temüjin. The actual father was a Merkit to whom Börte was given. Although Temüjin accepted Jochi as his legitimate eldest son throughout his life, it eventually became a source of tension among his children.

Another ramification of the Merkit attack was that Temüjin joined Jamuqa for the duration of a year. During this time he served as a lieutenant to Jamuqa and learned much about the techniques of steppe warfare.[9] Tension between Jamuqa and Temüjin, however, eventually drove the two apart. It is at this point that the charisma of Temüjin becomes very apparent. Although Temüjin and his following separated from Jamuqa, they were joined by several members of Jamuqa's forces. Although a few members of the Borjigin nobility joined Temüjin, commoners formed the majority of those who rallied to him, many of them barely above the status of slaves. In Temüjin they saw a figure that did not cater to the interests of the aristocracy.

This separation accelerated Temüjin's ascension to power. In 1185, after he and Jamuqa parted company, Temüjin's relatives elected him to be the khan of the Borjigin Mongols. While his patron, Toghril, and even Jamuqa congratulated him on his new title, the election was disingenuous. Typically, a ruler in the steppe was elected or chosen from among the leading figures of the nomadic aristocracy based on his experience and ability to provide for and protect the tribe. Once in power, the khan did not have absolute authority, but was expected to consult with those who raised him to power.[10] In 1185 Temüjin was young and with relatively little experience compared to his uncles and other relatives who elected him but he did possess enormous charisma. In truth those who selected him did so because they thought he was malleable and thus would serve as a puppet for their needs. Much to their chagrin, they learned Temüjin was most certainly not a puppet, particularly with strong-willed and smart women like his mother Hö'elün and wife Börte advising him.

Despite his election, Temüjin's troubles had only begun. Tensions increased between Temüjin and his *anda* Jamuqa. Eventually the two warred. Toghril, patron of both, did not participate. The two armies met in 1187 at the Battle of Dalan Balzhut with Jamuqa the victor. Temüjin fled after his defeat, perhaps into the Jin Empire.[11] Nonetheless, in some respects the battle strengthened him as many former followers of Jamuqa joined Temüjin, for the victor exacted a terrible vengeance on those who had left his army in previous years by boiling many alive. These extreme actions alienated many of those who had remained with him.

In the early 1190s Temüjin returned to Mongolia and apparently regained enough power to be a force in the steppe again. Although Jamuqa remained a threat Temüjin felt the time was right to deal with the Tatars who had steadily increased their power in the steppe. Indeed, even the Jin Empire in northern China had become concerned with their strength, perhaps an underlying reason for Temüjin's return. Thus the Borjigin Mongols and the Kereit, working in concert with the Jin, launched an attack on the Tatars in 1197. Caught between the pincers of the Kereit and Mongols on one side and the Jin armies on the other, the Tatars were defeated. Although their power was not completely destroyed, they ceased to be an immediate threat to all parties for the time being. As a result the Jin recognized Toghril as the major steppe ruler and Temüjin as one of his important vassals.

For the rest of the 1190s Temüjin's strength and influence grew. He and Toghril continued to fight the Merkit, as well as the Naiman in western Mongolia as the Kereit and Naiman were at war with each other. Temüjin also transformed into a capable military leader and on more than one occasion rescued his overlord, once from the Naiman and a second time restoring him to the throne after a rebellion. By 1200 Temüjin had established himself as the undisputed ruler of the Onan-Kerülen river basin, the territorial homeland of the Mongols. Conflict between the Borjigin and the Tayichiut Mongols was renewed and led to a major battle between the two tribes with Temüjin emerging victorious. The victory was not complete as many of the Tayichiut escaped, but their power was broken in the east.

A conclusion between Temüjin and the Tayichiut was not long in coming. Seeing the rise in power of Toghril, due partly to Temüjin's own success, a number of smaller tribes banded together in a confederacy against the two allies. As leader they chose a former client of Toghril's: Jamuqa. In 1201 the confederacy elected Jamuqa Gur-Khan or Universal Ruler and then marched against the Kereit and Mongols. At Köyiten the two forces met. Here Jamuqa's generalship proved less effective as Toghril and Temüjin defeated the confederacy. While Toghril pursued Jamuqa and brought him to submission, Temüjin followed the Tayichiut and defeated them although he nearly died from an arrow wound to the throat. The bulk of the tribe was incorporated into the Borjigin Mongols. To ensure that the Tayichiut would never threaten him again Temüjin executed the leaders of the tribe – beginning a pattern that would be a hallmark of the future Chinggis Khan. As an unexpected bonus the Onggirat, Börte's tribe, also joined Temüjin's following.

Riding a wave of success, Temüjin decided to finish the Tatars once and for all. They had taken part in Jamuqa's confederation against the Kereit and Mongols. With the addition of the Onggirat and Tayichiut the Mongols' strength had been greatly enhanced. It is at this point we also begin to see a transformation of Mongol warfare. Before attacking, Temüjin issued a remarkable order: no one would stop to plunder until he gave the order.[12] Typically, once nomadic forces reached the camp of the enemy they plundered it and rode off with their gains. The point of raids and attacks was not to decimate an enemy but rather to enrich themselves. Temüjin, however, saw a new reason for war: security against outside threats. He saw the wisdom, what modern observers would see as common sense, of securing a complete victory over the enemy before enjoying the spoils.

In 1202 Temüjin defeated the Tatars at Dalan Nemürges in eastern Mongolia near the Khalkha River. Much as he had done with the

Tayichiut, Temüjin ordered the destruction of the Tatar aristocracy. The commoners were then assimilated into the Mongols and distributed among the various clans to ensure they could not prove troublesome. Temüjin then dealt with his relatives. As they had elected him as ruler the Borjigin aristocrats considered Temüjin their puppet and did not pay attention to his prohibition on plundering during the attack on the Tatars. Temüjin corrected this and confiscated their booty – redistributing it among the rest of the Mongols.

At this point, although still a vassal of Toghril, Temüjin had become the master of eastern Mongolia. His sudden rise to power altered his relationship with Toghril, as the latter became increasingly wary of his protégé, concerned that Temüjin sought to oust him. Others fed this paranoia, such as Temüjin's senior relatives, upset that he had confiscated their share of the booty from the raid on the Tatars. Jamuqa also rejoined Toghril and spoke ill of his *anda*. Furthermore, Toghril's son Senggüm viewed Temüjin as a rival for succession to Toghril's throne. Temüjin's efforts to secure his relationship with Toghril did little to alleviate Senggüm's concern as Temüjin proposed that his son Jochi should marry Toghril's daughter Cha'ur and that his daughter Qojin should marry Senggüm's son Tusaqa. Senggüm was outraged by Temüjin's audacity as he viewed Temüjin's and, particularly, Jochi's social status as beneath his own. The conspirators then used the wedding proposal as an opportunity to try to destroy Temüjin; they accepted the proposal, hoping that the wedding party might be an occasion to launch an attack.[13] Temüjin almost fell into the trap, but Mönglik, a former vassal of Yisügei and who may have married Hö'elün, counselled him to be wary and seek more information. Due to Mönglik's intervention Temüjin saw through their designs. With this clear betrayal, conflict between the Kereit and the Mongols ensued. Although Temüjin suffered an initial defeat at Khalkaljit Sands in 1203, he managed to rally his forces and made a successful surprise attack on the celebrating Kereit camp Jer Gorge.

With the defeat of the Kereit in 1203 Temüjin's power and prestige increased tremendously; he now dominated central and eastern Mongolia. Furthermore, he assimilated the Kereit and increased his own forces; however, he did not exterminate the Kereit aristocracy. Most of them were treated honourably and given high positions. Having served as a vassal of Toghril for a number of years, Temüjin knew the Kereit aristocracy well. There was no true animosity between the Kereit and the Mongols, unlike that between the Mongols and the Tatars. Temüjin married many of the daughters and granddaughters of Toghril to his sons and followers, thus linking the Kereit closely to the Borjigin royal family. Toghril, however, escaped. His flight was short-lived, as a Naiman tribesman stumbled across the old khan and killed him without realizing who he had found. Senggüm, on the other hand, fled south into the kingdom of Xi Xia (modern Ningxia and Gansu provinces of China).

The final opposition to Temüjin's mastery of the steppe was the Naiman confederacy. The Naiman started the war between the two, seeing an opportunity to dominate the Mongolian plateau. They did not have a high regard for the Mongols and believed if they struck first they would easily defeat Temüjin's armies.[14] As the Naiman collected their forces and attempted to find allies among other tribes hostile to the Mongols, their plan leaked out. After considerable debate Temüjin led his forces westward to Chakirmaut or Naqu Cliffs in the spring of 1204. Meanwhile the Naiman had collected not only their own considerable strength but also the Merkit and an army led by Jamuqa composed of Mongol elements opposed to the rule of Temüjin.

Despite the Mongols' aggressive disposition the Naiman still outnumbered the Mongols. So on arriving in Naiman territory Temüjin ordered every man to light a campfire to conceal their true numbers at night. The ruse worked and delayed the Naiman attack. The confusion over the Mongols' true strength caused dissension among the leaders of the Naiman. The senior Naiman khan, Tayang Khan, wanted to lure the Mongols across the Altai Mountains, deeper into Naiman territory. His son Güchülüg and others urged a direct attack against the Mongols. Tayang Khan finally assented to this but it proved disastrous. The Naiman were crushed by the superior generalship of Temüjin as well as the disciplined forces that he developed as he conquered the steppe. The battle of Chakirmaut was the crowning achievement of Temüjin's army.[15] The victory, followed by a few minor skirmishes, crushed the Naiman and the Merkit, although Güchülüg and Toqtoa Beki, the Merkit chieftain, escaped westward into what is now Kazakhstan. The victory also broke Jamuqa's power. After being betrayed by his followers Jamuqa became Temüjin's captive. Temüjin executed the men who betrayed their former master but offered a pardon for Jamuqa. According to legend Jamuqa rejected it, sensing that the rift would remain great between them and requested a honourable death. Thus, honouring the taboo of shedding the blood of the aristocracy, Jamuqa's execution consisted of being rolled into a carpet and suffocated or having his spine broken.

Chinggis Khan at court, illustration from Rashid al-Din's *Jami' al-Tawarikh*. The scene shows not only Chinggis Khan's courtiers but also his *tuq* (military standard) on the right. The fact that the *tuq* (made from horse or yak tails) is white indicates that the gathering took place during a period of peace. A black *tuq* represented war.

With the defeat of the Naiman Temüjin's mastery of the Mongolian steppe was complete. With a relative peace established he was crowned as Chinggis Khan (Firm or Fierce Ruler) in 1206 at a grand *quriltai* or congress. At this *quriltai* Chinggis Khan, as he was henceforth called, began organizing his new empire as well as his army. With the *quriltai* Chinggis Khan also redefined what it meant to be a Mongol. During the process of unifying the Mongolian steppes he usually eliminated the aristocracy of his enemies, leaving his own family as the only viable nobility – one of the reasons why some of those who were defeated, such as the Naiman and Merkit, chose to leave Mongolia rather than to submit. Chinggis Khan then redistributed the defeated amongst the loyal military units, which were organized in units of ten, 100 and 1,000. Furthermore, he erased or at least subsumed older ethnic identities by creating the Khamag Monggol Ulus (roughly translated as All or United Mongol Nation). No longer was one a Kereit or Naiman, all of the people of the felt tents (the round *gers* or yurts of the nomads) were now Mongols. This identity became larger and eventually included all nomads under the guise of the Yeke Monggol Ulus

(Great Mongol Nation) as the Mongols expanded beyond Mongolia. Thus all steppe nomads became Mongols in identity, at least in the eye of the khan. Creating a new identity to replace old hostilities is not easy. Chinggis Khan found one way to bond the Khamag Monggol Ulus to his new state by creating teamwork exercises that involved invading his neighbours, not giving anyone time to rebel or resist the social changes he imposed.

Expansion of Empire

Whether or not Chinggis Khan intended to 'conquer the world' is debatable. Nonetheless, having stabilized the steppes of Mongolia, he did look at his neighbours as there were several immediate threats to his nascent realm. Potential dangers involved refugees who fled from Mongolia during the rise of Chinggis Khan, such as Senggüm of the Kereit, Toqtoa Beki of the Merkit and Güchülüg of the Naiman. All had been defeated by the Mongols but did not accept the new shift in leadership and fled. In addition the Jin Empire continued to meddle in the affairs of the steppe in an attempt to control the various tribes of Mongolia. Another group, the *Hoyin Irgen* or Forest People, existed to the north of Mongolia. They were actually a number of disparate peoples, including the Oyirad, Buriyat and the Kirghiz. They were different from the steppe tribes as they lived a semi-nomadic lifestyle, often establishing permanent villages and living more off hunting, fishing and limited agriculture rather than pastoral nomadism. In general the Hoyin Irgen tended to remain neutral in the wars among the nomadic tribes of Mongolia. Of course there were always exceptions, as a few had joined Jamuqa's coalition. For this reason and because of their proximity to the Mongols they were among the first to be conquered.

In 1207 Chinggis Khan sent his son, Jochi, with an army to the north to subjugate the Forest People. Quduqa-Beki of the Oyirad submitted and then acted as a guide for Jochi to the Tümen Oyirad who submitted to the Mongols at Shiqshit.[16] Quduqa cemented his relationship by marrying Chechiyegen, the second daughter of Chinggis Khan and Börte. His sons and daughter also married into the Chinggisid family. This use of marriage alliances became an important tool of Chinggis Khan to maintain control of tribal groups on his frontiers.

Jochi quickly secured the submission of the rest of the *Hoyin Irgen* in addition to the Oyirad.[17] In the Yenesei River valley the Kirghiz dominated the upper part of the valley while the Kem-Kemjiuts resided along the Kemchik tributary. Economically it was sensible for Chinggis Khan to incorporate it into his realm, as Muslim and Uighur merchants had imported furs as well as grain from this fertile region for years. Both the Kirghiz and Kem-Kemjiuts submitted rather than resist the Mongol army.[18] The Tümeds, who controlled the area of the Ija and Angara rivers, followed suit thus securing an economically important region and the Mongols' northern border.[19]

While Mongol forces secured the northern frontier, to the south lay more uncertainty in the various realms dominated by Chinese culture. While the bulk of the population was Han or ethnic Chinese, two of the three kingdoms were ruled by non-Han although influenced by Confucian and Chinese court practices. Militarily, the most powerful was the aforementioned Jin Empire, ruled by the Jurchen. To the southwest was Xi Xia (located in modern Gansu and Ningxia provinces) a Buddhist kingdom comprised of Han, Turkic and Tibetan populations: the latter, known as Tangut, being the ruling segment. Finally, further south and not sharing a border with the steppe, was the Song Empire, which had ruled northern China as well until the rise of the Liao Dynasty in the tenth century. While more populous and prosperous than the Jin Empire or Xi Xia, Song efforts to regain the north continually failed in the face of Jin military supremacy.

The first sedentary power that the Mongols invaded was Xi Xia.[20] The invasion of Xi Xia has often been viewed as a stepping-stone for the invasion of the Jin Empire or for economic reasons. The Mongols invaded, however, for reasons relating more to the security of Mongolia than as a practice run against a more powerful enemy or for economic gain, since the latter could be achieved through trade or raiding.[21] Although militarily inferior to the Jin Dynasty to the east, Xi Xia was a powerful state but the primary threat came from Xi Xia's influence in the steppe. It often served as a safe haven for deposed Kereit leaders due to trade ties and the potential of using Kereit refugees as pawns in Mongolia.[22] Indeed, Senggüm initially fled to Xi Xia before being forced to leave for pillaging parts of the kingdom.[23]

Chinggis Khan invaded Xi Xia in 1205, using Senggüm's presence there as a pretext.[24] It is also possible that he chose to attack Xi Xia to destabilize that kingdom while he secured Mongolia. By keeping a potential enemy, particularly one that harboured a rival, off balance Chinggis Khan kept his army away from Mongolia and bought time to firmly secure his own hold over his newly won kingdom.

Initially the Mongols raided the borders. The Tangut of Xi Xia, the ruling ethnicity of Tibetan origin, made only limited attempts to repel the more mobile Mongol armies. It was not until 1209 that Chinggis Khan began a true invasion of conquest. Several cities fell before the Mongols reached the capital of Zhongxiang in May of 1209. As the siege of Zhongxiang extended into October the Mongols remained unsuccessful at one of their first endeavours at siege warfare. They resorted to building a dyke to divert the Huang He or Yellow River into the city. By January of 1210 the diverted river almost collapsed the walls of the city, but the dyke broke and flooded the Mongol camp, forcing them to withdraw to higher ground. Nonetheless, the Tangut decided to negotiate with the Mongols rather than continue to resist.[25]

Meanwhile, tensions increased between Chinggis Khan's new state and the Jin Dynasty in northern China. Several tribes that bordered the Jin Empire switched their vassalage from the Jin to the Mongols, while others such as the Juyin simply revolted against the Jin.[26] The Mongols began their invasion of the Jin in 1211, partially to avenge past transgressions such as the Jin's execution of a Mongol khan prior to Temüjin's rise, but also simply for the plunder. Since Xi Xia was now a client of the Mongols, it was given Mongol protection against such raids. Although the Mongols devastated much of the Jin Empire, they withdrew to the steppe in 1212 and held only a small portion of it, primarily to control mountain passes connecting two realms. In addition they forced the Jin to pay a handsome amount in tribute.[27]

Peace between the two states was short-lived. In the autumn of 1212 Chinggis Khan once again invaded the Jin in a two-pronged attack. Tolui, Chinggis Khan's youngest son, led the second army. Both forces brought siege engineers with them. The Mongols withdrew to the steppe in 1214, once again having achieved a sizeable tribute payment as well as plunder. Perhaps more importantly the Mongols demonstrated that the Jin forces could not defeat them in open combat, nor could they rely on their fortifications to protect them, as the Mongols took numerous cities, slowly blockading the capital of Zhongdu (near modern Beijing). Again the Mongols did not occupy Jin territory but maintained a presence in strategic passes. It was now clear that the Jin could not launch an attack against the Mongols as they could not enter Mongolia, nor did they experience any lasting success against Mongol armies.

Not long after the Mongols left, hostilities resumed in 1214. As the Mongol presence moved further south and out of the mountain passes, the Jin emperor, Xuan Zong, moved his capital from Zhongdu to Kaifeng. Chinggis Khan viewed this as a breach of the peace treaty and felt that Xuan Zong could not be trusted, thus he ordered a new invasion. While Zhongdu continued to resist Mongol efforts to capture the city, Mongol armies continued their success in direct battles, repelling all attempts to relieve the Jin capital, forcing it to surrender in June 1215. As it increasingly appeared that the Jin emperor and his advisors had no concept of how to deal with the Mongols, several Jin generals switched sides while provinces rebelled against Jin rule after the fall of Zhongdu.

The fall of Zhongdu, combined with a Mongol invasion of Manchuria (the ancestral lands of the Jin), secured the north and northeastern portions of the empire for the Mongols. Although Chinggis Khan withdrew in 1216 to deal with a rebellion among the Hoyin Irgen, by 1218 most of the Jin Empire was in the hands of the Mongols. Increasing numbers of Jin generals, including ethnic Jurchen (the founders of the empire), as well as rebellious Khitans and Han Chinese, joined the Mongols. It seemed that the Jin Empire was on the verge of collapse but events in the west staved off defeat for another fifteen years.

While the Mongols had invaded Xi Xia and the Jin Empire, Chinggis Khan had not forgotten about the Naiman and Merkit refugees who had fled west. Indeed, when he invaded the Jin Empire, Chinggis Khan took the step of placing an army on the western borders of his empire to protect it from any possible attack from the Naiman leader, Güchülüg. In so doing he also gained new vassals in the west. As he became more powerful, the Uighurs of Turfan and some other smaller powers such as the Karluk Turks submitted to him between 1206 and 1209, joining the Mongol Empire through marriage alliances. Many of these polities suffered from attacks by the Merkit and the Naiman and sought a protector from their depredations.

After Güchülüg fled Mongolia, he eventually made his way into central Asia and entered the kingdom of Kara Khitai, where he was able to marry into the royal family. However, he and his Naiman tribesmen were no longer aided by the Merkit. In 1209 a Mongol army defeated the combined forces of the renegade Naiman and Merkit at the Irtysh River. The Merkit continued to flee westward and finally found refuge among the Qangli, a Turkic group that lived as pastoral nomads north of the Aral Sea. With the protection of the Gur-Khan of Kara Khitai, the Naiman were able to avoid the Mongols for a few years, but the Merkit were not as fortunate. In 1211 Güchülüg usurped the throne but did not openly rule until the Gur-Khan's death in 1213. An army led by two of Chinggis

Samukhaa at
Zhongdu, illustration
from Rashid al-Din's
Jami' al-Tawarikh.
For much of the
siege of Zhongdu
in 1215, Samukha
was in charge of the
blockade of the Jin
capital. The horses
in this illustration
are of the more
traditional Persian
presentation.

Khan's most gifted generals, Jebe and Sübedei, pursued the Merkit to the
Qangli territory and defeated both tribes. Jebe and Sübedei did not
attempt to incorporate the Qangli into the Mongol Empire at this time.
They merely completed their task and returned home.

This was not as easy as they had hoped. On their return journey
they encountered an army of the Khwarazmian Empire, led by its sultan, Muhammad II (r. 1200–20). The two generals had strict orders to
avoid engaging in combat with any other than those who sheltered the
Merkits but Muhammad II viewed them as a threat and initiated battle. By nightfall the battle was not over, but both sides retired for the
night. Under the cover of darkness the Mongols withdrew. Muhammad
was, however, clearly shaken by the encounter as his forces outnumbered the Mongols but were unable to defeat them. According to one
chronicler, 'the Mongols had filled Muhammad's heart with terror' as
he had never seen an army as ferocious in battle.[28]

Over time this fear faded as Muhammad extended his own empire into Afghanistan and Persia while sycophantic courtiers dubbed him a second Alexander the Great. Thus when the governor of the city of Otrar along the Syr Darya River massacred a Mongol-sponsored caravan in 1218 for espionage, Muhammad did not worry even though the Mongols were now his neighbours. Earlier that year the Mongol general Jebe overthrew Güchülüg's usurpation of Kara Khitai. The Mongols then pursued the prince until his death and annexed the former empire of Kara Khitai. Undoubtedly the governor of Otrar was correct in his suspicions as the Mongols used merchants as spies in addition to gathering intelligence from them through conversation. Chinggis Khan demanded retribution diplomatically, but Muhammad refused to deal with the Mongol ruler as an equal. Furthermore he executed one of the envoys and burned the beards of his entourage. Perhaps Sultan Muhammad believed that with the Mongols involved in a war against the Jin Empire they would not be willing to fight in central Asia too. Or perhaps he believed the praise his courtiers heaped upon him and trusted in the might of his army, which numbered around 400,000 men. In either case he was mistaken.

Once the news reached Chinggis Khan, he put his plans for eliminating the Jin on hold as he focused his attention on the Khwarazmian Empire. Assigning his trusted lieutenant Muqali to hold Mongol-controlled Jin territory and, if possible, finish off the Jin, Chinggis Khan amassed an army of approximately 150,000 horsemen to march west, the bulk of the Mongol army. Muqali, left with only 30,000 Mongol troops, augmented this force with thousands of Khitans, Jurchen, Tangut and Han Chinese.

The invasion began in the late summer or early autumn of 1219. The Mongols descended on Otrar, the site of the massacre. The city fell quickly and the governor was executed, ostensibly by having molten silver poured into his eyes and ears to sate his avarice. From Otrar the Mongols split into five forces. Each army struck different targets preventing the Khwarazmians from using their superior numbers in the field as they had to defend the numerous cities of the empire. One by one the cities of Mawarannahr (the region between the Amu Darya and Syr Darya rivers) fell. Muhammad soon fled across the Amu Darya. Chinggis Khan sent Jebe and Sübedei in pursuit while he continued with the destruction of the Khwarazmian Empire. Muhammad eventually escaped Jebe and Sübedei by fleeing to an island in the Caspian Sea, but died there in the most unregal fashion of dysentery or pleurisy, dressed in rags, in 1221. Meanwhile his son Jalal al-Din attempted to halt the Mongols. After some success against Mongol forces he attracted the attention of Chinggis Khan, who pursued him across Afghanistan to the Indus River and defeated him in battle. The prince, however, eluded capture by leaping off a cliff with his horse and swimming across the Indus into India, a feat that impressed even Chinggis Khan. The bulk of his army lacked the ability of their leader and was destroyed, although his harem now became the property of Chinggis Khan.

Although the Mongols had thoroughly defeated the Khwaraz-mian Empire, they gradually withdrew their armies from Persia and Afghanistan. Rather than trying to incorporate the entire empire, the Mongols annexed only Mawarannahr and set the Amu Darya River as their border. This became a trend in the Mongol Empire: only retaining a portion of their conquests so as not to overextend their armies. Meanwhile Jebe and Sübedei continued to ride westward, through the Caucasus Mountains. There they defeated a Georgian army. This encounter in 1221–2 had larger ramifications as the Georgians had planned to join the Fifth Crusade, but the untimely Mongol invasion prevented this. Although Jebe died crossing the mountains, Sübedei continued the ride. Before he rejoined the Mongol armies, in the steppes of modern Kazakhstan, he defeated Alans and Kipchak Turks, and later a combined army of Turks and Rus' or Russian princes at the Battle of the Kalka River in 1223. Not only did Sübedei defeat several armies and complete a circuit of approximately 8,050 km (5,000 miles), he accomplished this without the aid of reinforcements or modern navigational devices. Indeed, many of the nations he encountered were baffled by the Mongols since they did not know who they were, only that they simply came, destroyed and then vanished into the steppes. One bewildered Russian chronicler left this account of the mysterious opponents of the Rus' at the Kalka River, 'In the same year, for our sins, there came unknown tribes, and some people called them Tartars . . . Only God knows who these people are or from whence they came.'[29]

While Sübedei joined other Mongol forces in the steppes of Kazakh-stan, the Mongols continued other military activities such as dealing with a Tangut rebellion, which also caused them to withdraw from the Khwarazmian Empire. Although it is often said that Chinggis Khan destroyed Xi Xia because the ruler of the Tangut refused to provide troops for the Khwarazmian campaign, this is not quite accurate. The Tangut actually served the Mongols against the Jin until 1223, when

A Mongol general, 19th century, woodcut of a 13th-century drawing. The general's status is indicated by the yak-tail plume atop his helmet. This illustration is generally thought to be of the great Mongol general, Sübedei.

they rebelled and joined the Jin against the Mongols. Muqali died in 1223, forcing Chinggis Khan to return to the region to deal with the situation. Chinggis Khan did not invade Xi Xia until 1225 but overran the kingdom by late 1226. Only the capital remained by 1227. The Tangut had a small window of opportunity to drive the Mongols out when Chinggis Khan, now in his sixties, fell from his horse while hunting. His injuries slowed the siege as the princes and generals were more concerned with his health and urged him to end the siege and return to Mongolia. Chinggis Khan, however, pressed the siege. He died on 18 August 1227 due to internal injuries from the fall, but ordered his commanders not to reveal his death until the city fell and show no clemency. His sons and commanders carried out his orders without fail.

The siege of the Tangut capital of Zhongxiang, illustration from Marco Polo's *Livre de Merveilles*. Chinggis Khan died not as depicted in this illustration but from internal injuries sustained from falling from his horse while hunting. Polo's rendition is not surprising since virtually every account depicted Khan's death in a different way, from being struck by lightning or arrows, to during the consummation of a new marriage.

ÖGÖDEI

With the death of Chinggis Khan and the destruction of the Tangut kingdom, the next matter at hand for the Mongols was the selection of a new ruler. Although Tolui was possibly the best candidate in terms of military ability and leadership, ultimately the Mongol elite chose Ögödei and raised him to the throne in 1229–30. The prime reason for Ögödei's selection, in addition to Chinggis Khan's designation of him as his successor, was because of his temperament. Wise and calm, Ögödei possessed a talent for finding compromises between his more quarrelsome brothers, Jochi and Chaghatai. Even with Jochi's death in 1225 Ögödei was selected over Chaghatai, as Ögödei's talent for finding middle ground outweighed his alcoholism (which was notable even among the Mongols).[30]

Ögödei did not rest on his throne long. In 1230 the Mongol armies once again invaded the Jin Empire. With Muqali's death in 1223, many of the former allies of the Mongols wavered, deserting or joining the Jin. Muqali's lieutenants also proved to be less capable, thus the Mongols lost much of the territory they previously held. For the first campaign under his rule Ögödei focused less on simply regaining this land and showed more concern for the destruction of the Jin once and for all. With this in mind he and Tolui led armies into the Jin territory before dividing and striking multiple strongholds.

The death of Chinggis Khan, illustration from Marco Polo's *Livre de Merveilles*. This event would have taken place while suppressing the Tangut rebellion. According to the *The Secret History of the Mongols*, Khan ordered his death to be kept secret until the Tanguts were completely crushed. Here Khan is telling his sons that one arrow can be broken more easily than many.

Although Tolui died in 1231, the Mongols pressed on under the generalship of Sübedei. By 1231 the Jin held only eastern Henan and the Mongols took the capital of Kaifeng in 1233. Shortly before the fall of that city, the Jin emperor, Aizong (r. 1224–1234), fled to Caizhou. Unfortunately for the emperor, who ignored the advice of his commanders to flee elsewhere, Caizhou was poorly protected. The emperor quickly learned how unprepared the city was once the Mongols arrived. The siege began in October 1233 and continued until February 1234 when the city, flooded by a diverted river and the populace starving, submitted to the Mongols.

Even while Ögödei invaded the Jin Empire, the Mongols became active on other fronts. In 1230 he ordered the Mongol general Chormaqan to cross the Amu Darya River and resume the war against Jalal al-Din in the Middle East. Jalal al-Din fled before Chormaqan's forces into Transcaucasia (the area south of the Caucasus Mountains). While a detachment under his lieutenant Taimaz pursued Jalal al-Din, Chormaqan quickly gained the submission of the various polities of Persia by 1231, excluding Isfahan, which resisted until 1237. Jalal al-Din, after being pursued across Transcaucasia by Taimaz, was eventually killed by Kurdish peasants in 1231. Even with the threat of Jalal al-Din removed, the Mongols gave Transcaucasia only a brief respite. After consolidating Mongol dominion in Persia, Chormaqan invaded in 1236. Because of the invasions of Jalal al-Din, as well as the previous Mongol invasion in 1221–2, the Georgians and Armenians did not attempt to fight the Mongols in a field battle, realizing from previous experience that they lacked the ability to defeat the Mongols in the open. After a series of sieges Georgia and Armenia fell to the Mongols by 1239.

As Chormaqan entered Transcaucasia in 1236, an army of 150,000 Mongols, led by Sübedei and Batu, the son of Jochi, invaded the lands of the Kipchak Turks and the Bulghars on the Volga River. Despite a determined resistance neither the Kipchaks nor the Bulghars could resist the Mongol onslaught. Many of the Kipchaks fled before the Mongols, some of them reaching Hungary. Others were incorporated into the Mongol military machine.

In the winter of 1238 the Mongols advanced on the Rus' principalities, using the frozen rivers as roads. The fragmented Rus' discovered that they could not defeat the Mongols in open combat but learned that the Mongols were equally adept at siege warfare. One by one the Northern Rus' cities fell. In late 1238 and 1239 the southern Rus' cities also succumbed to Mongol attack, as did the Kipchak tribes of the Pontic steppes. The great city of Kiev, centre of Rus' civilization, was among the last cities to fall after days of continual bombardment from Mongol siege weapons. Of the major cities of the Rus' that did not submit when the Mongols approached, only Novgorod was spared from destruction due to a timely spring thaw that deterred the Mongol cavalry from progressing any farther north. Nonetheless, the Novgorodians saw the wisdom of submitting peacefully to the Mongols rather than incurring their wrath. Indeed, Novgorod became one of the Mongols most obedient vassals.

In 1241 Sübedei led the bulk of the Mongol army westward. It divided into two forces. The smaller force, commanded by Baidar and Qadan, invaded Poland while Sübedei and Batu led another across the Carpathian Mountains. At most Baidar and Qadan led 20,000 men, thus they sought to avoid direct engagement and conducted numerous raids. Eventually, though, they did fight a pitched battle at Liegnitz against a combined army of Poles, Germans and Teutonic Knights, a military order that emerged out of the Crusades in 1193. The Mongols destroyed this force before it could be reinforced by King Vaclav (Wenceslas) of Bohemia. The Mongol force then moved south to rendezvous with the main Mongol army.

Batu and Sübedei meanwhile forced their way across the Carpathians. The Mongols invaded Hungary via five routes. Unlike the Khwarazmians, the Hungarian King Bela IV did not wait for the Mongols in his castles. Rather, Bela marched with his army to a point at the Sajo River on the plain of Mohi. The Hungarian army was considered by many to possess the finest cavalry in Europe. Nonetheless, it proved to be of little use as the Mongols decimated it in April 1241. Using a rolling barrage of arrows and catapult missiles the Mongols seized a heavily defended bridge as another force made a rear attack by crossing at another point of the river. Soon the Hungarians found themselves trapped in their camp. The Mongols did not launch a final assault at once. Instead, they left a gap in their lines. The Hungarians took it to be an error on the part of the Mongols and began fleeing through it. In reality the gap was a ruse. With the Hungarians fleeing in a disorderly fashion that went from a trickle to a flood, the Mongol cavalry descended upon them, obliterating the Hungarian army. Mongol forces then spread throughout Hungary and into Wallachia and Serbia. King Bela IV barely escaped into the Adriatic Sea before Mongol troops arrived at his point of departure.

To all of Europe it appeared that the Mongols were on the verge of invading the rest of Europe but then suddenly they withdrew from Hungary. The exact reason remains a point of debate for scholars, but one cause that certainly played at least a minimal part was the death of Ögödei in 1240–1.[31] Ögödei's death drastically altered the Mongol Empire. It was under his reign that the Mongols began to conceive of conquering the world. Although this idea is often attributed to Chinggis Khan, in truth his actions seem to belie this idea. His goal seemed to have been more to secure the steppes of Mongolia from external threats than to dominate sedentary cultures. Raids and forcing sedentary states to pay tribute helped this process and were economically profitable. Ögödei, however, embraced the idea of conquest and encouraged the belief that Heaven had decreed that Chinggis Khan and his heirs should rule the world.

Ögödei also endorsed the creation of an effective administrative apparatus to rule the empire, which will be discussed in chapter Two. His role in laying the true foundations of the administration of the empire led to one of his key achievements – the building of the formal capital of the empire at Karakorum in the Orkhon River Valley in Mongolia. This provided a centre for the administration as well as dealing with ambassadors who came to submit – the Mongols had difficulty in understanding why they would come if not to submit. The creation of Karakorum not only assisted in the administration of the empire but also led to the creation of a commercial centre for it. Ögödei extended the *yam* or postal system created by Chinggis Khan throughout the empire as well as a logistical system to support it. His death, however, caused a crisis because he had not established a successor. Indeed, his death, due either to alcoholism or poison, also showed strains between the grandsons of Chinggis Khan.

Güyük and Regents

Ögödei's widow and sixth wife, Töregene, assumed the role of regent after Ögödei's death in 1241. Among her first obligations was to organize a *quriltai* in order to select a new khan. Her private choice was her own son Güyük, however she was slow to organize the meeting due to her desire for power. As the regent, Töregene essentially ran the empire. Those who disagreed with her ambitions, including many high-ranking ministers, ran the risk of death.

Töregene's rise to power is an interesting chain of events. She began her ascension in good faith. She gained the favour and protection of the senior member of the Chinggisid line, Chaghatai, Chinggis Khan's second son, in addition to other princes. They proclaimed that, since she was the mother of sons that had a right to the throne, she should be regent until the new khan was elected. The princes, perhaps in an attempt to curtail the regent's power, decreed that the old ministers would remain in their current positions in order that the old and new *yasas* or laws might not be altered.[32]

It appears that the other wives of Ögödei also wielded some power and influence though, as it was not until after Ögödei's beloved Möge Khatun died in 1241 that Töregene was able to control all aspects of the state. In addition she won over many of the Chinggisid family by bestowing numerous gifts and favours upon them.[33] Thus she increased her influence within the government. It must be remembered that at this time she still enjoyed the patronage and protection of Chaghatai, who as the senior prince wielded tremendous respect and influence in court matters. Secure in her position, she began to change the infrastructure of the government by purging those courtiers and ministers against whom she bore a grudge. And as her position was unassailable, no one could effectively oppose her endeavours.[34]

One of the key people she replaced was the able Khitan minister and governor of north China, Yelü Chucai. A former Persian merchant, 'Abd al-Rahman, became his successor. 'Abd al-Rahman gained the regent's ear by promising to double the revenue of the province through strenuous taxation.[35] He had accused Yelü Chucai of being too lenient with the population of China. Yelü Chucai's removal from office was a major divergence from the past leadership as he had been a very capable and trusted advisor of both Chinggis Khan and Ögödei. He died shortly afterwards in Karakorum at the age of 55, realizing that his counsel was now ignored.[36] Other ministers also found themselves at risk.

Meanwhile, Töregene also sought to bind some territories closer to her, building a base of support. The existing governor of Mawarannahr or Transoxiana, Körgüz, was arrested, imprisoned and replaced by Arghun, whose authority was expanded to all civil affairs of the Mongol Middle East.[37] With the appointment of Baiju, who she promoted over other lieutenants as military commander upon the death of Chormaqan in 1241, Töregene brought the region further under her control. While many of her appointees were chosen due to politics and corruption, some proved to be quite effective. Baiju, one of Chormaqan's lieutenants, proved to be an able general and extended Mongol influence into Rum (central modern Turkey). Arghun, unlike 'Abd al-Rahman, proved to be a capable and law-abiding minister. Arghun's image was tarnished, however, with the appointment of Sharaf al-Din as his undersecretary. Sharaf al-Din proceeded to tax the populace heavily and imposed taxes on widows and orphans on which 'there is no charge in the law of God nor impost in the yasa of Chingiz-Khan'.[38]

In addition to the purge of the ministries and governors of the empire, Töregene single-handedly orchestrated the election of her son Güyük to the throne. Although a son of Ögödei, it is unlikely that Güyük could have obtained the throne without the substantial efforts of his mother. Although the nominated heir, Shiremun, was not guaranteed the throne as all of the Mongol princes and generals voted, Güyük, however, seemed an unlikely candidate. He had a history of illness which certainly deterred some from supporting him.[39] In addition, it is doubtful that Ögödei would have ever considered Güyük as a candidate for khan. Güyük's animosity with Batu, another senior prince, was well known and not tolerated by Ögödei.[40] When this rivalry first came to the fore, Ögödei did not even speak to his son for several days, however, Töregene was able manipulate the situation to her advantage as regent.

As the princes gathered to elect the khan in 1246, Töregene garnered support behind the scenes. Pressing the issue of Shiremun's age, Töregene contended that his youth was a liability and Köten, Ögödei's second son who Chinggis Khan had suggested as Ögödei's heir, was sickly.[41] She downplayed Güyük's own illnesses while she lobbied behind the scenes to show that Köten's condition was more serious. Indeed, he died during Güyük's reign – albeit under somewhat mysterious circumstances. Thus Töregene elevated Güyük to the throne by carrying out a brilliant and subtle mud-slinging campaign that blurred reality.[42]

Güyük's ascension was not without contest. Chinggis Khan's youngest brother, Temüge Otchigin, made an attempt to forcibly seize the throne. He advanced upon the imperial court but withdrew when he heard Güyük was near.[43] Militarily, Batu was more of a threat, but he occupied himself with establishing his dominion over his newly won territories in the west and Güyük did not intervene. Batu, however, did attempt to stall the quriltai, since it technically could not start without his arrival as he was the senior prince after Chaghatai's death in 1242. Yet before he arrived the influence of Töregene prevailed and the princes selected Güyük as khan.

Although Güyük was now khan, Töregene continued to issue decrees. Only after Güyük was firmly in power did she relinquish her control in 1246. Two or three months later she died.[44] During the interim between Güyük's ascension and Töregene's relinquishment of power, Güyük became increasingly estranged from his mother, perhaps realizing that she had neglected the proper administration of the empire. Güyük began correcting this by restoring many ministers to their original positions, including those who had fled during Töregene's regency. He executed corrupt officials, such as 'Abd al-Rahman, the governor of Khitai, as the Mongols called northern China. Still, the empire lost two capable civil servants in the form of Körgüz, former governor of Mawarannahr, and the great minister of the empire, Yelü Chucai.

Although Güyük corrected many of the corrupt practices introduced by Töregene's regency, all was not well within the empire. Batu, the son of Jochi, and Güyük did not agree on many things. Much of their animosity stemmed from Jochi's questionable ancestry. Furthermore, the two had clashed during the western campaign. Only the presence of Sübedei prevented physical conflict. Güyük was sent back to Ögödei who, as mentioned earlier, became furious with his son. Güyük had not forgotten his feud with Batu. This was intensified by Batu's refusal to come to the quriltai for Güyük's ascension to the throne. Güyük did prepare an army, ostensibly to complete the conquest of Europe, but many suspected that it was to wage war against Batu. In the end nothing happened, as Güyük died in 1248.

Güyük's wife, Oghul-Qaimish, then assumed the regency. During her regency, which lasted until 1251, the empire came to a virtual standstill. As with Töregene, the Mongol princes commanded her to heed the advice of administrators, such as Chinqai. This, however, she failed to do. Indeed, she demonstrated very little interest in arranging a *quriltai*. Her own sons, Khoja and Naqu, perhaps out of frustration that their mother did not aid their ascent to the throne, eventually set up their own courts. Astonishingly, none of the three listened to the exhortations of the high-ranking bureaucrats. In addition they issued their own decrees, thus it was possible to receive three different orders from the self-proclaimed rulers. The increasing frustration of other members of the Mongol elite altered the status quo. Batu ordered a *quriltai* to be held under the auspices of his brother, Berke. Those present selected Möngke, son of Tolui and Sorqoqtani, as khan. Khoja and Naqu issued decrees saying that they did not recognize the election, which took place in their absence. Matters dragged on until a coup led by members of the Toluid and Jochid families ended the regency and ensconced Möngke Khan on the throne.

Despite the turnover in leadership and at times ineffective leadership of the regents and the brief reign of Güyük, the Mongols were active, albeit sporadicly, in expanding their empire. War against the Song Dynasty of southern China had begun during Ögödei's reign and continued in a sporadic manner throughout the 1240s. In the Middle East Baiju conquered the Seljuk Sultanate of Rum (modern Turkey) in 1243 and Mongol forces raided into Syria and the Crusader States, threatening Antioch. They also launched numerous raids against Baghdad, but with the lack of political stability the Mongols did not organize any large-scale campaigns of conquest. These, however, resumed under the leadership of Möngke Khan.

MÖNGKE

Oghul-Qaimish's inattention led to the coup in which Möngke (r. 1251–9) seized power with the backing of many of the Chinggisid princes in 1250. Under his reign the Mongol armies were once again on the march. The Mongols attained the zenith of their power during the reign of Möngke Khan. Upon ascending the throne, with the assistance of his politically wily and influential mother Sorqoqtani, and the military power of his cousin Batu, Möngke rectified the corruption that had entered the administrative practices of the empire during the regencies of Töregene and Oghul-Qaimish. Additionally, he purged many of the descendants of Ögödei and Chaghatai after they attempted a countercoup. Möngke dealt aggressively with any threat to the ascendancy of the Toluids.

Having restored the efficiency of the administration and removed threats to his power, Möngke set about expanding the empire. By this time the Mongols had approximately one million men under arms, ranging from nomadic horse archers, who made up the core of their armies, to engineers and siege artillery men, and of course infantry for garrisoning cities and fortresses that remained standing. The Mongols typically razed fortifications to the ground as they impeded the cavalry.

Möngke planned to carry out two major campaigns. Essentially, these were mop-up campaigns against powers that had not submitted previously. The first was led by Möngke himself, with the assistance of his younger brother, Khubilai (d. 1295). They invaded the Song Empire (1126–1279) of southern China. The Mongols had been at war with the Song since the reign of Ögödei but had made little headway. The geography of southern China, which ranged from mountains to flooded plains used for rice cultivation, made it unsuitable for cavalry warfare, and the Song's strongly fortified cities also stymied the Mongols' expansion. Although the Mongols had become exceedingly adept at siege warfare, the Song defenders were equally talented at defending their cities and using the latest technological advances, like gunpowder, against the Mongols.

The Mongols directed their second campaign against regions in the Middle East that had not seen the wisdom of submitting to the Mongols and those where the ruler had not come in person to demonstrate their obeisance. Two powers in particular concerned the Mongols. The first was the Nizari Ismailis of Alamut, in the Elburz Mountains of Iran, south of the Caspian Sea and in Quhistan in Central Iran. The Nizari Ismailis, Shi'a Muslims, known in the west as the Assassins, had been allies of the Mongols during the invasion of the Khwarazmian Empire as well as during the period of Chormaqan's rule of the Middle East. After 1240 the Ismailis viewed the Mongols as a threat – an accurate perception as the Mongols during the time of Ögödei had determined that Heaven had decreed they should rule the world. Furthermore, the Ismailis attempted to assassinate Möngke.[45] The second target of the

Mongol army, led by Hülegü, another brother of Möngke's, was the Abbasid caliphate of Baghdad. In theory caliph Mustasim ibn Mustansir was the ruler of the Islamic world as the successor to the Prophet Muhammad. In reality the Abbasid caliphate had shrunk considerably since its creation in the eighth century. Secular rulers sprang up in the frontier provinces to take power, at first with the blessing of the caliph, but then ruling with little regard for the caliph, as was the case of Sultan Muhammad ii of the Khwarazmian Empire. By the 1250s the caliphate was really a small kingdom centred on the city of Baghdad with little temporal authority beyond the surrounding areas.

Hülegü's campaign began at a leisurely pace as his army marched out of Mongolia in 1255. As they advanced, scouts and officials rode ahead to procure adequate pastures for them. This caused a redistribution of the *tammachin*, or troops stationed along the borders of the Mongol Empire. These advanced to new positions, leaving their former pastures to the Mongol prince. In addition, troops already in the Middle East began operations against the Ismailis. In 1252 Ket-Buqa, one of Hülegü's generals, began raiding Quhistan.

While Khwurshah, the Nizari Ismaili leader, did offer submission to the Mongols, he constantly delayed coming before Hülegü. While negotiations were carried out Ket-Buqa finally overran Quhistan, often using letters from Khwurshah to secure their formidable fortresses. Despite the obvious display of force Khwurshah still did not come in person to Hülegü, which angered the Mongol prince. As a result activities against the Nizari Ismailis intensified. Soon the greatest fortresses of the Nizari Ismailis, such as Alamut, surrendered to the Mongols. Khwurshah himself finally saw that all was lost and came before Hülegü. Hülegü then used the Nizari Ismaili leader to gain the submission of over a hundred other fortresses. Then, having little use for him, Khwurshah was executed, as were the leaders of the important families among the Nizari Ismailis. Many Sunni Muslims celebrated this; they had come to regard the Nizari Ismailis with dread as the Assassins were masters of disguise and could strike down notable figures even under tight security. Indeed, the Persian chronicler Juvaini, who also worked in the Mongol bureaucracy, revelled in the destruction of the much-feared Ismailis, who used assassination in order to intimidate and extend their influence in parts of the Middle East. Juvaini wrote:

> So was the world cleansed which had been polluted by their evil. Wayfarers now ply to and fro without fear or dread or the

inconvenience of paying a toll and pray for the fortune of the happy King who uprooted their foundations and left no trace of any one of them.[46]

Hülegü then moved against the Abbasid caliphate in Baghdad. Although Baghdad and the Abbasid caliphate had withstood several years of Mongol attacks, they remained independent and defiant of the Mongols. In truth, the outcome of the attack on Baghdad was never in doubt, at least by the Mongols. Previous attempts had amounted to little more than raids. The Mongols had not launched an assault on the city itself until the arrival of Hülegü. Even before the Mongols arrived the city's defences fragmented as internal rivalries robbed the caliphate of effective leadership. Indeed, Ibn 'Alqami , the *wazir* or chamberlain to the caliph, is thought to have been in league with the Mongols. Then of course there was the fact that caliph Mustasim was an incompetent more interested in pleasure seeking than matters of state. The caliph refused to capitulate but did little to defend the city and only came to terms after the Mongols breached the walls. The Mongols sacked Baghdad, ending the position of caliph among the Sunnis in 1258. Hülegü had the caliph executed by rolling him in a carpet and having him trampled, although some sources have a more colourful story in which the caliph starves to death with all of the treasure he did not spend on defences for the city.[47] The city was then given over to pillaging for more than 30 days.

Having brought the caliphate under Mongol rule, Hülegü moved his armies to the lush pastures of modern Azerbaijan. Most of the local princes of the region came and offered their submission, however the Ayyubid ruler of Aleppo and Damascus, al-Nasir Yusuf, was not among them. Hülegü set about rectifying this matter. The Mongol army descended upon Aleppo in January 1260. Despite its stout defences, after six days of concentrated fire by twenty siege engines the Mongols broke through. The citadel itself held for another month, although the city was turned over to pillaging for a period of five days. In the end Aleppo succumbed to the Mongols. After the fall of Aleppo other Syrian cities quickly fell. Al-Nasir, upon hearing of the Mongols' approach, fled from Damascus. Although Hülegü returned to Azerbaijan after Aleppo, his general Ket-Buqa continued the operations. Wisely, Damascus surrendered to the Mongols without a fight when they arrived in March 1260. Another Mongol force caught al-Nasir outside Nablus after a brief skirmish and used him to gain the submission of other fortresses. Then he was sent to Hülegü in Azerbaijan to show proper obeisance.

The citadel of Aleppo, which was an imposing fortress within the city. Although the city fell to the Mongols in 1260, after concentrated bombardment from trebuchets, the citadel held out for another month.

Hülegü, however, withdrew the bulk of his army in 1259–60 after receiving news that Möngke had died during the war against the Song. Meanwhile Ket-Buqa remained in Syria with a small army. Mongol control of Syria was ephemeral though. In Egypt the Mamluks, former slaves who had been trained specifically as soldiers, had come into power. They realized that they had little chance of defeating a determined invasion by the Mongols and thus decided to take the battle to the Mongols while they were unprepared. Having secured the neutrality of the Crusaders, who had provoked Mongol attacks on Sidon and in Galilee, the Mamluks advanced to 'Ayn Jalut, or the Well of Goliath, where they defeated Ket-Buqa in a hard-fought battle. The desertion of some of the Syrian troops from the Mongol side may have been the pivotal point of the battle. While this battle is often viewed as a turning point in history, since the Mongols advance was halted, it gains this position not so much due to the Mamluks' victory, tremendous as it was, but rather due to events that occurred in China.

In the eastern sphere of operations Khubilai was sent to open a new front against the Song in China. Möngke could not break through the northern defences, so he wanted to attack them from the southwest and force the Song to reposition some of their troops. Möngke ordered two out of every ten to serve under Khubilai and two out of every ten for Hülegü in 1252–3, although Khubilai's army was only one out of four armies sent against the Song.[48] The attack on the Song began in earnest in 1257 although mobilization began in 1255 and some attacks came even before.

The invasion started off well with all four armies making good progress on their respective fronts. It eventually began to bog down due to the terrain. In 1258–9 Möngke led a corps of 40,000 to 100,000 in a three-pronged attack from Shanxi into Sichuan. He captured Chengdu, Tongchuan and several mountain forts after determined attacks in 1258. In 1259, when Möngke moved against Hezhou, the prefect of the city moved the government to Diaoyucheng, which resisted the Mongols and stalled the Mongol offensive. During the course of the siege Möngke died either from an arrow wound or dysentery. Diaoyucheng, meanwhile, held out until 1279.[49]

During Möngke's invasion he had other commanders operating elsewhere in the Song Empire; most of these were not very effective except as raiders.[50] Khubilai laid siege to the city of Yauju and experienced many difficulties.[51] Much of the Mongols' difficulty in the Song campaign stemmed from the terrain. Haojing (1223–75), Khubilai's minister, believed that the Mongols in Sichuan were limited by the mountains and valleys as well as by the Song occupation of strategic places. This forced the Mongols to take circuitous routes, which were further complicated by guerrilla attacks, slowing them down. The difficulty of capturing mountain forts, particularly in Sichuan, forced the Mongols to take Sichuan only after capturing the rest of the Song Empire.[52] They encountered similar problems with the mountains and islands of Korea.

The Song campaign stalled further when Khubilai reached the Huai River and received the news of Möngke's death. Initially he dismissed it as false and pressed on, crossing the Yangtze River to capture O-Zhou. Only later did he receive information confirming his brother's death from Chabai, Khubilai's wife.[53] This news led to the dissolution of the Mongol Empire.

Möngke Khan's funeral in 1260, Mughal era. This scene probably did not take place but it does reveal a Mughal conception of the Mongol Empire.

2

DISSOLUTION OF THE EMPIRE

Due to the lack of a clear principle of succession, other than being descended from Chinggis Khan, warfare between rival claimants to the throne became increasingly frequent. Civil war erupted after Möngke's death as two of his brothers vied for the throne. As each sought the throne, tensions arose between Khubilai and his brother Ariq Böke, who had been left to rule as regent in Mongolia while Möngke campaigned in southern China. Both received the crown in separate *quriltais*; Ariq Böke's held in Mongolia, and Khubilai's in China. Thus civil war ensued, with Khubilai emerging the victor in 1264, but the damage to the territorial integrity of the empire ensured that it was forever destroyed. While most of the other princes nominally accepted Khubilai as the khan of the empire, his influence dwindled outside Mongolia and China. Khubilai and his successors, known as the Yuan Dynasty (1264–1370), found their closest allies in Hülegü and his successors. Hülegü's kingdom, known as the Ilkhanate of Persia, dominated Iran, Iraq, modern Turkey, Armenia, Azerbaijan and Georgia. Central Asia was ruled by the Chaghatayids, the descendants of Chaghatai, Chinggis Khan's third son, although often they were the puppets of Qaidu, a descendant of Ögödei and rival of Khubilai Khan. Meanwhile in the Pontic and Caspian steppes, descendants of Jochi, Chinggis Khan's first son, held power as the Jochid Khanate or Kipchak Khanate (so named after the majority of the nomadic population) and later as the Golden Horde.

THE EMPIRE OF THE GREAT KHAN

The history of Mongolia after the dissolution of the Mongol Empire is really the history of the Yuan Dynasty. Ariq Böke's unsuccessful challenge and claim to the throne of the Mongol Empire in 1260 was the death knell for Mongolia. Ariq Böke represented the interests of the old steppe elites, whereas Khubilai represented a new vision of empire focused more on the sedentary lands. With Khubilai's ascension to the throne the capital of the Mongol Empire moved from Karakorum in the Orkhon River Valley to northern China. He built two capitals. The first, Daidu, was located in the environs of modern Beijing. In many ways it symbolized Khubilai's empire. It was modelled after existing Chinese cities, although built and planned largely by non-Chinese.[1] Daidu served as his winter capital while another city was build roughly 200 km (125 miles) from modern Beijing. He named it Shangdu (the Upper Capital where he went in the summer) which appeared as Xanadu in Samuel Coleridge's poem 'Kubla Khan' and found a later incarnation in a film called *Xanadu* starring Olivia Newton-John as a Greek muse reincarnated as a roller-disco muse who helps build a roller-skating nightclub.[2] In retrospect the world may have been a better place if Ariq Böke had won.

Moving the capital from Mongolia had a deleterious effect on Mongolia. Quite simply, without the capital Mongolia became a backwater region of the empire. Khubilai and his successors did attempt to maintain support there simply because it remained an important troop reservoir – the importance of Mongol cavalry did not diminish over time. Indeed, there was concern that Mongols in Mongolia, as happened during the civil wars between Khubilai and Ariq Böke, could gravitate to the more conservative and traditional Mongol lords of central Asia. However, the Yuan Dynasty successfully prevented that from happening. As the civil wars dwindled after Khubilai's death in 1294, the fear diminished and less emphasis was placed on maintaining important ties to Mongolia.

Khubilai's repositioning of the capital did have a strategic sense that was not based solely on his gravitation towards northern china and Chinese culture. With the conquest of the Song Empire, Karakorum was simply not a central location from which to rule his new empire. Also, Karakorum was relatively insecure as Qaidu's forces, Khubilai's next major challenger, could reach it from modern Kazakhstan. Finally, the cost of maintaining a court in Karakorum befitting the status of the khan was prohibitive. Even in the days of his predecessors, 900 cartloads of provisions were required to feed the population. Shangdu and Daidu were better situated for provisions, more secure from western threats, and also better situated for ruling an empire that stretched from Lake Baikal to the Gulf of Tonkin. Although neither city was located near farmland Khubilai resolved the situation by extending the Grand Canal 217 km (135 miles), allowing provisions and other goods to arrive at Daidu efficiently and at lower cost.[3]

Indeed, as time passed the ruling dynasty increasingly assimilated aspects of Chinese culture and Buddhist influences and thus appeared very un-Mongol to the Mongols in Mongolia. In many ways Khubilai typified this. It is possible that his long life exacerbated the image of him transitioning from a Mongol khan into a Chinese emperor. Born in 1215, Khubilai lived an extraordinary 79 years – clear evidence that regardless of the age, the best medical care (and luck) made a significant difference in longevity. Although he ended as a corpulent emperor, often blind to the excesses of his government, Khubilai's early life did not presage this. Although he realized the importance of assuming the rule of a Chinese emperor, he never learned the language.[4]

Nonetheless, he realized he needed to walk in two worlds – that of the nomads and that of his sedentary subjects. So he adopted the dynastic name of Yuan (origin) and the dynastic calendar. His position was not original as preceding dynasties such as the Liao (907–1125) and the Jin (1125–1234), as well as Kara Khitai in central Asia, struggled to maintain their legitimacy over their nomadic armies while trying to rule a much more populous sedentary population.[5] Usually when the ruler lost his nomadic identity he was overthrown by the new,

Khubilai Khan hunting, miniature from Marco Polo's *Livre de Merveilles*. This illustration depicts a very European Khubilai Khan with idealized Mongol garb, which demonstrates Polo's description of Khubilai Khan's hunting – a large party, gyrfalcon and, of course, elephants. The depiction of the elephants demonstrates the lack of Europeans' familiarity with the animals at the time.

emerging dynasty; whether the new one was nomadic or sedentary mattered little. As emperor, Khubilai did not embrace the Chinese aspect of his identity entirely. Although he allowed the Chinese bureaucracy to remain somewhat in place, there existed a mirror Mongol administration staffed largely by non-Han – Mongols, Uighurs, Persians, central Asians and so on. While the Chinese ministers served their function to present Khubilai as the ideal Confucian sage-king, the Mongol administration actually ran the empire. Khubilai backed this image by building a temple to honour his ancestors, another to honour Confucius, and followed the practice of commissioning scholars to write the histories of preceding dynasties (Jin and Song).[6]

After consolidating his authority Khubilai resumed his campaigns of conquest. The war against the Song lasted until 1276. Only by adopting new technologies and adapting their style of warfare could the Mongols conquer the Song. Counterweight trebuchets from the west (which had been in use in Europe and the Middle East for almost a century) and an improved navy were the keys. Yet even before the Song Empire was conquered Khubilai attempted to extend his rule elsewhere. Korea became more firmly attached to the Mongol throne although it had been a tributary since the 1230s. Japan proved more troublesome. The first invasion was a probing attack but the second was a full-scale attempt of conquest that ended due to untimely (for the Mongols) typhoons. Khubilai also attempted to conquer Java, although this may have had more to do with overthrowing a usurper and restoring trade with the region than outright conquest.[7] Other efforts in Southeast Asia (modern day Vietnam and Myanmar) should be seen as a continuation of the Mongol conquests, although they also demonstrate Khubilai's power to bring those areas in to the orbit of his authority. From the perspective of Khubilai as a Chinese ruler, it was also restoring tributary relations with these states. Until the Mongol invasion, Vietnamese kingdoms had not paid tribute to China since the Tang Dynasty (618–907). While outright conquest failed not only due to fierce resistance but also the tropical climate, diseases and logistical failures, Mongol strength of arms also demonstrated that it was more prudent to send tribute than risk continued Mongol incursions.[8]

Although Khubilai did not conquer any territory beyond the Song empire, he demonstrated that his empire was the most powerful entity on earth. While the Mongol Empire was now fragmented, it still maintained a sense of unity through the *Altan Urugh* or Golden Family – the descendants of Chinggis Khan. The empire had always been viewed as the patrimony of the *Altan Urugh*. Although Möngke made the empire more centralized, as a patrimonial state, family members in other parts of the empire held appanages or collected income from distant sources. Thus it was possible that the ruler of the Jochid Khanate collected income from northern China while a prince ruling in Tibet could collect revenue from a town in Armenia. Indeed, during the war with Qaidu, Khubilai did not stop him from collecting his revenues from territories within Khubilai's domain – if he had, Qaidu could have reciprocated and the whole system may have unravelled. Undoubtedly, such a loss of lucrative income would have alienated other Chinggisids from Khubilai.

Although much of Khubilai's reign was fraught with war against the Song, foreign invasions and other khanates as well as internal rebellion, his rule set the foundations for the Yuan Empire. The Mongol ruling elite remained aloof from the Han Chinese population and tended to favour other populations within the empire. Tibetan Buddhism was favoured as a religion, although the practice of religious toleration continued. Although old age and possible depression after the death of his wife, Chabi, played a role in his increasing neglect of the affairs of state, allowing corruption to slip in, the empire was stable and flourishing.[9]

His successors inherited a vast empire of great wealth and power. Although Temür Öljeitü (r. 1294–1307), Khubilai's successor and grandson, followed Khubilai's general plan of ruling, he ceased the foreign adventures, undoubtedly saving the empire an immense amount of wealth and resources. (Khubilai's planned third invasion of Japan failed to launch because of a timber shortage and concerns about the onerous taxes on the Chinese peasants to pay for the expeditions.[10]) Temür Öljeitü, although he continued the war against Qaidu, which will be discussed further shortly, also strove to restore some semblance of peace through the Mongol Empire. He maintained good relations with the Ilkhanate, largely using the sea route around India and into the Persian Gulf. After Qaidu's death, relations improved with the Chaghatayid Khanate. Nonetheless, Temür Öljeitü's reign did not please everyone, as he increasingly ruled as a Chinese emperor, at least in the eyes of the more traditional Mongols.

After his death in 1307 Temür Öljeitü's nephew Khaishan (r. 1307–11) took the throne, signalling the beginning of a series of short-reigned rulers, with the exception of Khaishan's successor and brother,

Ayurbarwada (r. 1311–20). The other six, until Toghon Temür (r. 1332–70), lasted from a few months to five years. Although the empire continued to function, their reigns were marked by increasing friction between the pro-nomad and pro-sedentary factions. Ayurbarwada leaned toward the pro-sedentary factions. He encouraged the promotion of neo-Confucianism and re-established the use of the Confucian civil service exams that Khubilai had abolished. Nonetheless, Mongols continued to receive preference in the bureaucracy. Still, this did not assuage the concerns of the pro-nomadic faction in the court. As a result civil war and rebellion erupted periodically in the 1320s. As civil war preoccupied the court, the dissatisfaction of the population in the south garnered little attention.

Heavy taxation, resentment of Mongol rule and loyalties to the old Song Dynasty fuelled the sporadic rebellions in southern China. These began in 1279 with the fall of the Song, but were never completely crushed. The resilience of the rebels was in part due to the Mongols' lack of attention to the south. Eventually these often unrelated rebellions coalesced into a wider phenomenon known as the Red Turbans. The wars against Qaidu and pro-nomadic factions within the empire occupied much of the court's attention and thus prevented them from ever fully incorporating much of the former Song Empire into the Yuan. Instead they ruled it loosely. Furthermore, the climate and terrain prevented them from stationing large numbers of Mongol troops in the regions, thus relying on local Han garrisons. While many of these were commanded by Mongols and loyal to the Yuan, at the same time their loyalty could be suspect.

Thus, when Toghon Temür assumed the throne he inherited a myriad of problems and was unable to deal with any of them satisfactorily. Since the capital was moved from Karakorum an increasing dissatisfaction with the rulers had existed in Mongolia. Other problems included rebellions in southern China, wars on the frontier which were not dynasty threatening but still a drain on resources, widespread corruption within the government and the royal family and a series of natural disasters, including major flooding on the Huang He. Indeed it appeared the Yuan Dynasty no longer held the Mandate of Heaven, an idea crucial to maintaining the legitimacy of the dynasty. From the Chinese perspective the ruler was the Son of Heaven and as long as Heaven (*tian*) was pleased, it continued to confer its approval; this was evinced through prosperity, good harvests, success against enemies and so on. As the old adage goes, however, what Heaven

Mongol archer on horseback. Although this illustration is from the Ming era, it could still be representative of the 13th- and 14th-century Mongols. That the archer is partially disrobed suggests that he may have been in Yunnan, where it was much warmer than Mongolia, and where a sizeable number of Mongols were stationed during the Yuan era. His bow arm remains covered, in order to protect it against the bowstring.

gives, it can take away – or one can ascribe it to bad luck and poor administration. When Heaven removes its blessings from a dynasty, it then bestows the mandate on a new dynasty.

In essence Toghon Temür's reign was a lesson on how to lose the Mandate of Heaven, even though it was not entirely his fault as he inherited many of the problems. When the Red Turban rebellions toppled the Yuan Dynasty and the nascent Ming Dynasty (1368–1644), which evolved from one of the Red Turban factions in 1368, the Yuan Emperor Toghon Temür fled from China to Mongolia. According to legend, only six of the reported 40 *tümens* (ten-thousands) were able to escape. The rest were cut off and eventually surrendered. Even with the Ming's hatred of the Mongols, Mongol warriors were simply too important to massacre. If this legend is true, some scholars have pointed out that this also indicates a large demographic loss for Mongolia.[11] It must be remembered, however, that these 40 *tümens* were not stationed in Mongolia and thus cannot be considered a demographic loss for Mongolia. Indeed, many of them formed the so-called Yunnan Mongol population that still exists today in China, but this issue will be discussed in more detail in chapter Nine.[12]

Most of the troops Toghon Temür led back to Mongolia were soldiers, so he possessed a sizeable force of 40,000 to 60,000 men. Once in Mongolia he still viewed himself as the ruler, but without territory south of the Great Wall of China, which was later constructed by the Ming Dynasty. He headed towards the Onan-Kerulen River basin, the ancestral homeland of the Mongols, to assert his authority. At the same time he was pursued by the Ming army, in order to ensure that the Mongols did not launch a counterattack. Despite the loss of a vast amount of territory it was reasonable to assume the Yuan could re-establish themselves in Mongolia and perhaps launch a counterattack. This idea was illusory. Despite his presence in Mongolia, Toghon Temür found very little support for his claims as ruler there. The decades of antipathy towards the royal family manifested primarily in the descendants of Ariq Böke, who were the dominant figures in Mongolia. In addition to the still simmering feud between Ariq Böke and Khubilai, the Mongols of Mongolia simply viewed Toghon Temür and the returning Mongols as outsiders – essentially as Chinese and not Mongol. Thus war erupted between the two parties.

A third element entered the fray in the form of the Oirats, located around the Altai Mountains in western Mongolia. They had been a marginal group for much of the history of the Mongol Empire with little connection to the royal family, as the lineage of the Oirats was of non-Chinggisid descent. As their power increased in the late fourteenth century their own claims to the khanship and dominance over other Mongols was viewed as anathema. Indeed, as mentioned in chapter One, some Oirats traced their ancestry to the Kereit khan, Toghril Ong-Khan, despite having the name of one of the Hoyin-Irgen tribes (Oyirad) that was unconnected to the Kereit.

Warfare became endemic for much of the fourteenth and fifteenth centuries. The Ming emperors invaded Mongolia on several occasions with mixed results. Although they defeated Mongol forces, the Ming armies suffered constant attacks as they departed. Complicating the matter was the fact that the Ming could not sustain their presence in the steppe long term due to logistical issues. In addition the Ming attempted to play various Mongolian factions off against each other, a time-honoured tradition in Chinese foreign policy with the steppe, granting titles to rulers to legitimize them. The ultimate goal for the Ming was to weaken the Mongols through the policy of divide and rule, although their efforts were not always successful. To them it did not matter who they worked with – Chinggisids or Oirat leaders. Yet at the same time there was the risk that one leader could coalesce sufficient power to attack China. The attacks were not a large enough threat to topple the Ming Dynasty but nonetheless a danger. One example was the particularly dangerous Oirat leader, Esen (r. 1439–55), who created a nomadic empire that stretched from Lake Balkash to the borders of China.

After his death Mongolia again erupted in internecine warfare, particularly between Mongols ruled by the Chinggisids and the Oirats. Not until the rise of Dayan Khan (r. 1479–1517), selected as the 28th successor to Chinggis Khan, did stability return to Mongolia. Dayan, benefiting from his father Mandaghol's (r. 1473–9) unification of the Khalkha Mongols, one of the Chinggisid Mongol groups, defeated the Oirats and drove them out of what is now Mongolia. He then began to attack China and proved to be a serious threat until his death.

THE ILKHANATE

Elsewhere in the Mongol Empire the dissolution continued. As Ariq Böke and Khubilai fought, the rest of the empire fragmented. Central Asia, the area bequeathed to Chaghatai, became a separate khanate and resisted Khubilai's rule. It would be ruled at varying times by Chaghatayids or Qaidu, Ögödei's grandson and Khubilai's most formidable opponent. Meanwhile, Batu died in 1255 and his brother Berke (r. 1257–66) came to the throne after a short reign by Batu's son, Sartaq (r. 1256–7) and grandson, Ulaghchi (r. 1257). Berke quickly came into conflict with Hülegü. The stated reason was that Berke, a Muslim convert, was angered over the destruction of the Abbasid Caliphate. In truth it centred more on Jochid claims to territory in the Middle East that Hülegü now claimed as part of his own kingdom, known as the Ilkhanate of Persia, although the death of the caliph certainly didn't help matters. Hülegü and his successors were in the unenviable position of fighting not only the Golden Horde, as the Jochids were later known, but also the Chaghatayids. In addition the Golden Horde entered an alliance with the Mamluk Sultanate of Egypt and Syria, thus the Ilkhanate was surrounded by enemies with no direct route to

Boucicaut Master, Hülegü pursuing Berke, illustration from Marco Polo, *Livre des Merveilles* (15th-century edn). After the death of Möngke, civil war erupted between Berke and Hülegü over who had control of the lush Mughan steppe in Azerbaijan.

its sole ally, the Great Khan's empire ruled by Khubilai's new dynasty, the Yuan. This, however, led to an increased use of the sea route as illustrated by Marco Polo and Ibn Battuta.

While Hülegü and his successors recognized Khubilai as the khan of the empire, they used the title of Ilkhan, or subordinate khan. After Khubilai died in 1294, however, the Ilkhans continued the use of their title but ceased to be deferential to their cousins in the east. Due to a plethora of Persian, Arabic, Armenian and Georgian sources, we have a better picture of Ilkhanid history than of the Chaghatayids or Jochids. Of course, Rashid al-Din's *Jami' al-Tawarikh* would have us believe that prior to the rise of Ghazan Khan everything was essentially chaos and misrule. Then Ghazan Khan, with Rashid al-Din as his prime minister, set things to right. As George Lane wrote, 'the years before 1295 . . . have generally been dismissed as merely wasted decades of greed, anarchy, and mayhem'.[13] While there is some truth that Ghazan's rule might be considered a pinnacle, the Mongols did not run amok in the Ilkhanid state prior to his reign.

Wars against their neighbours occupied much of the Ilkhanids' time, particularly against the Jochids who desired the pastures and cities of Transcaucasia based on the idea that the Jochids had inherited the territory as far west as the Mongols horses' hooves had touched.[14]

Peter Jackson has demonstrated that in practice the Jochids did have some administrative claim to this territory prior to the arrival of Hülegü.[15] Nonetheless, with Hülegü's appearance in the region these claims ended in the eyes of the imperial court, albeit not from the Jochid perspective. There is some reason to believe that one of Hülegü's tasks in finishing the Mongol conquest of the Middle East was to curtail Jochid influence in the region, particularly due to the rise of Berke b. Jochi and brother of Batu (b. stands for 'son of', shortened from 'ben' or 'bin' as in Hebrew or Arabic names).[16] It appears that Möngke trusted Berke little and even Batu felt that perhaps Islam affected Berke's Mongol sensibilities.[17] Not all scholars agree on this interpretation. George Lane proposed the tantalizing idea that part of Hülegü's mission would be to carve a kingdom for himself out of Baghdad, Syria and Egypt.[18] The Mongol defeat at 'Ayn Jalut and the death of Möngke ended that possibility. Indeed, with the exception of Ghazan's brief conquest of Syria in 1299–1300, the Mongols never controlled Syria after 1260, much less Egypt.

Despite wars on multiple fronts consuming much of their attention the Ilkhanate slowly yet steadily created a rational state with minted currency,[19] negotiated with numerous European powers in search of an alliance against the Mamluks and centralized their rule. This included replacing and strengthening local dynasties when necessary – at times with direct Mongol rule.[20] Also, the Ilkhanids began to switch their armies over to the *iqta* or *timar* system, which consisted of the soldiers receiving revenues from land grants. This should not be misconstrued as the Mongol army becoming sedentary and switching to a medium or heavy Persian cataphract-style force as has been suggested.[21] Nor did the Mongols actually receive fiefs – that was not the purpose of the *iqta*. The *iqta* or *timar* holder did not 'own' or even manage the land. They simply received a portion of the revenue. The idea was that with a steady income from these lands (whether villages, markets or orchards), they would be less likely to plunder it or let their own flocks and herds destroy a farmer's field of crops. The Mongols, however, remained nomadic.[22]

At the same time, the Ilkhanid Mongols, as would their brethren in the Jochid and Chaghatayid khanates, converted to Islam, the religion of the majority of their subjects. Indeed, the Ilkhanate's acceptance of Islam during the reign of Ghazan Khan made it the first Mongol state to convert to Islam. The conversion had a substantial impact on non-Muslims within the realm. Christians, who at least viewed themselves as favoured prior to the conversion, saw a rise in persecution and Buddhist and shamanistic practices were abandoned. Yet outsiders did not really see the change as significant. European Christians still attempted to convert the Ilkhans to the 'right' form of Christianity and sought an alliance to regain the Holy Land. The Mamluk government and many religious scholars such as Ibn Taymiyya, within the Mamluk Sultanate, still viewed the Mongols as infidels and believed the Ilkhans' conversion was a ploy, and that the Mongols were wolves in sheep's clothing. The latter accusation does raise the question of whether the Mongols wore felt robes or *deels* in the Middle Eastern heat, although it may also explain their desire of other fabrics.[23] Nonetheless, the conversion of the Ilkhanate seriously threatened the Mamluks, who had a less than sterling pedigree as a leading Islamic dynasty based on almost continuous regicide. Indeed, a Ghazan proclamation after Islam became the state religion indicated that merchants could pass peacefully between the Mamluk Sultanate and the Ilkhanate. Furthermore, Ghazan claimed to have divine support for his rule – not a new idea as the Mongols claimed this since the time of Ögödei, but it was now couched in Islamic terms that could undermine support for the Mamluks. The threat was considered so great that the Mamluks even forged letters indicating that the conversion was false.[24] Curiously, the same polemicists politely remained quiet about the Mamluks' relations with the Jochid Ulus, which had some Muslims, but did not convert to Islam en masse until later.

Gradually peace fell across the Mongol Empire in the early 1330s, assisted by the conversion to Islam, which will be discussed in more detail in chapter Seven. This included peace with the Mamluk Sultanate. While military actions ended, a religious rivalry did develop between the two states.[25] For the aforementioned polemicists, peace did little to alter their views of the Ilkhanids, although the Mamluk government did take measures to muzzle their rhetoric.

Thus by the time of their last ruler, Abu Said (r. 1316–35), the Ilkhanate had finally achieved peace and stability on all fronts. Abu Said also had the longest and perhaps greatest reign of all of the Ilkhans. The termination of the wars allowed trade to blossom again. It had never stopped, to be sure, but now the Syrian and Transcaucasian borders were no longer a no-man's-land, allowing merchants and religious pilgrims of all sects to travel freely to Jerusalem as well as Mecca and Medina. Curiously, this stability and the long reign did not ensure the longevity of the empire. In the end, Abu Said failed in one crucial area as ruler – he did not produce an heir. With his death in 1335, generals and relatives contended for the throne. As internecine war erupted among the contenders, local dynasts achieved a measure of independence and out of one large empire emerged a number of independent polities.

THE CHAGHATAYID KHANATE

The demise of the Chaghatayid Khanate came not long after the end of the Ilkhanid state, or lasted considerably longer depending on how one labels the 'fall' of an empire. In some instances it is difficult to exactly identify the Chaghatayid Khanate. At the time of the dissolution of the Mongol Empire, a queen named Ergene (r. 1251–60) ruled the Chaghatayid Khanate. Confirmed in her position by Möngke in 1251, Ergene became regent by virtue of being the wife of Qara-Hülegü (r. 1242–6) during the minority of their son Mubarak-Shah. When civil war broke out between Ariq Böke and Khubilai she steered her realm into neutrality as her eastern borders touched both their domains. Unfortunately it was not a struggle she could avoid.

To secure more resources for his war with Khubilai, as well as to open another front, Ariq Böke supported another Chaghatayid prince, Alghu (r. c. 1260–65) to secure provisions from the Chaghatayid Khanate. While Ariq Böke's plan enjoyed some success, Alghu ultimately placed his own priorities ahead of his patron's. His rapacious attacks on Ergene's domains led the regent, as well as imperial officials (many of whom were waiting to see who was the actual emperor), to complain to Ariq Böke, forcing him to intervene against Alghu. These efforts failed as Ariq Böke could not fight both Alghu and Khubilai, causing Ergene to seek peace with Alghu. The peace treaty also resulted in their marriage. Although Khubilai sought to enlist the support of Alghu against Ariq Böke nothing came of the matter as the civil war ended in 1264.

In the end this mattered little as domination of the Chaghatayid Khanate entered the hands of Qaidu (1235–1301), a grandson of Ögödei and Töregene and one of the few Ögödeids to have escaped Möngke's purges. It appears that Qaidu's rise to power began with Alghu's efforts to expand his own authority in 1263.[26] After Ariq Böke's defeat, Qaidu then joined Berke against their common enemy Alghu, who had also encroached on the Jochid Khanate's territory.

Although the war between the two was a stalemate, several events occurred that opened the door for Qaidu to seize power in Central

Asia. Alghu died in 1265, as did Berke of the Jochid Khanate and Hülegü of the Ilkhanate in 1265/66. Meanwhile Khubilai was more concerned with consolidating his own empire. Qaidu then expanded eastward into the Tarim Basin, which was nominally under the protection of Khubilai. To deal with this threat Khubilai named Baraq (r. 1266–71) as the new Chaghatayid khan, effectively dismissing Ergene and Mubarak-Shah's authority. Again the war for the Chaghatayid Khanate stalemated with Qaidu dominating much of what is now Kazakhstan while Baraq Khan controlled south of the Syr Darya. The war came to an end in 1269 through a *quriltai* that included Baraq, Qaidu and Möngke-Temür, the ruler of the Jochid Khanate.

From this meeting emerged the so-called Talas Covenant. It was a peace agreement for central Asia and essentially recognized the interests (and power) of the Jochid Khanate. In essence, it divided the Chaghatayid Khanate between Baraq and Qaidu. Baraq received two-thirds of the revenues while the final third was shared by Qaidu and Möngke-Temür, although Möngke-Temür appears to have never received his portion of the revenue.[27] The division did not include Qaidu's own hereditary appanages. In addition territory was allotted to Qaidu and Baraq. This included pastures as well as settlements. For instance, Bukhara went to Qaidu, although it was deep in Baraq's territory. Although at times awkward, the agreement held.[28] The Talas *quriltai* also demonstrated that Khubilai was not considered a true Mongol, hence he was not invited, giving a clear criticism of his Sinicization and sedentary-centric policies.[29]

This allowed all three men to turn their attentions elsewhere. Baraq gravitated towards the Ilkhanate with an eye towards expanding his realm across the Amu Darya. Qaidu and Möngke-Temür encouraged Baraq, particularly as the Jochid ruler was at war with the Ilkhanate. The Ilkhan Abaqa, however, thwarted his efforts at Herat on 22 July 1270. When Baraq returned in disorder to Bukhara he sought support from Qaidu but found that many of his men had deserted to Qaidu. Furthermore, the Ögödeid prince made an alliance with Abaqa against Baraq. Abandoned both by his former ally and his army, Baraq died not long afterwards. Qaidu then assumed control of the Chaghatayid state, although he kept a Chaghatayid puppet on the throne in an unsuccessful attempt to mask his usurpation of power. With victory came the spoils, which included the imperial bureaucrat, Masud Beg, who had run the administration of the region since the time of Möngke.

Qaidu then turned his attention towards Khubilai, although he also had to fend off raids by the sons of Alghu and Baraq, launched from the Ilkhanate with the support of Abaqa, proving their alliance was temporary at best. While at times devastating, those raids were only a minor threat compared to Khubilai's power. As Qaidu never recognized Khubilai's claim as the Great Khan, their animosity was intense. While their war was far ranging, it was concentrated in modern Xinjiang in the People's Republic of China, particularly the Turfan region. Although the war continued for decades and often diminished into skirmishes as each ruler turned his attention to other matters, neither side gained a decisive advantage. Indeed, the war continued after Khubilai died and his grandson, Temür Öljeitü, took the reins of power. The final battle occurred in 1301 as Yuan forces invaded Qaidu's realm just south of the Altai Mountains. Initially Qaidu suffered defeat but with the aid of reinforcements he forced the Yuan back and the battle ended in a stalemate. The Yuan, possibly due to logistical problems, retreated but checked Qaidu's advance by burning the steppe. Qaidu, now in his sixties, died shortly thereafter.

With Qaidu's death an era of peace entered the remnants of the Mongol Empire. Temür Öljeitü was accepted as the undisputed khan of the Mongol Empire, although his real authority did not transcend his territory. This moment of Pax Mongolica also allowed the Chaghatayids to reclaim their authority. Du'a, a son of Baraq and Qaidu's former puppet, became the real power in the Chaghatayid Khanate although Qaidu's son Chapar ruled a reduced Ögödeid state to the north. Although Du'a had supported Chapar's succession, war began between the two of them with Chapar ultimately losing. Although an independent Ögödeid realm carried on in name, in reality it was increasingly subsumed by the Chaghatayid state.

After Du'a's death in 1307 the Chaghatayid Khanate spiralled into a series of succession struggles. Although most of the khans reigned five or more years, the civil wars and wars with neighbouring khanates weakened the khanate and prevented stability. Too often it faced a succession crisis and a border war at the same time. Thus war and power struggles became the focus of the Chaghatayid state until the reign of Tarmashirin (r. 1331–4). He was a Muslim convert and encouraged the Islamicization of the Chaghatayid Khanate. His attempts were not out of line with other events throughout the Mongol Empire. Indeed, the other khanates had converted to a single world religion (the Jochids and Ilkhanate to Islam and the Yuan to

Buddhism) in the waning years of the thirteenth and beginning of the fourteenth centuries. The Chaghatayid Mongols, like those in Mongolia, tended to be more conservative in nature and clung to the traditions of Chinggis Khan more readily than their brethren who lived in more diverse societies.[30]

Tarmashirin's policies met fierce resistance from the conservative factions, particularly beyond the Syr Darya. As Mawarannahr had been Muslim for centuries, nomads residing there had gradually adopted Islam, though more along the lines of Sufi variants than Sunni. Indeed, there is ample evidence that Tarmashirin was simply following the trend in the Chaghatayid Khanate as many of his officers and rank and file soldiers were already Muslims.[31] Tarmashirin's policies, religious as well as political and economic, ultimately led to his downfall in 1334.[32] Afterwards, while the Chaghatayid state continued, it rapidly decentralized with the conservative Mongols residing north of the Syr Darya remaining largely nomadic and shamanistic (although some converted to Islam) whereas Mawarannahr more or less went its own way under the control of various warlords – one of whom would become the Emir Timur, better known as Timur-i Leng or Tamerlane (r. 1370–1405).

Timur gradually consolidated power. Although descended from a Mongol tribe stationed in the region (the Barlas), he was more Turkic in origin, not a Chinggisid. While Timur married Chinggisid princesses and used the title of güregen or son-in-law, he never claimed to be khan and ruled with a puppet khan of Chaghatayid or Ögödeid origin, though everyone saw through the ruse. Meanwhile, to the north, the Mongols still claimed their authority, but the nobles there and to the south rarely gave them more than token recognition. Indeed, in Mawarannahr the Chaghatayids were seen more as bandits and marauders than as a polity. Timur's rule ended much of their threat although the Chaghatayid identity continued for another century. Timur's realm eventually encompassed much of the Chaghatayid state as well as the domains of the Ilkhanate while nomads from the former Chaghatayid domain comprised much of his army. His wars with the Jochid Khanate theoretically allowed him to conquer it as he defeated their armies in every encounter; however his lack of Chinggisid identity prevented him from ruling it or even attempting to incorporate it into his empire. In the end Timur came close to restoring the Mongol Empire but his death in 1405 en route to invading the Ming Empire in China prevented a restoration of Mongol rule. His own empire quickly splintered into smaller states ruled by his offspring (the Timurids). Whether or not his state and successors were a continuation of the Mongol Empire will be discussed in chapter Three.

THE JOCHID KHANATE

The civil wars between the Mongol kingdoms undermined the empire as the rulers continued to fight until the khanates disintegrated into smaller kingdoms or disappeared altogether in unabated internecine warfare. The first 50 years of the Jochid Khanate's existence, however, were focused on its war against the Ilkhanate. The Jochid Khanate or Golden Horde continued in some form into the eighteenth century. Over the course of centuries it fragmented until the Russians slowly absorbed its offshoots such as the Kazan Khanate (1552) and Astrakhan (1556) under Ivan the Terrible. The Crimean Khanate finally succumbed to Catherine the Great in 1783.

The Jochid Khanate was possibly the most diverse state in that it stretched across Eurasia from Bulgaria to modern Kazakhstan and had a population of Turks, Slavs and Finno-Ugric peoples with no one being dramatically more populous than the other groups, unlike the Yuan Empire. The Kipchak Turks may have held a slight edge in demographics – it was enough that many referred to the Jochid Khanate as the Kipchak Khanate, but it was nothing comparable to the Han population in China or the Iranian population of the Ilkhanate. Although the Jochid Khanate maintained much of its nomadic character it also adopted Islam and created major cities that dominated trade while controlling Turkic steppe nomads and the forest towns and villages of its Slavic and Finno-Ugric subjects. Nevertheless the culture of the ruling elite of the Jochid Khanate became increasingly Turkic rather than Mongolian.

While the geographic entity known as the Jochid Khanate can be seen on the map showing the post-1260 Mongol world, the exact political identity is more difficult to pin down. Within it, the khanate consisted of separate polities such as the Aq Orda, Köke Orda and Altan Orda, or white, blue and golden hordes, respectively. *Orda* or *ordu* means camp or palace in Mongolian and Turkic and is the source of the English word 'horde'. The exact location of each *orda* is difficult to define as some sources call the same place white or blue. The Altan Orda generally referred to the territory west of the Volga River, while the Aq Orda was the territory east of the Volga, extending into Kazakhstan. The Köke Orda, however, was a bit more nebulous as it sometimes included territory from the Aq Orda, but was usually considered to consist of the Siberian territories. The Altan Orda (*altan* or golden refers to its imperial status) tended to be the realm of the khan when the Jochid Khanate was united, however, the other *ordas* often acted autonomously and could impose their will upon the Altan Orda. The term Golden Horde, derived from Altan Orda, was only used to refer to the entire realm in the seventeenth century in the Russian sources. From there it entered common parlance among scholars and the general public. Most publications referring to the Jochid Khanate or Golden Horde focus on its relations with the cities of the Rus', or rather Russian relations with the Jochids. It is an odd situation as the Rus' principalities, while indubitably part of the Jochid Khanate, were generally viewed as backward by the Mongols and peripheral to their interests in the steppes and on the trade routes on the Volga River and the cities on the Black Sea coast. An increase in importance for the Russian territories came only in the later fourteenth century as Moscow's status increased and fractures appeared in the unity of the Jochid Khanate. This is not to say that the Mongols did not value their Russian territories, but rather these territories were simply not as important in terms of wealth or geopolitical strategy as the other khanates. Nonetheless, the Rus' were not simply client states or vassals as is often indicated on maps in history textbooks, but a fully incorporated part of the empire.

The steppe was the natural focus of the Jochid Khanate due to the large population of Kipchak Turk nomads. They provided the bulk of the Jochid armies. Also as the Mongols themselves continued to be nomadized, locating their capital camps in the steppe was logical. Cities such as Sarai and New Sarai sprung up along the Volga River, much like Karakorum in Mongolia. Located along the northern Silk Road, they served not only as trade centres but also as locations for the bureaucracy that administered the empire. Trading colonies on the Black Sea coast, particularly on the Crimean peninsula, became increasingly important as the primary trade routes for Italian merchants as well as the Jochid's line of communication with the Mamluk Sultanate in Egypt, its vassal or ally – depending on whether you were in Cairo or Saray.[33]

Although the Jochid Khanate did not convert to Islam until the fourteenth century, from the reign of Berke it had an increasingly Islamic slant to its government. The arrangement with the Mamluk Sultanate and Berke's patronage of Islamic scholars led to an increasing presence of Islamic influences in the government in terms of function-aries, bureaus and protocols. This north–south axis was crucial to Berke's war against the Ilkhans over pastures in Transcaucasia. While seemingly trivial from a modern perspective, the amount of pasture one owned also meant wealth in livestock (consider ranch wars in the American West), as well as being able to position troops and thus extend one's control. The Mamluks had little love for the Mongols in Persia and thus provided a second front. Meanwhile, the Kipchak population of the Jochid Khanate also provided labour for the Mamluks as Italian merchants bought Kipchak slaves in the Black Sea area and sold them in the ports of the Mamluk Sultanate. These were then trained as Mamluks, or slave-soldiers. All of this was possible through the Byzantine Empire regaining Constantinople (which had been in Latin or Frankish hands since the Fourth Crusade of 1204) in 1260. The restored Byzantine Empire, however, was not initially part of the alliance system as the Ilkhanate was its neighbour. Emperor Michael Paleologus, being sandwiched (the Jochid Khanate bordered the Byzantines on the border with Bulgaria) between the two super-powers, sought to remain neutral. The Jochids, however, sent a raiding party into Byzantine territory – this convinced the emperor which side was more dangerous.[34] With the Bosphorus Straits now pro-Jochid, the ties between the Jochid Khanate and the Mamluk Sultanate were secure.

Berke's death in 1266/7 did not end the southern focus of the Golden Horde. Berke's nephew or grandnephew Möngke-Temür, who figured so heavily in the early history of the Chaghatayid Khanate, was the next khan. Although not a Muslim, he continued many of the policies of his predecessor including contact with the Mamluk Sultanate. This should not be surprising as it kept pressure on the Ilkhanate. And, as discussed earlier, he was able to involve the Chaghatayid Khanate against the Ilkhanate as well, thus fitting his southern strategy. It should not be forgotten, however, that the Jochids viewed the Mamluks as vassals although the Mamluks saw their relationship as an alliance between equals.

Möngke-Temür's early reign was dominated by Noghai, a general who controlled the western frontiers of the Jochid Khanate and played the role of kingmaker. His power was so great that he became a virtu-ally autonomous entity within the horde. Throughout his career as the top Jochid commander he ensured that neighbouring states knew the military strength of the Jochid Khanate as he led forces against not only the Ilkhanate but also into Poland and Hungary and often intervened in Bulgaria to shore up Jochid influence. As a result Bulgaria recognized Noghai's authority over the khan's. Möngke-Temür could never wrest the mantle of authority away from Noghai and had to share it. As a result Noghai continued to be an influential force during the reign of Töde-Möngke (r. 1280–7), another Muslim ruler. So great was Noghai's influence that it was often difficult to tell who was truly the ruler of the state. Unrelated to Noghai's influence, it was during Töde-Möngke's reign that the Jochid Khanate became increasingly Turkic, reflecting the growing separation of the empire. While Mongolian may have been used by some, coins minted in the Jochid state had Turkic inscriptions and Turkic came into increasing use in the court as well.

Noghai's power reached its apogee during the reign of Telebogha (r. 1287–91), during which Noghai was openly co-ruler. Unfortunately for Telebogha, the young khan demonstrated some signs of independence, so Noghai killed him. Noghai then raised Telebogha's son Toqta (r. 1291–1312) to the throne. During the first part of his reign Toqta played the role of the deferential puppet, but as he matured he came into open conflict with his 'guardian'. Noghai's death in 1299 prevented civil war from consuming the khanate. Nonetheless, the damage was still great.

Much of the remainder of Toqta's reign consisted of restoring the territory and authority of the Jochid Khan. To this end he made some advances against the Ilkhans, although more through diplomacy than military action. Still, he reduced the power of Noghai's heirs and brought Bulgaria back into the orbit of the Jochid's rule. He also dealt a humbling blow to the Genoese who vied with the Venetians for trade access in the Black Sea. In 1308 he sacked Kaffa. The Genoese were able to re-establish their position there, but according to the terms set by Toqta.

Although Toqta initiated the Golden Age of the Golden Horde, Üzbek Khan (r. 1313–41) ruled it. The Jochids did not extend their empire during his reign, but peace with the Ilkhanate allowed it to flourish as the khanates re-established the Pax Mongolica across the empire. Nonetheless, Üzbek Khan did have other concerns as the Rus' princes grew increasingly restless. Russian principalities had long been an afterthought to the Jochids – primarily a resource to exploit for troops and revenue. Although some attempts at breaking from Jochid rule were made, they ultimately failed as Üzbek Khan played princes against each other until he finally appointed Yurii Danilovich, of the rather small and inconsequential city of Moscow, as the Grand Prince, primarily to serve as the Mongols' 'man on the spot' in the region and to counter the power of the stronger principality of Tver.

Üzbek also led the conversion of the Jochid state to Islam, which may have played a role in the dissatisfaction of the Eastern Orthodox Russians. The conversion did not occur overnight, but an increasing number of the nomadic population converted, including Üzbek Khan, who then made it the official religion of the khanate, although he did not force it upon his *dhimmi* subjects, like the Orthodox Russians (*dhimmah* refers to non-muslim subjects granted rights under an Islamic State). Nonetheless, when Ibn Battuta visited the Golden Horde, he found arguably the most powerful Islamic state in the world.[35]

Yet even as the Jochid Khanate blossomed the harbingers of its demise began to appear on the fringes of the state. As the Ilkhanate fell in 1335 Turkic beyliks took advantage of the power vacuum, among them the obscure Osmanli polity, perhaps founded by refugees from the Jochid realm, as will be discussed in the next chapter. To the west, Poland again was on the rise after gaining some respite from Jochid attacks. In the northwest, Lithuania took advantage of Jochid inattention to extend its own influence into areas formerly under Jochid suzerainty. Poland and Lithuania eventually unified, making a state that could contend with the Jochid Khanate, although their unification had more to do with Germanic expansion than with the Mongols. Towards the end of Üzbek's reign Moscow became increasingly dominant in the north as the Mongols' tax collector.

Üzbek's son and successor Tinibeg's reign was brief (r. 1341–2), as Janibeg, his brother, usurped the throne. Janibeg (r. 1342–57) attempted to reassert Jochid power beyond his borders, yet had the unfortunate timing to rule a state when the Black Plague struck, undermining the foundations of the state and weakening it politically, militarily, culturally and economically, as will be discussed in chapter Eight. The Black Plague exacerbated brewing tensions and rivalries within the Jochid Khanate. After Janibeg's death there was a quick succession of rulers and succession squabbles. During this period, the Altan, Aq and Köke Ordas acted increasingly as separate entities. In the meantime other powers strove to fill the vacuum caused by the internal Jochid power struggle. Lithuania continued to dominate western areas neglected by the Jochids while Moscow steadily increased its dominance over other Russian cities, albeit still under the guise of a loyal subject of the khans. Civil war prevented the Jochid state from reasserting its authority and when a ruler did emerge, such as Mamai, a non-Chinggisid general, their authority was not always accepted.

The great Muscovite victory at Kulikovo Pole, or Kulikovo field, along the Don River did not liberate Russia. Although Dimitri Donskoi (he earned the epithet Donskoi, meaning 'of the Don', with his victory here) defeated Mamai in 1380, it did not end Mongol dominance, though Mamai lost further support among the Mongols and was ultimately killed. Moscow quickly learned that it was still a subject with the rise of Toqtamysh (r. 1377–95), a protégé of the Emir Timur in central Asia. With the aid of Timur, Toqtamysh became the preeminent power in the Aq Orda. From there he extended his domain into the western Jochid Khanate and emerged as the sole ruler of the Jochid Khanate. He then sacked Moscow, putting it back under Mongol authority for another 100 years.

Although a protégé of Timur, their relationship quickly soured, largely because as a Chinggisid and legitimate ruler and general in his own right Toqtamysh could not exist in Timur's shadow. Timur, in the eyes of a strong Chinggisid ruler, was nothing more than a pretender. Certainly Timur used his own Chinggisid puppets, but other than his initial rise to power in the White Horde, Toqtamysh's achievements were his own. Thus the old feuds resumed as Toqtamysh attempted to take Azerbaijan and to reclaim areas in central Asia that once belonged to the Jochid Khanate. Although Timur defeated him on a few occasions Toqtamysh always recovered and even participated in an alliance with the Mamluks and Ottomans against Timur. Ultimately they all failed and Toqtamysh met defeat at the Terek River in 1395. He once more escaped but could not regain his throne. Timur sacked both Sarai and New Sarai, burning the cities – the primary reason why we have so little documentation from the Golden Horde.

Timur's actions had far-reaching consequences as will be detailed in chapter Three. After his victory he placed a puppet on the throne but did not attempt to rule the Golden Horde, possibly realizing that the Jochids would never accept a non-Chinggisid ruler. After Timur's death in 1405 the Jochid state fragmented while Lithuania and Moscow also became involved in the affairs of the steppe. In 1480 Moscow finally ended its subservience to the Mongols and by 1502 the Jochid state officially ended. Successor states continued to exist until 1789, but by 1502 the last true part of the Mongol Empire had disappeared – or had it?

3

THE WORLD OF 1350:
A GLOBAL WORLD

In Shakespeare's play *Much Ado About Nothing* the arrogant and confirmed bachelor Benedick offers his support and loyalty to Don Pedro.
Don Pedro was modelled on Peter III (1239–1285), King of Aragon. To
prove his fealty Benedick offers to pluck a hair from the beard of the
'Cham' (Khan).[1] Although the play is set in the thirteenth century and
is thus contemporary with the Mongols, and indeed Peter did have
some diplomatic contact with them, it is clear that Shakespeare is
making a reference that his audience could easily understand. Even by
1600, when the play was being performed, the identity of the ruler of
China was still not perfectly understood – at least in England. The
Portuguese had their stations at Macao and at Nagasaki Bay in Japan.
Portuguese-supported Jesuits also operated in China and Japan. The
Portuguese certainly knew the ruler, although not through direct contact, but the English had little access to East Asia and thus no way to
know that the Mongols no longer ruled China. For most of Europe little had changed in the knowledge of Asia since Columbus failed to
reach China and India.

Yet with the disappearance of the Mongol Empire, or perhaps
the fading, as it 'disappeared' or 'fell' at varying times and rates, the
post-Mongol world was noticeably different in terms of geography,
culture, religion and technology. As will be discussed, many of the
changes can be traced to the Chinggis Exchange. Nonetheless, one is
quite justified in asking, what did the post-Mongol world look like?
A number of successor states arose, directly attributable to Mongol
influence, but other geographic changes also resulted. Although the
majority of the Mongol Empire still existed in 1350, the Ilkhanate
ended in 1335 and by 1350 the chaos had settled enough for new polities to emerge. This is where the discussion of the post-Mongol
world begins.

SUCCESSORS AND HOW THE WORLD CHANGED

Examining a map demonstrates the most obvious change. As mentioned in the Introduction, the Mongols erased from the geopolitical map a number of kingdoms and empires along with a number of smaller polities. Just among the major powers we see the disappearance of the Jin Empire, the Tatar confederation, the Kereit, the Naiman, Xi Xia, Kara Khitai, the Khwarazmian Empire, Bulghar, the Kipchak confederation, Abbasid Caliphate, Ayyubid Damascus and Aleppo, the Ayyubid kingdom of Egypt, Mosul, Seljuk Sultanate of Rum, Vladimir-Suzdal, Kiev, the Ismaili state of Alamut and Quhistan, the Song Empire, Da-Li, Cilicia and the Principality of Antioch.

Some states re-emerged or became strengthened due to the Mongols, such as Georgia, Armenia, Trebizond, the Byzantine Empire, Novgorod, Tver, the Teutonic Knights of Prussia, Hungary and the Sultanate of Delhi. Granted, the Mongols did not conquer all of these states but the Mongol presence directly impacted them negatively or positively at some point. For instance, Antioch and Cilicia grew due to Ilkhanid support but these states then became the targets of the Mamluk Sultanate. The Mamluks could not risk a major invasion of Mongol territory but found the Ilkhanate's smaller and weaker vassals suitable substitutes.

The appearance of the Mamluk state was dependent on the Mongols as well. The Mongol invasions created the abundance of Kipchaks available to the slave trade. King Louix IX's Seventh Crusade ultimately resulted in the rise of the Mamluks in 1250, but for the next decade they struggled with internecine feuding while also maintaining the façade of Ayyubid power by keeping an Ayyubid (a relative of Salah al-Din or Saladin) prince on the throne. Only the Mongol arrival in Syria forced the disparate Mamluk factions to unite and place a strong leader, Qutuz, openly in charge of the state. After the Mongol defeat at Ayn Jalut, another amir, Baybars, assassinated Qutuz. Baybars solidified the Mamluk state by transforming it into a power directly opposed to the Mongols and the Crusaders. He developed a standard operating procedure of eliminating Crusader holdings whenever a Mongol attack was not imminent. Baybars also placed a special emphasis on destroying Cilicia and the Principality of Antioch and Tripoli, both vassals of the Mongols. A nightmare scenario of a major Crusade launched in conjunction with an Ilkhanid invasion haunted the Mamluks. Eliminating that possibility became a necessity.

Although the Crusader kingdoms and the Ilkhanate disappeared, the Mamluks remained a power until 1517 and faced a number of successors to the Mongols in the Middle East before falling to perhaps their most powerful successor.

Several states emerged out of the ashes of the various Mongol khanates, but not all of them were successors. One instance was the Sarbadarids (1337–86) in western Khurasan. Consisting of local landowners and supported by an alliance with the Shaikhiyya, a Sufi sect that incorporated messianic Shi'ism, these were not Mongols or Turks, although some members may have been. They were not a successor power as they did not use Mongol ideology or symbols to secure their legitimacy but remained a distinct but local entity that lasted until Emir Timur arrived in 1380. The true successors had distinct ties to the Mongols, either being founded by Chinggisids or commanders tied to the Mongol khanates. The use of aspects of governance from the Mongol khanates, whether through ideology, genealogy or governing structures to establish their legitimacy served as another qualifier. Finally it should be noted that some scholars may dislike the use of the term 'state' to describe these polities as many were simply nomadic confederations. Historians of the steppes have long recognized that nomads simply do not conform to European, Middle Eastern or Chinese definitions of state, but it is clear that they viewed themselves as independent powers and acted as such.[2]

A number of diverse successors came from the demise of the Ilkhanate and, as Andre Wink notes, adopted aspects of the Ilkhanate.[3] Among these aspects, and perhaps of the utmost importance, was the revived concept of Iran. As mentioned earlier, Persian culture blossomed under Ilkhanid patronage. Tied to the use of Persian culture and the stiffening of borders during the internecine post-dissolution wars, a clear concept of Iran emerged. While the Ilkhanate was certainly larger than Iran, it is notable that the concept of Iran not only solidified during the Ilkhanid period, but continued after the Ilkhanate ended. Tabriz, capital of the Ilkhanid state, remained the place of legitimacy while Mongol lineage, political concepts, symbols and practices remained critical to successors securing and maintaining power. Fifteenth-century successors such as the Kara Qoyunlu (1375–1468) and Aq Qoyunlu (1375–1508), both Turkoman tribes, adhered to these criteria.[4] As the Turkoman confederations lacked Chinggisid lineage they did not use the term khan, but *padishah-i-Iran* or *kesra-yi-Iran*. Implicit in their actions was that they were the rulers of the Iran that emerged from the Ilkhanate and that, although they were not Chinggisids, they still had a connection to the Mongols. More importantly, in adopting Mongol governance structures and symbols, it must be recognized that their subjects expected a Mongol connection in a legitimate ruler. It should be noted too that the successors worked with what they knew, the Mongol system, rather than inventing a new paradigm. Nonetheless, might did not make right. It could allow you to gain power but more was needed to secure it and maintain a ruler's credibility – utilizing Mongol symbols and structures allowed them to obtain that credibility.

Around Baghdad and Tabriz coalesced the Jalayirs (1336–1432). This post-Mongol state claimed descent from the Jalayir Mongol clan and *mingans*. The depredations of Timur seriously weakened them and ultimately left them exposed to Timurid rule and then domination by the Kara Qoyunlu, their former vassals. A similar story awaited the Chobanids (1335–57), so named after Amir Choban (*d.* 1327), a high-ranking general and would-be kingmaker in the twilight of the Ilkhanate. The Chobanids created a state in Azerbaijan that dominated most of

Muhammed ibn Mahmudshah al-Khayyam, Mongolian archer on a horse, *c.* 1400–25, drawing. Although this Persian illustration comes from the post-Mongol period, the successors of the Ilkhanate still dressed and fought much like their predecessors.

the former northwestern Ilkhanate. Their rule was particularly oppres-
sive and they vied with the Jalayirids for control of Tabriz.[5] The
Chobanid dynasty ended in 1357 when the Jochids conquered Tabriz.

Into this chaotic scene emerged a true successor to Chinggis Khan
in all but genealogy, Amir Timur or Timur-i Leng, better known to the
Western world as Tamerlane. Despite being disabled from an arrow
wound to one of his legs gained in his youth, Timur was a relentless
campaigner and often appeared to spend more time traversing his
empire on campaign than in his capital, Samarqand. His career has
been described in chapter Two, but it is important to note that he re-
established much of the Mongol state, combining parts of the Chaghatayid and Ilkhanate khanates. Furthermore, he used his status as *güregen*
or son-in-law as well as Chinggisid khans to cement the legitimacy
of his state in the eyes of the conquered. Indeed, most of his detrac-
tors viewed him as an illegitimate ruler not because of his Mongol
connections but as an infidel, but then central Asian Sufism received
little sympathy from the traditional *ulama* in the Middle East as they
often viewed it as a deviation and blasphemous. Although Timur died
in 1405, his empire lasted in some form until the early sixteenth century.
After his death it immediately splintered, with the western portion
almost immediately lost to the Kara and Aq Qoyunlu. The eastern
portion in Central Asia and eastern Iran lasted longer and stabilized.

In addition to his struggles against the Jochid ruler, Toqtamysh,
Timur defeated various Iranian successor states, the Mamluks, the
Sultanate of Delhi and the other powerful successor state – the
Ottomans. Although Timur's defeat of Bayezid at Ankara in 1402 left
the Ottoman Empire in shambles it did recover. Indeed the Ottoman
Empire proved to be the longest lasting successor to the Mongols,
ending in the First World War peace treaties in 1923, although it ceased
to be a successor state long before then. The origins of the Ottomans
remain somewhat obscure. The antecedents to the Osmanlis arrived
in Anatolia as refugees from the Mongol invasions of central Asia in
the 1220s or perhaps at a later period.[6] Others have postulated that the
Ottomans may have arrived from the Pontic steppe after Noghai's fall
from grace in 1299, that an *Ataman* or non-Chinggisid leader led 10,000
households out of Crimea via Kaffa and they eventually settled in the
vicinity of Sogud in Anatolia.[7] In this scenario the name Ottoman
derives not from Osman but from the title Ataman.

Regardless of their origin, we know that the Osmanlis coalesced
into an identifiable polity around Osman b. Ertogrul in about 1290.

With the final destruction of the Seljuk Sultanate of Rum in the late thirteenth century the Mongols ruled Anatolia loosely, which led its governor, Sülemish, to rebel in 1298. This rebellion was crushed the following year but after 1300 Anatolia was low on the Ilkhan's list of priorities, allowing a number of *beyliks* to emerge, among them the Osmanlis or Ottomans, who were subservient to the Mongols.[8]

For their early history, the Ottomans used many Mongol institutions but substituted Osman, rather than Chinggis Khan, as their historical founder. Over the centuries they found new ways to legitimize their authority. With the conquest of Constantinople they could claim the title of caesar and claim to be a successor of the Roman/Byzantine heritage. The conquest of the Mamluks in 1515–17 allowed the sultan to claim the title of caliph, thus strengthening their claims to be defenders of the religion. Many sultans also played up their roles as *ghazis* or holy warriors, even if their actions did not always substantiate that claim. It is notable that the Ottomans never claimed the title of khan despite their steppe heritage, perhaps recognizing their non-Chinggisid origins, but rather opted for the Islamic title of sultan. Of course, with their meteoric rise, they soon established their own legitimacy and ceased to be regarded as a successor to the Mongols but as an entity in their own right.

The Safavid Empire was the rival of the Ottomans for Middle Eastern dominance. Found by Shah Ismail, its roots were also found in the Ilkhanate. The Safavi Sufi founder, Shaykh Safi al-Din (*d.* 1334) received patronage from Ilkhans Ghazan, Öljeitü and Abu Said. Safi al-Din also frequented the households of Rashid al-Din. Due to his connections his Sufi order flourished in Azerbaijan. The prestige of his connections to the Ilkhans and the wealth the order accumulated due to Mongol patronage enhanced the status of his family and gave legitimacy to Safi al-Din's descendant, Ismail. Ismail also benefited from familial ties to the Aq Qoyunlu, which he ultimately destroyed in 1508. Ismail began as the head of the *kizilbash* or 'Red Hats', as the Safaviyya Turkomen members were often called due to their distinctive headgear.

Öljeitü's conversion to Shi'a Islam planted the seeds for Shi'ism as a national religion and it was gradually incorporated into the Safavi order. Thus, by the time of Ismail's rise to power, he embraced a millenarian approach to Shi'ism that helped fuel the *kizilbash* with a distinct ideology. As the leader of the Safavids, Ismail captured Tabriz by defeating the Aq Qoyunlu. By capturing the former Ilkhanid capital the Safavids established their legitimacy. Ismail conquered the rest of Iran by essentially following the borders of the Ilkhanate and defeating Timurid rulers. Although Turkic, the Safavids adopted Persian ideas of kingship, which elevated the ruler above his *kizilbash* chieftains. Again the ruler did not adopt the title of khan, as it had become a title reserved for Chinggisids. Although Öljeitü began Iran's movement to Twelver Shi'ism, the Safavids cemented it by replacing the Mongol heritage with Shi'a Islam.[9]

The Jochid Khanate lasted until approximately 1502 when the Great Horde met defeat at the hands of the Crimean Tatars. It had fractured earlier as discussed in chapter Two. After 1502 a number of new powers existed in the former Jochid domains. Most were of Chinggisid descent such as the Crimean, Kazan, Kasimov, Astrakhan, Sibir, Uzbek and Kazakh khanates. Other groups also existed like Noghai, Lithuania and Muscovy; the latter emerged as a major player by collecting taxes for the Mongols. Mongol support for this formerly insignificant village was crucial in the face of more powerful neighbours such as the Russian principalities of Tver and Novgorod. In terms of a successor state all of the Chinggisid states continued Mongol practices and Muscovy continued many on its own.

In the wake of the Black Plague and the political weakening of the Jochid Khanate after Timur devastated it, the Lithuanians dominated much of the western Pontic Steppe, particularly what is now Ukraine. With the Union of Kreva in 1386 Lithuania united with Poland, which transformed Lithuania into a Catholic state. Polish concerns regarding the Teutonic Knights in Prussia gave Lithuania a westward interest, but did not hamper its expansion into the steppe. Taking advantage of the vacuum caused by the fracturing of the Jochid Khanate, Lithuania found itself in conflict with the Crimean Tatars and Muscovy (who often formed an alliance).[10] With the Ottoman expansion Lithuania and Muscovy found a common enemy. It created an odd situation where Muscovy sent tribute to the Crimeans, while the Crimeans submitted to the Ottomans as the Ottomans transformed the Black Sea into an Ottoman Lake by dominating the coastline.

Lithuania became a Mongol successor only in terms of territory. The Crimean Khanate's claim was due to its Chinggisid lineage as well as for destroying the Great Horde. It now appeared to be the dominant steppe power. But although it remained a powerful player into the sixteenth century, Muscovy emerged as the most potent state in the western steppes. Although Muscovy gained its status by dominating other

Russian city states, including Novgorod and Tver, it also contended with the steppe powers. The Kasimov Khanate (1452–1681) came under Muscovite protection in the fifteenth century largely in preference to domination from Kazan. Indeed the Kasimov Tatars accompanied Muscovite troops in raids against the Kazan Khanate. The Muscovite Tsar, Ivan iv (the Terrible), ultimately conquered the Kazan Khanate (1438–1552) in 1552 and then Astrakhan (1459–1556) in 1556. Internal politics undermined much of their resistance to Muscovy. The conquests were part of a larger competition between Muscovy and the Crimean Khanate. In the sixteenth century these two powers vied for influence over Kazan and its lucrative control of the fur trade. Often a junior member of the Crimean royalty ruled Kazan. As Crimean influence expanded in the sixteenth century some lesser steppe powers, such as the Noghai, turned to Moscow as a counterweight. Increasingly steppe nations referred to the Russian tsar as the Tsagaan Khan or White Khan, a reference to imperial authority. The Tsars never referred to themselves as this, perhaps because of their lack of Chinggisid lineage, but did not prevent others from using the title, letting neighbouring powers confer legitimacy upon the Russian ruler rather than claiming it for him. At the same time Russian expansion and military strength could not be ignored, thus giving Moscow legitimacy in the eyes of the steppe powers. At the same time those steppe powers that once turned to Moscow as a counterweight against Crimean dominance soon found themselves under an even more powerful Russian state.

The Crimean Khanate (1441–1783) maintained its independence from Russia until 1783 when the Russian empress Catherine the Great annexed it. However, it did not go quietly. Independently and as an extension of the Ottoman Empire, Crimea was the terror of Russia's southern frontier with raids reaching as far east as Astrakhan and some raids entering the suburbs of Moscow to the north. In 1571 the Crimean khan Devlet Giray (r. 1551–71) even burned many of the suburbs, imperilling the existence of the city of Moscow. Crimea at times also exerted suzerainty over non-Chinggisid groups like the nomadic Noghai and the Kuban Tatars, which enhanced its power. As mentioned above, their suzerainty over others was not always welcomed. Crimean power was enhanced by its relationship with the Ottoman Empire, however; as the Ottomans learned, controlling Crimea was not the easiest of tasks.

Ottoman efforts to bring Astrakhan and Kazan directly into its orbit failed when the Crimeans passively resisted an Ottoman scheme to dig a canal from the Don River to the Volga in 1563. While Devlet Giray was a vassal to the Ottomans, he had no intention of seeing the Ottoman sultan's authority extend beyond the Black Sea coast and diminish Crimean influence in the steppe. Indeed, the Crimeans raided and made treaties with Cossacks, Muscovy and Lithuania and often violated those made between the Ottomans and those states. Although the Ottomans could influence the Crimean khans, Ottoman presence in Crimea also diminished the khan's authority over his Karachi Beys (subordinate nobles). Thus they sometimes carried out their own agenda, with or without the khan's support. Nonetheless, Crimea's ties to the Ottomans served as a useful buffer. When engaging the Crimeans, other states risked Ottoman intervention. Only when Ottoman power was sufficiently weakened could the Crimean Khanate be overcome but until then it remained a powerful actor in the Pontic Steppe.[11] A Chinggisid ruled Crimea until 1783 when the Russian khan Sahin Giray deposed him – partly as a result of the annexation but also because of his ineffectiveness as a ruler. One could argue that Crimea was a continuation of the Mongol Empire, but considering Crimea submitted to the Ottomans in 1524 when Ottoman sultans appointed the Crimean khans it could no longer be considered truly independent.

The Sibir Khanate (1490–1598) arose out of the enigmatic Köke Orda (Blue Horde) of the Jochid Khanate. Founded by Ibak, a descendant of Shayban b. Jochi, Sibir subjugated the Mansi, Nenets, Khanti and other less powerful groups living in the Siberian forests. As a result they paid the *yasak* or tribute of furs. Very few records provide history of the Sibir Khanate. Nonetheless it was a successor state or continuation of the Mongol Empire – though the lack of documentation prevents us from knowing the full story. Situated on the Irtysh River, Kashlyk, the Sibir capital, became the pre-eminent power in western Siberia, although internecine fighting between two Chinggisid branches (the Shaybanids and Taibuginids) within the khanate prevented many external affairs. Nonetheless, in moments of peace Sibir competed with the Kazan Khanate on its western borders for influence over the Noghai Tatars in the region, but with Kazan's fall a more powerful neighbour entered the picture.

Its demise came with the expansion of Muscovy and competition for the valuable fur trade with northern Siberian peoples. Tsar Ivan IV granted licence to the Stroganov family to trap furs and build outposts along the Irtysh and Ob rivers. As the Stroganovs encroached on the territory of the Sibir Khanate, these outposts suffered many raids. To protect Muscovite interests and end the competition, cossacks commanded by Yermak (d. 1585) received sanction from Muscovy to move into Sibir territory. Although Yermak defeated Kuchum Khan, the ruler of Sibir (r. 1563–98), in 1582 and captured Kashlyk, Kuchum regrouped and pushed the cossacks out in 1584. Not until 1598 did the Muscovites completely overwhelm Sibir, opening up all of Siberia to Russian dominance. Kuchum fled to the Noghai territory where he died.

Although the Sibir Khanate held an extensive amount of territory it had been limited to the taiga or forested region between the Ob and Yenisei rivers, largely due to the Uzbeks and Kazakhs. Their presence in the southern steppes also prevented Russian penetration of the steppes until the eighteenth century. The etymology of the name Uzbek has not been completely resolved, but it is thought that they took their name from Üzbek Khan, the great Jochid ruler. The khans of the Uzbeks were descendants of Shayban, a son of Jochi. Under Abdulkhayr Khan the Uzbeks were united into a formidable force. Not all of the Uzbek clans, however, accepted his rule. These became known as 'those who departed', or Kazakhs, led by Janibek Khan and Kerey Khan in 1456. Both were Chinggisids. With the rise of the Kazakhs and Uzbeks other remnants of the Mongol Empire suffered. The Chaghatai largely disappeared as an entity as the Uzbeks and Kazakhs encroached and incorporated their pastures.

Under Muhammad Shaybani the Uzbeks crossed the Syr Darya River. In 1506 they defeated the last Timurid, Babur, a descendant of both Timur and Chinggis Khan. Despite his best efforts to reclaim Mawarannahr he had to settle for a kingdom in Afghanistan and northern India. Babur finished what his great grandfather had started by destroying the Sultanate of Delhi along with a number of other Muslim and Hindu kingdoms. While the resulting Mughal Empire continued many Mongol governing principles, it used Islamic and Indian practices as well. Again one could question whether it was a successor to the Mongol Empire; although some have viewed it as a continuation, this claim is tenuous. Babur's Chinggisid lineage came from his mother's side, thus limiting his claim to be khan. In any case the dynasty came to an end with the Sepoy Rebellion in 1857, although the empire had splintered after 1720 with the emperors ruling an ever smaller realm and receiving only token recognition from former vassals.

In the meantime the Uzbeks established a strong state in Mawarannahr but suffered from poor timing. To the north the

Kazakhs formed a khanate that at its height could summon 200,000 warriors. To the south were the Mughals. Once they stabilized they fended off Uzbek attacks, although Uzbek expansion did occur in parts of Afghanistan. The Mughals also found a useful ally against the Uzbeks in the Safavids. In an attempt to expand into Khurasan across the Amu Darya River Muhammad Shaybani met defeat at the hands of Shah Ismail at Merv in 1510. Ismail followed steppe tradition and made his skull into a drinking goblet. As Muhammad Shaybani attempted an alliance with the Ottomans against the Safavids, Ismail sent his stuffed head to the Ottomans to signal the failure of their plot. The drinking goblet came into good use after 1514. Sultan Selim I, who gained the sobriquet 'The Grim', defeated Ismail at the Battle of Chaldiran thanks to his use of cannons which broke the Safavid ranks of horse-archers. Afterwards, Ismail grew despondent and engaged in heavy drinking. Considering that he viewed himself as the Mahdi, who was not supposed to be defeated, his actions are understandable. At least he had his goblet to remind him of his glory days.

Thus on those fronts the Uzbeks were limited. A new threat emerged on the eastern frontier in the form of the Oirats, western Mongols who seemed willing to fight all challengers – Uzbek, Kazakh, Chinese or Mongol. And if those were not available, they fought amongst themselves. The situation of the Uzbeks worsened when in 1556 Astrakhan fell to Tsar Ivan IV. This brought new Chinggisids into the region and set up more succession issues. Despite being refugees the Astrakhan Chinggisids, known as the Janids, still carried considerable clout. Although the Uzbek Empire rose in a period when it was surrounded by dynamic neighbours, the Shaybanid Uzbeks also enjoyed success after the death of Muhammad Shaybani. Ubaydullah Khan (r. 1533–9), proved to be the most talented of the Shaybanid khans. Although unable to expand beyond the Amu Darya, Ubaydullah ensured the Uzbeks continued to be a menace the Safavids could not ignore. Much of the destruction of Khurasan's productivity can be traced to the wars between the Uzbeks and Safavids rather than the Mongols proper. Although he was killed by a relative in a battle over the city of Khiva, Ubaydullah's strong will and leadership is apparent in the events that occurred after his death. His greatest success, however, was maintaining the unity of the Uzbek Khanate despite the independent attitude of the Uzbek notables.

After Ubaydullah's death his relatives fought more amongst themselves than against their neighbours – each trying to turn their particular appanages into an independent state. Certainly periods of consolidation and unity existed, as during the reign of Abdullah Khan II (r. 1583–98), but only through Abdullah's iron-fisted rule. While his subordinates chafed under his rule, trade and agriculture prospered. In addition he extended the Uzbek state deeper into present day Xinjiang with the conquest of Kashgar. Meanwhile Khurasan resumed its place as a war zone between the Uzbeks and Safavids. Abdullah Khan's death in 1598 ended Shaybanid rule in Mawarannahr, however. His successors died months after he did, leaving the empire to his brother-in-law, Jani Khan, one of the Astrakhan Chinggisids, who abdicated in favour of his son, Baqi Khan (r. 1599–1605).

The Janid dynasty failed to hold the empire together. Ultimately the Uzbek Khanate broke apart into three khanates. The Janids ruled from Bukhara, core of the former Uzbek Empire, which became known as the Khanate of Bukhara (1500–1785). The Khanate of Khiva (1539–1920), which gained a modicum of independence when Ubaydullah died in 1539, remained under Shaybanid control. The Khanate of Kokand (1709–1883) emerged in the Ferghana Valley. Further divided and unable to meet the challenges of more dynamic powers such as Nadir Shah's (r. 1736–47) rapid expansion from Iran, all three khanates saw the rise of new dynasties with the Mangits in Bukhara, Qungrats in Khiva and the Mins in Kokand. Weakened and somewhat isolated due to the existence of the hostile Mughals, Safavids, Kazakhs and Oirats, these successors ceased to be a threat in the grand scheme of things. In the nineteenth century the Russian Empire devoured them although Khiva maintained a semblance of autonomy until the Bolshevik Revolution. In 1921 the Chinggisid ruler of Khiva was removed from the throne.

While the Uzbeks crossed the Syr Darya, the Kazakhs stayed in the steppe where they remained a potent force but lost their independence in the 1700s after gradually coming into the Russian orbit. Yet for almost 300 years they remained a force with which to be reckoned. As indicated earlier, the Kazakhs came into being in the fifteenth century when Janibek and Kerey rejected the authority of Abulkhayr Khan and, taking advantage of Oirat attacks on the Uzbeks, split from the Uzbeks. It is difficult to establish the exact date for the foundation of the Kazakh Khanate, but it is safe to say that it existed in the last quarter of the fifteenth century.[12] Although fighting with the Uzbeks consumed much of the Kazakhs' early existence, by 1500 the two khanates came to an agreement although conflict still flared occasionally. Under Kasym

Khan (r. 1511–18), the Kazakh Khanate reached its peak. Under his rule other nomads joined the Kazakhs including several Noghai groups as well as Naimans and Argyns from the former Chaghatayid Moghuls.[13] Kasym's khanate stretched from the Yaik or Ural River in the west to Semirechie in the east and northward to the Irtysh River, bounded to the south by the Syr Darya. The sudden expansion of the Kazakh Khanate under Kasym and perhaps a legacy of the Kazakh's rejection of Abulkhayr Khan's efforts at centralized authority among the Uzbeks prevented long-term unity for the Kazakhs. Three hordes or *ordas* formed almost immediately after Kasym's death: the Great Horde (*Ulu Jüze*) in Semirechie, the Middle Horde (*Orta Jüze*) in the steppe zone above the Syr Darya and the Siberian taiga, and the Small Horde (*Kishi Jüze*) located east of the Yaik or Ural River. Although some semblance of unity remained in the late sixteenth and seventeenth centuries, as evinced when the Kazakhs attempted to wrest Mawarannahr from the Uzbeks, it was ephemeral. Under the leadership of Tevkkel Khan (r. 1586–98) the Kazakhs captured several cities but failed to take Bukhara by siege in 1598. In the absence of a strong khan the hordes behaved increasingly independently and by the eighteenth century it was clear that the Kazakh Khanate no longer existed except in name.

The Kazakh downfall occurred in the mid-seventeenth century with the arrival of another successor state, the Zunghars or Oirats. Although the Kazakhs initially held off the Zunghars, the ensuing wars that lasted into the eighteenth century wreaked havoc across the steppe as the Zunghars and their spin-off confederation, the Kalmyks, took over the pastures and animals of the Kazakhs. The Zunghar threat forced the Kazakhs to once again unify or face extinction. Tauke Khan (r. 1680–1718) led the three hordes in a desperate struggle against an increasingly powerful Zunghar Empire forming in the Tarbagatai region and western Mongolia. From the mid-seventeenth century Zunghar raids carried off livestock, but by 1698 Zunghar raids into the Lake Balkhash region increased. The Kazakhs soon lost the Ili River basin. Tauke Khan's efforts to resist the Zunghar were fruitless when in 1718 he led a combined army of the hordes to resist the Zunghars in a three-day battle at the Aya Guz River, just north of Lake Balkhash. With the Kazakh defeat the Zunghars advanced and defeated a second Kazakh army of the Middle Horde just north of Tashkent. Trapped between the Kalmyks to the west and the Zunghars and defeated on all sides, this period in Kazakh history became known as the *aktaban shubrundy* or Great Disaster.[14]

After the death of Tauke Khan in 1718 the Kazakh Khanate irrevoc-ably split again into the separate hordes, with both the Great Horde and Middle Horde at times subject to the Zunghars. For the rest of the eighteenth century the Kazakhs struggled to remain independent of the Zunghar, Russian and Qing empires. Particularly in the face of the Zunghars and Kalmyks, the Small Horde turned to Russia for assist-ance. Realizing that the incorporation of the Kazakhs into the Zunghars threatened Russian possessions, the Russians were only too glad to help. The khan of the Small Horde, Abulkhayr Khan, submitted to the Russian Tsar in 1730. While the Kazakhs were not always the most loyal of vassals, in the end the Russians slowly inveigled their way into Kazakh politics. Gradually the other Kazakhs, pressed on all sides, turned to the Russians for protection from the Zunghars. Although the Qing Empire ended the Zunghar threat in 1758, the Russian presence in the steppe was sufficient to prevent a resurgence of a Kazakh Khanate. By 1822 the Kazakhs could no longer select their own khans, who tended to live as 'guests' in Russian cities. Thus the sultans, non-Chinggisid aris-tocracy, gained some authority but the damage was done. By 1846 the Kazakhs were part of the Russian Empire.

In the east it is difficult to consider the Ming as a successor state to the Mongol Empire and it was not, particularly as the Ming Dyn-asty built the Great Wall to fend off attacks from the Mongolian successors to the Mongol Empire, but the Ming still functioned differ-ently from the Chinese kingdoms prior to the Mongols. Although it did renew tribute relations with former clients of the Yuan, the Ming remained xenophobic yet at the same time continued some Mongol institutions such as the *sheng* or provinces. Mongol rule completely altered the provincial level of administration. The Yuan created eleven provinces, which the Ming redrew to fifteen, and the Qing expanded to eighteen provinces, but the governing structures were from the Yuan period.

Nonetheless the rise of the Ming dramatically transformed the region. For the first time in 300 years China proper (not southern Mongolia or the area between the Great Wall and the Gobi Desert, eastern Turkestan or Tibet) was united and ruled by a Han dynasty. Since the 900s northern China had been ruled by non-Han such as Khitans, Jurchens and Mongols with the northwestern portion by Tangut and then Mongols. Indeed the region of modern day Beijing had been outside Han control since the tenth century. Professor David Robinson points to the Ming establishment of Beijing as its capital as a shift in Han mentality as it had not been a traditional centre for the Chinese.[15] For the Ming, however, the necessity to have a political centre close to the steppes in order to ward off Mongol attacks and perhaps maintain influence in Korea to counter Mongol loyalties there also played a factor. Korea certainly felt the impact of the Mongol Empire. It is thought that perhaps the Mongol invasion may have assisted in transforming Korea into the 'Hermit Kingdom'.[16] Just as the Ming tended to be xenophobic as a result of Mongol rule, its Korean contemporaries also began a policy of greater isolation.

While China consolidated under the Ming, the Northern Yuan Dynasty fell apart. Not until the rise of Dayan Khan as the 28th successor to Chinggis Khan in 1479 did stability return to Mongolia, albeit briefly. Dayan, benefiting from his father Mandaghol's (r. 1473–9) unification of the Khalkha Mongols, defeated the Oirats who had expanded from western Mongolia into central Mongolia. Dayan Khan drove them out of what is now Mongolia as well as putting pressure on the Ming. Unification was fleeting however as his nine sons quarrelled for succession after his death in 1517 and laid the foundation for divisions between the Mongolians that still exist. One of Dayan's actions divided his realm into two parts consisting of six *tümens*, three in each part. These *tümens*, the Chahar, Urianghai, Khalkha, Ordos, Tümed and Yüngsiyebü became the groupings of Chinggisid Mongolia. Although the Mongols recognized the leader of the Chahar as the khan, the other leaders viewed him as first among equals. Soon all six leaders assumed the title of khan. This had the adverse affect of diminishing the importance of the title as it now meant simply the leader of any of the six divisions.

By the sixteenth century Mongolia (northern and southern) was in a state of controlled chaos with various Borjigin (not only Chinggisid but also led by descendants of Chinggis Khan's brothers) led tribes fighting each other, the Ming and the Oirat. In southern Mongolia (which comprised much of the modern Inner Mongolia Autonomous Region) Dayan's grandson and ruler of the Tümed Mongols, Altan, established a new line of legitimacy with Buddhist support through the Dalai Lama's confirmation of Altan as khan, theoretically raising him above the other Chinggisid princes. Although he was able to assert his authority over most of the other Mongols, as often was the case with the Chinggisids, this unity was ephemeral. Nonetheless, the internecine warfare among the Borjigin aristocracy forged a common identity for the Mongols, as those nomads ruled by a Borjigin, especially a Chinggisid, prince, that distinguished them from the Oirats and gave rise to the modern identity of Mongolians.

By the seventeenth century only two true successors remained – the Zunghar confederation and the Qing. The Qing gained support from eastern Mongols due to their distrust of the Chahar Khan, Ligdan's intermarriage with the Manchus, and the fact that with the defeat of Ligdan the Manchus gained the jade seal of Chinggis Khan. The Manchu script was based on the Mongolian Uighur or vertical script authorized by Chinggis Khan in 1204. Other ties included the shared Tibetan Buddhist religion, recognizing the Dalai Lama as the premier religious authority. These factors and marrying Chinggisid princesses gave the Qing legitimacy that was cemented by the Dalai Lama conferring the title of khan upon the Qing ruler. This Qing could be rightfully viewed as the Altan Khan or Golden Khan. As gold is also the colour of imperial authority the very title suggests greater legitimacy than the title of khan that the various Chinggisid khans used.

Also in the east vying for the legacy of the Mongol Empire were the Zunghars. While not a direct successor to the Mongol Empire, the Zunghars were the successor to the Oirat confederation of the fifteenth century, which formed in the wake of the collapse of the Yuan Empire. From the sixteenth to eighteenth centuries the Zunghars contended for domination over Mongolia, Tibet, the Kazakh Khanate, the Uzbek khanates and even into Siberia. The Zunghars were the last great steppe power and in this sense they must be considered a successor state. Their armies fought along similar lines and used governing structures based on those of the Mongol Empire. The fact that the Dalai Lama also conferred the title of khan on Zunghar rulers also gave them the legitimacy of a successor. Like the Qing the Zunghars could never carry the same authority as the Mongol Empire but they could be successors to its heritage and legacy.

With the defeat of the Zunghars in the eighteenth century, however, the Mongol Empire and its successor states truly ended. Although the Russian Empire continued to expand into central Asia and across Siberia, it was no longer functioning as a steppe power but as a European imperialist state. The Qing also ceased to be a successor. As Peter Perdue argues, the defeat of the Zunghars eliminated the major threat to the Qing not only militarily but also in terms of legitimacy.[17] Both vied for hegemony in the Tibetan Buddhist world of Inner Asia. In order to defeat the Zunghars the Qing had to mobilize tremendous resources of men, material and animals. With the

Zunghar threat removed in 1757 the Qing Empire faced no external threats until the Opium Wars when European imperialism intruded upon China. Russia was not a threat as it wanted to trade and in any case did not have sufficient military forces in its eastern provinces to threaten the Qing. The removal of the Zunghars also decreased the importance of the Mongols to the Qing. The fact that the Mongols could desert to the Zunghars, or even reassert a Chinggisid Dynasty, hovered like a spectre in the back of the minds of the Qing emperors. The Qing needed the Mongols' support in order to defeat the Zunghars and to conquer China. China was easier to conquer than the Zunghars but, once the Zunghars met defeat, the Qing turned their attention to the most populous part of their empire. Although the Qing emperor continued to play the role of an Inner Asian khan, increasingly he acted as a Chinese emperor. Although it was in keeping with the actions of Khubilai Khan, it is not what Chinggis Khan would have done.

LINGERING MONGOL INFLUENCE

Although the empire disappeared and a wide range of successors came and went, the influence of the Mongol Empire lasted much longer. In the early nineteenth century Alexander Burnes, a British adventurer and officer of the British East India Company, entered Afghanistan. A government official known as an 'elchee' was sent to greet him.[18] Burnes may not have given the official's title a second thought, but it was a Mongolian title – elchi, meaning ambassador. Clearly it was a holdover from the Mongol Empire. The question is how did it stay in Afghanistan and why was it being used in a Pashtun dynasty? The logical explanation is that it became embedded in the culture not only through the Mongol Empire but also from its use in the Timurid, Uzbek and Mughal empires.

Other Mongol influences remain in Afghanistan. The ethnic group the Hazaras and certain segments of the Aimaks are a holdover of Mongol rule. Indeed, despite the current rhetoric of Afghanistan being the graveyard of empires, the Mongols conquered and ruled Afghanistan for approximately 150 years. The Hazaras take their name from the Persian word for thousand, the equivalent of a mingan (Mongolian military unit of one thousand). The Aimak are diverse nomadic and semi-nomadic groups of mixed descent, including Mongol. Oddly enough, Mongolian soldiers are once again on the march, this time however as peacekeepers who serve in Afghanistan and Iraq or participate with the United States and other countries in the war games in Mongolia known as Khanquest.

Unbeknown to most of the world, Chinggis Khan was quite active in the twentieth century, manipulating world politics or at least serving as a pawn in events, even serving in the Second World War. Harold Lamb's biography of the great Mongolian leader in 1927 reintroduced Chinggis Khan to Westerners, but in East Asia he became a pawn in East Asian politics as Japan, China and the Soviet Union competed for the support of Mongolians in the region. Although Japan and China vied for the attention of the Inner Mongolians, much of what they did had the potential to influence sentiments in Mongolia.

Japan and China both attempted to influence Inner Mongolian popular opinion by venerating Chinggis Khan. The Japanese constructed a large temple (more than 762 sq m/2,500 sq ft) to Chinggis Khan in Ulanhot during their 1931–45 occupation of Inner Mongolia. The Guomingdang or Chinese Nationalist Party protected the sacred relics of Chinggis Khan held at Ejen Khoroo by moving them from the Ordos to Gansu in an effort to preserve Inner Mongolian support. Not to be outdone by the Guomingdang or the Japanese, Mao Zedong and the communists called upon the Inner Mongolians to resist the Japanese in the spirit of Chinggis Khan.

This effort to claim Chinggis Khan did not impact Mongolia directly, but the use of his image and identity demonstrated the importance not only of Chinggis Khan but also of the Mongolian people at this stage of the war. Considering the popular belief at the time in Japan that Chinggis Khan was actually a Japanese samurai who ventured into the steppes,[19] one might wonder how Japan have used the Chinggis Khan relics as propaganda in Mongolia – especially as they periodically espoused a pan-Mongol movement, much to the chagrin of the Soviets.

The Soviets also placed an importance on Chinggis Khan during the Second World War. To maintain Mongolian loyalty Chinggis Khan received the endorsement of the Soviets, just as they used Russian national heroes such as Alexander Nevskii in propaganda to stoke patriotism in the face of German invasion. With the end of the Second World War the Soviet leadership also changed its perspective. Nationalist propaganda lost favour at the end of the war in part because of the fear that national heroes, particularly non-Russian ones, might become rallying figures against communist rule. As a

Soviet satellite the Mongolian government followed Soviet examples in 1949, condemning Chinggis Khan as a reactionary and feudal lord while painting his campaigns as nothing more than plundering expeditions that exploited the people.

Milder rhetoric surfaced after the death of Stalin in 1953 but government circumspection did not cease altogether. Quite simply, unless one wrote in an anti-Chinggis tone, a manuscript would not be published – but at least the secret police rarely paid a visit. Events in Inner Mongolia made the complete condemnation of Chinggis Khan in Mongolia relatively short. In the long run the Chinese communists' efforts to harness the aura of Chinggis Khan were successful. The communist defeat of the nationalists in China gained Mao the relics of Chinggis Khan. Mao returned these to Ejen Khoroo in 1954 with pomp and grandeur. Two years later the Chinese government built a mausoleum (almost 465 sq m /5,000 sq ft) to house the relics and began restoring the Japanese-built Temple of Chinggis Khan in Ulanhot. With China keen on renewing relations with Mongolia, Chinese favour of Chinggis Khan had the potential to sway the public.

Mongolia's government reconsidered its position on Chinggis Khan, especially as 1962 marked Chinggis Khan's 800th birthday. No one is positive of the birth date; Western scholars mark it either as 1165 or 1167, but in Mongolia 1162 remains in vogue. Although Tsedenbal, Mongolia's prime minister, did not fully endorse it the Mongolian Academy of Sciences gained permission to study the issue. The first effort to honour Chinggis Khan was innocuous, with commemorative stamps, an academic conference and an editorial in the state newspaper, Ünen (Truth). The next step was bolder with the creation of a 11-m (36-ft) tall stone monument adorned with Chinggis Khan's portrait, erected near the birthplace of Chinggis Khan at Gurwan Nuur in the Khentii aimag (province).

Since Mongolia became the second communist state in 1921 it followed the Soviet lead in most matters. For this event, however, Mongolia did not consult the USSR. Soviet historians criticized the academic conference. In China the reaction was quite different. Although some Chinese historians criticized Chinggis Khan, others praised him. Their reaction, however, did not reflect the context of Mongolia, but rather Chinggis Khan's role in Chinese history – particularly as a unifier. Also in 1962 Inner Mongolians held their own conference on Chinggis Khan, which caused new tensions between the Soviet Union and China. At this conference some scholars suggested that Mongolia be reunited with China, resulting in vociferous criticism from the Soviets. The Soviets continued their negative portrayal of Chinggis Khan not only by continuing their criticism of all the 1962 events but by taking offence at the Mongolian scholars who dared to criticize Soviet historical studies of Chinggis Khan. The fact that the Mongols conquered Russia in the late 1230s and dominated it for 200 years certainly played an unspoken role in Soviet policy. In the end Tsedenbal defused much of the situation by dismissing Daramyn Tomor-Ochir, a party official, as the scapegoat for the whole affair.[20]

Mongolian scholars, though, did not escape the Soviet Union's wrath. X. Perlee, one of the greatest, refused to play by Soviet rules. As a consequence he was imprisoned, and when not in jail the government denied him permission to perform research outside Mongolia. The fact that he was Tomor-Ochir's teacher also placed a target on his back. Relatives of scholars came under scrutiny by the government as well. Many faced demotion or the loss of their jobs. Meanwhile the territory around Chinggis Khan's birthplace became a Soviet tank base with restricted access.

Chinggis Khan remained a part of the sub-plot during the Sino-Soviet split. The Soviets denounced any Chinese scholarship that presented a favourable view of Chinggis Khan. Not all of the hostility stemmed from Russian or Marxist views of Chinggis Khan, though. Some of the negative reaction was because the Chinese scholars insinuated that if not for the Mongols, who introduced aspects of Chinese civilization to Russia, the Russians would have remained ignorant savages.[21] In 1975 Tsedenbal ridiculed Chinese fascination with Chinggis Khan, linking it to ideas suggested in the Inner Mongolia 1962 conference where some advocated reunifying Mongolia with China. Thus honouring Chinggis Khan placed Mongolia's independence in peril. Neither side (Soviet or Chinese) truly favoured Chinggis Khan's role in their history. While the Chinese promoted his image in the 1950s and early 1960s, overall, outside of Inner Mongolia, they had little interest in the topic. The Cultural Revolution of the late 1960s and early 1970s reversed the situation completely as Inner Mongolian scholars and others associated with studying or praising Chinggis Khan found themselves targets for persecution while the temple at Ulanhot and the mausoleum both suffered extensive damage.

Throughout his life Chinggis Khan faced adversity and overcame it. In death he carries on the tradition. In 2005 the mausoleum received a US$30 million dollar facelift and now attracts millions of visitors, mainly

Han Chinese. Accordingly the mausoleum's temple has been altered to suit Han tastes and to frame Chinggis Khan as the progenitor of a Chinese dynasty, not a foreign one. For instance, motifs include dragons rather than horses, wolves and eagles. Mongolians and Inner Mongolians are uncomfortable with this co-opting of their ancestral hero.[22]

As evinced above, the Russians have often felt insecure about their relations with the Mongols. The so-called Mongol or Tatar Yoke has been blamed for keeping Russia backwards vis-à-vis the West. This has been proved quite convincingly to be a myth.[23] Yet good myths are difficult to forget. As part of a campaign against mounting alcoholism in Russia, politicians and scientists now blame the Mongols. Much of this has to do with the image of the Mongols, which has rarely been positive. Russia still struggles with its relation with the Mongol Empire. Some view it as protecting Russian culture and Russian Orthodoxy from an expansive medieval Catholic Christendom. Mongols provided support to Alexander Nevksii's efforts against Swedish Crusaders and the Teutonic Knights.[24] Others in post-Soviet Russia are nervous of nationalist sentiments among Buryat Mongols. Unlike China, there are no monuments to Chinggis Khan in Russia, but the prospect of one does make many nervous. Curiously, the Russian and Buryat educated classes tend to view Chinggis Khan more positively than the working classes. Thus there are some Russians, along with Buryats, seeking to claim Chinggis Khan. In addition to the Chinese and Mongolian claims to his resting place, there are those in Russia who claim that Chinggis Khan's grave is located in Buryatia, somewhere around Lake Baikal.[25] Most, however, view this as myth and point out another concern. According to one news report:

> Buryats, however, are not enthusiastic about the search for the grave, said German Galsanov, a news anchor at Arig-us Television, a private network named after the site of Genghis's mother's birth. 'What's the point?' he asked. 'We're not going to learn anything more.'
>
> He recounts a story that is popular in the former Soviet Union: that in 1941 Soviet archeologists broke into the grave of Tamerlane – a descendant of Genghis who had his own empire – in Samarkand, Uzbekistan. Two days later, Germany invaded the Soviet Union. 'So if that's what happened when we opened up Tamerlane's grave,' he said, 'imagine what will happen when we open up Genghis Khan's?'[26]

Mongol Image

As the story above indicates, despite the Mongol impact on world history they are primarily remembered for destruction. Although centuries have passed, the Mongols are viewed as an unstoppable force bent on destroying all that they encountered, particularly 'what they did not understand'.[27] Indeed, this view not only permeated the scholarly literature until the past few decades, it persists in popular literature as well as the popular imagination. One can look at the most innocuous forms of popular entertainment, from movies to comic books to see this display. In the popular Marvel Norse superhero comic book *Thor*, after encountering a series of setbacks, Thor's alter-ego, the lame Dr Donald Blake mutters, 'The only thing that could make this day worse would be if Genghis Khan and the Mongol horde ran me over.'[28] In the Scooby-Doo movie *The Reluctant Werewolf*, while Scooby and the eponymous Shaggy compete in a Transylvanian car race, Dracula attempts to foil their efforts by unleashing Genghis Kong, a combination of King Kong and Chinggis Khan.[29] In the cartoon series *Spider-Man and His Amazing Friends*, in an effort to defeat Spider-Man a villain puts him in an arena with the deadliest warriors of history – thus Genghis Khan appears.[30] Although many other examples exist, one might turn to the *Wizard of Oz* to find that the Wicked Witch's guardsmen are garbed in suspiciously Mongol-like accoutrement. Finally, in the movie *Red Dawn*, just before Russian paratroopers land on the high school campus in Michigan, a high school history teacher wrote Genghis Khan on the blackboard – foreshadowing the United States' doom.[31] In all instances, the 'worst thing' one could be confronted with was some incarnation of Chinggis Khan and the Mongols. Indeed, the G-Word or Genghis Khan appears to be the avatar of this image, while Chinggis Khan is the historical figure.

That this view permeated popular media in the twentieth century is not surprising. Indeed, it would last until the twenty-first century, and still lingers. Much of this has to do with Western and Eastern stereotypes of 'barbarians' (that is any non-sedentary cultures), Orientalism, the concept of the 'Yellow Peril' and, of course, the Mongols' own actions. With wars against Japan, Korea and China, and a looming one with Vietnam, it is not surprising that in the epic film about Chinggis Khan, rather than using an Asian actor, John Wayne played Temüjin with his eyebrows taped up. As Ruth Dunnell pointed out, 'Among the descendants of people who suffered the brunt of the Mongols' brutal

onslaught in the early thirteenth century, the verdict on the Mongols
varies according to prevailing political or religious needs.'[32] Often the
Mongols remain a useful *bête noire*. In 2003 the American invasion of
Iraq was unflatteringly compared with Hülegü's destruction of Baghdad,
a comparison missed by most Americans as most had no idea of who
or what a Hülegü was. Yet most of the population of the Middle East
understood the connection and that it was not meant as a compliment
(although one might wonder how the American generals viewed it).[33]
Even prior to this, Osama bin Laden and other Salafists attempted to
paint the United States of America as a threat to Islam of the magni-
tude of the Mongols through reference to Ibn Taymiyya.[34] Ibn Taymiyya
(1263–1328), an Islamic scholar in the Mamluk Sultanate, viewed the
Mongols as the greatest threat to the Islamic world – and this was after
they had converted to Islam.

   While it is true that blame must be attributed to the Mongols themselves, it is somewhat curious that other destructive groups have not
had the same level of stigma attached to them. Some celebrate this
identity of menace as evinced by the rise of a motorcycle gang known
as the Mongols, who sought to rival the Hell's Angels. Other historical
groups seem to fall short. Certainly the Vandals garnered some recognition. Perhaps only Attila and the Huns or Hitler's Nazis have gained
the same level of infamy.

   The dawn of the twenty-first century witnessed plenty of
changes. Mongolia was now truly independent for the first time since
1696 when the Qing Empire absorbed it. Chinggis Khan quickly
became, and rightfully, the father of the nation. As such Chinggis
Khan was the embodiment of all things positive – he had made
Mongolia great once and it would rise again, albeit not as the largest
contiguous empire in history. Thus the Mongols recognized the more
positive aspects of the Mongol Empire and not just the body counts.

   Today in Mongolia one cannot avoid the legacy of Chinggis Khan
and the Mongol Empire. To the Mongol he is the father of their state
and to outsiders he is easily the most identifiable figure in Mongolian
history, even more so since 2006, which marked the 800th anniversary
of the founding of the Mongol Empire by Chinggis Khan in 1206. His
face and presence is everywhere. Travelling to Mongolia you arrive at
the Chinggis Khan Airport in Ulaanbaatar. Then you can take a taxi to
Chinggis Khan Bank to exchange money, which will bear Chinggis
Khan's visage on every note from 500 *tögrögs* and above. During the
process you might ride down Chinggis Khan Avenue. Need a place to

lodge? Try the Chinggis Khan hotel. Hungry? Dine at the Chinggis restaurant and quench your thirst with a Chinggis Beer – a very nice German-style lager. The next day you might find yourself tired. A Chinggis Khan energy drink would be in order. After visiting all of the Chinggis Khan tourist sites, perhaps you'll end your day with a night-cap of any of the variety of vodkas bearing Chinggis Khan's image.

Meanwhile the Great Khan has been observing your activities in Ulaanbaatar as his face adorns a hillside overlooking the city. His pres-ence is ubiquitous and prominent as a memorial pavilion in Sukhbaatar Square overshadows the statue of the city's and square's namesake. A five-metre-high (16-feet-high) statue sits in the middle, surrounded by statues of his successors and a couple of exquisitely sculpted Mongol warriors. It is indeed quite impressive. The size of the palace and statue clearly demonstrates Chinggis Khan's significance and the country's direction for the future. Significantly larger than the tomb and statue of Sukhbaatar, the hero of communist Mongolia, the pavilion signifies that the communist period is a lesser part of Mongolia's past. In 2006 rumours floated about renaming Ulaanbaatar to Chinggis Khan City. Yet all of this pales in comparison to the towering metal statue in the steppes outside of Ulaanbaatar. A 40-metre-tall (130-feet-tall) statue of Chinggis Khan rises above the steppes. One can even enter it and observe the steppe from a platform between the ears of his steed.

The use of Chinggis Khan as a historic symbol and one of national pride is of great importance. At the same time, since the fall of commun-ism in Mongolia, the Mongolians have also been doing quick studies in advertising. Unsurprisingly this has led to some concern over exactly how the Chinggis Khan 'brand' should be used. While Chinggis Khan vodka is interesting, what should one do about Chinggis Khan toilet paper? Should there be any restrictions on the use of Chinggis Khan in advertising? Yet the Mongolians are not the only ones who want to use his cachet – Russia, Kazakhstan and China have all sought to tap into the legacy of Chinggis Khan. As a result, in 2006 the Mongolian legis-lature, the Ikh Khural, discussed the nature of this problem as well how to control it.

Chinggis Khan's importance to Mongolia should not be under-estimated. He has come to symbolize the ideas and hopes of Mongolia as does the legendary 'Once and Future King' Arthur for Britain. There are several legends of Chinggis Khan[35] that correspond with a tradition in many cultures termed as the 'sleeping warrior' by Lord Raglan.[36] In summary, in the 'sleeping warrior' legend, a resting hero from the past will awaken from his hidden location and aid his home-land in a moment of great distress.

Considering that Chinggis Khan is the founding father of Mongolia, there can be little surprise at his rising popularity in Mongolia. The Mongolian nation has lasted longer than the empire itself. What is notable is that most Mongolians rarely speak of Chinggis Khan's deeds outside Mongolia, but rather of his statesmanship, vision and laws. To them the importance of the conquests is secondary to the institutions that he gave to the Mongols. This is not because they are apologists for the brutality of the conquests but rather that they realize the importance of his other activities. As a result, since 1990 he has become the ultimate symbol of Mongolian nationalism. Furthermore, Chinggis Khan is not only the father of the country, but many – includ-ing academics and politicians – view Chinggis Khan as the reason why Mongolia has successfully transitioned into a democratic state. In the eyes of many Mongolians the framework for democracy was created by Chinggis Khan by having his successors elected.[37] While the historical validity of this belief is rather dubious as only descendants of Chinggis Khan could rule, it demonstrates a rationalization and a justification of why democracy has taken root. By tracing it back to Chinggis Khan, democracy is justified and becomes part of the customs and culture of Mongolia. Clearly, Chinggis Khan's importance and that of the Mongol Empire cannot be ignored. The founder of the empire has served as a symbol to Mongolia, although the image has varied through the years. In this context it is not surprising that Inner Mongolians look to Chinggis Khan and others have tapped into his virtues.

Like Mongolia, Kazakhstan found itself an independent state with the collapse of the Soviet Union. Rather than looking at Janibek Khan or Kasym Khan as the father of their country they too turned to Chinggis Khan. Hundreds of Kazakhs have had their DNA tested or lobbied to have their names included in a book listing those of Chinggisid lineage.[38] Kazakhstan was the primary participant in the production of the film *Mongol*, a biopic concerning the rise of Chinggis Khan. Part of the purpose of the film was to educate Kazakhs in their past with Chinggis Khan as their hero.[39]

This more benign view of Chinggis Khan is becoming less of an oddity to Westerners. Although scholars of the Mongol Empire have known the complete picture of Chinggis Khan for decades, it had not carried over into the public perception, although it is changing. One rea-son is due to the success of an American scholar, Jack Weatherford, whose *Genghis Khan and the Making of the Modern World* sat high on the *New York Times* best-seller list for several weeks. An anthropologist, he tapped into the Mongolian sentiment. Rich in cultural insight, although at times a bit haphazard in historical accuracy, Weatherford painted a more optimistic view of the Mongol Empire. He is not the only scholar to recognize the more positive achievements of the Mongols. Indeed, virtually every book on the Mongols has a legacy section (indeed you are reading one now) that goes into long-term effects. A key to this change of events has undoubtedly been the rise of world history as a discipline, which has been slowly yet enthusiastically embracing the Mongols as a harbinger of a global history and a significant catalyst changing the world, as will be illustrated in Part Two. When I teach modern world history I use the Mongol Empire as my starting point. Not only because it is my speciality, but also because it serves as a har-binger of globalization, modern warfare and the alteration of the map of Eurasia. Furthermore, what other empire shares connections with John Wayne, the Dalai Lama, Christopher Columbus and William Shakespeare?

PART TWO

THE CHINGGIS EXCHANGE

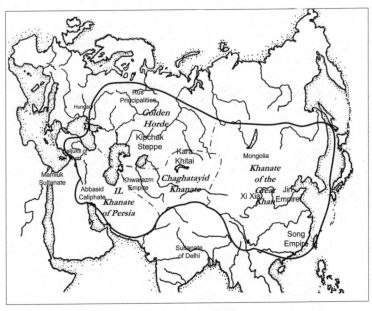

Post-Dissolution Empire.

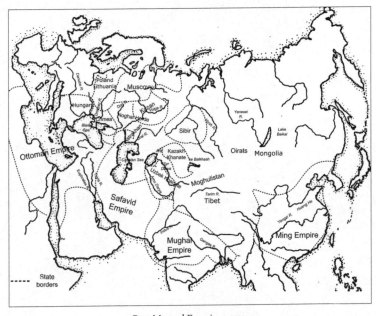

Post-Mongol Eurasia, c. 1550.

4

PAX MONGOLICA
AND TRADE

It is well established that the Mongol Empire had a great deal of interest in promoting trade. A unified empire that stretched from the
Carpathians to the Sea of Japan provided secure travel routes and
reduced the number of tariffs and taxes that merchants paid as they
crossed the various Eurasian travel routes. Indeed, it was said that a vir-
gin carrying a gold urn filled with jewels could walk from one end of
the empire to another without being molested. Perhaps this was a slight
exaggeration, but it did convey the point that the Eurasian trade routes
were more secure than they had ever been, and new routes flourished
as well, beyond the traditional Silk Road. Yet what is less understood is
how the Mongols achieved this. Certainly establishing the largest contiguous empire in history helped with security, but what would attract
merchants from the main trade routes to the court of the Mongol
khans? While the Silk Road did pass through central Asia, Mongolia was
not just off the main highway, it was beyond the back roads.

However, trade existed between the pastoral nomads of Mongolia
and sedentary kingdoms for centuries. Little is known about the trade
between the tribes of Mongolia and the Liao, Jin or Xi Xia states in the
eleventh and twelfth centuries other than that goods that might be
used for war were banned from entering the steppe, although that did
not stop many entrepreneurs.[1] Most of the trade took place in border
towns in what is now Inner Mongolia and through 'tribute missions'.
Few merchants actually risked going into the steppe, particularly
north of the Gobi Desert, since it involved too many risks for large
caravans. Indeed in the pre-Mongol period trade with the Chinese
kingdoms often started with the threat of raids. From the perspective
of the nomads, 'war and trade are not in contradiction; on the con-
trary, trade involves war, because military actions are needed to create
the possibilities for trade'.[2] There were three basic categories of obtaining goods in the pastoral nomadic–sedentary commercial relationship.

The first was that nomads traded clandestinely with China, which meant that it was not sanctioned by the imperial government. Most nomads carried out this form. The second category went through official channels: the nomads submitted to the authority of the emperor, at least nominally, and paid tribute and traded at approved locations. This form benefited the nomadic leaders as gifts from the tribute went directly to them, which could then be kept or given to subordinates. The final form was that the nomads raided the borders and seized goods, which benefited the rank and file as they gained a share of the spoils, although they also incurred substantial risk in this dangerous method of procuring goods.[3]

CHINGGIS KHAN AND EARLY CONTACT

The rise of the Mongol Empire altered the traditional methods of nomadic-sedentary trade, not only eradicating many states that sought to dominate and control the trade routes, but also creating a change in mindset. This change regarding how the Mongols conceived of trade was crucial. As Janet Abu-Lughod has demonstrated,

> unification does not necessarily reduce the overall costs of transit, but it has the potential to do so, depending on policy choices. The chief contribution made by an administration based on 'law and order' is a reduction in unpredictable protection rent. By eliminating competing tribute gatherers and by regularizing tolls, unification makes transport costs calculable.[4]

Yet not even a decision on policy is sufficient, particularly in a region that is marginal in intercontinental trade. A change in mindset is necessary. Whereas the nomads had previously gone to established trading centres with a few traders venturing deep into the steppe, the Mongols created a scenario where the trade came to them.

Early in his career Chinggis Khan established important contacts with the few Muslim merchants who did business in the steppe. Indeed, after one setback in 1203 while fighting the Kereit, Chinggis Khan regrouped at Lake Baljuna. There he made an important contact with a Muslim merchant named Asan (Hasan) who was at the lake watering the wethers, or castrated sheep, that he used to trade for sable and squirrel pelts.[5] From this it can be determined that a fur trade existed between Muslim central Asia and Siberia and that one route went through central Mongolia. Asan became a relatively significant figure during Chinggis Khan's reign. As Igor de Rachewiltz points out though, a Sartaq or city-dwelling Muslim from central Asia does not import sheep to Mongolia in order to trade for pelts. Most likely he brought goods to Mongolia in order to trade and purchased the sheep there to take to the Hoyin Irgen or Forest People around Lake Baikal. The pelts were the ultimate goal but required transactions along the way into order to cover the expenses of the journey.[6] Nonetheless, Asan's actions were but a harbinger of the model of how trade in the Mongol Empire would be carried out.

With the rise of Chinggis Khan a gradual transition occurred in the security of the trade routes. Chinggis Khan encouraged trade and liked to talk to the merchants who visited his camp. While part of this was to glean intelligence about distant lands and what the merchants observed, he also realized the importance of trade to his nascent kingdom. His desire to restore and promote commerce in Mongolia began almost immediately after he unified the steppe. At the *quriltai* of 1206 he posted guards called *qaraqchin* on the trade routes to protect merchants. Stationed regularly, they ensured the safety of caravans but also carried out other duties. One of their primary duties was to screen merchants and expedite or re-route their journey to Chinggis Khan, wherever his camp was at the time, if they had merchandise that interested the Great Khan.[7] With Mongol expansion into central Asia the Mongols not only gained the fealty of the Uighurs and Qarluq tribes, but also secured the trade routes from Amaligh (located in modern Kazakhstan) to the east.

When Muslim merchants from central Asia arrived at Chinggis Khan's camp, they found not only a ready customer but also a wily business partner. Indeed, one such merchant known as Balchikh brought beautiful fabrics to Chinggis Khan and demanded three *balish* of gold for each piece. Chinggis Khan refused and was enraged at the business practices of the merchant, saying 'Does this fellow think that fabrics have never been brought to us before?'[8] He then revealed to the merchant the wide variety of fabrics the Mongols already possessed and ordered his guards to confiscate the goods from Balchikh. At first this may seem a disastrous policy for promoting trade, but the ruse worked as the other merchants then understood who they were dealing with and offered their goods as gifts, probably hoping to escape with their lives. Chinggis Khan, however, then paid a *balish* of gold for every piece of *nasij*, or gold brocade, and a silver *balish* per two pieces of *zandanichi*, or cotton cloth. It was clear the Mongols would pay a fair value for the goods but would not be cheated or exploited. Chinggis Khan then invested in their return journey and encouraged his generals and princes to do the same, with each providing gold and silver as well as two or three people (Muslims) from their own retinue to form the caravan. Chinggis Khan then sent a message to Sultan Muhammad, the ruler of the Khwarazmian Empire, seeking terms of trade and safety for merchants travelling between their two domains.[9] The Mongol-sponsored caravan was truly an international affair consisting of Muslim merchants from the Khwarazmian Empire and beyond, including some Indians.

This trade caravan was massacred in 1218 when it returned to the Khwarazmian border town of Otrar as the governor (rightly) suspected that the merchants were also spies for the Mongols.[10] The incident provoked a war which resulted in Mongol expansion into central Asia and the Middle East and the destruction of the vast Khwarazmian Empire, which previously stretched from the Zagros Mountains to the Syr Darya. The massacre violated the sensibilities of Chinggis Khan and his idea of government. He had made great endeavours to promote trade and if caravans he sponsored were massacred indiscriminately it undermined his goals and reputation for providing security. Yet there was more to it than simple pride. Thomas Allsen commented that 'the incident was not merely an affront to [Chinggis Khan's] dignity and an open challenge to Mongolian arms; it was at bottom a pocket book issue, and it is this grievance, more than any other, that provoked retribution'.[11] Chinggis Khan and his princes had invested in it. Individually no one invested large amounts, only a few *balish* of gold or silver each, although we do not know how much Chinggis Khan invested himself. Indeed the Mongol financing of the caravan comes across like the proverbial club of little old ladies who pool their money to buy stocks.[12]

The war demonstrated Chinggis Khan's basic trade policy. He promoted trade and sought fair prices. In the process he reversed the old standards of trading between the nomads and the sedentary people. Whereas the Mongols and other nomads previously did not have sufficient quantities of luxury goods and often had to resort to trading or brokering deals with traders in the borderlands, now they possessed new wealth and wanted to spend it. Furthermore they wanted luxury goods, but remained in the steppe so that merchants had to come to them rather than the reverse. Thus the Mongols had to pay for the price of transportation, and it also began a change in attitudes about commerce. While merchants could expect to recover the cost of transportation, nonetheless they still had to cover their expenses while en route to the Mongol camps. Now that more merchants ventured into the steppe, we see more of them following the trading model of Asan the Sartaq – buying bulk goods along the way and selling them elsewhere. With improved security and the guaranteed purchaser of bulk and luxury goods at the other end of the trade route, as Allsen wrote, 'long-distance bulk trade became in these circumstances an economically sound proposition'.[13]

ÖGÖDEI AND KARAKORUM

Although change in Inner Asian commercial activities began under Chinggis Khan, the key change came during the reign of Ögödei (r. 1230–41). He established the Mongol capital of Karakorum in the Orkhon River basin, a region that had a long history of importance in Mongolia.[14] By building his capital here Ögödei further legitimated Chinggisid and Mongol authority, not only with the location's historic importance, but its strategic importance in central Mongolia rather than Chinggis Khan's old capital of Avarga in the Onon-Kerülen River basin.[15] In 1230 when Ögödei assumed power the site of Karakorum was almost the centre of the empire, which stretched from the Amu Darya to the Sea of Japan. Khubilai Khan later moved the capital, partly because with the conquest of China Karakorum was simply too far removed in order to rule effectively. Another reason was that although Karakorum was the capital and at an ideologically strategic location, in terms of logistics it was poorly situated. Some 900 cartloads of provisions came to the capital daily in order to feed the inhabitants.

The Mongol khans did not actually reside at Karakorum. Rather they remained in their nomadic camps in the pastures near the city. Indeed the papal envoy John of Plano Carpini never entered Karakorum but went directly to Güyük's camp. Although William of Rubruck visited Karakorum, his encounters with Möngke Khan took place in his camp a few days journey from Karakorum. On some matters of state they would come to their capital. Yet for the most part the khans seem to have viewed Karakorum as perhaps a garage, basement or attic. In a sense it is where they kept their stuff. And, as we all know, storage space is crucial for anyone. Observers noted that near the palace in Karakorum were many large barn-like buildings that stored both

Ögödei Khan, illustration from Rashid al-Din's *Jami' al-Tawarikh*. Ögödei was the second ruler of the Mongol Empire, and was largely responsible for the stabilization of the empire as well as the conception that it was the Mongol's right to rule the world. This illustration shows the khan, presumably in Karakorum, receiving tribute.

provisions and treasure.[16] Thus the Mongols not only had the largest empire but also the largest walk-in closets.

Of course part of their 'stuff' was treasure and loot – plunder brought back from pillaging but also items purchased from merchants. Another part of their 'stuff' was artisans brought back to Mongolia. The Franciscan monk and unofficial emissary of the French king Louis IX, William of Rubruck, saw many Chinese craftsmen in Karakorum. He observed that they paid taxes in silver and in goods and that they all followed the same craft as their fathers did.[17] William arrived in Karakorum in 1253, so these appear to be second-generation Karakorum residents, perhaps brought back during Ögödei's conquest of the Jin Empire in northern China in the early 1230s. William insinuated that all of the sons following the occupation of their fathers was not simply tradition, although it was the norm for most of the medieval world, but Mongol decree.[18] In the Mongolian production centres all sons followed their father's occupation with no opportunity to pursue another vocation as sometimes occurred outside the empire. Thus the Mongols ensured that they had the goods they desired. Many of the artisans who came to Mongolia as a result of the conquests became part of a military-industrial complex, so to speak, to make weapons and armour for the Mongols. Other artisans made luxury items such as *nasij,* the gold threaded silk brocades that the Mongol nobility cherished and often bestowed on guests as a symbol of honour.[19]

Karakorum itself was a planned and organized city. During heavy snows the Mongol government even arranged for snow removal, according to William of Rubruck.[20] Nonetheless, it apparently was not a large city. William of Rubruck noted that if one excluded the khan's palace, the city was smaller than St Denis, a village on the outskirts of Paris with a population of approximately 10,000 people.[21] Whereas William of Rubruck may not have been overly impressed, one must still take into account that, although Karakorum was located in Mongolia, the vast majority of the population were foreigners. It was truly a polyglot city. Besides the palace and the royal warehouses the city also possessed two major commercial districts. One hosted the previously mentioned Chinese artisans. The other was a market, located near the palace and dominated by Muslim merchants, although other merchants and envoys also flocked there. The market appears to have dealt in luxury as well as mundane goods but not foodstuffs. One could purchase millet and other grains (when available) by the east gate; the south gate had a market for oxen and carts, presumably because it faced China; sheep and goats were sold at the west gate; at the north gate one could buy horses. Curiously, one does not see any mention of a camel market, perhaps because their value was easily three times that of any horse. In addition there were the buildings of the government for the chancellery and scribes. The city also hosted twelve 'pagan' temples, which could include Buddhist and Daoist shrines. William also noted two mosques and one church, belonging to the Church of the East or Nestorians. Indeed Karakorum was a hotbed of missionary activity.[22]

Much of the success of Karakorum as a commercial centre must be attributed to the policies of Ögödei. During his reign he established the storehouses for luxury goods ranging from ingots of gold and silver to satin, as well as granaries for the grain that came as tax payments. He also issued decrees on selecting guards and people to be in charge of them. This may not seem that unusual a step, but one must remember that Ögödei was establishing a permanent base to store goods. Although nomadic societies have always acquired goods, they still had to move them around, so large quantities were rarely sought or kept for the long term. Ögödei realized the amount of goods coming to the Mongol court had to be managed and organized and created a new branch of government in order to take care of it. He also selected people from each *mingan* (unit of 1,000), presumably so that one group would not monopolize the position and take advantage of it. Each *mingan* now had representation.[23]

Ögödei established a few other institutions instrumental in facilitating commerce. In many areas, including the *chöl* region, or Gobi

The interior of Erdene Zuu, the monastery sponsored by Altan Khan. It was built on the ruins of the old Mongol capital of Karakorum and marks a true transition from the final vestiges of the Mongol Empire to Buddhist Mongolia.

A *yam* station. The *yam*, or postal system, kept the Mongol Empire connected from modern Turkey to Korea. This recreation has two Mongolian horses at a *ger* or yurt. *Yam* stations could be large, but most of them were usually as simple as this one. The *tuq* in the background shows black tails, indicating that the empire was in a state of war.

Desert, he established wells with brick walls so animals could not fall into them and foul the water.[24] The Gobi had long hindered trade north of China, but Ögödei's primary concern in doing this was for the people and their herds as well as ensuring that he could send armies to northern China if necessary. Nonetheless the wells no doubt encouraged trade as they made the route significantly easier.

Another institution that Ögödei created was the *yam* or messenger system. Although Chinggis Khan may have established a rudimentary version, Ögödei extended it and linked it to other parts of the empire as well as creating the means to maintain its efficiency.[25] This included having stations with 24 horse-keepers at each post. Part of the efficiency was due to Ögödei's decree that assigned units of one thousand households to provide the *yamchin* (those who manned the *yam* stations which kept the postal horses known as *ulagh*), the storehouse attendants and granary keepers with provisions in addition to carts, oxen and horses for use.[26] Finally, he extended the patrols that routinely travelled the main routes and not only ensured the safety of the routes but also reported to the khan what items might be coming via the caravans.

But first Ögödei had to attract the caravans to Karakorum. For this he had a simple plan – he opened the doors to the storehouses. According to Juvaini, a Persian in the employ of the Mongols, this had the effect of drawing moths to a flame:

> And from all the corners of the earth there had come mer-
> chants, and speculators, and seekers of governorships and
> appointments, and all returned having attained their goal and
> object, and succeeded in their wishes and desires, and received
> the double of what they had in mind. How many a poor man
> became rich, how many a pauper wealthy and prosperous! And
> every obscure person became a man of great account.[27]

Much of Juvaini's writings in regard to Ögödei's excessive generosity must be viewed through the lens of Juvaini's own life. He was a Muslim whose own homeland was conquered and ruled by the Mongols. Although he found himself in their employ, like his father before him, he also had to reconcile the fact that the Mongols were infidels and Dar al-Islam, or the abode of Islam, that is to say the lands ruled by Islamic law and Muslim rulers, was shrinking rapidly. During the thirteenth century several Muslim thinkers came to rationalize this by determin-ing that although the ideal situation was to be ruled by a just Muslim king, it was better to be ruled by a just ruler of any religion than to be ruled by a tyrant. So, while by virtually all accounts Ögödei's character was one of generosity and good nature, it also shows that Ögödei was truly a just ruler. The instances that Juvaini relates also provide signifi-cant data for Ögödei's interest in commerce.

Indeed, much to the consternation of his officials, Ögödei repeat-edly paid top dollar for any item that crossed his path. In one instance an arrowsmith had fallen on hard times and was in debt. He offered to sell Ögödei his arrows so that he could end his debt of 70 *balish*. In return he would supply Ögödei with 10,000 arrows every year. Ögödei gave him 100 *balish*. Not only did Ögödei demonstrate his generosity but also secured a contract to supply the Mongols with more arrows.[28]

Juvaini also records other instances of generosity and business brilliance:

> When he seated himself upon the throne of kingship and the
> fame of his kindness and generosity was spread throughout
> the world, merchants began to come to his Court from every

side, and whatever goods they had brought, whether good or bad, he would command them to be brought at the full price. And it usually happened that without casting a glance at their wares or inquiring the price he would give them all away.[29]

Naturally his advisors attempted to thwart his excessive spending but to no avail.[30] Even when they paid a fair or more than fair amount, if it was less than what Ögödei thought was appropriate, he increased it.

While Ögödei's actions may seem foolish and contradictory (very unlike Chinggis Khan), there was some brilliance to them. Ögödei knew he could not live forever. After all, if his father failed in that endeavour, then how could he succeed? Yet by excessive spending he brought international commerce to Karakorum. What merchant would not risk travelling there when they knew that, regardless of what they brought, they would be paid twice its value after determining the cost of transportation? Ögödei's brilliance was not only in creating the infrastructure for trade within the empire but also in making Karakorum the focal point of that trade.[31] Merchants continued to flock to the city long after his death, even when more pragmatic figures sat on the throne and the rewards stabilized to more reasonable amounts.

ORTAGHS, INTERREGNUM AND RESTORATION

Ögödei's plans became a reality but with some unintended consequences. As the empire grew so did the merchants' influence in the court, particularly Muslim merchants who dominated much of the overland trade. Some came to Mongolia seeking capital for investment, others just to sell. Merchants often formed partnerships known as *ortaghs* with Mongol aristocrats, enabling them to enjoy official patronage and have a steady investor, which allowed both parties to profit. Many of the *khatuns* or Mongol queens routinely invested their private wealth into commercial ventures. In addition the Mongol khans permitted the merchants to use the postal routes and stations as long as they did not impede military and government traffic in the time of Ögödei. His successor Güyük (r. 1246–8) continued Ögödei's policies and routinely purchased items at 10 per cent or more over the price.[32] Oghul-Qaimish (r. 1248–51), Güyük's wife and regent, also favoured merchants and even princes who became merchants. Merchants now flocked to the Mongol capital though this eventually led to corruption that wreaked havoc on the bureaucracy.

The *gerege* or *paiza* was the passport or
document used by travellers and messengers
on the Mongol *yam* or postal route. The
material and shape of the *gerege* indicated
the privileges of each traveller – the better
the material, the more rights they had. This
one is made of gold.

The antecedents for this corruption lay in the regency of Töregene,
Ögödei's wife and regent (r. 1242–6). The regency of Oghul-Qaimish
exacerbated it as many merchants moved into the bureaucracy through
purchasing office and the regent's encouragement of tax-farming. While
the Mongolian queens had long been investors in the *ortaghs*, the
number of *ortaghs* increased tremendously in the 1240s with a resulting
increase in *yam* traffic as the *ortaghs* were also issued *paizas* or *gerege*,
the passes or passports that allowed one to use the services of the *yam*.
Corruption became rampant with the proliferation of *gereges*, creating
an economic disaster for the families that provided support for the *yam*
stations. Instead of simply being able to stop and rest at the *yam* posts,
the merchants could use them at the same level as imperial emissaries
and princes – commandeering provisions and animals and expecting
the support families to feed and shelter the entire entourage.

As a result many of the nomads near the *yam* stations became impoverished and/or moved away. The same occurred where the *yam* route passed through sedentary areas. Peasant villages and fields were abandoned to avoid the onerous demands of the *ortaghs*. Much of the crisis was due to Oghul-Qaimish's inattention to the affairs of governance. Although she followed the practices of Töregene by heavily investing in commerce and the sale of offices, she did not control the distribution of the *gerege*. The lack of regulation and general neglect of affairs of state led the Chinggisid princes to also invest heavily in the *ortaghs*. Some went so far as to become *ortaghs* in order to increase their wealth.[33] Thus now senior and junior princes (*aqa* and *ini*) also handed out the all-important *gerege*. The lack of regulation over the *yam* passports ultimately led to a breakdown in the communication system that bound together an empire that stretched from the Sea of Japan to the Carpathian Mountains. In addition, due to the inadvertent decentralization of the government, the princes sent out their own *elchis* or messengers/envoys to issue and carry out decrees.

The fourth Mongol khan, Möngke (r. 1251–9) ultimately restored order and curtailed the corrupt mercantile practices. It is notable, however, that he did not attempt to destroy the *ortaghs*, or merchant–Mongol prince partnerships, but simply rein them in from damaging the interests and institutions of the state. One of his first steps was to recall all of the *paizas*. He forbade the other princes to issue *yarlighs* or decrees and rescinded all *paizas* from the time of Chinggis Khan, Ögödei and Güyük. Furthermore he banned the princes from engaging in any matter concerning the 'financial administration of the provinces without first consulting the agents of the Court'.[34] Möngke effectively limited the *aqa* and *ini* from damaging the state through commercial interests. By recalling the *paizas* issued by his predecessors and ruling that only the imperial government could issue them he returned the use and regulation of the *yam* to imperial control. According to the Persian chronicler and administrator Juvaini,

> the order was given that *paizas* should not be given to merchants so that a distinction might be made between them and those engaged in affairs of the Divan [government]. That merchants should make use of *ulaghs* was inequitable in the extreme, and for that reason the people were not to be inconvenienced in this way.[35]

Thus the merchants lost the imperial passports that allowed them to use the *ulaghs* as well as the right to demand services from the *yam chin* or the supporting population. Furthermore, he removed the tax-exempt status the merchants had gained, enrolled them in the census and made them pay taxes as their status dictated with other subjects of the empire.[36] In this manner Möngke ended the massive deregulation of commerce that occurred during the interregnum period and consequently the harm it did to the empire.

Having taken care of the provincial corruption, Möngke then addressed corruption due to the *ortagh* system at central government level. He ordered the *elchis* to stay on the routes and not enter villages and towns where they had no business. Furthermore he curtailed the amount of provisions anyone could take, thus alleviating the burden of the herders and peasants who supported the *yam* stations. The *ortagh* were given similar restrictions on their demands while using the *yam* system. While they no longer carried the *paiza*, merchants still travelled the routes as these were still the best commercial routes due to the *ulaghs* and protection provided by the Mongols. Nonetheless, the days of lavish feasts and commandeering of animals for caravans were over. If they stopped at a station or village they had to pay for new animals or any provisions and lodging. At the same time Möngke respected the contracts made by the *ortaghs* with the government and paid any debt owed to them. Thus while the *ortaghs* had enjoyed a brief period of unrestrained influence and prosperity at the expense of the subjects of the empire, Möngke's regulation of the trade routes and check of the avarice of the Chinggisid princes at the expense of the empire returned an overall prosperity. His financial reforms brought a higher degree of centralization to the sprawling empire and allowed it to continue to grow through his conquests. Although his reforms prevented the misuse of imperial resources, they did not hamper trade. They may have even improved it by reducing the power of the *ortagh* and levelling the playing field for other merchants.

POST-DISSOLUTION

With the death of Möngke the Mongol world gradually split into four separate realms. Although they hypothetically remained united through the recognition of the khan who ruled the greater portion of East Asia, including Mongolia, in reality the states inexorably spiralled apart. Nonetheless they remained connected as independent states in new ways. The principal method was through war as the new khanates engaged in lengthy civil wars with at least one of their neighbouring khanates at any given time. The second was through trade. Indeed, despite frequent warfare the Pax Mongolica largely remained, as the various factions of the Altan Urugh or Golden Family still collected revenue from various parts of the empire. Thus, even as the Chaghatayid Khanate might fight the Yuan Khanate in East Asia, rents and income owed to the Chaghatayid Chinggisids were still paid, just as the Chaghatayids sent payments to the Mongol court in China. As evinced by the travels of the Venetian Polo family, trade across Eurasia remained possible even during times of war. Tying the loose ends of the empire together was the *yam*. The postal stations still functioned and merchants used the routes knowing these still tended to be the quickest and most efficient. However, war between the khanates could alter the routes, as experienced by the Polo family.

In the early 1260s Nicolo and Maffeo, father and uncle respectively of Marco Polo, travelled from the Black Sea to the court of Khubilai Khan. This journey, however, occurred only because their way back to Venice was blocked by war between Berke, the ruler of the Jochid Ulus, and Hülegü, the ruler of the Ilkhanid realm in the Middle East. As war waged back and forth on both sides of the Caucasus Mountains, it made the route from Bulgar, a city on the upper Volga river, to Sarai, on the lower Volga, where the Polos went to trade with Berke, so precarious that they chose to venture east rather than return west. Eventually they arrived in central Asia. While in Bukhara they

Khubilai Khan granting Niccolo and Maffeo Polo a golden *gerege* or *paiza* to facilitate their journey back home – and to return to his court, 14th century.

encountered an envoy from Hülegü on his way to Khubilai Khan's court, so the Polos joined his entourage and were safely escorted to the presence of Khubilai Khan.[37] Indeed war more than once caused a change in the Polos' travel plans. When the Polo family, including Marco, sought to return to Italy after seventeen years in the service of Khubilai Khan, wars in central Asia forced them to take the sea route. Again they travelled in the company of government officials, this time escorting a princess from Khubilai's court to the Ilkhanid court.

Although Marco Polo served as a government functionary in the Yuan Empire, and not as a governor as he claimed, his travels reveal much about trade in the Mongol Empire. Certainly his opinions reflect his own interests and interpretation of Mongol concerns and should not be taken to necessarily reflect the actual intent of Khubilai's foreign policy, or all aspects of Khubilai's goals. Still, when discussing areas that Khubilai attempted to conquer, Polo lists the commodities and wealth that each possessed. If nothing else, he was aware of the commercial and economic benefits that conquest had. Furthermore, some of the attempts to conquer were commercially driven. Khubilai's first attempt to conquer Japan, or at least the city of Hakata, in 1274 was to deprive the Song Dynasty of trade connections there and the revenue they reaped from the Japanese trade. Considering that the funds derived from the Song-Hakata trade aided Song resistance to Mongol conquests it was a wise move on Khubilai's part to eliminate it.[38]

Trade also partially motivated expansion into Southeast Asia as well as Java. Part of this was to restore tribute that had been previously paid to the Song Dynasty and that now Khubilai hoped to claim. This tribute cannot simply be viewed as 'protection money' or as recognition of a patron–client status. For centuries tribute missions consisted not only of formal diplomatic relations but also negotiations on trade and, of course, actual trade between merchants during the diplomatic missions. Often the tribute relations were simply a façade of diplomacy with the real emphasis placed on formalizing trade relations.

Polo indicates that avarice consumed Khubilai Khan when he heard of the wealth of Champa, or central Vietnam. After conquering it in 1281, although Mongol control was fleeting, the Mongol reaped tribute in elephants and rare woods.[39] Furthermore, the Song had previously traded extensively with Champa as well as with Java. By forcing the recognition of Mongol rule and power, Khubilai attempted to restore, albeit forcibly, those trade relations. Again, Polo's description of trade goods ranging from rare woods like ebony to drugs and spices indicate that he had a focus on the trade opportunities and, considering the long-standing Mongol emphasis on protecting and encouraging trade, it is likely that the Mongols also viewed their invasions as opportunities to secure resources or perhaps as gunboat diplomacy to open trade. In any case while fears of invasion may have lingered they did not stop commerce.[40] In 1976 an early fourteenth-century ship bound for Japan and financed by the Ashikaga *bakufu* (Shogunate) and a Tofukuji Zen temple in Kyoto was found near Korea. Its cargo of 20,000 pieces of porcelain and 28 tons of copper coins indicate that trade between the empire and Japan was not small-scale.

While Khubilai's overseas expeditions of conquest failed, ships from the Mongol Empire traversed the sea lanes between China and India. The great traveller Ibn Battuta hoped to depart from India to China on these ships whereas Polo travelled from China to India on them. While trade was the official action, diplomacy accompanied them as evinced by the fifteen diplomats sent by Toghon Temür (r. 1333–68), the ruler of the Great Khanate who Ibn Battuta encountered. Of course the gifts exchanged in these diplomatic ventures included not only fine luxury goods from their respective kingdoms, but also human ware – slaves, dancers, singers and so on. Chinese junks transported Indian goods back to the Mongol Empire as well as various stops in between, including pepper from Malabar – the Western extent of direct trade from the Great Khanate with India.[41]

The Chinese junks returned to the great trading cities of southern China like Canton. While the trade was carried on Chinese ships most of the merchants were not Han Chinese, but rather Muslims and Jews, including not only Chinese converts but also Arabs, Persians and central Asians who moved to coastal China. As a result when Ibn Battuta arrived in China he found not only Muslims, but also a Muslim quarter complete with mosques, madrasas and qadis. These establishments were part of the *ortagh* system discussed earlier. After the defeat of the Yuan Dynasty in 1368 the *ortagh* system in China more or less collapsed and the Muslim settlements shrank in size and influence, partially due to Ming xenophobia, as well as the end of Mongol preference for non-Han personnel.

Although the Mongol Empire split into four major states, in the fourteenth century it still played an important role in intercontinental trade despite warfare between the khanates. This can clearly be seen through the travels of Ibn Battuta. In the course of these travels the

Moroccan scholar ventured through all four khanates and gave descriptions of what he encountered. Although some are not very detailed, sufficient data may be teased out to offer a glimpse of commerce during the fourteenth century.

While we know much less about the Jochid Khanate, we do know that it sat at the nexus of a number of trade routes. In addition to routes connecting it to central Asia and the Middle East, northerly routes connected it to the Baltic trade as well as the Siberian and Arctic fur trade. The wealth of commerce that transited through the Golden Horde cannot be figured precisely, but if Ibn Battuta's count of 200 ships in the harbour of the Crimean port of Kaffa (then a Genoese colony) is accurate, it was an immense sum.[42] In addition to the usual luxury goods of silks and spices, Italian merchants also carried amber, furs, timber, grain and slaves from various parts of the Jochid Ulus. From the Black Sea they carried the goods to the Middle East, the ports of North Africa and Italy.

The Pontic ports were not the only cities that emerged as major trade centres. New Saray, the capital of Üzbek Khan, built by him around 1330, was a thriving centre of trade until the central Asia conqueror Timur-i Leng destroyed it, partly in order to re-route trade routes to his capital of Samarqand. It was the meeting point of merchants travelling the Volga River who brought in grain, furs, timbers and slaves and the caravaneers who carried silks, spices and other luxuries from east to west. In addition, artisans also produced leather, metal, woollen and silken goods. Horses from the Jochid Khanate departed from New Saray and Urgench to be sold in India.[43]

The north–south trade to the Baltic should also not be discounted. The Rus' princes bought items from throughout the world, as evinced in the archaeology,[44] paying not only in silver but also in amber. Jochid trade then extended beyond their empire. Through Novgorod, merchants from around the Baltic, particularly the Hanseatic League, did business with other merchants in the Jochid Khanate. Actions in the Mongol Empire could have a tremendous impact on areas as distant as England. For instance, when the Mongols invaded Europe the London fish markets collapsed as Baltic merchants did not come to buy fish. Instead they remained at their ports, ready to evacuate a terrified citizenry in case the Mongols appeared on the horizon.[45]

The destruction of Baghdad rendered it a provincial city of little importance; however the establishment of the Ilkhanid court at Tabriz transformed that city into a major transit point along the Silk Road. In addition it took business away from Baghdad, making recovery even more difficult. Tabriz meanwhile linked routes from the Middle East, Mediterranean, central Asia and Indian Ocean. Indeed Ibn Battuta remarked that the bazaar of Tabriz was one of the finest in the world in terms of selection and variety of goods.[46] In addition to Muslim merchants who resided in the capital, Genoese, Venetians and other Europeans operated in the city, marking the first true European trading colonies in the interior of Asia. Prior to this Italian trading centres had been restricted to the Mediterranean and Black Sea coasts. These merchants were not always dealing with middlemen either. In 1320 the Ilkhan Abu Said signed a commercial treaty with Venice.

The wealth the Mongols brought to the city via commerce and the simple fact that it was the capital transformed it into a metropolis of at least 200,000 people. Throughout its existence the city expanded. Under Ghazan Khan it saw new planned suburbs added, including mosques, madrasas, Ghazan's mausoleum and numerous homes for officials. It truly became the focal point of the Ilkhanid's activities, so much so that it even survived Öljeitü's efforts to move the capital to Sultaniyya.

Areas outside the Mongol Empire also benefited in trade, although undoubtedly some would have preferred not to have the Mongols influence trade in the way they did, as artisans, merchants and others fled from them. Although Cairo benefited from being the political capital of the Mamluk Empire, it also benefited from serving as a nexus point for trade between the Mediterranean and Red seas. Its role as a trade centre was cemented with the decline of Damascus after Ghazan Khan sacked it during the Ilkhan's invasion of Syria in 1299–1300. Numerous artisans, merchants and others took refuge in Cairo. The talent, skill and wealth they brought helped transform Cairo into 'the most cosmopolitan center of civilized culture anywhere in the Dar al-Islam'.[47]

Damascus recovered quickly with the cessation of hostilities between the Ilkhanid and Mamluk states. It resumed its role as a hub between Anatolia and the Black Sea region to the Arabian oases and from the Levant to Persia and even India. Damascus, throughout the Mamluk period, also prospered due to the Mamluk–Ilkhanid war prior to Ghazan's attack, as it served as the Mamluks' Syrian capital. Although it historically had been the centre of Syrian activity, with almost 50 years of war and tension between the two Middle Eastern powers it had become a resplendent city and second only to Cairo in importance for trade and government; in terms of education it may have outstripped Cairo. Peace between the Mamluks and Ilkhanate also led to the return of Chinese goods to the Middle East. Although the trade never truly stopped, due to the sea routes through the Red Sea, the lack of caravan trade did limit availability, but the return of the Pax Mongolica allowed it to resume with security making goods relatively affordable.

While Chinese goods were always desirable, Chinese influence also affected the economy of other parts of the Mongol world. During the reign of Gaykhatu Khan the Ilkhanate switched to paper money. While today we accept scraps of decorated paper as money, the medieval Persian world was not ready for such a radical idea. Merchants in the bazaars rejected it completely and the economy shut down despite the efforts of the government to force the adoption of the paper script. This concept of using a currency other than gold or silver, but backed by it, was limited to the Mongol Empire. During the reign of Muhammad Tughluq, Sultan of Delhi, due to the dearth of silver in India copper coins were issued as currency, their value being backed by gold – a clear imitation of paper money. Yet while the Mongols may be credited with expanding the use (at least temporarily) of paper money and the concept of state-backed currency outside China, they must also be recognized for expanding its use throughout China.

This currency experiment was not the only monetary change the Mongol Middle East underwent. The Mongols did return to the dinar and dirhem system, but it was not the same as the pre-Gaykhatu system. The traditional monetary system in the Islamic world consisted of gold dinars and silver dirhems based on the Byzantine and Sasanian systems respectively.[48] The ratio of dirhems comprising a dinar varied in time and region. During Ghazan's reign in the Ilkhanate the gold dinar was replaced by a silver dinar, which consisted of six silver dirhems.[49] It is possible that the emphasis on a silver currency was connected with the easy availability of silver from the Anatolian mines.[50] Although the Ilkhanate and the Yuan Khanate no longer shared similar paper currency, Ghazan's monetary reforms were still congruent with that of the Yuan as 10,000 silver dinars (known as a *tûmân*, a word introduced into Persian from the Mongolian *tümen* or 10,000) matched a Chinese *tael*. As Bert G. Fragner notes, this switch back to the dinar not only changed the monetary system but also served as a demonstration of the Ilkhanate's authenticity as an Islamic state by using Islamic currency models.[51] Remarkably, the system also proved quite durable as vestiges of the Ilkhanid system appear in modern Iran. Although currency consists of 1,000 dinars to the rial, ten rials (10,000 dinars) is still called a *tûmân*.[52]

As with the currency of Iran, the Mongol emphasis on trade cannot be overlooked in terms of contributions to world history. Not only did the Mongols encourage and promote trade, they also fostered, even if indirectly, a thirst for new products and goods. While silk, spices and porcelain had been imported to Europe for ages, the existence of the Mongol Empire changed trade considerably. Goods were much cheaper and more abundant due to the security the Mongols provided. Even after the dissolution of the Mongol Empire it was easier to travel and pay taxes and tariffs to four governments rather than the dozen or so that existed prior to the Mongols. Indeed, the Mongols built numerous caravanserais, the modern equivalent of truck stops, across Eurasia where merchants and other travellers could rest. Granted, many of these existed prior to the arrival of the Mongols, but they increased them and often established them at regular intervals. Furthermore, the Mongols also established patrols that maintained security throughout most of the so-called Silk Road. Then with the collapse of the Mongols and the rise of other states often hostile to European interests, such as the Ottomans who were often at war with Venice, or hostile to other states, such as the Safavids to the Ottomans, the trade routes collapsed or at least withered. Security was compromised and prices increased, eventually leading a number of intrepid Europeans to seek new travel routes. One such was the Genoese sailor Christopher Columbus who travelled west to seek India and the land of the Great Khan. As we know Columbus eventually discovered or rather accidentally bumped into another continent. The fact that he sought the land of the Great Khan also indicates that knowledge of the east was weak to say the least, considering that the Mongol Yuan Dynasty collapsed in 1368, almost 130 years prior to Columbus's voyage. Furthermore, Polo still served as Columbus's primary source of information on Asia and Columbus carried a copy on his third voyage in 1498, perhaps hoping to figure out why he still had not found the Great Khan. The fact that Polo's thirteenth-century guidebook still served as the equivalent of a Fodor's guide is quite remarkable.

5

NEW FORMS OF WARFARE

The rise of Chinggis Khan revolutionized steppe warfare through the introduction of strict discipline, new tactics, the creation of a military academy and the adoption of a decimal organization.[1] He refined centuries-old traditional steppe tactics, allowing the Mongols to operate on wide-ranging fronts with consistent success at the tactical, strategic and operational levels. An unexpected result was that his military revolution impacted the development of warfare for centuries.

The Mongol art of war was based on a simple component: the horse-archer. This warrior was primarily armed with a double recurve composite bow that possessed incredible penetrating power and range. Its range was well over 300 m (984 ft), but usually it was used in battle at shorter ranges, typically under 150 m (492 ft). Arrows shot from the bow seemingly had no trouble penetrating chain mail and other armour.[2] In conjunction with a string of three to five horses, the well-disciplined Mongol soldiers easily outmanoeuvred their opponents while unleashing a hail of death. For the most part the Mongols were lightly armoured, although their lamellar armour made from overlapping plates of leather or metal gave better protection against arrows than chain mail. Although the horse-warrior had been present since the ancient period, the Mongols were the most proficient at combining the mobility of horses with firepower.

Fighting primarily as light horse-archers, the Mongols perfected the timeless tactics of the steppe such as encirclements and feigned retreats. Their tactics maximized their archery skills and mobility, allowing them to stay out of range of their opponents' weapons. As with other steppe-based armies, the Mongols initiated combat at bowshot range, gradually drawing closer and typically only directly engaging the enemy at close quarters at a decisive moment when the enemy's formation broke or weakened. Their tactics ensured that they did not require superior numbers but relied on mobility, firepower and subterfuge to gain victory.

A common tactic was the arrow storm or shower in which they enveloped their enemy then shot a hail of arrows with the intent of disrupting enemy formations. The target of the arrow storm was not an individual, but rather they loosed their arrows at a high trajectory into a predetermined 'killing zone' or area target, emphasizing concentrated firepower. While the practice of concentrating firepower existed prior to the Mongols, they used it to its maximum effect in all aspects of war, including siege warfare.

The Mongols also combined the arrow storm with hit-and-run tactics known as the *shi'uchi* or chisel attack, similar to the *caracole* tactic of fifteenth- and sixteenth-century European warfare. The Mongol units sent waves of men against enemy formations. As each wave charged, they shot several arrows and retreated before making contact with the enemy, circling back to the Mongol lines before making contact. They released their final shot roughly 40 to 50 m (130 to 165 ft) from the enemy lines before wheeling around. This was close enough to pierce armour but distant enough from the enemy to evade a counter-charge. They changed horses to keep their mounts fresh. This was often used in combination with other manoeuvres.

The practice of double-envelopment of the enemy, a traditional method employed in the steppe, stemmed from the Mongols' training in the *nerge* or battue style of hunting. The warriors formed a circle around and constricted their prey, driving them towards the centre and forming a dense mass from which it was difficult to escape. The Mongols did not always require large numbers of troops to achieve this. Their archery skills and mobility allowed them to encircle an enemy force even when they were outnumbered. Whenever possible, the Mongols preferred to surround their enemies by using the *nerge*. Once Mongol scouts made contact with the enemy, the main Mongol force extended its lines over as great a distance as possible so as to overlap the flanks of the hostile force. At times this extended for miles until they encircled the enemy. Gradually the circle contracted, herding everything towards the centre. As skirmishes occurred, scouts constantly relayed intelligence to the Mongol commanders.

They also used the *nerge* as part of their invasion strategy, as demonstrated against the Rus' principalities. After the capture of the city of Vladimir in 1237 they sent their *tümens* out in *nerge* fashion, reducing every town and fortress they encountered and gradually constricting their circle, which extended for hundreds of miles. At times they intentionally left gaps in their *nerge*, apparently allowing the enemy a means of escape. In reality the gap served as a trap. In their panic to get away the enemy often discarded their weapons to flee faster and rarely maintained discipline. This was the tactic that destroyed the Hungarians at Mohi in 1241.

Initially a weak point for the Mongols, siege warfare quickly became a strong suit as they learned quickly and incorporated engineers into their armies. These were either conscripted or came to the Mongols voluntarily, although Mongolian engineers existed. Nonetheless, for the entire existence of the Mongol Empire, the Mongols were largely dependent on Muslim and Chinese engineers who manned and manufactured artillery and other siege equipment. On occasion, such as in the Russian campaign and in Europe, catapults appeared in field battles as well as at sieges.

Psychological warfare was always a strength for the Mongols and they employed it frequently. After realizing it was more efficient to convince a city or fortress to surrender without resistance rather than be drawn into a siege, the Mongols gained a reputation for massacres if a city resisted. The use of massacre must be seen not as wanton blood lust but as a calculated tactic that served several purposes. It discouraged revolts behind Mongol lines and also as helped spread propaganda and misinformation about the size of their armies. They used rumours of their ferocity to maximal effect through spies and survivors, causing other populations to become intimidated and choose to surrender rather than risk the alternative.

To confuse and intimidate their enemies the Mongols also used subterfuge. They lit numerous campfires and tied branches to the tails of their horses to stir up dust in order to mask their numbers. The Mongols also mounted dummies on their spare horses and rode in single file to disguise their numbers at a distance. On other occasions they herded oxen and horses into enemy lines to disrupt them. In the resulting confusion the Mongols attacked. Whenever they could the Mongols weakened their opponents by promoting rebellion or discord among rivals and by courting the support of oppressed minorities (or majorities). While the Mongols made good use of their reputation for extreme brutality, they took pains to portray themselves as liberators when circumstances warranted.

Their tactics made them an efficient and deadly army, while actions at the strategic and operational level left them without peer until the modern era. They engaged in strategies of high mobility. While the Mongolian horses were surpassed in terms of strength and speed by sedentary armies, they were without equal in endurance. Furthermore, the Mongols had access to virtually limitless numbers of horses. As the average Mongol trooper possessed three to five mounts he could remain mobile even if a single mount was lost or tired. Their mobility permitted the Mongols to embark on a style of warfare that was not copied again until the twentieth century with the use of motorized vehicles.

Before an invasion the Mongols made extensive preparations in a *quriltai* where they planned the upcoming war and appointed generals to lead the invasion. Prior to the decision, they accumulated intelligence by using merchants who benefited from the Mongols's protection of the trade routes. During the *quriltai*, mobilization of the army began and they established rendezvous points along with a time schedule. Although the planning of the campaign was a major component the Mongol generals maintained a high degree of independence, enabling them to complete their objectives on their terms while abiding by the timetable. This allowed the Mongols to coordinate their movements and concentrate their forces at prearranged sites.

The invasion began by attacking in several columns and in a set pattern. First, a screen of scouts covered the invading forces and constantly relayed information back to their main column. Through adherence to their pre-planned schedule and use of scouts, the Mongols marched divided but could come quickly to each other's aid and thus fight united. Furthermore, because their forces marched in smaller concentrations, columns stretching for miles did not impede them. They used their mobility to spread terror, to the effect that rarely were their opponents ever really prepared to concentrate their forces when the enemy appeared on many fronts at the same time.

The use of a multi-pronged invasion also fitted into their favoured method of engaging the enemy. They preferred to deal with all field armies before moving deep into enemy territory. Reaching this goal was rarely difficult, as the enemy usually sought to meet the Mongols before they destroyed an entire province. Furthermore, the use of columns screened by scouts enabled the gathering of intelligence allowing the Mongols to locate enemy armies more rapidly than a single army could.

By concentrating on the dispersion and movement of enemy field armies, the assault on strongholds was delayed. Of course, smaller fortresses or ones they could surprise easily were taken as they came along. Among the best examples of this was the Khwarazmian campaign. The

Mongols in pursuit of other enemies, miniature from Rashid al-Din's *Jami' al-Tawarikh*. Although this illustration represents a 13th-century battle, the warriors are dressed in 14th-century Ilkhanid clothing.

smaller cities and fortresses were taken before the Mongols eventually captured Samarqand. This had two results. First, it cut off the principal city from communicating with other cities. Second, refugees from these smaller cities fled to the last stronghold bringing reports from the defeated and destroyed cities, reducing the morale of the inhabitants and garrison forces of the principal city while also straining its resources. Food and water reserves were taxed by the sudden influx of refugees. The Mongols were then free to lay siege without the interference of a field army, as it had been destroyed. Finally, the capture of the outer strongholds and towns provided the Mongols more raw materials in the form of labour, to man the siege machines or to act as human shields for the Mongols.

The Mongols also always tried to destroy the enemy's command structure. This was carried out by harrying the enemy leaders until they dropped. Chinggis Khan first used this policy in the wars of unification in Mongolia. In his first few encounters he failed to do this and defeated enemies regrouped and began conflict anew. Afterwards, it became a standard operating procedure. Being constantly on the move, the enemy leader was unable to serve as a rallying point for his armies. In addition the enemy's armies had to keep moving to find him. In many reports, perhaps exaggerated, the enemy leaders were only a few steps ahead of the Mongols. The Mongols also acquired new intelligence on other lands as the fleeing enemy would run in the opposite direction from the Mongol armies. The Mongols always dispatched a special force to pursue them and other forces were also sent to the outlying regions. In some cases these regions were areas independent of the kingdom invaded by the Mongols, but this did not exclude them from Mongol attention.

For many, the Mongols were not another army – they were a force of nature, a punishment sent by god, the forerunners of the apocalypse. In the face of overwhelming death and destruction their enemies struggled to find ways of fending off the Mongols. Some succeeded, most did not. The Mongols transformed and influenced the means of waging war throughout the world for centuries.

Mongols pursuing enemies, illustration from the Saray album. All the characters are dressed as Mongols. While this depiction may simply show the artists' knowledge of armour and weaponry at the time, it is also a commentary on the influence and spread of Mongol military advancements and accoutrement through Eurasia.

IMPACT ON THE CRUSADES AND THE MIDDLE EAST

In the period of the Crusades a great deal of cross-cultural exchange occurred, both consciously and unconsciously. The fact that it overlapped the period of the Mongols only intensified the exchange through the addition of another variable. As with all exchanges, rarely was it monodirectional. Islamic and Christian societies did not only receive ideas or impetus for change from the Mongols. Indeed, the Mongol Empire gained new military knowledge, among other things, from the Levant.

One such exchange was the counterweight trebuchet. For the Mongol Empire, the standard trebuchet had been man-powered and of simple design. Essentially it consisted of a basic upside-down U-frame with an arm attached. A stone or pot of flammable material was loaded on one end while men pulled ropes connected to the other. To improve range or use a heavier missile, more men were added. The counterweight trebuchet, however, was of a much more complex design and came in variations. The basic design included a box on one end (the counterweight) filled with rocks. When released it dropped and pulled the arm upwards which in turn pulled a long sling from underneath the trebuchet with its missile. At the apex of the arm's arc the sling opened, flinging its missile. With the counterweight and the velocity caused by the sling's arc, missiles flew with greater force, causing more damage and allowing use of heavier missiles.

Although in use in Europe and the Middle East since the late twelfth century, it did not arrive in East Asia until the 1270s, though it was probably used by Mongol forces in the Middle East prior to 1260. Marco Polo attempted to take credit for its arrival in China, but it is quite certain that Muslim engineers in Mongol employ brought the weapon as the city of Xiangyang fell in 1273, a few years prior to the arrival of the Polo family.[3] Its arrival most probably hastened Khubilai Khan's conquest of the Song Dynasty.

The Mongol impact on warfare during the Crusades also manifested in more apparent ways. The first was the Mongol invasions of the Middle East and Europe with Sübedei's *reconnaissance en force* occurring during the Fifth Crusade. Rumours of the army of the mysterious Prester John or rather his grandson King David, ruler of the east, reached the Crusader army, laying siege to Damietta. Furthermore, King David was only a few days' march from Antioch. This played a factor in some strategic decisions at Damietta and ultimately contributed to the failure of the Fifth Crusade (1217–21).[4] The Mongol appearance in the Middle East during this time impacted on the Fifth Crusade in another way. This Crusade, unlike some of its brethren, had an operational strategy. While the main crusading army struck Egypt, allies (Seljuk Turks and Georgians) were to attack northern Syria to prevent Ayyubid armies coming to the aid of Egypt. The Georgians were to play a major role in this; however, Sübedei's army devastated the Georgian army – perhaps playing on their emotions by using the King David identity. It is said that the Mongols approached bearing crosses. While it is plausible, it seems unlikely the Mongols knew the Prester John legends and the Georgians probably simply mistook one variety of Mongol *tuq* or standard as a form of crucifix.[5] In any case the Georgians were crushed and unable to participate in the Crusade. Indeed, the Mongol appearance began a downward spiral for the Georgians for roughly two decades after establishing itself as a powerful regional kingdom. Furthermore, because of Georgia's inability to attack northern Syria, Ayyubid forces could attack the Crusader states on the Levant, thus worrying King John Brienne of Jerusalem and his barons and driving a wedge between the European Crusaders and those from the Levant.

Although the Mongols then disappeared across the mountains, by no means were they finished with the Crusades. The primary objective of the Mongols' invasion of central Asia in 1219, which led to Sübedei's invasion of Georgia, was the destruction of the Khwarazmian Empire. In this endeavour they succeeded. Although Sultan Muhammad died on an island in the Caspian Sea, his son Jalal al-Din escaped to India only to return after the Mongols vacated the region. However, his appearance attracted their attention again and led to Chormaqan's invasion. The Mongols destroyed Jalal al-Din's army again in 1231 but Khwarazmian forces survived. They eventually became a potent regional mercenary force used by the Seljuks, Ayyubids and others in the vicinity. They were hired by Egypt to augment Sultan al-Salih's (r. 1240–9) forces in the internecine wars of the Ayyubids and to counter the Franks who joined the army of Damascus, Kerak and Homs. Their eagerness to join the Egyptians may also have had something to do with Mongol expansion in the region. Indeed, with the Mongol conquest of the Seljuk Sultanate and intimidation of the cities of the Jazira region, leaving the region probably seemed wise, particularly as their prospect for employment diminished. En route to Egypt they sacked Jerusalem, which had been returned to Christian hands in 1229 through the mediation of Frederick II, thus denying it to the Crusader states forever.[6] The Khwarazmians then joined Sultan al-Salih and defeated a combined army of the Kingdom of Jerusalem, Damascus and Kerak at the battle of La Forbie or al-Harbiyya in 1244. For the Crusaders it was a devastating defeat, second only to Hittin in 1189.

Although al-Salih conspired with the Prince of Homs to destroy the Khwarazmian mercenaries (which he did) as the Sultan viewed them as too much of a menace to everyone (which they were), the Mongols continued to affect the Middle East indirectly. Their conquest of the Kipchak Steppe flooded the slave markets of the Middle East with Kipchak Turks who were then purchased as mamluks, or military slaves. Although it was King Louis IX's Seventh Crusade that led to the mamluk coup in Egypt in 1250, it was the Mongol conquest of Syria in 1258 that transformed them into a major power as the Mamluk Sultanate.[7] Prior to this the Mamluks kept an Ayyubid prince (albeit a minor) on the throne to provide legitimacy for their rule, as they otherwise had no claim to the throne. With the arrival of the Mongols, however, the child was quickly removed and the Mamluks gave up all pretence. Their claim to the throne was then cemented with their victory at 'Ayn Jalut in 1260. Afterwards they were seen as the Protectors of the Faith – an image they promoted through the patronage of religious leaders and scholars as well as a building programme. Furthermore, recognizing the threat should the Crusaders ever ally with the Mongols, the Mamluks made a concerted effort to eliminate the Crusader states once and for all – a policy that had not been followed since the death of Salah al-Din in 1193. The Mamluk Sultanate proved a constant irritant to the Mongols of the Ilkhanate and the Mamluks succeeded in removing the Crusader states with the destruction of Acre in 1291. By razing coastal fortifications and using a scorched earth policy along the Mongol frontier, the Mamluks prevented any possible conquest from west or east. By taking advantage of the Ilkhanate's preoccupation with the Jochid and Chaghatayid khanates, the Mamluks were able to eliminate the Crusaders as well as clients of the Ilkhans, such as the Kingdom of Cilicia, one by one, destroying Mongol influence in the region. This forced the Mongols to attempt alliances with European powers, but they were often too engaged in European affairs to launch a new Crusade or, in the Papacy's case (as will be explained later) more concerned with the salvation of the Mongols' souls than military affairs.

Part of the problem undoubtedly rested with the Mongol invasion of Europe in 1240 during which the Catholic kingdoms of Hungary and

Poland were devastated. Mongol scouts were encountered as far west as Vienna and most correspondence with Mongol officials inevitably included ominous phrases about what would happen if European rulers did not submit. The Mongol invasion resulted with numerous calls for a Crusade. Nothing actually materialized, but would-be Crusaders, particularly those who lived in central and eastern Europe, were allowed to commute their vows to man the frontiers whenever a rumour circulated that the Mongols were approaching. Pope Innocent IV also sought to build an anti-Mongol coalition to protect Europe from further encroachment. More often than not, however, those who would have fought the Mongols ended up in the Baltic as part of the *reysens* or seasonal, almost package-tour, raids of the Teutonic Knights against the Prussians or, in the case of Lithuanians, fighting against the Teutonic Knights.[8] Nevertheless, the menacing presence of the Mongols to the east, particularly the Jochid Khanate which invaded eastern Europe on several occasions, kept fear alive in the breast of many Europeans. Although the Ilkhanate and Jochid Khanate were separate entities and the European crowned heads realized it, it is questionable as to how the average person viewed the Mongols – separate or were they all the same? Thus, if nothing else, the Mongol presence from 1240 onward contributed to the continued lack of manpower for the Latin states in the Levant. Although it is not possible to get a precise number of the men who went east or stayed at home out of fear of a Mongol attack (or at least used that excuse to secure an indulgence), it is evident that after the thirteenth century German and Hungarian participation in crusades to the Levant dwindled. Other factors, to be sure, played a role in this, but the lurking fear of a massive pagan and almost incomprehensibly fearsome army just beyond the frontier distracted many would-be Crusaders from journeying elsewhere.

The Mongols also altered warfare in the Middle East in the actual selection of weapons as well as execution of tactics. First and foremost was the spread of the curved sabre. This occurred elsewhere as well, but the sabre became the preferred cavalry weapon throughout the Middle East and indeed the world largely due to Mongol success. This trend starts in the thirteenth century and by the sixteenth century the sabre is ubiquitous.[9] Although the sabre first arrived from the east with the arrival of the Turks, other societies preferred to keep their straight-bladed swords. With the arrival of the Mongols and for centuries afterwards, however, the sabre became the almost exclusive weapon of the mounted warrior. The curved blade made it perfect for a mounted attack as it allowed the rider to slash and follow through as he rode by. A straight blade was less effective in a slashing attack and better suited for a downward hacking attack. In an attack in which the rider slashed and kept on riding, the straight sword was likely to become either embedded in the target or jar the attacker so he became unbalanced or lost the weapon.

The Mongols transitioned much of the Middle East into steppe warfare. Although horse-archers had played a vital role in Middle Eastern warfare since the Parthians defeated Crassus at Carrhae in 53 BC, the primary cavalry force was not horse-archers but lance-wielding riders who might be classified as medium cavalry. This transition occurred under the Sassanids and during the time of the Arab conquests, and continued under the Abbasid state. The arrival of the Seljuks altered the situation with the infusion of nomadic horse-archers. However, the core of the Seljuk army came from *iqta* and *timar*-based armoured cavalry.[10] The bow remained an important weapon but it was not always the primary weapon. This remained the case for most of the people of the Middle East and central Asia such as the Ghaznavid, Khwarazmians and Ayyubids. Only in areas of a large Turkic nomadic population, such as Anatolia, did the horse-archer become the dominate element on the battlefield, although contingents were found in all armies (including those of the Crusader states in the form of the Turcopoles).

The initial Mongol armies in the Middle East were light horse-archers. While some may have worn armour, the Mongol trend was for lamellar armour. Even the metal varieties of lamellar tended to be fairly lightweight and allowed for the mobility the Mongols preferred. The Mongols did use medium and heavy cavalry tactics at times, but these were provided by auxiliaries such as Armenians and Georgians. When the Mongols themselves charged, it tended to be for a killing blow after the enemy's ranks had been decimated by archery. Historians have speculated the Mongols transitioned to a more traditional medium cavalry in the face of their defeats by the Mamluks. Scholars have speculated that the light horse-archer could not compete against the Mamluks due to the latter's heavier armour which allowed them to engage in close combat and shock tactics, combined with their proficience in archery.[11] Indeed, the Mamluk soldier was designed to be able to engage heavy shock troops like the Knights Templar and Hospitaller as well as the horse-archers of the Mongols and thus had to

counter two styles of fighting. The scholars who espoused this transformation from light cavalry did so based on the idea of Ghazan Khan's
military reforms and repeated references to assigning *iqtas* and *timars*
to finance the soldiers. Reuven Amitai, however, has convincingly
demonstrated that this is not accurate.[12] As explained earlier, *timars*
were assigned primarily as a way to fund the army and prevent them
plundering the peasantry and townspeople of the Ilkhanate. At no time
do we see an actual transition. The successors to the Ilkhanate, such as
the Jalayirs, Kara Qoyunlu and Aq Qoyunlu, were horse-archer armies,
as were the armies of the Chaghatayids. Even the Ottomans had large
numbers of horse-archers until the Janissary infantry became the
mainstay of the army. The Safavids, who challenged the Ottomans,
used horse-archers to carve their empire. Only with the advent of effective field cannon, as at the battle of Chaldiran, did the nomadic horse-
archer cease to dominate the battlefield.

Yet did the Mongols not learn from their defeats by the Mamluks?
One must remember that while the Ilkhanate Mongols were enemies of
the Mamluks, their primary enemy was always another Mongol state –
the Jochid or Chaghatayid khanates who fielded nomadic armies. As
demonstrated in their conquests, non-horse-archer armies rarely defeated the Mongols. In the case of the Mamluks several factors played a role
in their success. Man for man, they were better warriors – their whole
life revolved around military training. This declined after the Mongol
threat receded but even during Napoleon's invasion in 1798–9 they
proved a challenge. Second, having rebuffed the Mongols on numerous
occasions the Mamluks knew their fate should the Mongols ever conquer them. As mentioned earlier, they sought to deprive the Mongols of
pasture and practised a scorched earth policy. And in the instances of a
number of sultans the Mamluks enjoyed superior leadership and, at
times, luck, which should never be discounted on the battlefield. Indeed
the fact that so many battles were close testifies to the fact that the
Mongols never viewed their style of warfare as inferior to that of the
Mamluks, nor did successor states, as the horse-archer remained the
dominant warrior east of the Euphrates.

DELHI AND INDIA

The Mongol presence in India transformed the Sultanate of Delhi as
well. While the antipathy between the Mongols and Delhi was not like
that of the Ilkhanate and the Mamluks, it still existed. The Mongols had

had a presence on the borders of Delhi since the 1220s, when Chinggis Khan conquered the Khwarazmian Empire, until the rise of Timur. Nonetheless, the Mongols never invaded the sultanate until 1241. Prior to this they had conquered Lahore and Multan but these cities recognized Khwarazmian authority. Chinggis Khan saw little reason to attack Delhi as it remained neutral in the war with Khwarazm.[13] After Jalal al-Din fled into India after his defeat by Chinggis Khan, the Mongol ruler requested permission to cross through the Sultanate of Delhi in pursuit of him. Although the Mongols sent an embassy to Delhi, we do not know what happened to it.[14] As the Mongols did not attack Delhi it is probably safe to assume the embassy returned to Chinggis Khan safely. Indeed, Peter Jackson postulates that Delhi may have made a token submission to Chinggis Khan and Ögödei.[15] Nonetheless, during the reign of Ögödei, the Mongol general Mönggetü did raid Sind in 1236-7, only to withdraw in the face of the arrival of Delhi's army.[16]

After the Mongols withdrew from the Indus Plain Delhi extended its borders to the mountains. Although the Mongols captured some cities and even raided across the Indus River a few times, they never truly conquered and held anything south of the Peshawar for a long period of time.[17] Nonetheless, the Mongol presence transformed the military of the Sultanate of Delhi. Although of Turkic origin, with an emphasis on cavalry, the Sultanate of Delhi had a large infantry, since much of India was not suitable for horse breeding. The threat of the Mongols and their mobility forced the sultanate to find a counter to them. In the view of Simon Digby:

> The survival of the Delhi Sultanate in the face of Mongol attacks depended upon an adequate supply of battle horses to mount the army when the export of horses from Mongol controlled central Asia was cut off and possibly to some degree upon war elephants, used in the line of battle and inspiring great awe, which the Mongols did not possess.[18]

The Mongol threat also limited the sultanate's military actions against neighbouring Hindu states. Some scholars believe that Delhi's domination of India was stalled in the shadow of the Mongol menace to the northwest, forcing the sultans to keep their armies close to Delhi and the frontier.[19] It is clear that due to the Mongol threat the military of the sultanate became formidable. Indeed, according to Juzjani, the sultanate even waged a *jihad* to drive the Mongols out of the region west of the Indus. On 6 Muharram 656 H. / 13 January 1258 , an army gathered outside Delhi to liberate Multan, which it successfully did.[20] The Mongol threat only subsided after 1329; during that year the Chaghatayid khan Tarmashirin threatened the environs of Delhi. Sultan Muhammad Tughluq (r. 1325–51) forced him back across the Indus. With the collapse of the Ilkhanate and the general chaos in the Chaghatayid Khanate after Tarmashirin's death, Delhi became relatively secure and only dealt with the occasional raiding band, not full-scale invasion. Unfortunately this lull seems to have given the Sultanate of Delhi a false sense of security because in 1399 the central Asian conqueror and Chinggisid-wannabe, Emir Timur or Timur-i Leng, sacked Delhi and carried incalculable wealth back to Samarqand. The sultanate never fully recovered and this eventually set the stage for the arrival of the Mughals (Persian for Mongols) led by Babur, a descendant of Timur and Chinggis Khan. Thus the Mongols, in a sense, would rule much of India until 1857 when the British officially ended the Mughal royal line after the Great Sepoy Rebellion.

EASTERN EUROPE

Eastern Europe, particularly what is now Russia and Ukraine, endured Mongol rule longer than any other region. Centuries of contact with other steppe powers prior to and after the collapse of Mongol hegemony over the region gave it a familiarity with steppe warfare. This influence continued well after the rise of Muscovy and the formation of a definitive Russian identity. Testament to the influence of the Mongol military system is found in the fact that the Slavic principalities of Eastern Europe had frequent contact with steppe nomads and used them as allies and auxiliaries but did not readily adopt the steppe warfare technique prior to the Mongol arrival. Indeed, the Kipchaks and other nomads often had to worry about Rus' encroachment into the steppe.[21] Not until the Mongol period did steppe warfare begin to change military thought in the region. Previously, there was no need to fight like the nomads; while the Kipchaks and Pechenegs were worthy adversaries, they could be countered. The Mongol style of warfare, however, was unlike anything the Rus' had encountered and one for which they had no answer. In short, not to adapt meant no chance of defeating the Mongols. Prince Danilo of Galicia and Volynia began refitting and reorganizing his military forces with the intent of rebelling against the Mongols – observing that if the Mongols defeated their old martial methods easily, in order to defeat the Mongols, one had to fight as them.[22] Indeed, in 1254–5 he campaigned with some success against the Mongols. What is notable is that he followed the Mongol example of campaigning in winter.[23]

Many, if not all, of the Rus' principalities under Mongol control emulated the Mongols. As the Rus' warriors were incorporated into the Mongol military, the transition was assisted by increased familiarization with Mongol warfare. Initially, however, the Rus' fought in their own formations and traditional style. Over time, however, the Rus' began to organize their armies along similar lines and used steppe nomad tactics and weapons[24] including not only adoption of the composite bow, but Mongol style sabres and lamellar armour for both men and mounts.[25] Indeed, there were occasions when Mongol forces, although just how many is a matter of conjecture, appeared to be fighting under the command of Rus' Prince Alexander (Nevskii) of Novgorod.[26] Muscovy was perhaps the most successful in this transformation. Indeed, Moscow also adopted aspects of Mongol administration. Under Prince Ivan III (the Great) (r. 1462–1505), Moscow instituted the *yam* postal system and applied it in much the same way as the Mongols. Its use continued well into the nineteenth century.

The advent of gunpowder weapons did not make an immediate change for Eastern Europe. Poland, Hungary and Muscovy still had primary threats in the form of the various offshoots of the Golden Horde and the Lithuanians who fought in a similar manner to the Mongols with masses of horse-archers. Even after Poland and Lithuania merged in a marriage alliance it did not fundamentally alter their method of fighting. The Polish-Lithuanian cavalry remained a scourge of the battlefield. Among the Russians the nobility fought as horse-archers, rather than shock cavalry as their pre-Mongol ancestors did. In order to counter the Crimean Tatars and other steppe powers, Ivan IV needed cavalry. Although he created the *streltsy* or musketeers in the sixteenth century, their primary role was to defend the string of forts on the southern frontier against nomadic incursions, not to engage them in open warfare. The *streltsy*'s battlefield success was noted more in engagements in siege warfare and in the Baltics. To augment his own cavalry drawn from the nobility Ivan turned to other sources. The growing importance of the Cossacks as well as the use of Tatar light cavalry by Muscovy emphasized the need for troops experienced in steppe warfare. It was not until the time of Peter the Great that Russia's military focus began to shift from the steppe to

Europe as its primary concern, in part because the steppe became less of a threat.

Although the political and military focus shifted to the west in the seventeenth century, Mongols still played a role in the Russian military. Kalmyks or western Mongols who migrated to the Volga River in the early 1600s played a key role in the defence of Russia's southern frontier. With the decline of the Ottoman threat to the south and the defeat of the Crimean Tatars in 1789, it appeared the horse-archers of the steppe had finally lost value as a military unit; however, the Russian conquest of central Asia during the nineteenth century renewed interest. Mikhail Ivanin (1801–74), a Russian military officer who gained an appreciation of steppe warfare when he served against the Khanate of Khiva, saw some benefit in steppe tactics even if it was no longer a dominant form of fighting. In 1846 he published *The Art of War of the Mongols and the Central Asian Peoples.*[27] He placed an emphasis on mobility and the use of cavalry tactics by the Cossacks. The imperial military academies soon incorporated it into their curriculum and it remained in use not only in the Russian Empire but in the military academies of the Red Army until the Second World War, as will be discussed later in this chapter. Ivanin's efforts, combined with other reforms, proved quite effective and only diminished as Russia's failure to industrialize undermined its logistics, as demonstrated in the Russo–Japanese War, 1904–5.

EAST ASIA AND GUNPOWDER

As noted earlier, warfare in East Asia noticeably changed with the arrival of the counterweight trebuchet. Yet this was not the only change. The Mongol invasion of Japan caused a substantial change in the method in which samurai engaged in warfare. Prior to the Mongol invasions the samurai primarily engaged a single enemy in combat to test their martial prowess. The Mongols, however, did not engage in single combat. Rather they operated in large units and used concentrated firepower to eliminate enemy formations. Rather than a single opponent, a samurai faced a unit. Even the best of swordsmen would ultimately be defeated by sheer weight of numbers. It was only after the samurai switched to unit tactics that they levelled the playing field.

The most significant change, however, was the advent of gunpowder weapons. It is well established that gunpowder was discovered in China and indeed the Mongols first encountered it during their invasions of the Jin Empire. Gunpowder weapons had been in use since at least 1044 when a compendium of military knowledge, *The Complete Essentials from the Military Classics (Wujing Zongyao)*, was published. It is likely that gunpowder weapons (a variety of bombs) were in use to some degree as early as the tenth century as gunpowder itself was invented in the ninth century.[28] Its manufacture remained a closely guarded secret during the Song Dynasty and it does not appear to have been used in their eleventh-century wars, but by the twelfth century gunpowder weapons such as firelances (originally a primitive bamboo tube flame-thrower, later attached to a spear) became ubiquitous in the Song arsenal.[29] Rockets were added to the mix in the twelfth century although their inaccuracy limited their effectiveness. While all were daunting weapons whether using incendiary or explosive gunpowder, the Mongols found ways of countering and using it to their advantage.

Although the spread of gunpowder is directly related to the rise of the Mongols and the Pax Mongolica, it is unclear whether the Mongols themselves contributed to the spread. Some historians have claimed the Mongols used gunpowder weapons, essentially bombs hurled by catapults, in the Middle East and perhaps Eastern Europe; unfortunately there is no definite documentary or archaeological evidence to confirm it. Considering the Mongols rarely met a weapon they did not like, we can be certain that if they found a way to transport it safely it would have been incorporated into their arsenal outside China. Nonetheless, it remains speculation. Weatherford mentions the Mongols' use of gunpowder as a matter of fact, but provides no evidence to support the ubiquitous use he claims. Iqtidar Khan is confident that the Mongols used gunpowder on their western campaigns and cites several passages in the Persian sources, which could be translated as gunpowder weapons, however, as he admits, these terms can also be translated as more conventional weapons, including naptha. Khan also proposes that the Mongols are responsible for the spread of gunpowder into India as the Sultanate of Delhi adopted its use by 1290. This is plausible as there is evidence that gunpowder, at least in the form of fireworks, was in use in central Asia in the later part of the thirteenth century.[30]

Much of the speculation arises from the fact that one thousand Chinese engineers accompanied Hülegü to the Middle East in the 1250s. This is simply not sufficient to prove that the Mongols used gunpowder missiles in their conquests of Alamut or Baghdad. Several serious issues prevent us from accepting that the Mongols used it. None of the sources mention the use of gunpowder weapons at the sieges.

Nor do witnesses mention gunpowder or describe it. Juvaini, who was present at the siege of Alamut, does not mention any reference to gunpowder or explosions. As a member of Hülegü's administrative staff and later governor of Baghdad, he was in a position to know these things. One passage excites the imagination:

> From the towers bows sent up swift-feathered shafts, and a *kaman-i-gav*, which had been constructed by Khitayan crafts-men and had a range of 2,500 paces, was brought to bear on those fools, when no other remedy remained; and of the devil-like Heretics many soldiers were burnt by those meteoric shafts. From the castle also stones poured down like leaves, but no more than one person was hurt thereby.[31]

Two things come to mind here. First that we have the Chinese (Khitayan) craftsmen building the so-called ox-bow (*kaman-i-gav*). Then there are the 'soldiers burnt by those meteoric shafts'. At face value it could mean gunpowder weapons, particularly incendiary ones. When taken in context with the rest of Juvaini, it means little more than that the Mongols had a very powerful ballista. Juvaini's book is resplendent with flowery phrases. It is a masterpiece of imagery and allusions. Could their opponents be burnt? Quite certainly, but good, old-fashioned naptha also did the trick and had done so for centuries. Simply because Chinese siege crews were present does not mean that they used gunpowder weapons.

Arguing that the chroniclers of the Mongol Empire omit reference to it, as gunpowder might be a state secret, fails as neither Juvaini nor Rashid al-Din appear to be shy about gossip or discussing military matters. Rashid al-Din, who also had a scientific bent, should have shown a keen interest. As another highly placed person in the Ilkhanid administration, he was also in a position to know about secret weapons or, as one might expect after an explosion, not-so-secret weapons. Certainly, if it had been in use, by 1300 it was no longer a secret weapon and thus could have been described in a book written for the Mongol court. The more damning evidence is the omission of gunpowder weapons in sources hostile to the Mongols on these campaigns. They simply do not mention it. This is most surprising for if the Mongols had used it at Baghdad, Alamut or anywhere outside China, this would have been the first recorded use of gunpowder weapons. Furthermore, the resulting explosion would have been memorable even if it had been a single missile hurled from a tre-buchet. However, the sources do not record anything like this. As the military theoretician and erstwhile nemesis of Bugs Bunny, Marvin the Martian, once said 'Where is the Earth-shattering ka-boom!? There was suppose to be an Earth-shattering ka-boom!' Alas, the sources are silent as well.

Nonetheless, the Mongols used it in their wars against the Jin, the Song and in their invasions of Japan. All the sources hostile to the Mongols refer to it in the eastern theatre of operations. As for the Jin and the Song, its use should not be surprising. In Japan there is picto-rial evidence and, more importantly, archaeological evidence.[32] So why did they not use it outside East Asia? Logistics may be the simple answer. Ceramic bombs have to be transported. Even packed with care to prevent breaking, they would have been difficult to carry. The weight of iron bombs may have limited their practicality. The Mongols usually built their siege weapons on site – either from local materials or reassembling one carried on camel back. While the Mongol *ger* or yurt might have been conveyed on a large cart, there is no indication that other equipment was. As the *gers* on carts were domestic residences of the nobility, it is unlikely that war materials were stowed in them. Troops rode on horseback. There is only one instance of troops being hidden in carts – during Shiremun's ill-fated coup against Möngke.[33] Otherwise, everything was hauled on camel-back. Considering the need for other supplies, the Mongols may have decided gunpowder weapons did not merit hauling them hundreds, if not thousands, of miles across Asia. Use in China was easier as they could be transported via ship to Japan or along the coast to Korea or southern China. Furthermore, as they were in the arsenal of the Song, the Mongols could always use captured stores.

Another consideration is the production of gunpowder weapons. In China the material was at hand or procurable. Once the Mongols moved outside China those who would make the gunpowder entered an unknown world. For instance, how does one say 'Where can I pro-cure *xiaoshi* 消石 or 硝石 (saltpetre)?' in Armenia?[34] The language and conceptual barriers would have been immense as the Armenians (or anyone else) would have no idea of what the engineer needed as gun-powder technology was unknown to them.

Finally, was there a need for gunpowder weapons outside of China (or even in China)? In China it was a simple matter of availability. Were they effective? Perhaps, although they did not prevent the Mongol conquest of China. Thunder-crash bombs were certainly more effective against earthen fortifications than stones hurled from a traction trebu-chet. Yet, as discussed earlier, when counterweight trebuchets appeared in China, formerly impregnable cities fell – which did not happen even with gunpowder weapons. Outside China, traction trebuchets gave way to counterweight trebuchets, allowing heavier missiles to crush walls much more rapidly. Aleppo's defences were destroyed after five days of concentrated trebuchet bombardment. It should be noted, however, that incendiary gunpowder weapons also played a role in Mongol war-fare in East Asia. Yet once in the Middle East the Mongols had access to naptha. Indeed their control of the Mughan plain situated them near petroleum deposits that had bubbled to the surface since ancient times. Of course, flammable weapons were easily made, but naptha was the most effective weapon other than Greek Fire, the recipe for which van-ished centuries earlier. Considering all of this it is unlikely the Mongols even needed gunpowder weapons to take the fortifications. Indeed, they used local materials for missiles and siege engines, and even efforts to remove all stone within the vicinity did not prevent them from being resourceful.[35]

It is known, however, that the Mongol Empire was the primary transmitter of the knowledge of gunpowder whether directly, through its use in war, or simply because most major trade routes ran through it. While it is unlikely that Europe gained its knowledge of gunpowder directly from the Mongols, we do know that it appeared there only after the Mongol invasion. Most probably merchants, perhaps even the Polo family, travelling through the Mongol Empire carried the recipe back. Of course this eventually led to European dominance over much of the world after the year 1500. Indeed, Roger Bacon (1220–1292) recorded a version of a gunpowder recipe in his *Opus Maius* in 1266. It is known that he knew fellow Franciscan monk William of Rubruck, who did travel to Mongolia. Although William's account does not mention gun-powder, is it possible that he found 'the secret' or another member of his party carried it back? It is tempting to speculate that Jean of Plano Carpini was the industrial spy as his mission contained an espionage component. Yet he must be dismissed, as gunpowder does not enter his account of the Mongol military and as his work contains suggestions on how to fight the Mongols, it is clear that he was willing to do any-thing to stem the Mongol threat. If he had it undoubtedly he would have given the recipe to someone who may have used it. It seems unlikely that Roger Bacon, a Franciscan, would be that recipient. William, on the other hand, was primarily there to proselytize. Perhaps where he failed in one area, he succeeded in another.

Although knowledge of gunpowder reached Europe and India in the thirteenth century, albeit at different times, it remained more of a curiosity until cannons were developed. The archaeological evidence reveals that firearms existed in the Yuan Empire by 1290 and perhaps in the 1280s.[36] While pictorial evidence suggests that cannons may have existed prior to this, it is not conclusive; these weapons may have been an early flamethrower. Considering that there are no reports of cannons of any sort being used to fend off the Mongols it seems implausible that they appeared more than a few years prior to the archaeological data. More importantly, the advent of the cannon appears to have been a Mongol initiative. Regardless, the technology quickly spread and cannons of similar design appeared in Europe and in Southeast Asia in the early fourteenth century.[37] While independent discovery is always a possibility, the similarities in design make this unlikely. A more plausible scenario is that the information travelled across Eurasia via merchants, envoys or other travellers.

In his study of the spread of firearms Kenneth Chase demonstrated that the Mongols are tied to the rise of European hegemony by more than spreading gunpowder via trade routes.[38] The Mongols had an impact on neighbouring areas based on their own tactics and weapons. As the composite bow of the nomads out-competed muskets and other early firearms in terms range and accuracy, not to mention rate of fire, nomadic armies decimated firearm-wielding infantry. In addition, the nomads were too mobile for early cannons; not until the sixteenth and seventeenth centuries did cannon-manufacturing techniques advance to producing easily manoeuverable artillery pieces. Earlier cannons were simply too heavy or, in some cases, not sufficiently durable to transport across the steppe. Thus if you bordered a steppe power in the fourteenth and fifteenth centuries firearms simply were not efficient weapons.

In western Europe, however, warfare was less focused on mobility and more on shock tactics or siege warfare and rarely engaged steppe nomads. A concern of the European cavalry was to protect themselves against increasingly powerful crossbows, the English longbow and eventually early firearms. As a result the knight became less mobile and the rest of the army consisted of masses of infantry. Early cannons and firearms, however, could be effective against the knights and infantry in a way they could not be against the steppe nomads.

Eventually the knight disappeared while light and medium cavalry appeared to counter the artillery. Cannons, however, were not field weapons even in late medieval Europe for the same reasons they were not effective against nomads at the time. Furthermore, kings were virtually the only nobility that could afford the expense of making cannons. As European castles continually improved against traditional siege weapons, rulers became dependent on cannons to smash fortifications to bring recalcitrant vassals into line or defeat their enemies.

Similar events occurred in China. The cannon first appeared in the Yuan Empire and gunpowder weapons became a regular, although not common, part of warfare as the Red Turbans drove the Mongols out and the Ming Dynasty replaced them. Cannons, however, played only a small role in the defeat of the Mongols. Indeed, the Red Turbans and then Ming's use of cannons was primarily limited to siege warfare and battles in south China. For the reasons described above, the Ming did not use cannons extensively on their northern frontier with the Mongolian tribes. Cannons remained an ineffectual weapon against mobile units.

Nonetheless, gunpowder-based weaponry became increasingly ubiquitous in some areas, but the ramifications of bordering a steppe zone were great. Countries sharing borders with steppe nomads had less development in gunpowder weaponry until their prime military focus shifted against sedentary states. Only then did the technology improve. Towards the end of the seventeenth century field artillery pieces became more mobile, thus providing support for musket-wielding infantry. The cannons easily disrupted steppe cavalry formations and possessed a greater range than the composite bow. Only then did steppe warfare decline as the dominant form of warfare, but that is not to say the nomads did not attempt to field their own artillery. Indeed, in the wars between Kangxi (r. 1662–1722), the Qing emperor and Galdan Khan (r. 1678–97) of the Oirat there was the curious instance where the Qing used cannons made by Jesuit monks pitted against cannons made by Lutheran Swedes and used by an Oirat Mongol in a battle that would dictate who was the most powerful Buddhist ruler. It should be further noted that these cannons were not carried on carriages – bouncing across the steppe they would have broken down. Instead they were carried on camels wearing protective felt armour to defend against arrows and small arms fire. Ultimately, the better logistics of the Qing state carried the day in 1696.

Yet it should be noted that only one gunpowder state formed a truly effective method of dealing with horse-archers prior to the 1600s: the Ottomans. This may have been because of their need to not only deal with the strongly fortified cities of the Habsburg in Europe, but also the horse-archers of the various powers on their eastern border, ranging from the Aq Qoyunlu and the Safavids (defeated at Chaldiran in 1514) to the Mamluk Sultanate (conquered in 1516 in Syria and Egypt in 1517). Gradually, other Eurasian states like Muscovite Russia, the Safavids and Mughals learned from the Ottoman example, while the Qing were in a unique situation of being a semi-nomadic society that conquered both the sedentary as well as the nomadic and melded different military systems into one that could fight both nomadic and sedentary opponents. Thus, until archaeology proves otherwise, I remain a sceptic. Philology is not sufficient to prove the presence of gunpowder weapons outside China in the pre-dissolution Mongol Empire.

MODERN WARFARE

After the carnage resulting from static trench warfare on the western front of the First World War and new developments in mechanized warfare, the inter-war period saw a re-evaluation of Mongol warfare. The advent of tanks and aircraft allowed a mobility that could possibly replicate the Mongol style of fast-moving and deep-striking tactics. Captain B. H. Liddell Hart, a British officer, conceptualized combined formations of tanks and mechanized infantry that could operate independently and in advance of the main army. This mobile strike force could cut enemy communications and supply lines, thus paralyzing the enemy's army.[39] As with the Mongols, the adversary would then be only able to react and incapable of offensive action. Liddell Hart interpreted Mongol tactics correctly, but overlooked a key objective in Mongol strategy, which was the annihilation of the enemy's field armies. Liddell Hart, however, may have witnessed enough death in trench warfare in the First World War and hoped to avoid the large death tolls of that war.

Initially, Liddell Hart's idea of using the Mongol emphasis of mobility and firepower came to fruition with the Britain's first experimental tank brigade. Its successful performance in exercises, along with Liddell Hart's chapter on Chinggis Khan and Sübedei in *Great Captains Unveiled*, influenced General Douglas MacArthur, us Army Chief of Staff, to propose a similar development in the American army in a 1935 report. Although MacArthur recommended the study of the Mongol campaigns for future use, his advice went unheeded until the Second World War. Unfortunately, his suggestion came at the end of his term. His more conservative successors lacked his vision but also lacked the means to carry out the plan within the US Army at the time.[40] After the Second World War Liddell Hart continued to advocate applying Mongol warfare with tanks, calling for a combination of swifter light tanks and the firepower of heavier tanks to allow for speed and flexibility in attack.[41]

Another British military theoretician, Major-General J.F.C. Fuller, also viewed the tank as being a modern 'Mongol' and encouraged the use of self-propelled artillery. He, unlike Liddell Hart, also emphasized the role of airplanes in ground attacks. Despite advocating the adoption of Mongol tactics, Liddell Hart's and Fuller's ideas did not come to fruition among Western militaries initially. Farther east, however, others made practical use of similar yet distinctively different ideas before British, French and American militaries began to incorporate these ideas beyond a few experimental units.

The German Wehrmacht's blitzkrieg strategy of the Second World War bears remarkable similarities to the Mongol art of war and not by accident. Part of the development of the blitzkrieg originated from information gained from the Soviets as a result of the Rapallo Pact of 1923, the operational doctrine of Soviet Marshal Mikhail Nikolayevich Tukhachevsky (1893–1937), who emphasized 'employment of forward aviation in concert with rapidly moving tank columns'.[42] Under this idea, Soviet concern with warfare was the 'seizure and maintenance of the offensive over a long period of time'[43] also known as the Deep Battle. These ideas stemmed from the long military influence of steppe warfare in the Russian and Soviet academies. While Liddell Hart and Fuller unsuccessfully reconceptualized warfare in the west, Tukhachevsky developed his own system independently. Nonetheless, their strategies are virtually identical and have their origins in the Mongol system.

The Soviet Deep Battle system shared the Mongol goals of hampering the enemy's ability to concentrate their armies, forcing them to react and incapacitating offensive actions. Thus by 1937 the Soviets possessed a Mongol army in a doctrine and tactical sense due to the work of Marshal Tukhachevsky and Mikhail Vasilyevich Frunze (1885–1925) in developing the Deep Battle strategy.[44] Stalin, however, purged the officer corps of the Red Army the same year, culminating with the execution of Tukhachevsky, leaving the army in disarray. Tukhachevsky's tank armies, the centrepiece of Deep Battle strategy, became infantry support, much as they had been used in the First World War. Stalin's strategy to defend every inch of Soviet territory resembled that of Muhammad Khwarazmshah II's but with the Wehrmacht playing the role of the Mongols. And it remained that way until the Germans overextended themselves and Marshal Georgii K. Zhukov took over command of the Red Army, having successfully used Deep Battle strategies and other Mongol tactics at Khalkin Gol (in Mongolia) in 1939 against the Japanese.

Until then the Wehrmacht's devastating blitzkrieg strategy dominated the early warfare of the European theatre. While influenced by Soviet developments in the 1920s, independent German advances occurred as well. Two German officers, General Hans von Seeckt and General Heinz Guderian, played the most significant roles in creating a force designed specifically for the blitzkrieg. Seeckt organized the Reichswehr (the German army between the First World War and the establishment of the Wehrmacht). Recognizing the deficiencies of his smaller army he focused on flexibility. To this end subordinate officers were trained to quickly assume command positions and replace their superiors in case of death or the incapacitation of a commanding officer. Thus a major was expected to effectively command a division should his general die. This practice was then extended to non-commissioned officers so that they could assume the leadership of their unit.[45] Although this idea was probably based on Napoleon's practice that every soldier carried a marshal's baton, meaning that anyone in his army could advance to the highest rank, it had antecedents in the Mongols's own leadership practices.

The Mongol influence, albeit indirect, is more apparent in Seeckt's operational strategy. His writings from 1921, before the Rapallo Act, state 'that what would matter in future warfare was the use of relatively small, but highly skilled mobile armies in co-operation with aircraft'.[46] Seeckt's conclusion came from his experience in the First World War as well as listening to his subordinates in the Reichswehr. The reduction of the German army after the First World War, Polish hostility and the looming threat of the Red Army also convinced him that a static, defence-minded military would fail if Germany was invaded.[47] As with other theoreticians, he desired to avoid the static warfare of the First World War and, much like the Soviets, focused on mobility that allowed for operations that overwhelmed the enemy, forcing them to react. Furthermore, the purpose of the attack was to annihilate the enemy before they could counter the attack. This was particularly suitable for the terrain of Germany's eastern borders. In essence he had to substitute mobility for mass with the reduction of troops in the inter-war period. Interestingly, General Seeckt also included traditional cavalry, albeit armed with light machine guns and carbines, in his military plans for hit and run tactics and other manoeuvres.[48]

General Heinz Guderian, a subordinate of Seeckt, studied the works of Fuller, Liddell Hart and Giffard LeQuesne Martel, all of whom emphasized the tank as an offensive weapon that was supported by other units (whether artillery, infantry or air power) and not vice versa.[49] As with all who appreciated the development of the tank, Guderian believed they would restore mobility to warfare. As has been discussed, Fuller and Liddell Hart were greatly influenced by the Mongols and thus Guderian, at least indirectly, carried these ideas into the German blitzkrieg, although the foundations laid by Seeckt and exchanges with the Soviets were of more importance.

Guderian's idea of warfare greatly resembles a Mongol operation. He believed that tanks were best used en masse, rather than as support units, and for striking quickly so that they hit the enemy's defences before the enemy could intervene or deploy effectively. Much like the Mongol practice of using auxiliaries to finish off isolated fortresses, Guderian indicated that once the defences had been penetrated by the panzers, other units could carry out the mop up duties, particularly of any static defences.[50] Mongol influence in modern warfare remains very apparent, albeit indirect. Indeed, many commanders of the recent 2003 Iraq War may have realized that their actions mirrored the theories of these theoreticians, but probably not their ultimate root in the Mongols. Yet other Mongol influence remains by fuelling the popular imagination in warfare. According to Colonel Keith Antonia (now retired) of the us Army and inductee into the Ranger Hall of Fame, Commander of the 75th Ranger Regiment, Colonel David L. Grange, Jr (now retired Brigadier General), developed an exercise based on Mongol training.

During Antonia's days as a Ranger, Colonel Grange evaluated all of the captains in the regiment by having them go through a programme designed to test the 'the mettle, endurance, will, ability to operate under physical and mental stress, and potential of every captain in the Regiment. He modeled the programme after the training regimen that

[Chinggis] Khan's most elite warriors endured to prepare for combat. He called it "Mangoday" [sic].'[51] Antonia indicated that they took part in a 72- hour live and simulated fire exercise. After arriving at Fort Benning, Georgia, the Rangers were assembled into teams and given an objective. They practised and then were flown to their destination in the swamps of Florida. With heavy loads, they then moved to an ambush site, conducted the drill and returned to the swamp camp. Their meal on the first day consisted of a bouillon cube and hot water.

They then received the next phase of the operation. This was to rescue a downed fighter pilot in the mountains. After a rehearsal they flew to the Appalachian Mountains in North Georgia, located the pilot (who was injured), recovered a cache of weapons and ate a meal of a ball of rice and a sardine. Then they carried their heavy loads (approximately 80 to 100 lb), recovered weapons and the pilot with a broken leg to their extraction point. After returning to another base they received their third mission, which involved another plane flight and an intensive march near Fort Benning. All of this was accomplished in 72 hours.

During the mission review Colonel Grange explained the rationale for the exercise. According to Colonel Antonia, this was based on elite units in the Mongol army:

> He described how [Chinggis] Khan created his elite Mangoday warrior battalions. He told a story of how one day [Chinggis] Khan's small army was outmanoeuvred by a far superior Chinese force. To overcome the odds he decided to use psychological warfare. He asked his generals to choose 50 of the best soldiers in the army. He instructed them to ensure that they were all volunteers and not married. He wanted these 50 to have no thoughts of wives or children when he sent them to their fate. [Chinggis] Khan gathered the 50 together and instructed them to attack the Chinese army to the front which consisted of thousands of enemy soldiers. He told them to kill as many of the Chinese as they could. They attacked the Chinese and killed a thousand before the last of Khan's warriors fell. Upon seeing the small, aggressive, fearsome and frenzied Mongol force kill so many of his soldiers, believing that the rest of the Mongols were just as fearsome, the Chinese general decided to withdraw his forces, leaving [Chinggis] Khan's army to fight another day.

After that, [Chinggis] Khan began training battalions of elite Mangoday warriors who would have a similar ethos and spirit as those first 50. Their task progressed in difficulty over time. At first, they were well fed, had a lot of rest, movements were short and tactical problems simple. Each day, they were fed a little less, received a little less sleep, marched a little farther and the complexity of the tactical problems increased. In the end they were required to march for days with no food or rest, and attack a simulated enemy under a complex set of conditions. Those who persevered became Mangoday warriors.

Col. Grange told us that he wanted to see how we operated under the stress of little sleep and little food while carrying heavy loads and moving long distances. He wanted us to remember what it is like for a soldier to carry a machine gun, recoilless rifle, mortar or radio so that as commanders, when we planned our future movements, we took the soldier's load into consideration. He also wanted to see how we reacted in a fluid environment with an elusive enemy and changes of missions and unknown factors.[52]

Grange's 'Mangoday' training and legend may have been based on an Israeli Palmach exercise. Antonia later saw an Israeli pamphlet relating similar information. The existence of such pamphlets has been confirmed to the author by others who underwent Israeli military training. Unfortunately the sources do not indicate any training similar to this legend. In the popular media concerning the Mongols there has been mention of the Mangudai, Mönggedei or Mangoday troops. It is not known where this term originates. Perhaps it is derived from *möngke-de* (eternally) or *manglai* (vanguard). As the Mongols were renowned for their stoic endurance and achieving tasks thought impossible for their contemporary sedentary opponents,[53] perhaps the term originates from a corruption of *Monggol-tai*. That is to say, being like a Mongol. The most likely etymology is *Manghut-tai* – to be like a Manghut. The Manghut were among Chinggis Khan's best troops during the wars in Mongolia. They were usually positioned against the best units of his opponents.[54] Ultimately the origins of the term or even the existence of such a group in the Mongol military is irrelevant. What remains germane is the fact that the Mongols' success continues to inspire military planners to ask, 'What would Chinggis do?'

6

THE MONGOL ADMINISTRATION

An oft-used story about the Mongol Empire was that Yelü Chucai, the recently acquired Khitan administrator who quickly became the leading civil authority within the empire, informed Chinggis Khan that he could conquer from the saddle, but not rule from it. The moral was that the Mongols needed to curb their more violent tendencies and rule or, rather, let others who knew better do the job for them. While the story might be true, it probably is not. It gets muddled since some versions have Ögödei receiving the words of wisdom rather than his father. Second, it is a common trope in the chronicles any time a steppe-based empire dominated China – a 'civilized' bureaucrat needed to introduce the 'barbarians' to bureaucracy and governance. It did serve its purpose, however, in illustrating the point of developing a rational governmental system. Indeed there is a great deal of timeless truth to it as evinced by the Iraq War and Afghanistan – it is a great deal easier to conquer a country than to rule it, particularly after you have destroyed many of the existing institutions. In addition, this story and others written by other bureaucrats (Juvaini, Rashid al-Din and so forth) convinced scholars for decades that the Mongols relied heavily on existing administrative structures and allowed local authorities to manage the day-to-day affairs of the empire. Thus the Mongols were viewed as using hands-off management.

For instance, David Morgan wrote in the original edition of his classic and still standard work, *The Mongols*, as well as in an article which sensibly asked as a title, 'Who Ran the Mongol Empire?' that the Mongols, while destructive, were pragmatic. Thus while the Mongols ran the empire they left institutions largely intact allowing sedentary people, particularly the Uighurs and Khitans, to take the lead in administering the empire.[1] Professor David Morgan, however, is also notorious for, after some years of reflection, pointing out that the historian David Morgan is wrong, much to the consternation of his undergraduate students. He did this in an article in 1996, which contradicted his book, the previous article and decades of other scholars' work. In 'Mongol or Persian: The Government of Ilkhanid Iran', he reversed his conclusion after reassessing the sources.[2] Indeed, while local dynasts and government structures remained in place, the Mongols were much more hands-on than previously thought. The most obvious evidence is that the 1206 *quriltai* goes into great detail on the assignment of military units and households as well as the rules and regulations for various positions within Chinggis Khan's bodyguard, adding up to over a chapter of detail about the creation of the Mongol administration. *The Secret History of the Mongols* provides more details on administration than on military tactics.

A proper study of the Mongol administration from beginning to end has yet to be published, primarily because it is indeed a daunting subject. Nonetheless, we have a fair idea of how it worked and it appears to be somewhat standardized across the empire. The Mongols, however, allowed for considerable nuance in their style of governing. What follows is an overview of the Mongol administration, how it worked and also how it changed over time. Readers will note that Persian, Turkic and Mongolian terminology has been used over Chinese terms. This is in part due to the languages I used in my research but also to the fact that these were also the languages the Mongol government used. Chinese sources are undeniably important but the pre-dissolution Mongol Empire had an aversion to the language.

ORGANIZATION OF THE MONGOL ADMINISTRATION

At the top of the Mongol hierarchy sat the khan. Although he was all-powerful and in theory his commands could not be refused, the khan relied on many people not only to carry out his decrees but also to maintain support or 'buy in' so that others would follow his commands. The khan was not an autocrat but elected to his position, albeit from a limited pool of candidates. After the ascension of Chinggis Khan, only Chinggisids could contend for the throne, but there was a vetting system where attributes and bases of support were determined before the khan was chosen. As discussed in chapters One and Two, often the process was challenged by mud-slinging and politicking behind the scenes – in essence, the political campaign techniques of the modern era. While a khan could name his successor it did not guarantee the nominee a throne.

Chinggis Khan and his sons as displayed in a Persian miniature, 14th century. This illustration could be a depiction of the time when Chinggis Khan divided his empire between his sons and named Ögödei as his successor.

A key component of the upper levels of the Mongol system of governance was the *ordo* and *inju* system. The *ordo* was the palace camp of the khan. Other Chinggisid princes, including the descendants of Chinggis Khan's brothers, and their wives also maintained *ordos*, which could vary in size. Thus in addition to the imperial *ordo* there were four representing the four sons of Chinggis Khan and then one, decreasing in size, for each grandson, and so on. Each wife also had her own *ordo* in the vicinity of her husband's. Each *ordo* had a household staff of not only slaves, servants and guards but also administrative personnel which comprised just part of the *inje* (Mongolian) or *inju* (Persian).[3] In addition to the household the *inje* consisted of subjects, landed property and inherited people such as slaves, subjects and wives, that the preceding khan bequeathed to the next. The division between people and land is important. From the Mongol perspective, while territorial acquisition was important, control over a population held greater significance. To a certain extent the empire was run as a family business and the subjects in many ways were just a different form of livestock. While the Chinggisid *ordos* were assigned to certain *nutaqs* or pasturelands, the exact territorial borders of these appanages tended to be vague. At times the khan might allot *inje* territory to non-Chinggisids such as administrators, governors and other loyal servants of the empire.

The establishment of the *ordos* accomplished several goals for Mongol expansion. It spread the Chinggisids with their followers throughout the empire and thus extended the control of the empire. The Chinggisids ran their *ordos* autonomously but were still subject to imperial command. In some sense the empire functioned as a federation of Chinggisid princes with the khan serving as the glue that held them together. Decrees came from the imperial palace or Altan Ordo in Mongolia although, as discussed in chapter Two, on a few occasions during periods of ineffective leadership the other *ordos* acted more independently. Indeed, the fluid nature of the Mongol administration aided in the dissolution of the empire. As each *ordo* had its own administrative apparatus it was possible to assert an increasing amount of autonomy during moments of weak central authority.

The ultimate source of central administration emerged from the *keshik* or bodyguard and household retainers of the khan, following the frequent process in the pre-modern world by which companions of warlords became heads of administrative offices.[4] The *keshik* was part of the *inje* and apart from it. Initially comprised of *nököd*, or the companions and followers of Chinggis Khan, even after his death the *keshik* still served as a training ground for generals and administrators. Chinggis Khan first formed the *keshik* in 1203, when it consisted of 70 day guards, 80 night guards and 1,000 men who accompanied Chinggis Khan into battle.[5] In the 1206 *quriltai* this expanded to 10,000 men consisting of 1,000 night guards, 1,000 *qorchin* or quiverbearers, 7,000 day guards and the 1,000 battle guards.[6] During battle the majority usually remained to guard the khan's camp and household. The dramatic increase also tied the newly united Mongolia and later other areas to the Mongol Empire. Commanders and subject rulers sent their sons and younger brothers to serve in the *keshik*, thus also making them hostages as the khan now had control over their lives. At the same time it allowed the khan to come to know these men and judge their character. Thus if a ruler did not abide by his wishes the khan could remove him from the throne and replace him with a *keshik*-trained relative with whom the khan had developed a personal bond. More than not, from their years of serving in the *keshik*, these sons became extremely loyal to the Mongol Empire and helped solidify Mongol control when they returned to their homes.[7]

Every khan formed his own *keshik*, although after Ögödei at least part of the *keshik* became the core of the successor's bodyguard, ensuring a smooth transition as well as continuity of the institution. Yet by forming his own *keshik* the khan ensured that it did not become a praetorian guard that chose the khan. It allowed the khan to stamp his own personality on the unit, which was important since the members of the *keshik* were more than just guards. When not on active duty they held positions as household staff – tending to the flocks and herds, cooking, serving drinks, holding the khan's cup. The menial labour allowed the khan and the *keshik* commanders, who were non-Chinggisids, to judge the characteristics of their men as well as keeping the *keshikten* (members of the *keshik*) humble. Yet by serving the khan food and drink or looking after his personal possessions strong ties were made, as the khan came to know each individual and developed a level of trust. A crucial factor is that as they had previously served in the *keshik* they demonstrated their loyalty to the khan and, in return, the khan knew their capabilities and could assign them to the appropriate task outside the *keshik* in either military or administrative roles. In order to maintain these ties the *keshik* member often served a tour of duty either as an officer or as an administrator away from the court but returned to the *keshik* upon completion of his duties.[8] Imperial agents needed the khan's support in order to carry out their orders in distant *ordos* as their presence often intruded upon the authority of the local Chinggisids.

With the dissolution of the empire the other leading princes formed their own *keshik* on the model that Chinggis Khan provided.

Khubilai Khan actually increased his *keshik* to 15,000 men, although it was reduced in the later empire to less than 1,000 men.[9] Over time the four *keshik* commanders became increasingly important in matters of state. Uli Schamiloglu has called these individuals the *qarachi beys* (also spelled *kharachi*) and traced their influence in the Jochid Khanate as well as in its successors, particularly the Crimean Khanate. Although the khans always needed the 'buy-in' of the generals and other princes, as the *qarachi beys* emerged their unified effort could actually thwart the khan's designs, often requiring their signature on decrees to make them official.[10] How often the interests of the *qarachi beys* coincided varied but they could serve as a check on the khan's power. This check arose as part of a transition from assigning positions based on merit to one based on family. Certain families inherited the position and eventually accumulated power. One successor state of the Ilkhanate, the Jalayirs, evolved from their status as *qarachi beys*. In central Asia Timur's clan, the Barulas, also emerged from the *keshik* as a commanding family. While not the cause of his rise the prestige of the Barulas and their connections certainly assisted Timur.

In the context of the Chinggisid Exchange this system carried significant influence into the post-Mongol world. The diffusion of Chinggisid princes throughout Eurasia helped maintain the prestige of that lineage as well as the idea that only Chinggisids could use the title of khan. This perception lasted well into the seventeenth century. Furthermore, the institutions of the *keshik* and the later *qarachi beys* continued as integral parts of successor states, although the exact influence and power of the *qarachi beys* varied through time and space. What was the norm in the Crimean Khanate in 1550 was not necessarily the same in Iran in 1370. Nonetheless, these derivatives of the *keshik* shaped the sociopolitical and military culture of the former Mongol Empire. While the sources are quiet in regard to the role of the *keshik* post in Yuan Mongolia, the *keshik*'s influence there is apparent. As Christopher Atwood has written, Mongolian identities bear the hallmarks of the *keshik* divisions: the Khorchin tribe comes from the quiverbearers (*qorchin* or *khorchin*), while the Torghuds, a division among the Oirats, is derived from the day guards (*turgha'ud*); finally in Inner Mongolia there is a Kheshigten banner, a clear derivative of *keshik*.[11]

While the princes of the various *ordos* managed their *inje* or *inju* lands and subjects, the empire also contained lands known as *dalai* (sea) and other territories. The latter consisted of territories that submitted to the Mongols voluntarily and thus preserved the local ruling dynasts.

Nonetheless, over all *dalai* lands and submitted territories, a Mongol-based governance structure existed, incorporating imperial, regional and local elements under its umbrella. Furthermore, as the Mongol Empire was a conquest empire, territory and people were incorporated into the empire as it expanded. The Mongols used a dual administrative scheme – military and civilian. Initially military forces governed newly conquered lands. As a region stabilized and the empire expanded these lands were switched to civilian administrators, although it is difficult to say if the local population appreciated the difference.

As nomads the Mongols organized people rather than land, although the latter could occur. The *mingan*, or unit of 1,000, was the first organizational tool the Mongols utilized.[12] It not only served as the basic military unit for the Mongol Empire but also as a unit of taxation and levy. Units of 1,000 men or households worked well for the decimal-focused Mongols, yet as the empire expanded they integrated more sophisticated governance structures.

A critical institution through which the Mongols governed newly acquired lands was the *tamma*.[13] Initially, on the administrative side, the Mongols concerned themselves with the mobilization of manpower for military units as well as procuring goods for rewarding those who partook in the raids and wars. Chormaqan's force in Iran was such an organization and Grigor of Akanc wrote that the Mongol force under Baiju stationed in Azerbaijan was also a *tamma*.[14] Always established on the fringes of the empire, on the border between nomadic and sedentary cultures, the *tamma* could launch further attacks and extend Mongol influence beyond their borders.[15] Members of the *tamma* were known as *tammachin* (singular *tammachi*).

As the empire frontiers stabilized the *tamma* ceased to be an effective administrative structure as its purpose was primarily military. The pace of transition from military to civilian administrators varied from region to region, but eventually the transition happened. Although this change seems progressive, a *tammachi* did not always want to leave his current position as some had served at their post for several years. Nonetheless, they did move. With the switch to civil authority *darughachin* (singular *darughachi*.) or governors, accompanied by *bichigchin* (scribes) arrived in the region. Eventually an administrator known as the *yeke jarghuchi* replaced the *tamma* commander.[16] Their function revolved around the collection of tribute as well as resolving local disputes. During the conquest phase administrating conquered territory through the *mingan* units made sense but as the needs and goals of the empire evolved so did the administrative institutions. A civil administration emerged whose purpose was not solely concerned with the military but with the actual governance of the conquered territories. As many of the highest ranking *darughachin* and *yeke jarghuchin* came from the *keshik*, their personal bonds with the khan ensured their authority and the fact that they reported to the khan provided credibility even in the face of other nobles.

The terminology for the civil administrators of the Mongol Empire adds to the difficulty of understanding how the Mongols ran their empire. Throughout the sources three titles are mentioned in several places. Most often the chronicler referred to the terms without further explanation, and modern scholars have struggled to define them. One problem is that each term originates in a different language, *darughachi* from Mongolian, *basqaq* from Turkic and *shahna* from Persian. The second problem is that in some places the terms seem to serve as synonyms while in other sources it is implied that their meanings are not the same. The final problem is that their meanings evolve and change over time.

The clearest indication that the terms *basqaq* and *shahna* were synonyms appears in the pre-Mongol era of Turkestan. During the war between Muhammad Khwarazmshah and the Gur Khan of Kara Khitai, Tört Aba the governor of Samarqand is described as a *shahna* in one place, but shortly after Juvaini refers to him as the *basqaq* of Samarqand.[17] While it is possible that Juvaini simply utilized terminology in current use in the Mongol Empire, it seems unlikely the Mongols would have altered local terminology in order to create a new bureaucratic ranking system. It is also clear that *darughachi* and the *basqaq* were the same office. The *basqaq* was an official in the Kara Khitain Empire, while the Mongols first used the term *darughachi* between 1206 and 1214 in northern China.[18] Although Chinggis Khan initiated the use of the *darughachin*, Ögödei expanded their presence. Their primary purpose, as Buell notes, 'seems to have been integration of local administrative systems based on these cities, and much was simply taken over unchanged at the time of conquest, with the imperial establishment at large'.[19] The presence of the *darughachin* extended beyond northern China, as 72 *darughachin* were present in the portion of Kory under Mongol control.

According to Carpini, after a conquest the Mongols placed *basqaqs* in countries where they supervised the region and encountered rebellion.[20] In Russia the institution of *basqaq* began in 1245. The Mongols stationed *basqaqs* in the forest zone, although the khans of the Golden Horde later recalled them. Yet when they were present the *basqaqs* collected or farmed out taxes to whoever would bring in the highest yield and conscripted troops.[21] The difference in terminology is due to the fact that in East Asia ethnic Mongols were the primary actors whereas in the western region of the empire Turkic was the lingua franca and thus Carpini and others adopted the terms the Turks used rather than the Mongolian terms, just as *shahna* tended to be used more in the Persian world.

No matter whether the populace referred to the individual as a *shahna*, *basqaq* or *darughachi*, the imperial governors were placed in the cities and regions of the sedentary world and were responsible to the khan. They supervised local governments as well as collected taxes and sent revenues to the khan and could lead local armies if necessary. 'And, most important, there they linked local power structures (and administration) through their offices with [the khan's] central establishment.'[22] In so doing the *darughachi* served as the intermediary between imperial authority and local dynasts. A primary responsibility of the *darughachi* in which he worked closely with the local ruler was to oversee and carry out the registration of the population in a census. The census was carried out on a fairly regular basis and often the census-takers were protected by a local dynast: Alexander Nevskii, the prince of Novgorod, being the most prominent in the historical record. As the local ruler provided guards for the *darughachi* and his *bichegchin* or secretaries as they registered the population for taxes and military service purposes it tied the local ruler to the empire. In addition to security, the local dynast also provided administrative support if necessary.[23] If harm befell the *darughachi* or his men during the process the local ruler faced repercussions including execution.

Like many terms, the meanings of *basqaq*, *darughachi*, and *shahna* changed through the course of time. Charles Halperin, discussing the terminology in the Jochid Khanate, noted that by the fourteenth century the *basqaq* had become the equivalent of a nineteenth-century British colonial viceroy, while the *darughachi* had become more similar to a state department desk officer who advised but lacked operational responsibilities. Thus, although the *basqaq* and *darughachi* held synonymous meanings at one point, by the fourteenth century the two terms were no longer synonymous, although few are in agreement on exactly how they changed.[24] Istvan Vasary has rightly, in this writer's opinion, determined that the meaning of *darughachi* changed over time and

place but always had a common feature: the *darughachi* was a chief official or a superior of a territorial or administrative unit. Vasary assumes
that 'as the chief task of civil administration in a feudal nomadic state
like the Golden Horde was to assure regular taxation of the subjects,
the daruga's [*sic*] function was surely connected with taxation.'[25]
Nonetheless over time the terms changed slightly in each of the post-
dissolution khanates along with their job responsibilities so that *basqaq*
and *darughachi* were no longer synonymous, and in some regions only
one term was used, such as *shahna* in the Middle East.

Although the *darughachi* interacted with the local ruler, the latter
often had a great deal of autonomy as long as they abided by the
Mongol rules such as paying tribute and taxes, providing troops and
coming to the khan's *ordo* to show their obeisance to the khan. In addition to the local dynasts, other local administrators existed. At the
time of the establishment of the Mongol Empire into sedentary lands
the Mongols lacked administrative skill and personnel in dealing with
sedentary subjects but as they sought to control the troop reservoirs
of the steppe they also commandeered the sedentary administrative
reservoirs for functions of governance. In governing the conquered
territories the Mongols often used local notables as administrators,
particularly at the local level. They needed people with language skills
and knowledge of local customs. In China and Persia the Mongols did
not always use local administrative structures but often promoted others into the administration even though they sometimes had no previous experience, particularly at regional or provincial levels that were
more connected to the imperial level of the government. The key to
advancement from the local strata of administration to the regional or
imperial level, however, was mastery of the Uighur script used to
write Mongolian. They would replace 'local elites, whose status was
validated by mastery of indigenous literary and cultural traditions,
with those who possessed the inclination and skills outside their own
cultural and linguistic milieu'.[26]

The Mongols often allowed the native rulers to retain their positions and territories for two reasons. The first was that by giving
foreign rulers a chance to be part of the empire the Mongols could
avoid unnecessary military actions. Second, due to the Mongols' lack
of experience in administration they wanted to recruit others with
those talents. At the same time, when discussing lack of experience one
must keep in mind that at the local level the Mongols did not attempt
to enforce a new system of administration, but rather to create a

syncretic form of government by placing their own imperial personnel as a new strata of administration while maintaining individuals who were familiar with the locality. As time progressed each region became more firmly attached to the empire and the governance became more homogenous. Yet by 1260 this had not taken place through the entire empire.

As Thomas Allsen has demonstrated, under Möngke the administration of the Mongol Empire underwent substantial transformation.[27] Möngke's major reforms served to lessen the burden on the sedentary population of the empire and organize trade and agriculture to its own benefit. In addition Möngke sought to restore imperial authority over the appanages of the Chinggisids and reduce the amount of devastation to property and people in war zones in an effort to maintain and preserve the economic prosperity and long-term vitality of the newly conquered lands.[28] Möngke insisted on keeping damage to a minimum since he recognized the Mongols stood to benefit more in the long term through taxation than they would in the short term through plunder and preying on their subjects. Although Möngke's reforms originated as a result of the mismanagement of the empire during the regencies of Oghul-Qaimish and Töregene, they continued in the same direction the Mongol administration of the previous khans had taken, in intent if not practice. This may be a sign that the Mongol khans evolved from being rulers of an empire that centred on controlling people in the traditional steppe sense into rulers focused on territorial rule with a rational and coherent administration.

TAXATION

Just as the empire had been divided into khanates, *ordos*, military districts and civilian administrative districts to control the conquered lands, in order to maintain control of the fiscal resources of the empire the khans gradually divided the sedentary portions of the empire into fiscal regions. By Güyük's reign the empire consisted of three revenue districts: northern China, Turkistan and Khurasan-Mazandaran.[29] Although nomads existed in all three regions, these regions primarily consisted of sedentary populations. Even Turkistan cannot be viewed as being strictly nomadic as the population of Mawarannahr and the numerous cities along the Silk Road provided an enormous amount of wealth for the empire. The Rus' territories did not have a specific governor like northern China, Iran and

Turkistan, however, in 1257 an Onggirat named Kitai was selected to be *darughachi* or governor.[30] At a higher level the fiscal administrative territories emerged as secretariats, ruled by a civil government. Most of the senior officials of the secretariat were Mongols, with a few Uighurs during Möngke's time. It is notable that no Han Chinese presided at the decision-making level. By Möngke's reign more Mongols had administrative experience, making it possible for Mongols to govern their empire. Of course, many of the leading figures in the administration were not Mongols.

Prior to the establishment of a formal taxation system the Mongols typically plundered their sedentary subjects.[31] In early Mongol society tribute was formalized and payment came in the form of goods and services which demonstrated the subjection of an individual to an overlord, whereas a levy was extraordinary and used to fulfill a specific need.[32] Eventually, the Mongols set a tithe at approximately 10 per cent of possessions including manpower for the military or other service. Additionally, when on campaign Mongol commanders demanded goods or levied what they needed from subjects, typically those they had recently conquered. This was known as the *alba qubchiri*.[33] The *alba qubchiri* differed in its application for nomads and sedentary populations. Depending on the era, *alba qubchiri* could also mean service such as in the military, particularly for nomads.

During the reign of Ögödei the taxation system became standardized, primarily due to the influence of the Khitan official Yelü Chucai and Mahmud Yalavach, a central Asian. In 1235–6 Yelü Chucai and Shigi Qutuqu conducted a census of Northern China. Yelü Chucai determined that this was perhaps the best method of demonstrating the importance of the sedentary population to his nomadic overlords. By providing a forecast of tax revenue for the khan, the Mongols saw the benefits of taxing rather than plundering. In central Asia Mahmud Yalavach adopted the reforms of Yelü Chucai of 1229, although pre-existing systems also influenced his model. They continued to be used until 1239 or 1240, after which the Mongols transferred Mahmud Yalavach to northern China. Mahmud Yalavach's reforms, while similar to those of Yelü Chucai, differed in certain aspects and became the standard for most of the empire. Yalavach's system was based on *qubchir*, a poll tax on adult males paid in cash. Originally a 1 per cent tax on herd paid in kind, with a sedentary population it evolved into a poll tax that the Mongols levied when needed. The rate varied over time and was often based on the means of the household. Yelü Chucai's version centred

THE MONGOL CONQUESTS IN WORLD HISTORY

on households after the Chinese custom, although he did include a poll tax after 1236, perhaps due to central Asian influence. In addition another tax known as *qalan* was imposed. The Mongols collected this as military service owed by local rulers but it also referred to an exemption from military service. The *qalan* was often paid in kind rather than cash.[34]

Another imperial tax was the *tamgha* (stamp or seal), a customs tax or value-added tax placed on goods. Generally speaking, merchants paid it on a transaction at a rate of 5 to 10 per cent. An official stamped the goods showing that it had been paid. The *tamgha* was an important part of facilitating trade as it allowed merchants to pay significantly lower rates than in the pre-Mongol era when they paid customs and tolls in every realm they passed through.

Perhaps the most onerous tax was that paid to the *yam*, particularly in periods of administrative malfeasance. Nomads and villages in the vicinity of the *yam* paid a tax in horses and supplies to maintain the post station. Before Möngke's reforms the tax was collected repeatedly and often merchants and officials using the *yam* imposed on the hospitality of the nomads and villagers with excessively large retinues, crippling the local economy to the extent that the local population fled, rendering the *yam* ineffective.

By the mid-thirteenth century taxation was a combination of local taxes (whatever was used in that particular region) and new levies applied two or three times a year, often two or three years in advance. Möngke carried out reforms to end this practice. He created a new system of Mongol-inspired tribute to which all adults were subject. In addition traditional taxes were paid, such as the Islamic *kharaj* or land tax. The new taxes included agricultural taxes, from which nomads were exempt, and duties on trade. One important aspect of these reforms was the further concentration of power at the imperial centre, as regional princes were bypassed and a representative of the central government collected the revenue. In theory extraordinary collections did not happen. Möngke's system formed the basis of taxation used by the other khanates after the split of the empire.

MONGOL ADMINISTRATION IN THE CHINGGIS EXCHANGE

This chapter has provided a basic delineation of the Mongol administrative apparatus. At the lowest level, what occurred in Mongol Armenia differed from Mongol Manchuria. The fact that the Mongol government had inherent flexibility allowed it to adapt for cultural and regional differences. Governance was more consistent over a broader swath of territory as the imperial government through its taxation and creation of fiscal districts and secretariats provided stability to the empire. The consistency not only benefited the Mongols but also the merchants, the military and even the subjects of the Mongols.

While the roles of the *darughachi*, *basqaq* and *shahna* ceased to be synonymous in the post-dissolution world, much of the Mongol administration carried on, evolving or adapting new regional features such as the Islamic *diwan* or bureaus in the Ilkhanate and Jochid Khanate. Meanwhile, in Yuan China, the Confucian exams returned for civil service appointments. In essence the Mongols provided new models of their own innovation as well as from their conquests for their successors to emulate or ignore as they chose. Many of these positions continued through the centuries throughout the former domains of the empire.

7

RELIGION AND THE
MONGOL EMPIRE

The thirteenth-century Mongols are an anomaly in history in that
when a world or universal religion came into contact with a traditional religion, the followers of the traditional religion usually converted,
either by choice or by force. On the surface this may not be surprising, since the Mongols's imperial policy on religion was one of toleration – a rare instance in the pre-modern and perhaps even in the
modern world. As one examines this phenomenon more closely, the
Mongols may not be so unique in their policy of toleration. As Michal
Biran has demonstrated the Kara Khitai also carried out a policy of
religious toleration in their empire. Indeed, religious toleration appears
as a long-standing tradition in Inner Asian empires, perhaps due to it
so often being a crossroads for many religious systems.[1]

One might consider the Mongols simply as the grandest and most
important in this list of Inner Asian empires, as they exported their
practice of religious toleration from Inner Asia to the rest of the Mongol
Empire. Even when one religious practice had considerable influence
in the upper levels of the Mongol Empire, such as the Church of the
East, also known as Nestorian Christians, it rarely had any noticeable
detrimental impact on the Mongols' views of other religions. Indeed
they remained incredibly tolerant of all religions. Being primarily
shamanistic in the first decades of the empire, they did not possess a
comprehensive religious canon that dictated morality or provided an
exclusive worldview with an emphasis on the afterlife. Traditionally,
shamanism focused on spiritual matters that directly impacted the
mundane world and related to real life issues such as illness and other
tragedies. The afterworld was very similar to the mundane. Salvation
of one's soul did not exist, excepting instances where one's soul was
stolen by an evil spirit. The soul was necessary in the mundane world
but in the afterlife one was just another spirit and not at risk for eternal
damnation.[2] Thus the Mongols 'were open to any sort of religious

practice or ritual which might help them find success in realizing their immediate needs'.[3]

The Mongols established relations with religious communities throughout their empire. As suggested earlier, they had multiple reasons for doing so. The principal reason was strategic as well as practical, as sympathetic rapport with religious leaders reduced the threat of hostility and rebellion among the conquered. Thus the Mongols exempted clergy of all religions from taxes. Also, religious buildings were usually spared from destruction during invasions by Mongol armies, providing the town submitted. Of course, if a city refused to surrender then no one's safety was guaranteed. Furthermore, the khans asked the clergy to pray for them.[4] While locals often construed this as the Mongol khan converting or courting their religion, the Mongols did it for all out of respect for all religions, although it remained tied to the *realpolitik* policies of the Mongols.

In traditional Mongol religion one tried to avoid offending spirits for fear of supernatural retaliation, thus honouring the rituals of all religions and being included in prayers was simply a form of spiritual insurance against offending another spiritual power. Furthermore, inclusion in the prayers also demonstrated the legitimacy of the khan's authority as it had the official backing of the local religious elite. The inclusion of the ruler's name in the *khutba*, the Friday sermon in Islam, was a centuries-old practice that indicated the legitimacy of the ruler. Similar practices existed in other religions.

Beyond their own policy of religious toleration the Mongols attempted to preserve peace between the religious sects within the empire. This should not be construed as a philanthropic ideal, but rather one of strategic necessity. When the Mongol general Jebe pursued the Naiman renegade Güchülüg into central Asia, the Muslim population greeted Jebe as a liberator. Under the rule of Güchülüg, a Buddhist, the Muslims felt persecuted. As Michal Biran has demonstrated, much of the oppression stemmed less from actual religious motivation than Güchülüg's secular policies but it was viewed as religious bias.[5]

The Mongols, led by Jebe, defeated Güchülüg but this did not lead to a persecution of Buddhists. The Mongols were not interested in becoming involved in religious strife. Jebe decreed that all should follow the religion of their ancestors and not attempt to persecute others for their beliefs.[6] Other than manipulating religion for political purposes the Mongols had very little interest in doctrine. Their policy came down to the fact that everyone had the freedom to worship in their respective religion but if it threatened the stability of the empire or Mongol supremacy, they had no compunction about reacting with violence. They would not tolerate any religion's claims to spiritual supremacy over the whole world since it conflicted with their own claim to world domination.[7] This originated with the rise of Chinggis Khan and the Mongol Empire and a religious-based ideology of conquest known as Tenggerism.[8] Through this ideology it had been confirmed by Heaven (*Tenggeri*) that Chinggis Khan and his successors were to rule the earth. Anyone who defied them defied the will of Heaven. Whether or not Chinggis Khan truly believed this is unknown – his conquests demonstrate his actions were more reactionary than bent on world conquest. Ögödei, however, appears to have taken Tenggerism to heart. Yet, while Tenggerism was a religious ideology, it was one for Mongols, not something that one could convert into. Indeed, it allowed for other religions to exist – although as subjects in the empire and not challengers to the authority of the Mongols. As such, the Mongols had no issues with other religions as long as their clergy did not attempt to prevent the will of Tenggeri.

As the Mongol Empire was the most powerful state in the world, it was natural that other powers sought to find some type of relationship with it and indeed, even convert it to their religion. Christendom was no exception. Since the advent of the legend of Prester John, Western Europe had sought an Eastern Christian ally against the Muslims. Initially, many thought the Mongols were the armies of Prester John but after the invasion of Hungary the Europeans quickly realized their mistake. This did not, however, prevent them from dreaming that the Mongol khans might convert to Christianity. Indeed, with rumours that a few of the Mongol princes, such as Sartaq b. Batu, were Christians, and even more princesses and queens, the papacy had reason to believe the Mongols could be converted.[9] The papacy, like clergy from other religions, believed that if the ruling elite converted, the masses would follow suit.[10]

Due to their hopes of converting the Mongols and a very real concern about possible Mongol attacks on Christendom, the so-called Mongol missions took place. Pope Innocent IV dispatched several friars to the Mongols with a message in two parts. The first reproached the Mongols for their attacks on Christians and informed them that if they did not desist they would surely face the wrath of God.[11] The second, however, outlined the tenets of the Catholic faith and the reasons why the Mongols should convert.[12]

These attempts to convert failed despite Pope Innocent IV's best intentions, primarily because he, and probably the rest of Europe, lacked a proper understanding of steppe diplomacy and the power of the Mongols. Güyük's response to Innocent's overtures was remarkable not only in its brevity and clarity but also in its ominous tone. The core of Güyük's message was that the Mongols had conquered all who opposed them and who did not submit to Chinggis Khan and the successive khans:

> God ordered us to destroy them and gave them up to our hands. For otherwise if God had not done this, what could man do to man? But you men of the West believe that you alone are Christians and despise others. But how can you know to whom God deigns to confer His grace? But we worshipping God have destroyed the whole earth from the East to the West in the power of God. And if this were not the power of God, what could men have done? . . . But if you should not believe our letters and the command of God nor hearken to our counsel then we shall know for certain that you wish to have war. After that we do not know what will happen, God alone knows.[13]

Upon receiving Güyük's letter, Pope Innocent IV sent a second message stating that he had no intention of war, and that he only sought the salvation of the Mongols' souls. Unfortunately he also undermined his own attempts at conciliation by still insisting that the Mongols risked the wrath of God. It is quite clear that Innocent IV failed to grasp that this argument could not sway the Mongols as they believed Heaven was on their side. This was further magnified by the fact that from the Mongols's perspective the pope was not the sole representative of God on earth.[14]

Pope Innocent IV was not the only Christian leader who attempted to establish some sort of accommodation with the Mongols. King Louis IX sent expeditions to the Mongol khans seeking an alliance with them against the Muslims. These too failed as the Mongols viewed them as offerings of submission to Mongol power.[15] In truth, the Mongols had every reason to view King Louis' diplomatic efforts as a token of submission; for all of his zeal and efforts in winning the Holy Land for Christianity his failures outweighed his minimal successes. In the minds of the Mongols it would be logical for King Louis to submit in order to gain assistance against his enemies, especially after the debacle of the Seventh Crusade (1248–50).

Thus the early efforts of Christians to convert the Mongols, or at least to draw them closer, were unmitigated failures. Much of the blame, if blame can be placed, may be found in the papacy's attitude towards other religions. Western Europe, despite its involvement in the Crusades, was still a backwater civilization compared to the rest of the world. Its mindset, as a whole, was more closed than the Franks in the Holy Land, or the Muslims they struggled against, or even the Rus' who were already under Mongol dominion. The Latin Europeans, with the exception of those on the frontiers with Orthodoxy in the east and Islam in Spain and Sicily, did not have enough contact with other cultures to recognize cultural barriers in communication, whether religious, diplomatic or any other. The Western European tended to consider himself superior to any member of another ethnic group, culture or religion he encountered. Indeed, the papacy berated Muslim rulers for not allowing Christian missionaries to proselytize in their domains, despite the fact that Pope Innocent did not consider that this obligation should be reciprocal.[16] Thus the Catholic missionaries, and indeed the various popes, scoffed at the native traditions and even the erring ways, in their view, of the Nestorian Christians. It also caused them to warn of divine retaliation while attempting to guide the Mongol khans toward the Catholic Church. To the Westerners, there was one path to take: the Catholic path. There was simply no alternative.

This is not to say that this path was necessarily straight and narrow. Pope Innocent IV did attempt to alleviate some conversion worries for infidels and heretics. In 1245 he issued a papal bull, similar to one issued by Pope Gregory IX in 1235 which granted missionaries special privileges in order to facilitate conversion.[17] The four most important privileges were the right to hear confession anywhere, absolve excommunicates, dispense converts from various kinds of irregularities in ritual and basically to make conversion as easy as possible without straying from the Catholic path. In addition the bull included a list of eighteen different groups of people, including ethnic groups and religious sects, which were targeted for conversion. Predictably, considering the size of the Mongol Empire, most of these groups resided in Mongol controlled lands.

Even with the new privileges the Catholic missionaries failed to gain influence over the Mongols. The narrow view and self-conceived superiority of the Westerners probably had the most deleterious effect on their conversion attempts. The presence of the Nestorian Christians did not help matters as it provided the Mongols with something of a model of Christianity. Despite the number of Mongols who were Nestorian Christians the Mongol khans had little respect for the Nestorians in general.[18] Still, the Nestorians were more open to other cultures and syncretism in general. G. W. Houston wrote that 'it was unlikely that the Nestorian missionaries held these same prejudices [as did the Catholics], as [the Nestorians] freely incorporated the customs of the local religions into their brand of Christianity'.[19]

Anatoly Khazanov had another but related opinion toward the failure of the papacy to convert the Mongols:

> It seems to me that one of the main reasons for their failure was connected with their claims on the supremacy over temporal and ecclesiastical authorities of the converts. The nomadic rulers were afraid that the conversion to Christianity would put their independence in danger.[20]

Both scholars are correct, at least in part. The Nestorians did have an advantage over the Catholics as their brand of Christianity was more syncretic and able to adapt to various cultures as Houston suggests. Furthermore, the Nestorians did not hold any temporal or spiritual authority over the Mongols as Khazanov correctly observes did the papacy over Catholic Europe. On the other hand, I must disagree with Khazanov that the Mongols were afraid they would lose their independence by converting to Catholicism. There is plenty of evidence suggesting that the Mongols would not tolerate any threat to their power, whether from a secular source or a religious figure. Chinggis Khan executed Teb Tengri, a powerful shaman, after his attempts to seize more political power.[21] The Mongols ended the Abbasid Caliphate, as the caliph was a figure who could, at least in theory, claim spiritual and temporal authority. Considering the papacy's efforts to place itself above temporal rulers, it is not unlikely the pope would have met the same fate as the caliph if the Mongols had reached Rome. Events, however, occurred that persuaded the papacy that the Mongols could be converted.

CHRISTIANITY

One can understand why so many Christian missionaries thought the Mongol Empire was ripe for conversion. Mongolia, although off major routes of exchange in most eras, was not isolated from other religions even before the Mongol Empire. Around 1009 contact through missionaries and merchants had gradually converted the Kereits of central Mongolia to Nestorian Christianity. In that year the Nestorian patriarch in Baghdad received a letter from Ebedyeshu, the metropolitan of Merv, announcing that the Kereits wanted priests and deacons who could baptize them. Exact numbers are uncertain, but it was thought that 20,000 Kereits converted. Many Naiman, Merkits and Önggüt also converted, although Christianity co-existed with shamanic practices.

As a result, after the incorporation of the Kereit, Merkit, Önggüt and Naiman tribes into the Khamag Monggol Ulus, Nestorian Christianity was widespread but not dominant among the Mongols. Nonetheless the vast majority of the Mongols maintained their native beliefs.[22] Though the Nestorians were not a majority they had a significant impact on the Mongols, particularly as many of the wives of the Mongol elite were from the Kereit and Naiman, in addition to a few high-ranking officials in the administrative apparatus. Indeed, Ögödei Khan's (r. 1229–40/41) primary minister, Chinqai (d. 1252) was a Nestorian Christian. In addition, Sorqoqtani (d. 1252), a Kereit princess as well as the wife of Tolui; Töregene (d. 1246), a Merkit and the wife of Ögödei; Oghul Qaimish (d. 1252), a Merkit and wife of Güyük Khan (d. 1248) were also Nestorian Christians. Over time the papacy viewed the Christian wives of the khans as a route to the conversion of the khan. The success of the missionaries in this route, however, proved minimal.[23] Nonetheless, a Nestorian Christian influence existed in the upper circles of the empire.[24]

After the dissolution of the Mongol Empire a new relationship began between the Mongols and Western Europe, with alliance in mind. During this phase, however, the Mongols primarily initiated contact and the papacy became more wary of accepting the Mongols's overtures as optimism for converting the Mongols waned. To be fair, the papacy did attempt new methods in converting the Mongols. Still there were stumbling blocks of a religious nature. When the Mongols offered a marriage alliance with Bela IV of Hungary, Pope Alexander IV vigorously instructed him to decline. Alexander admitted that the Mongol military machine was truly an intimidating factor to face, but he correctly realized that such an alliance would eventually lead Hungary into Mongol servitude. Two reasons supported Alexander's rationale. The primary reason was that the Mongols were not Christians and therefore, from the papacy's perspective, could not be trusted. As the Mongols were not baptized, why would they respect an oath sworn on a Christian relic? This was the normal method of cementing an alliance. The second reason, and the more accurate, was that a marriage alliance could make Hungary a vassal of the Mongols and not an equal ally.[25] As discussed earlier, this was a standard procedure for the Mongols. The daughters of the khans served as de facto rulers or enforcers on behalf of their fathers.

Nevertheless these issues did not deter the papacy's hopes of converting the ruling elite, preferably the khan, believing the masses would follow. Although the previous history of relations with the Mongols suggested conversion would not happen, the papacy clung to this dream because of the number of Christians in the upper ranks. It was not unfounded, as much of the optimism for the conversion of the Mongols was directed at the split of the Mongol Empire. The Ilkhan-ate initiated negotiations with Rome, primarily because they sought allies against an encirclement of hostile states. In 1274 envoys of the Ilkhan Abaqa took the first step in removing one of the major stumbling blocks in making an alliance: they received baptism. Therefore they were no longer infidels and could negotiate on behalf of Abaqa.[26]

Not satisfied with this initial step the papacy continued to place conversion of the Mongols over the existence of the Latin kingdom in the Near East. As with their relations with the Greeks, they extended the promise of a military alliance in return for conversion. James Muldoon demonstrated that this arrangement had a severe flaw, writing 'As the papacy became less able to provide military aid for the Greeks and others who sought it, popes seem to have become more insistent on submission to the papacy before making promise of aid they could not provide.'[27]

With the papacy unable to fulfil their part of the bargain, such as providing an offensive against the Mamluks of Egypt, the Mongols had little reason to convert. The papacy faced other problems in the conversion efforts. Even when the Mongols seemed to be genuinely interested in Christianity there was a dearth of Christian missionaries to go to the Mongol lands – the most famous example of this being the experience of the Polo family. When the Polos returned from the court of Khubi-lai Khan in 1269 they carried a message from the Great Khan for the pope. Khubilai asked him to send one hundred educated men to teach him about Christianity. The pope was only able to send two friars who turned back once they reached Mongol lands.[28] One cannot truly blame the missionaries. With the abundance of stories and rumours spread about the Mongols being the children of Gog and Magog, coming from Hell, and any number of tales about their behaviour, the idea of travelling and remaining in Mongol lands for years must have been a terrifying experience for any prospective volunteers.

Thus the popes were often restricted to conversion via correspondence with the Ilkhans by sending letters explaining the Christian doctrine to the ruler. In 1291 Pope Nicholas sent one to Tegüder or, as known by his baptismal name, Nicholas, son of the Ilkhan Hülegü.[29] In this missive Pope Nicholas warned him that when converting others to Christianity he should not make significant changes in lifestyle. Pope Nicholas specifically warned against changes in dress as this would be a very obvious change and cause for dissension between converts and others. Pope Nicholas, unlike his predecessors, realized that it was important for the convert to be both Mongol and Christian, and not just Christian.[30] Unfortunately for the Christians, this realization came too late.

ISLAM

Although Christianity failed to make inroads in converting the Mongols, another religion did: Islam. Initially, however, Islam did not have any more success at proselytizing than Catholicism. While the Muslims of Khotan viewed the Mongols as liberators from Muslim oppression when the Mongols invaded the Khwarazmian Empire, most of the Muslim world (as well as Christian) viewed them as a punishment from God for their sins. Indeed the Mongols were a calamity that wrought a crisis of faith for many Muslims. Dar al-Islam, which had expanded since the establishment of the 'umma or Islamic community in Medina by the Prophet Muhammad in 632, suddenly began to contract before the onslaught of a pagan army. Some Sufi groups, however, saw the Mongol invasion as God's justice – punishing those unjust rulers who had persecuted the 'Friends of God', or the Sufis.[31]

Until the dissolution of the empire, however, few Mongols converted to Islam. The first known Muslim Mongol, and the most important prior to the death of Möngke, was Berke b. Jochi. All of the Muslim sources agree on Berke's faith, and non-Muslim sources support this idea if they do not directly state his religion. The true issue is that it is not certain at what point he became a Muslim as the sources indicate that he was one since childhood or openly professed his belief when he became the ruler of the Jochid state.[32] Regardless of the moment he professed Islam, all sources agree that his conversion of Islam came through the efforts of a Sufi from the Kubrawiyya order, Shaykh Sayf al-Din Bakharzi.[33]

Persian miniature of Chinggis Khan speaking at the Friday Mosque in Bukhara. Upon capturing Bukhara in 1220, he informed the citizens of the city that he had invaded as a punishment for their sins because he was the Scourge of God.

Gradually others converted to Islam following Berke's example with Berke's brothers, Toqa-Temur and Berkecher, as well as Berke's wife Chichek Khatun among the first. Non-Chinggisids also converted. Although exact numbers are not known, a respectable portion of the aristocracy and military allegedly converted to Islam.[34] Nonetheless, after Berke's enthronement in 1257 the Jochid Khanate did not suddenly become a Muslim state overnight. Although Berke's successor Töde-Möngke was also a Muslim, thus indicating some continuation of the religion at the highest levels, it must be kept in mind that most of the evidence supporting the growth of Islam in the Jochid territories is found in Mamluk sources. With its own precarious legitimacy, the Mamluk Sultanate may have very well exaggerated the spread of Islam in order to rationalize an alliance and diplomatic relations with an infidel state. Professor Devin DeWeese noted that many of the claims of conversion to Islam appear to be more a tool to gain concessions and advantages from other parties, both in the Jochid Khanate and outside, usually the Mamluk Sultanate.[35] Indeed, the fact that Töde-Möngke did not adopt an Arabic name suggests that although interest in Islam grew it was still not universally accepted by all of the 'core base' of the ruler's supporters – that is to say, the nomadic population. The fact that Töde-Möngke and Berke did not change their names or add an Islamic element indicates that Islam remained very much a secondary aspect of their identity.

Thus while Islam made some progress it is difficult to gauge its importance beyond the upper levels of Mongol society in the Jochid Khanate. Certainly Islam had been at least familiar to the Mongols since the days of Chinggis Khan as he dealt with Muslim merchants from his early reign. Nonetheless between 1206 and 1260 there was little impetus for the Mongols to consider Islam as a viable religion. Under the reign of the Möngke a new offensive began in the Middle East. The Mongols had no true interest in the destruction of Islam, particularly when one considers their own practice of religious tolerance. Still, two Islamic powers existed that defied Mongol sensibilities by not recognizing their rule – the Shi'a Nizari Ismaili' sect in Iran and the Abbasid Caliphate. With the destruction of these two powers there was little reason for the Mongols to convert when Heaven was clearly on their side. Furthermore, if Islam had become widespread in the Jochid Khanate or anywhere else in the Mongol Empire, later conversions by Mongol rulers would have carried less importance.

After the dissolution of the empire Islam steadily gained influence beyond the Jochid Khanate. In 1295 the Ilkhanid Baydu publicly converted to Islam, although he never prayed or fasted publicly. His proclamation may have simply been to gain the support of Mongols and Turkic leaders who were Muslim or had Islamic inclinations. Baydu, nevertheless, marked a shift in Ilkhanid religious policy. The Ilkhan Ghazan made Islam the state religion. Again, this may have been because the rank and file had already converted to Islam.[36] Even if Ghazan's conversion was sincere, which it appears to have been, and making the religion the state religion simply reflected the facts on the ground, it remained a radical shift in state policy.

Due to the policy of religious tolerance some Ilkhanid religious groups, primarily Christians, believed the Ilkhans favoured them, perhaps simply because they were not being persecuted. Yet with the Ghazan's reign Islam clearly became the favoured religion. Buddhist temples, some built during the reign of Hülegü (1260–5) were destroyed or transformed into mosques. Nestorians experienced persecutions, although other Christians such as Armenians appeared to have suffered less, perhaps due to being a majority in their own regions. Yet in many ways this should not be unexpected. The most ardent defenders of the faith and oppressors tend to be the recently converted, perhaps revealing a deep-seated motive to prove their sincerity of belief.

During Ghazan's reign Sunni and popular Sufi variants of Islam became the religious preference, with the exception of a brief period when Öljeitü Khan (r. 1304–16) ruled. He never met a religion he did not like: he was, at various points, Christian, Buddhist, an adherent of several Sunni forms of Islam, and finally a Shi'a Muslim. As the latter he persecuted Sunnis. His successor Abu Said (r. 1316–35) returned the official preference to Sunni Islam. While the conversion to Islam meant the end of widespread religious toleration in the traditional Mongol style, other believers were still treated as *dhimmah* and could continue to practise their faith; it also meant that the Mongols assumed the role of patron of the arts, particularly in the Persian vein. Furthermore, Islam became more widespread throughout Iran as many Buddhists departed and other religions became clearly inferior in terms of social and legal status.

Despite having the first Muslim ruler among the Mongol states the Jochid Khanate was the second to become a definable Islamic state. Islam did not become the dominant religion until the conversion of Üzbek Khan in 1313. While it appears that an ever increasing portion of the nomadic population viewed themselves as Muslim, many of the elites rejected the use of the shari'a, which Üzbek attempted to impose over Chinggis Khan's *yasa* (law) with the establishment of Islam as the state religion.[37] Although Üzbek quelled the rebellion, primarily as he had the support of the rank and file, it nonetheless demonstrated that not all supported the idea of abandoning traditional beliefs.

Finding balance between the *yasa* and shari'a was a challenge for all rulers and also demonstrated the limits of religious toleration. A core issue could revolve around a meal. Traditional Mongol custom was to slaughter an animal by making an incision in its chest to squeeze or rip the heart or aorta, killing the animal by internal haemorrhage and attempting to keep the blood within the animal. This was so as not to waste the blood which could be used for sausages and other food. It may also have to do with the Mongolian custom to prevent blood from going into the ground as it traps the soul according

A Mongol prince studying the Quran, illustration from Rashid al-Din's *Jami' al-Tawarikh*. This image reflects the conversion of many Mongols to Islam in the Ilkhanate as well as the Jochid Khanate.

to shamanic belief. The kosher or *halal* method practised by Jews and Muslims, however, consists of cutting the jugular vein on the neck so the blood drains out while blessing both the meat and the process. Obviously the two methods cannot be reconciled or combined. At various times and throughout the Mongol Empire the *halal* method was banned, often leading to a wave of persecution against Muslims, perhaps instigated by Chinese or others jealous of increasing Muslim influence in government positions or in trade.[38] The incidents may also reflect the Mongols' own struggles to accommodate other legal systems into their own governing structures. At the same time this conflict gave ammunition to outsiders who would never accept the Mongols' conversion as they constantly veered from accepted Muslim practice. The most virulent attacker was Ibn Taymiyya who ceaselessly damned the Mongols and called for resistance to them. Furthermore, as they were not Muslims in his view, he argued they should be killed as well as any who dealt with them.[39] Part of the issue revolved around who converted the Mongols. Sufis, with their syncretic practices, were not Muslims in the eyes of Ibn Taymiyya and his ilk, therefore the Mongols could not be either. Although the Mamluks silenced Ibn Taymiyya on occasion his ideas did gain an audience, including among extremists today.[40]

In central Asia conversion to Islam came late. Although the region of Mawarannahr had been predominately Muslim for centuries, other parts of the Chaghatayid Khanate adhered to their traditional beliefs – both shamanistic and Buddhist. Indeed, it is somewhat difficult to say if the Chaghatayid Khanate ever became a Muslim entity. Certainly by the fourteenth century Mawarannahr had, but it is not clear that the rest did. Usually Tarmashirin's conversion is marked as the turning point but even as late as 1339 Yisün-Temür Khan protected Buddhist monasteries.[41] Nonetheless, Tarmashirin's conversion from Buddhism may have been an effort to bolster his support among Muslim merchants and connect central Asia to other lucrative markets. However, as illustrated above, the complete conversion of the region did not happen. Indeed, the Mongol elite ultimately killed Tarmashirin for trying to replace *yasa* with shari'a. His successors even converted mosques into Buddhist temples. Although the western portion of the realm (Mawarannahr) had extensive contact with the Islamic Jochid and Ilkhanid states, the eastern portion had more contact with the Buddhist world of the Yuan Empire. Indeed, despite the long-standing Islamic contact in Mawarannahr, one might only consider it fully Islamic with the advent of the Timurid age. Johan Elverskog makes a convincing proposal that the Chaghatayid never fully converted to Islam due to their geographical position. He notes that the rural versus urban sectors of the khanate played a role. Islam in central asia tended to be an urban phenomenon.[42] Certainly Sufis did venture into the steppe but where Islam was most successful was in the cities where the mosque and madrasa system along with displays of public piety had the most impact.

In addition to conversions among the Mongolian and Turkic nomadic populations, the Mongol conquests also led to changes in Islam for the Muslim world. One of the most notable changes was that the centre of religious authority, as with culture, moved from Baghdad to new locations. With the fall of Baghdad in 1258 refugee scholars, *fuqaha* (singular *faqih*, jurist) and other members of the *ulama*, or learned elite, fled elsewhere – primarily to Cairo. This was but the final wave of mass refugees since the Mongols entered Dar al-Islam in 1219. As a result Cairo and Delhi became the new cultural and religious centres of the Muslim world. Mecca and Medina remained the centres of pilgrimage for the pious, but Cairo, Damascus and Delhi – all just outside the Mongol Empire – became the centres for religious educa- tion and destinations for all scholars. The first two cities lay within the Mamluk Sultanate while Delhi was the capital of an eponymous sultanate. Both bolstered their legitimacy by keeping the Mongols at bay, thus becoming defenders of the faith, but also by serving as patrons for the religious elite by building mosques and madrasas. As a result Cairo and Delhi moved beyond being political centres to become religious, cultural and educational centres of the western and eastern portions of the Islamic world. Indeed, the arrival of so many learned figures, belle-lettrists and religious authorities transformed Delhi from a military camp into a sophisticated cosmopolitan city and a leading centre of knowledge. Meanwhile, Baghdad was, as Ross Dunn so aptly wrote, 'reduced to the status of a provincial market town'.[43] Indeed, Dunn attributes Cairo's massive population partly to the refugees from Mongol conquered territory.[44] Other factors included it being the capital of the Mamluk Sultanate as well as a nexus of trade between the Mediterranean and Red seas. Cairo's position as a centre of religion was cemented with the Mongol sack of Damascus during the Ilkhanid invasion of Syria in 1299–1300 during the reign of Ghazan Khan.

Thus, even as the Mongols converted to Islam and became a part of Dar al-Islam, they remained somewhat outside it, at least from the Sunni perspective. Oddly, with the reign of Öljeitü in the Ilkhanate, Shi'a Muslims began to accept the Mongols as legitimate rulers due to Öljeitü's own affiliation with Shi'ism. Outside the Mongol Empire, however, many refused to accept the Mongol conversion, regardless of whether it was Shi'a or Sunni. The final Mongol experience with Islam was quite a change of circumstance compared with their first appear- ance on the scene in Dar al-Islam. Instead of being the end of Islam the Mongols actually expanded its reach and forms.

BUDDHISM

Despite initial encounters with Buddhism in Xi Xia and Tibet the Mongols never had any true inclination towards Buddhism until the time of Khubilai Khan. Certainly individual Mongols may have been interested in it, but it was just another religion to them. Nonetheless, Buddhist temples representing a Tangut Buddhist sect as well as other sects existed in Karakorum. High-ranking lamas from Tibetan sects as well as Chinese Chan Buddhists travelled to meet Chinggis Khan as did many other religious leaders.[45] In one instance the meeting resulted in the Chan Buddhist monk Haiyun being given authority over all Buddhists in China, later confirmed by both Güyük and Möngke. Ögödei also granted the Buddhists (and Daoists) tax exempt status in 1229 which, as Klaus Sagaster wrote, 'was a measure of political importance, since in the last years of the Jin dynasty, Buddhists had largely suffered prejudice to the advantage of the Confucians'.[46]

Tibetan Buddhism did not gain influence until the 1240s, although the Mongols surely encountered it through adherents of Tibetan sects in Xi Xia. The increase in contact came about with Köten's (r. 1206–51), a son of Ögödei, conquest of Tibet, which included the destruction of a few monasteries and death of hundreds of monks. During the course of the conquests his general Doorda encountered the representatives of a number of sects and suggested that Köten invite one of the leaders to his camp. Köten decided upon the leader or *pandita* of the Sa-skya sect, Kun-dga'-rgyal-mtshan (1182–1251).[47] While the encounter may have had some religious undertones, Köten's true purpose was political. As the leaders of the various Buddhist sects of Tibet wielded tremendous secular authority as well as religious, bringing the Sa-skya Pandita under Mongol influence extended Mongol control in Tibet. This is not to say that Kun-dga'-rgyal-mtshan was an unwitting pawn. He used his opportunity at Köten's court to proselytize as well as to use his medical skills, which proved to be another avenue for Buddhist contact with the Mongols. Furthermore, his association with Köten allowed the Sa-skya to remain the dominant group in Tibet; during the reign of Möngke the Sa-skya Pandita was given authority over all Buddhist sects in Tibet.[48]

In the western portion of the empire Buddhism expanded into Iran. It had existed in eastern Iran centuries prior but had more or less vanished. It also continued in the steppe through the Kara Khitai Empire, which the Mongols annexed in 1218. Yet just before Mongol expansion Buddhism dwindled in northern India and Afghanistan with the campaigns of the Ghaznavids and then the Ghurids, resulting in an exodus of Buddhist scholars to Tibet. With Tibet as the central nexus of an increasingly popular tantric Buddhism and the security brought by the Pax Mongolica, it is not surprising that it spread beyond the 'tantric' bloc of Tibet, Kara Khitai and the Gansu corridor. The fact that the Persian chronicles are rife with tales of Buddhists oppressing Muslims indicates a widespread Buddhist presence.[49] Most, if not all, of these tales appear to be exaggerations, nonetheless they do reflect an increase of Buddhist presence if not among the Mongols themselves, then in the court and throughout the empire. One must also consider that the Mongols's practice of moving populations may have caused some of these issues. The sudden intermingling of alien faiths certainly caused tension. It also reflected a 'jockeying between religious traditions and in many cases these feuds became intertwined with the internal political struggles of the empire'.[50] The importance of the Uighurs within the empire undoubtedly gave rise to some of these fears. The Uighurs of the Tarim Basin, who dabbled with Nestorian Christianity as well as Manichaeism, eventually settled on Buddhism. With their submission to Chinggis Khan in 1209, being in the pleasant situation of having one foot in the sedentary world and another in the steppe, they became crucial members of the early Mongol bureaucracy.[51] As with other religions, the Mongols sponsored the building of Buddhist temples and monuments. Naturally the Uighurs' importance also transformed them into a locus for other Buddhists seeking to gain Mongol influence. The population of Besh-Baliq, the Uighur capital, increased to 50,000 people.[52]

While the faithful of any religion may have worried about converting the khan, all of the khans appear to have been content walking a middle path between all religions. In the Ilkhanate, Hülegü sponsored three Buddhist temples even as he funded the observatory of Nasir al-Din Tusi, the brilliant Shi'a scientist. His successors continued the practice with some additions, such as Gaikhatu incorporating Buddhist ceremonies in their court rituals. Most curiously, Ghazan Khan who, more than anyone else, transformed the Ilkhanate into an Islamic state, was raised a Buddhist by his father Arghun. Even after Ghazan converted, Buddhism survived. His successor Öljeitü (a good Buddhist Mongolian name) also converted to Islam, but Buddhists within the Ilkhanate did take a stab at bringing him back to their true faith. As part of the *Jami' al-Tawarikh*, Öljeitü commanded Rashid al-Din to not only include histories of the Mongols but to expand it to a history of the world. This included a sizeable section on Buddhism. Thus a Sunni administrator wrote, with his research team that included Buddhists, a history of Buddhism for a Shi'a Mongol khan.

It is evident that Buddhists found support throughout the empire. Indeed, during the reign of Möngke all of the major Buddhist sects found a Chinggisid patron, usually Toluids.[53] The various patrons supported them financially not only in Tibet but in their respective territories as well. This support extended into non-Toluid regions as well. As noted earlier, in the 1330s Buddhist monasteries were protected in the Chaghatayid Khanate, and as late as 1326 a Buddhist temple was restored. The longevity of Buddhism in the Chaghatayid region is not surprising considering that much of it was formerly part of the Kara Khitai Empire and Uighurstan was next door, and at times part of the Chaghatayid/ Ögödeid realm during the reign of Qaidu. Indeed, although Mawarannahr became almost exclusively Islamic, the eastern portions converted much more slowly, thus Buddhism and shamanistic practices never fully disappeared even after Tughluq Temür Khan (d. 1363) converted to Islam in 1354. Still, his conversion was to Sufism rather into Sunni Islam. Furthermore, his conversion did not end the religious toleration of the region as Buddhists fell into the *dhimmi* category. Buddhism continued to flourish in the region well after his conversion. As discussed above, the rural existence of the eastern khanate and connections with the Yuan assisted in maintaining the Buddhist identity of the region. The Jochid Khanate also had its share of Buddhists. During the reign of Toqtogha Khan (r. 1290–1312), a number of Uighur Buddhists served in the Jochid administration.[54]

In East Asia Buddhism flourished. Khubilai had long harboured an interest in Buddhism and even inquired of Chan Buddhist monk Haiyun whether it was possible for a religion to subdue the world. He inquired about Buddhism, Daoism and Confucianism and naturally Haiyun replied that Buddhism was capable of doing so. Yet Buddhism prospered not only due to court support but also due to the Pax Mongolica. As it had for centuries, the Korean peninsula continued to serve as a conduit for Buddhism, particularly between China and Japan. Monks from Japan came to leading Buddhist temples in the Yuan Empire, demonstrating, as David Robinson notes, contact between Japan and the Mongols did not end with the Mongol invasions of Japan in the late thirteenth century.[55] Indeed the number of monks coming from Japan often reflected less the relations between the Mongols and Japan but rather the internal stability of the Yuan. During the Red Turban rebellions in the waning decades of the Yuan Empire, not only did fewer monks come to the continent but also many who had resided for years returned to Japan to escape the chaos. Ironically, the rebellion that caused Buddhist refugees evolved from a millenarian Buddhist cult known as the White Lotus.

Although Khubilai Khan patronised Haiyun, the leader of the Chan Buddhists, it was under Khubilai that Tantric Buddhism became particularly popular in the Yuan Empire. Although Khubilai Khan had continued to practise religious toleration he had a definite predilection for Buddhism and it sometimes it got the better of him. The religious debates he so enjoyed gained a much more combative edge compared to those during the reign of Möngke. In a debate between Buddhists and Daoists the losing side (the Daoists) had their heads shaved and were urged to convert to Buddhism, although his mother Sorqoqtani apparently chastised him on how this veered from tradition and forced him to relent.[56] Buddhist officials also gained increased patronage. Indeed, the 'Phags-pa Lama became one of Khubilai's most trusted advisors and introduced the eponymous script that became the official alphabet of the Yuan Empire, even if it virtually disappeared after the Yuan collapse.

Their association began during Möngke's reign. During his campaign against Da-Li in 1251 Khubilai entered Liangzhou, where the Sa-skya Pandita resided. Wishing to converse with the esteemed lama, Khubilai invited the Sa-skya Pandita to join him. Illness prevented them from meeting but instead the Sa-skya Pandita sent his nephew 'Phags-pa to Khubilai. The young man impressed him and they met again in 1253 when Khubilai returned from Da-Li. By this time Sa-skya Pandita had died and 'Phags-pa had succeeded him. At this time Khubilai became a devotee of his teachings.[57] At the same time the 'Phags-pa Lama's relation with Khubilai Khan became more complex; religion intertwined with politics. By remaining at the Khubilai's court the 'Phags-pa Lama served as a hostage. His status in the Tibetan Buddhist world ensured the good behaviour of the powerful lamas and elites in Tibet as well as ensuring that doctrine was in line with the Mongol concerns. Khubilai Khan also used the 'Phags-pa Lama to further Mongol authority over all Buddhist sects by declaring him Grand Preceptor of Buddhism – essentially transforming him into the highest Buddhist authority not only in Tibet but the entire empire.[58] In 1270 the monk received the title of Imperial Teacher, which became a position that lasted for the duration of the Yuan Empire. Furthermore, he was appointed as the minister for the Office of Buddhist Affairs in 1288. The 'Phags-pa Lama cannot be viewed as simply a pawn as it also increased the status of his own sect as well as his authority. At the same time it was not without risks as most of the Buddhists in China were Chan Buddhists (from which Zen Buddhism is derived), favoured under Möngke Khan. Nonetheless, as a Buddhist Khubilai had some inclination to unify the various Buddhist sects – not only to bring harmony to the religion but also to strengthen his control over the Buddhist population.

As with many efforts to forcibly unify disparate elements, it resulted in conflict. Chan Buddhists were removed from positions within the empire in favour of Sa-skya Buddhists. Holding a variety of positions also meant a variety of duties, which necessitated a very large budget along with privileges. This irked not only the Chan Buddhists but Confucian administrators, who felt slighted along with Daoists, who were at times persecuted. The fact that the Buddhist monks also took advantage of the privileges given to them did not ameliorate the growing tensions within the empire. Not all of the favoured monks were from the Sa-skya sect but by and large they came from Tibetan sects which gave the hostility a precise focus. Despite the unintended consequences Khubilai's actions helped spread Buddhism among the Mongols. Several works were translated into Mongolian and also into Chinese, with some entering Chan Buddhism as important texts, such as 'The Explanation of What Should be Known' (*Shes-bya-rab-gsal*).[59]

Khubilai also met with other Tibetan Buddhists such as the Karma Paksi, Chos-kyi-Bla-ma (1204–1283), the hierarch of the Karma bKa'-brgyud-pa sect. Meeting in 1255, their encounter was not as favourable as Khubilai's discussions with 'Phags-pa. One might suspect that as a devotee of 'Phags-pa Khubilai's adherence to a rival doctrine had something to do with it. Nonetheless, Karma Paksi did have favourable relations with Möngke. Khubilai and Karma Paksi's animosity did not end, however. After Möngke's death Karma Paksi supported Ariq Böke over Khubilai. Again, one cannot help but wonder if religious rivalry was the root of their animosity.[60] Unlike in Europe where the authority of the pope often conflicted with that of monarchs, Khubilai was the supreme ruler and it was good to be king. The Karma Paksi escaped execution in 1264 but was left more or less confined to his monastery in Tibet. His successors, however, did interact with the Karma sect as well as others.

After Khubilai Buddhist favouritism continued with a particular interest in Tantric Buddhism from Tibet. Chinese sources tied it to the weakening of the Yuan Empire, particularly the Mongols' indulgence in Tantric sexual practices. The sources claimed it sapped their vigour and diverted their attention from the matters of state. While some of the accusations have merit, the extent is questionable and some appears to be sour grapes from supporters of Chinese Buddhism, Confucianism and Daoism. The fact that the Mongols selected a foreign religion over a Chinese one, in the minds of the Han population, clearly indicated faulty thinking. Nonetheless, it had very little to do with the decline of the Mongols, although the financial resources committed to Buddhist activities definitely played a role. Indeed, although with the decline of the Yuan Buddhism faltered among the Mongols, it regained importance in the 1500s.

It is wrong to suggest that Buddhism vanished in the northern Yuan state. Monasteries in Mongolia were built and also refurbished. The lack of financial resources that the northern Yuan provided did limit some activities, nonetheless Sa-skya, Karma and other sects still proselytized amongst the Mongols. Still, it had to compete with shamanism and monasteries were often targets of plunder not only during the wars with the Ming Empire but also during the civil wars between Mongol princes.

As the various Chinggisids fought to gain supremacy in the steppe, as well as contemplating restoration of Mongol rule in China, Buddhism re-emerged. As suggested above, it is difficult to say that it ever completely disappeared, although with the Yuan retreat from China the monasteries of Tibet did not have easy access to Mongolia, isolating it somewhat.[61] Nonetheless, with the resurgent Mongols Buddhism gained new impetus. On one hand the Ming Empire promoted Buddhist proselytization among the Mongols with the faulty belief that it would quell their warlike nature – a Pollyanna-ish approach to reducing Mongol frontier raids. Rather than having peaceful Mongols to the north they found Mongols plundering the frontier and giving part of the booty as tithes to their new faith, once again proving politics and religion rarely mix well. Of greater importance, however, was the establishment of relations between a Chinggisid prince named Altan and the dGe-lugs-pa sect of Tibet. Although his wife converted to Buddhism, Altan remained somewhat non-committal in his religious dealings. Nonetheless, after Altan's success against Ming armies, many (both Tibetan and Chinese) Buddhists viewed him as a potential saviour against Confucian persecution of Buddhists, despite his lack of commitment. Although a number of priests came to his capital of Köke-khot (modern Hohhot or the Blue City), the most significant was Sonam Gyatso, the head of the dGe-lugs-pa or Yellow sect. It was revealed that Altan was the reincarnation of Khubilai Khan and thus the khan of all Mongols. Altan, in turn, awarded

Tsam dance. Altan Khan's conversion to Buddhism spearheaded a vigorous process of converting the 16th-century Mongols to the Yellow Sect (named after the colour of their robes and hats) of Tibetan Buddhism. Despite considerable oppression, traditional beliefs did not end as evinced in the Tsam dance, which incorporated many pre-Buddhist figures such as the White Old Man (far right), a powerful earth spirit.

Sonam Gyatso the title of Dalai Lama, or Oceanic Priest, noting his piety and wisdom. Although Altan Khan remained unconverted, he promoted and protected Buddhists. His conversion came, however, after a dGe-lugs-pa monk cured his gout, after the traditional remedy of sticking the ailing foot in the opened chest of a slave or horse failed. With this change in religion and healthcare reform, Altan became an ardent promoter of Buddhism, and Tibetan Buddhism became the primary religion of the Mongols.

Conclusion

A fair question to ask is why the Mongols did not convert to a world religion until after the dissolution of the empire. And then, why Buddhism and Islam? Part of the answer may be found in how the Mongols viewed themselves. It is clear they believed that Heaven, or *Möngke Köke Tengri*, had decreed that Chinggis Khan and his sons were to rule the earth. As stated earlier, this belief has been coined as Tenggerism.[62] A component of Tenggerism also included the idea that just as there was only one god or heaven, there could only be one khan on earth.

At first the Mongols' primary foes were nomads who were of similar culture and usually practiced the same shamanistic beliefs as they did. Although the Naiman and the Kereits had Nestorian Christians, it is uncertain just how deep their Christian beliefs ran. It appears that it was more of a syncretic form, including aspects of traditional steppe beliefs. As the empire expanded the Mongols encountered civilizations that had more sophisticated religious practices, which focused more on the concerns of the afterlife than on the mundane. Coming from an environment in which the afterworld and the present world were very similar it is quite possible that the Mongols saw very little use in adopting something that placed an emphasis on the afterworld. After all, if one were a khan in the present world, one would still be a khan in afterworld.

Moreover, from Chinggis Khan's perspective, what protection did these religions provide to their believers? He had defeated the Nestorian Christians, Ong-Qan, Khan of the Kereit and the various khans of the Naiman. He had unified the tribes of Mongolia as was prophesized by Qorci.[63] As the Mongols conquered more nations, this only validated Heaven's decree that the Mongols would rule the earth. Furthermore, the Mongols had witnessed how religion could be an instrument of division. The Muslims of Khotan welcomed them, preferring an unknown ruler to the Buddhists who persecuted them. What incentive was there to convert to any of these religions of the conquered people? Naturally the Mongols did not wish to offend any religion, so they did not persecute it.

Through the course of time many observers believed the Mongols gradually turned to monotheism. In part this may have been due to their references to *Mönkge Köke Tengri*, and how they worded their messages to foreign powers.[64] However, with the idea of Tenggerism evolving into a more complex form of religion in the mid-thirteenth century, as suggested by Sh. Bira, it truly became a form of monotheism.[65] Indeed, Bira asserts that Mongolian Tenggerism was the driving force behind the Mongol conquests.[66] One must be wary of such an assertion, however. While indeed the Mongols did believe it was their manifest destiny to rule the world as decreed by *Tenggeri*, whether it was because of a religious zeal from Tenggerism or simply that it explained their unparalleled success is another question and research puzzle altogether. Still, it is questionable if non-Mongols understood Tenggerism in the same context. Khazanov wrote that the Mongols' 'trend towards monotheism could reflect not so much their own religion's evolution but a desire of their observers, who professed different monotheistic religions'.[67]

In conclusion, there are several reasons why the Mongols were able to resist conversion to a world religion until the breakup of the Mongol Empire. The first was that they believed they were ordained by the heavens to conquer the world. The concept of Tenggerism is a powerful one. In this context the Christians' God, the Muslims' Allah and all other concepts of heaven or a divine spirit could be neatly incorporated into Tenggeri. The interpretation of how one addressed Heaven was of little consequence, as suggested by Möngke Khan when he said, 'But just as God gave different fingers to the hand so has He given different ways to men.'[68] Thus why would one convert when they all worship the same god? The various theological debates that took place before the khan must have been amusing and puzzling to the Mongols as the participants philosophized and debated.

This leads to the second point. Since they worshipped the same god, there was no reason to persecute someone on religious grounds. Thus it was natural that the Mongols were amazingly tolerant of all religions during a time when religious tolerance was rare. This tolerance extended to any religion, as long as it did not threaten their authority by making political claims that threatened Mongol power.

Third, in the case of Islam and Christianity there was simply no reason to convert; the Mongol armies destroyed all that opposed them. These religions did not appear to offer any strategic gain. Of course the Mongols did not persecute these religions but there was no convincing argument to entice conversion to their interpretation of worshipping the one god.[69]

Finally, another reason for Christianity's failure to convert the Mongols was a cultural issue, which may have extended to Islam as well – perceived prohibition of alcohol. In the case of Islam this might have been more apparent but of course the definition of what alcoholic drinks were prohibited also varies with schools of law and variations of Sufism. In Christianity no prohibition existed, however a perception of one did. William of Rubruck encountered this on his journey to the court of Möngke Khan. While at the *orda,* or camp, of a Mongol commander named Scatatai, located somewhere in the Pontic Steppe, William encountered a Muslim who wished to convert to Christianity, presumably a Turk. This individual, however, feared he could not do so as if he did he would then not be able to drink *kumiss,* or fermented mare's milk, which comprises much of the nomads' diet, particularly in summer.[70] William, who grew quite fond of *kumiss*, tried to convince him otherwise, but to no avail. Indeed, William met several Christians there who professed the same sentiment including Greeks, Rus' and Alans. Not only could Christians not drink *kumiss* but if they did they were no longer Christians and 'their priests reconcile them as if they had denied the faith of Christ'.[71]

While it is not certain if the Mongols had heard this, many Christians in their empire viewed *kumiss* as not being kosher, so to speak. This too needs to be viewed through the lens of religion. As the Mongols were infidels, then for these Eastern Christians their favoured drink must certainly be ungodly. And without doubt a priest would point out the fact that *kumiss* was not to be found in the Bible. For Catholics, such as Friar William who enjoyed *kumiss* or even John of Plano Carpini, who did not care for it, since they previously did not have regular contact with the steppe cultures, it was simply a novelty.[72] Nevertheless, as the Mongols had more contact with these Orthodox Christians, if the Mongols had converted to Orthodox Christianity they would have had to abstain from *kumiss*, a vital part of their culture and, in a sense, lose their 'Mongolness'.

Only after the unity of the Mongols dwindled did religion begin to play a factor as each khan sought an advantage over his opponents. One may also return to the topic of Tenggerism and wonder, if Tenggerism gave rise to the notion of a divine right to rule the world did the dissolution of the empire undermine the core beliefs? With the offspring of Chinggis Khan fighting each other rather than conquering the world, one may question if the princes and the common nomads still believed in Tenggerism as a religion. With a crisis of faith many may have sought solace in another religion. While some conversions may have been sincere, most initial ones were strategic political conversions rather than borne of devotion. Eventually this plan backfired. The conversion to world religions made the Mongols too similar to most of their conquered subjects, thus the rulers became much like the ruled and assimilation followed in much of the former Mongol Empire.

Yet even as the Mongols converted to Islam and Buddhism, in many areas persecution of religious minorities was fairly rare. In the cities of the Jochid Ulus such as al-Qarim, Kaffa, Sudak and Tana one would find Christian churches and Muslim mosques without any sense of oppression from the government. The local inhabitants, however, may have felt otherwise, yet the Mongol khans still tended to favour a pragmatism that favoured their interests. In the trading ports of the Black Sea the

Mongols had little interest in alienating the Italians who carried goods to the rest of the Western world. The Italians, in turn, saw little reason to anger the Muslim rulers who allowed them to profit so greatly.

Khazanov wrote that Islam was more successful in gaining adherents because the converts did not have to give up their ethnic affiliation or change their way of life – exactly what Pope Nicholas began to realize.[73] Over time the majority of the Mongol khanates made Islam the state religion, with only the Khanate of the Great Khan (East Asia) accepting Buddhism. As a result Islam spread over a larger geographic region than ever before. This was largely due to the growth of Sufism. Previously Sufism was often persecuted by rulers at the instigation of the *ulama*, or the more conservative religious elites of a region. Sufism, being more syncretic, was often seen as veering dangerously towards heresy. However, during the disruption and chaos of the Mongol invasion and a degree of spiritual crisis in the aftermath, the emotive spirituality of Sufism as found in the Sufi brotherhoods (t riqah) and Sufi-derived popular religion provided more tangible comfort and expression than the staid Sunni practice.[74]

Perhaps the key lesson in examining the Mongol Empire and its relation with religion was that the religious tolerance of the Mongols was born from its situation at a crossroads of religion and the nature of shamanism. With the advent of Tenggerism, the creation of the Yeke Monggol Ulus, the use of Chinggis Khan's *yasa* and the military dominance of the Mongol Empire, a distinct Mongol identity appeared. To adopt another religion often meant, at least from the Mongols' perspective, losing that identity. Thus 'foreign' religions gained few converts. To the Mongols those religions, whether Catholicism, Greek Orthodoxy, Judaism, Sunni or Shi'a Islam and many forms of Buddhism meant not only a change in belief and world view, but also a distinct cultural transition that diminished their 'Mongolness' if not in their own eyes, then in the eyes of other Mongols. Furthermore, when the Mongols converted, it was not because the religion, whether Islam or Buddhism, had similarities to shamanism, but rather the particular form of religion they adopted was syncretic and allowed the incorporation of cultural aspects that otherwise were foreign to religion. In this manner the Mongols did not lose their identity. Instead they became Mongols who happened to be Muslims or Buddhists (or in earlier instances, Christians) rather than a Christian, Muslim or Buddhist whose Mongol identity was subsumed in religious identity. Another possibility or factor was that both Islam and Buddhism supported mercantile activities. Although the Mongols had extensive contact with the Genoese and Venetians, Franciscan missionaries, with their vows of poverty, and the church's rather dismissive attitudes towards merchants, could not have been seen as advantageous to the trade-minded Mongols. Islam, on the other hand, has always been favourable to merchants. Buddhism has also been historically amenable to trade and, indeed, spread largely to merchants and monks travelling with their caravans.

8

THE MONGOLS AND THE PLAGUE

I heard that in the previous year, 1347, an innumerable horde of Tartars laid siege to a very strong city inhabited by Christians. The calamitous disease befell the Tartar army, and the mortality was great and widespread that scarcely one in twenty of them remained alive. After discussing it among themselves, they came to the decision that such a great mortality was caused by the vengeance of God, and they resolved to enter the city which they were besieging and ask to be made Christians. Accordingly the most powerful of the survivors entered the city, but they found few men there for all the others had died. And when they saw that the mortality had broken out among the Christians as well as among themselves, because of the unhealthy air, they decided to keep their own religion.[1]

And thus efforts to convert the Mongols to Christianity were once again thwarted due to bacteria's proclivity towards non-denominational beliefs. Call it bubonic plague, the Black Plague or Black Death, the result was the same – death for most who encountered it.[2] The plague was perhaps the most deadly result of the Mongol Empire and the Chinggis Exchange. Although the Mongols did not cause it directly, it is difficult to imagine how it could have spread so rapidly without the aid of the Mongol Empire; in return, it hastened the end of the empire. Just as ideas, goods and travellers benefited from the Pax Mongolica and the trade routes established and protected by the Mongol Empire, so could disease. The plague probably started in the steppes of central Eurasia – random outbreaks still occur today but, unlike in the fourteenth century, modern medicine can contain and cure it fairly easily.

Why the steppe? It is the most logical place, although some have suggested that it came to Mongolia with Mongols returning from the conquest of the kingdom of Da-Li (modern Yunnan) where they encountered the plague that had originated in the neighbouring Himalayas. Another possible location is the Great Lakes region of central Africa although this is certainly not the origin of the bubonic plague of the fourteenth century.[3] Having the plague originate in the Himalayas seems a bit tenuous; if the Mongols brought it back in the mid-thirteenth century, then where are the body counts that should have accompanied it en route to Mongolia? They do not appear for almost a century. As it devastates northern India after entering from central Asia, it seems unlikely that it originally came from the Himalayas. Furthermore, bubonic plague is a disease of small mammals, such as marmots which live on the Inner Asian steppe; the fleas that live on this ground-burrowing rodent often hold a bacillus, *Yersinia pestis*, that causes bubonic plague – so named as buboes form on the neck, armpits and groin.

If the bacilli entered the lungs it became pneumonic plague and spread through sputum. Whereas the bubonic form is 60 per cent lethal, the pneumonic form offers a 90 per cent likelihood of death. Generally speaking, the disease stays with the fleas and the marmots or other small mammals. Most nomads learned to avoid the sick marmots (identifiable by the buboes should a hunter kill them). Most probably died in their burrows, where the fleas then found a new host among the other marmots. Among humans the disease has an incubation of two to eight days, culminating with a fever of up to 105°F. The patient then suffers from convulsions, vomiting, giddiness, intolerance to light and pain in their limbs. Not surprisingly, the patient is often dazed. Two or three days after the fever begins the skin becomes splotchy and buboes appear around the flea bite and lymph nodes. If left alone the buboes will eventually burst. If the patient does not die of exhaustion, heart failure or internal haemorrhage they recover after eight or ten days of suffering. There is also a chance that it can enter the lungs and become the pneumonic form of plague, thus increasing the likelihood of spreading. One would suspect that for marmots and other small mammals the symptoms are similar although, as with humans, immunity can occur. In such cases plague-bearing marmots exist without the symptoms.

In order for the disease to spread beyond the marmot burrow the bacilli must be transmitted to others animals or humans. *Yersinia pestis* is a non-motile and non-sporing bacteria requiring an assistant of sorts to spread it.[4] The flea, usually *Xenopsylla cheopis*, is that helper.[5] Not all fleas carry the bacteria so when dealing with marmots it is a bit of a gamble. Should the flea carry the bacteria, it builds into a solid mass in the flea's stomach so that when engorging blood, the blood has nowhere to go and causes the flea to vomit into the bloodstream, including some of the *Yersinia pestis*, and infecting the victim. If infected the cute, cuddly and (for our Mongolian hunter) tasty marmot will not survive. So where is a poor flea to go?

While no one is certain how the disease spread, a safe bet is that a Mongol hunter killed a marmot, as marmots were (and still are) a favoured meat and often used as rations for the army. *Yersinia pestis* could have spread either by the hunter eating an infected animal or, more likely, the fleas left the dead marmot and found a new host – the Mongol hunter.[6] It was a logical choice. While more than 300 mammals (most of them small) are susceptible to *Yersinia pestis*, some are not. Indeed, cats, sheep, cows, goats and horses are difficult to infect and, at least in the case of horses, fleas do not care for them.[7] Thus, the flea jumps to the Mongol hunter. While modern (and some medieval) humans tend to be hygiene conscious, the Mongols were not known for their cleanliness.[8] Furthermore the fleas had a better chance of survival on the Mongols than by leaping on their dogs. Except in the summer the weather in the steppe is too cold for much of the year for fleas to survive or their eggs to hatch.[9] In a nice warm *ger* or yurt, however, one could find a safe haven. From a single Mongol the flea and its eggs could eventually spread along the trade routes from the steppes of Mongolia to the Black Sea port of Kaffa, from which the Black Plague spread to the Middle East and Europe.

Kaffa and the Plague

Although the plague came to the Mediterranean world from Kaffa, on the Crimean peninsula, the plague did not originate in that Genoese trading colony. We know the plague came from the east, following the trade routes. Tombstones in a Nestorian Christian graveyard in Issyk Kul (in modern Kyrgyzstan) indicate the plague struck this town along the northern caravan route in 1338–9, although there is no evidence of what *Yersinia pestis* was doing prior to this incident. As marmots live in the region, Issyk Kul could be the starting point for the entire event. The bubonic plague also seems to have been present in the region in the sixth century, again contradicting a Himalayan origin.[10] The plague reached Kaffa in 1346 during a siege by the Jochid Mongols.

Janibek Khan decided to lay siege to the city in 1343/4 in order to settle a trade dispute that began after the murder of a Mongol in the Venetian colony of Tana. Due to Mongol reprisals the Venetians abandoned Tana, the population fleeing to Kaffa by ship.[11] The Mongols pursued them to Kaffa. It is most likely that the plague reached the Mongols either through reinforcements who arrived from other areas in the eastern portion of the Jochid state or merchants who came to the camp, again coming from the east. By 1346 the Jochid Mongols had increasingly converted to Islam, although many still adhered to shamanism. As the plague struck they still had to deal with the dead in the proper manner. For the common Muslim Mongol soldier this meant their body had to be washed and buried within seven days. Meanwhile, shamanistic Mongols were taken into the steppe and left exposed to nature. It is easy to speculate that the next victims were those who handled the bodies as the fleas moved from one host to another. Soon no one would want to have contact with the bodies yet they still had to be removed from the camp. The death rate may have been too great to have dealt with the dead properly.[12] Ever practical in the ways of war, the Mongols devised a solution.

It may have been a fine day for a Genoese merchant as they sat outside a tavern in Kaffa, drinking wine made from the grapes grown in region and perhaps snacking on caviar from local sturgeon. Certainly the siege lay outside but it seemed unlikely that the Mongols would destroy the town as they reaped a tremendous amount of revenue from the trade that passed through Kaffa, although they had sacked Kaffa in 1298/9 and 1308. The fact that it was a port city meant that escape was relatively easy. Hopes were high that diplomacy would win the day and new terms would be set, thus while frightening and risky, the prospect of a Mongol siege in 1346–7 was not quite the same as it would have been a century earlier when Mongol diplomacy consisted of a three-word ultimatum: surrender or die. Suddenly from out of the clear blue sky an object falls and hits your table. Chunks of body, blood and pus from the buboes splatter over the area. It is not raining bodies but in order to dispose of the dead the Mongols decided to use them as trebuchet missiles. What is the splatter radius of a roughly 70–80 kg (150–170 lb) body hurled 100 m (330 ft) from a trebuchet and falling at 9.8 m (32 ft) per second per second?[13] Large enough to terrify the citizenry of Kaffa.

According to Gabriele de Mussis, our major source for the events at Kaffa, 'What seemed like mountains of dead were thrown into the city, and the Christians could not hide or flee or escape from them, although they dumped as many of the bodies as they could in the sea . . . No one knew, or could discover, a means of defense.'[14] This was clearly a sign for a normal self-respecting merchant to vacate Kaffa. As a result a number of ships left Kaffa to its fate. Of course the merchants were possibly infected through the spread of the bacilli of exploding buboes from the hurled bodies, and rats that picked up infected fleas from the Mongol camp or ships bringing provisions to Kaffa. Thus the exodus from Kaffa became a fleet of death. There is only one exit from the Black Sea – through the Straits of Bosphorus. Merchants being merchants stopped at Constantinople. From there they travelled to Egypt and then returned to Italy. Three ships arrived in Genoa on 31 December 1347, but were expelled after it became clear that death stalked the ships. Rather than a homecoming, the townspeople chased the galleys off with flaming arrows and missiles.[15] From Genoa the galleys travelled to the port of Messina in Sicily in 1348 and the eastern Mediterranean coast was infected.[16] The western Mediterranean followed suit. There was a slight chance that this could have been avoided if the galleys had been quarantined in Genoa, but from there the disease spread to Europe, although it is likely another ship would have brought it to the rest of Europe. As goods, people and rats disembarked, the plague went with them either as bacteria already lurking in the humans or in the fleas on the rats (and people). By 1349 the plague had reached as far north as Scotland. On a more positive note, the hopes of a diplomatic solution to the siege came true. Terms on Kaffa were reached between the Jochid Khanate, Genoa and Venice in 1347.

IMPACT ON THE WORLD

Numerous books have been written about the impact of the plague in Europe. David Herlihy, Norman Cantor and others contend that it transformed Europe.[17] Their cases are convincing. The resulting population collapse created a social response that changed society. Wage labour arose or increased in frequency, doubt in the church increased, new saint cults appeared and medicine advanced because the old beliefs and methods simply did not or could not function in post-plague Europe. In short, the plague with its devastating death toll fundamentally altered the European world.

Some of the most notable effects were due to the population shortage; some occupations now accepted women. Indeed, beer and ale production in the late fourteenth and mid-fifteenth centuries became dominated by women.[18] Wage labour increased as manors lacked sufficient labour to plant and harvest, thus in order to attract people wages had to be offered. When wages were not high enough revolt occurred. This should not be surprising. With an average of 50 per cent mortality, it must be kept in mind that some locations had lower death rates but some were much higher. In order to draw people where they were needed, there had to be an attraction. Cash payment is certainly one. Labour shortages also created a necessity for labour-saving machines, primarily improving upon ones that already existed.[19] With cash payment peasants could now own land. Few, however, had enough money to buy land and thus rented the land they worked. With the lack of farmers some land turned to pasture, which benefited the wool industry of England and Flanders. Yet even this could be rented out by landowners, often exorbitantly as recorded in the nursery rhyme, 'Baa Baa Black Sheep': One for his master (the king's taxes), one for his dame (the land lord or lady), and one for the little boy who lived down the lane (the peasant received the remaining third of the wool yield).

Education changed as well. As the bubonic plague was an equal opportunity infector, the educated classes also decreased. Some 30 universities existed in Europe before the plague; 24 remained afterwards.[20] Contributing to the demise of universities was that plague made travel difficult. Naturally towns did not welcome strangers during this time of turmoil. Thus some universities closed simply due to lack of students. In the wake of the plague, however, wealthy patrons founded new ones to accommodate local students. Since there was less of a need for a lingua franca as students tended to be local, using the vernacular language, rather than Latin, gained new prominence.

Galenic medicine with its emphasis on the four humours (blood, black bile, yellow bile and phlegm) could not explain the plague and cures prescribed by Galenic physicians had no effect. These physicians believed bad air or miasma transmitted the disease (true in the case of pneumonic plague) so many attempted to keep air out of dwellings. Some remedies included trying not to breathe or lying in a certain way. Surgeons went around wearing ornate masks filled with incense to purify the air while waving wands of incense in an attempt to rid the air of impure elements. While they certainly gave inspiration to later interpretations of wizards and sorcerers, their patients died. With the failure of Galenic medicine, a new empirical medicine evolved with an emphasis on anatomy. This was good but most of the new practitioners were also barbers.

The Catholic Church also changed dramatically. New emotive patron saint cults evolved with an apocalyptic emphasis. Of particular importance was St Roch, who apparently was infected with the plague (in depictions of the saint, he points to his bubo), yet was also able to cure it. It is also in this period that flagellants appear en masse. These zealots believed, as did many, that the disease (like the Mongols) was a punishment from God for their sins. Thus they duly whipped themselves as penance. Some even believed that blood drawn from the flagellants' ardour could cure the plague and perhaps even raise the dead. The flagellants were openly defiant of the church, which seemed helpless against the plague. Unfortunately some were also anti-Semitic. While many viewed the plague as a punishment from God, some believed the Jews had something to do with it, although it was also a good excuse to plunder local Jewish communities. As outsiders, medieval Jewish communities were frequent targets, some accused of spreading the plague through sorcery or poisoning wells. Therefore many Jewish communities fled western Europe (particularly the Holy Roman Empire) to Poland, where King Casimir found use for their commercial talents. Once again the Mongols brought misery to the European Jews – in the thirteenth century another popular hypothesis to explain the Mongols had been that they were the Biblical Ten Lost Tribes. Fear swept through the Holy Roman Empire that Jewish communities invited the Mongols to invade and secretly stored weapons and other material to aid them. The seemingly inevitable pogrom followed.

With the plague-induced crisis in faith, one might have some sympathy for the church. On top of these new challenges it had other issues with which to contend. Due to the dire need to provide last rites the church had to ordain new priests to replace the fallen. The urgency of replacing priests sometimes resulted in ill-trained priests, at times ignorant of Latin or the proper rites. The use of the vernacular increased in services as did heretical views. To correct this the church increasingly recruited from universities, where the students had a strong foundation not only in Latin but also theology. Nonetheless, they also studied other fields, such as philosophy, which entertained beliefs the church considered anathema. In this period some of the roots of not only the Renaissance but also the Reformation were laid.[21]

Much has been written on the plague in Europe, yet virtually all of Afro-Eurasia also suffered. Few realms escaped it. Indeed, as it left the Mongol Empire the plague infected the Middle East not only via the Kaffa refugees but also from other directions. It crept out of central Asia and entered the former Ilkhanate before winding its way into India and to Anatolia, which also received it from Constantinople. Then it made its way south through Syria, seemingly adopting Mongol strategy and striking in a pincer fashion. As in Europe, it was considered the punishment of God, but carried out by jinn. Others viewed it as a reward from God – in a sense, martyrdom for the believers. As Michael Dols demonstrated, there was a lack of consensus in the exact purpose of the plague in the Middle East.[22]

In 1348 Ibn Battuta encountered the plague as he attempted to return home after years of travelling abroad. While in Aleppo he heard how the plague, arriving from Egypt, struck Gaza, allegedly killing 1,000 people every day.[23] It then struck Ascalon, Acre and Jerusalem in short order. Taking refuge in holy places such as the al-Aqsa mosque did nothing to stave off the plague.[24] Rather than wait for the disease to travel up the coast or arrive from Anatolia Ibn Battuta attempted to go to Damascus, farther inland. He had only reached Homs when he heard the disease killed 2,000 a day in the Syrian capital. Other reports put the death toll at a more reasonable 100 per day.[25] Nonetheless the population of the city dropped by 30,000 people from 80,000 before it was over. According to most accounts Cairo lost approximately 200,000 people from a population of half a million. As elsewhere in the world, if the plague entered a house, within two days its inhabitants were dead. Funeral processions caused traffic jams throughout the city and the bodies of the dead were ignominiously piled along the roads. So empty were certain towns and quarters that the call for prayer was not completed for lack of muezzin and the faithful.[26] By the end of 1348 the entire Levant coast and the interior fell before the plague – an achievement that eluded the Mongol armies.

As in Europe cash became king. Those dealing with the dead possessed the means of making a lucrative living, providing they stayed alive. Quran readers were in short supply and often booked back-to-back ceremonies due to demand. Porters and gravediggers also found themselves in 'skilled' labour positions. Indeed, gravediggers made as much as five times as a Quran reader on a single victim.[27] At harvest time, due to the lack of peasants, labourers were hired with promises of 50 per cent of the crop. Often, though, the very Mamluks who were to supervise the harvest ended up doing the work due to the dearth of workers. The Mamluk state suffered from a tremendous loss of revenue not only from the loss of life and subsequent loss of taxes but in many areas it was estimated that half of the cultivated land went unattended during the plague years. Many occupations also temporarily disappeared as people abandoned traditional trades and devoted themselves to the more lucrative occupations of dealing with the dead, which certainly appeared to be the rising occupation. Rather than dealing in distant trade others satisfied their commercial needs by buying and selling the goods of the dead. Due to the shortage of labour, wages rose and the state ordered others to resume their normal occupations due to the lack of water bearers and even laundresses.[28] Prices of commodities fluctuated as they did in Europe.

Unlike Europe, the rural poor did not make the same advances with land ownership. Recurring outbreaks continued to depopulate rural regions. It is true that the urban population also suffered but the urban institutions, particularly the governmental ones, were more developed than those of Europe. Thus with depopulation the government continued to function, even if at a more limited level, whereas in Europe the lack of centralized authority weakened the rule of law and allowed change to occur. In the Middle East, once the region sufficiently recovered, it was back to business as usual for the most part. The lack of an apocalyptic vision in Sunni Islam prevented the rise of millenarian cults that also acted as agents of change, unlike Catholic Europe.[29] While the plague might have been a punishment or reward, most Muslims knew that God would do as he would. And if the disease occurred due to sin, then there was little one could do to stave off the punishment or earn penance. Furthermore, in Islam original sin does not exist, so the plague was not a punishment for all humankind. While not all Muslims were or are as fatalistic as this might suggest, the currents of this thought caused people to act differently than an apocalyptic view might. Finally, while the plague spread, in the Middle East and the Islamic world in general one does not see the demographic shifts as people fled from plague. Cities were not vacated and society as a whole was not disrupted. As indicated above, depopulation on an incredible scale occurred but the plague did not disrupt and transform society. In short, Islamic society was better situated to cope and continue in the face of the plague than Christendom. Nonetheless, this was not the same for all regions. The Mamluk Sultanate survived, although it is arguable if it ever fully recovered. The plague certainly contributed to the continued breakdown of powers in the former Ilkhanate, leaving it ripe for Timur's conquest. Meanwhile, it is during this time that an obscure Turkic *beylik* emerges in Anatolia. There is a case to be made that the plague played a role in the foundation of the Ottoman Empire.[30]

One of the most intriguing aspects of the Black Plague as it exited the steppes is the reports that humans were not the only victims but livestock, rats, cats and dogs also fell before the disease. In Constantinople dogs, horses, birds and rats died.[31] Other sources note that the plague spared neither man nor beast. Many recognized the rat as part of the problem. The desire to get rid of rats during the time of plague was recorded in the story of the Pied Piper of Hamlin.[32] Rather than taking the children as payment, we should see the Pied Piper as the Grim Reaper killing the children with the Black Plague. The fact that livestock also died from plague, though some are more resistant than others, has led to some speculation that the disease was anthrax, or that anthrax and other diseases also occurred. Undoubtedly in such unhygienic situations other diseases contributed to the death toll. But, as noted above, most livestock are less susceptible to the plague. As the plague existed in the steppe, the livestock of the nomads may have been more resistant to it simply from occasional exposure. In areas that were marmot-free this did not apply. As livestock often shared the dwellings of their peasant owners, more inter-species diseases were shared than in the more sparsely populated steppe. With the exception of the frailest infant animals nomads did not share their tents with their cattle. It is one thing to share a room with the plough ox, but quite another to share with 100 sheep and goats, a dozen horses, a few cows and the random camel. Thus when this strain of bubonic plague hit the Mediterranean world, it entered a world of little resistance.

IMPACT ON THE MONGOL EMPIRE

A proper assessment of the plague's effect on the Mongol Empire has yet to be made. The following is but a brief foray expanding on the discourse in the existing scholarship. Even before the plague hit Kaffa it had already devastated other parts of the empire as it made its way across Eurasia. Merchants carried it to oasis towns and the *khans* or bazaars of the trading cities along the Silk Road. No doubt merchants and other travellers facilitated the spread of disease in an attempt to flee when the Black Death walked the marketplaces and streets of the cities. Even after its peak in the late 1340s the disease did not go quietly. In China the Mongol Empire saw outbreaks in 1353 and 1354. One must remember that in addition to the massive number of deaths other effects were omnipresent as society, the economy and even the state suffered. The plague had little preference for its victims. In all areas of the Mongol Empire it is highly likely that the plague played a major role in collapse. The Yuan Dynasty lost China only fourteen years after the last plague outbreak.

In the case of the Jochid Khanate the plague came from the east and struck all of its major cities located along the trade routes. Saray, Astrakhan and other cities all suffered. Reports from the Crimea indicated that 85,000 people died in 1346 – this does not include the death toll from Kaffa.[33] While the disease then departed from Astrakhan and other regions of the Jochid Khanate to enter the Caucasus and Armenia before reaching the Middle East, it also ventured north. By 1349 it reached Pskov and Novgorod. By 1352 virtually every Russian city experienced the Black Plague with typical results. In some instances, as at Pskov, it visited twice. Similar occurrences were recorded throughout the Jochid Khanate, with the last wave of plague occurring in 1396. Indeed, Uli Schamiloglu estimates that the plague roiled the Jochid Khanate in 1346, 1364, 1374 and, finally, 1396.[34]

As Schamiloglu has indicated, in Europe the plague killed 33 to 50 per cent of the population and approximately a quarter to a third of the population of Egypt, so it is not unreasonable to expect that similar numbers existed in the Mongol Empire.[35] Although the Jochid, Chaghatayid and Yuan khanates did not disintegrate, the plague caused turmoil. The armies of the Mongol states weakened. Although the nomads generally suffered less than sedentary populations the khanates had urban centres and troops near these locations. Any army, as evinced by the Mamluks, that lost a third of its manpower suffered in more than just numbers. Veterans, generals and heroes alike could suffer alongside new soldiers. Considering that the core of the Mongol army in all areas of the empire remained horse-archers drawn from a nomadic population, the loss was tremendous. Throughout the empire the loss of soldiers and government officials surely affected the Mongols' ability to govern in any khanate.[36] In addition the second half of the fourteenth century experienced several outbreaks of plague with a corresponding decline in population. Sedentary populations could lose the same percentage but due to their larger populations they retained 'strategic depth' and thus recovered faster.

These factors certainly impacted upon the Jochid Khanate. Schamiloglu has clearly demonstrated that plague was possibly the most important factor in its decline. The plague struck just after the long and successful reign of Üzbek Khan. The periodic waves of the plague must have made it difficult to maintain control. During this time, as previously discussed, the leadership of the Jochid Khanate was precarious with a number of murders and usurpations. Political murder and machinations changed the ruler but the military and Jochid governing institutions remained in place, at least until the plague damaged them to the point that it could no longer govern an empire the size of the Jochid Khanate. While the plague also affected the Russian principalities, the fact that the Mongols now had more limited resources meant that they had to decentralize some authority. Thus Moscow benefited. On the western frontier, Lithuania also benefited, since the Mongols, with their stretched resources and political fragmentation, were rarely able to challenge intrusion on the distant northwestern borders.

Similar situations occurred in the Chaghatayid and Yuan states. The breakdown of authority allowed the continued drifting apart of the Chaghatayid state. In the Yuan Empire it assisted in the rise of the Red Turbans with the destruction of strong government authority. The Black Plague may have also contributed to the millenarian beliefs of the White Lotus sect. All of them also suffered from the loss of technical expertise. The Yuan Empire, however, due to its larger population, could have recovered if given a chance. The Red Turban rebellion ensured that the recovery never occurred. In the Chaghatayid and Jochid khanates the disruption of trade and the loss of technical expertise in their cities was irreplaceable. Mawarannahr recovered, partially because of the rise of Timur and his relocation of artisans to central Asia. The Jochid Khanate did not, for even as the plague ended, Timur hit it, albeit provoked by Toqtamysh, in the midst of its recovery. Timur destroyed Saray and other cities and carried off the skilled artisans. Between the plague and Timur, the Jochid Khanate stood little chance of a complete recovery. Too much loss of life and talent meant that the Jochids' grasp on their periphery was slipping from their hands. Largely due to the plague and its repercussions, the Jochid state separated into smaller khanates.

9

MIGRATIONS AND
DEMOGRAPHIC TRENDS

The Mongols are often associated with depopulating entire regions. Although scholars doubt the veracity of these reports in terms of exact numbers, it is clear that the Mongols, in a more pragmatic sense, were quite adept at resource management. Even if they did not kill as many as the sources suggest they certainly did not blanch at the idea that others thought they did. Juzjani recorded an anecdote about an imam who survived a fall from the walls of Herat. Tolui, amazed that the man emerged unscathed, believed him to be an auspicious individual and took him to Chinggis Khan. After some time with the imam, Chinggis Khan asked the cleric if the world would remember Chinggis Khan. After some moments of consternation the imam asked for the security of his person. Chinggis Khan affirmed he would be safe no matter what the answer, and the imam replied 'A name continues to endure where there are people, but how will a name endure when the Khan's servants martyr all the people and massacre them, for who will remain to tell the tale?' The statement angered Chinggis Khan but after he regained his composure he said:

> I used to consider thee a sagacious and prudent man, but, from this speech of thine, it has become evident to me that thou dost not possess complete understanding, and that thy comprehension is but small. There are many kings in the world, and, wherever the hoofs of the horses of Muhammad, the Aghri, have reached, there I will carry slaughter and cause devastation. The remaining people who are in other parts of the world, and the sovereigns of other kingdoms that are, they will relate my history.[1]

Clearly, the Mongols were not averse to massacres when it suited their purposes. Yet they also impacted on populations in other ways. For instance, when Hülegü's army marched into the Middle East the Mongols took steps to secure pasturage for their animals, which undoubtedly had consequences for farmers and nomads along the route:

> And elchis were sent on in advance to reserve all pasturage and meadowland wherever the World-King's troops might be expected to pass, from the Qanghai mountains between Qara-Qorum and Besh-Baligh; and all animals were forbidden to graze there lest the pastures might be harmed or the meadows injured. And all the garden-like mountains and plains were banned and prohibited and the teeth of cattle were prevented from browsing thereon. And in the countries from Turkestan to Khorasan and uttermost Rum and Georgia grass fell into the category of 'but to this tree come not nigh', so much so that whoever fed a bale of it to his beasts was obliged to forfeit them; until in truth, grass (giyab) became sin (gunab) and of verdure (sabzi) there was satiety (siri). The elchis then departed in order to remove themselves, consisting as they did of a whole army, from the meadows and pastures to places through which the King's troops would not pass.[2]

In addition to Mongol armies already operating in the region, such as that of the Mongol general Baiju which moved to Anatolia from the Mughan steppe due to this order, other nomads had to vacate these regions, moving into other pastures and displacing other nomads, or into arable areas where they disrupted farming as their sheep ate the grain before harvest. The Mongol advances changed the demographics of every area they entered. This chapter is not a close examination of census figures, but rather an examination of the impact of the invasions on populations and how the demographics of the Mongol Empire and its frontiers changed. The sources often put the death toll from the conquests in the millions. While one must be careful with the numbers in ancient and medieval sources, it is safe to say that if the numbers are not exact, they are at least at a level suggesting one had not previously seen or even conceived of such devastation and loss of life. While it is easy to become enamoured with the efficiency and effectiveness of the Mongol military, the impact on trade and culture and the overall impact of the Mongol Empire, it should never be forgotten that the Mongols had little regard for the lives of those they conquered. As long as they resisted they were rebels before the will of *Tenggeri* (Heaven) who decreed that Chinggis Khan and his successors should rule the earth. As such, the empire was their property to do with as they desired. As indicated by Chinggis Khan in the quotation above, the Mongols were not concerned with a bloody reputation. Indeed, they understood the value of fear and propaganda very well and preferred it if that reputation preceded them.

Nonetheless, the Mongols also greatly impacted upon their era and the future through direct and indirect control of populations through less, although still terrifying methods, such as those that they used to secure sufficient pasture for the advance of Hülegü's army. They relocated populations as they needed. They also turned people into refugees who fled before the Mongols, whether to avoid destruction or simply because the Mongols, as in the instance of Hülegü, needed them to move. What follows is an examination of some of those instances.

MONGOLIA

Curiously, Mongolia is often overlooked in the history of the Mongol Empire after 1206. Certainly attention is drawn to the Mongolian plateau in regard to travellers going to Karakorum, but not to what else occurred there. Perhaps the most noticeable effect would be the change in identity. After 1206 no longer was Mongolia comprised of dozens of tribes but a single Mongol nation – the Khamag Monggol Ulus, later expanded to the Yeke Monggol Ulus or Great Mongol Nation/State. While Chinggis Khan's restructuring of Mongolian tribal society into decimal units did not completely erase old tribal identities, it diluted them while also asserting a Mongolian supra-tribal identity. Without Chinggis Khan it is unlikely that that Mongolians (at least as we know them) would exist today. Although the wars of unification certainly led to a drop in population, not only in human lives but also livestock, recovery seems to have been quick and massacres of the defeated (like the Tatars) were probably overstated, with just the aristocracy being annihilated. The identity of the tribe was tied to the most dominant element with outsiders joining the group relatively easily (although not always willingly).[3]

With the Mongol expansion, the demographics changed again. For one, Mongol units spread across Eurasia. Some scholars have contended that the Mongol expansion was due to climatic factors – a drying up of the steppe that led to conflict and necessitated expansion out of the steppe. The reality does little to validate such environmental hypotheses.[4] With respect to the desiccation of the steppe, the fact that the Mongols built their capital in Mongolia as well as imported thousands of artisans to live there, as will be discussed below, undermines the idea that Mongolia became uninhabitable. Granted, the Mongols imported food, but the Mongol rulers still nomadized near Karakorum and held large *quriltais* there which brought hundreds of leaders and supporters back to Mongolia regularly.

Nonetheless, Mongol units did expand outward, so naturally the Mongolian population in Mongolia potentially declined. It does not appear, however, that it was significant. It must be remembered that when Chinggis Khan reorganized the military, society was also divided into *mingans* and *tümens*. Thus when Chinggis Khan assigned territory, the bulk of the military was assigned to his youngest son, Tolui. At the 1206 *quriltai*, 95 *mingans* were assigned and these did not include the Hoyin Irgen.[5] His sons and some relatives received territorial assignments that moved them out of Mongolia. Jochi, Chaghatai, Ögödei and Tolui received 9,000, 8,000, 5,000 and 5,000 people (not just soldiers) respectively. Jochi, Chaghatai and Ögödei received pasturelands (*nutag*) outside Mongolia. Military commanders were also assigned to them who had already been assigned *mingans* and even *tümens*. When those are totalled, probably fewer than 100,000 Mongolians left Mongolia permanently at this time.

But what proportion of Mongolia's population was this? Scholars disagree over population estimates for Mongolia at the beginning of the thirteenth century.[6] Their numbers range from as low as 500,000 to 2,500,000. Why is there such a wide discrepancy? Of course, to estimate the population figures for a region that did not carry out a census at that time, much less maintain demographic records, is extremely difficult. Still, it is possible to make a fair estimate. Most scholars have taken the census figures for Mongolia around the turn of the twentieth century (1,000,000) and based their calculations on this. Considering the small total population that most scholars have arrived at, such numbers could only provide a relatively small army at best. Furthermore, as warfare had been rampant in the region in addition to other disorders, it was natural that the population count as well as the army would be smaller than in the early twentieth century. Fortunately, we know that the Mongol army at the time of the coronation of Chinggis Khan in 1206 numbered 95,000 men.

As the 1206 numbers are based on the assumption that one male in every family in Mongolia between the ages of 15 and 70 participated in the Mongol army, it is fairly simple to extrapolate an approximate population of Mongolia. The typical household in Mongolia is usually estimated to be five people; thus if one per five served in the military, the population of Mongolia should be approximately 475,000, which is lower than all of the other figures. However, can this number be accepted? Between 7 September and 6 October in the year 1241, Shigi Qutuqu conducted another census that yielded a total of 97,575 ethnic Mongol troops and a population of 723,910.[7] This gives roughly 7.4 members per household. With this new average of one soldier per seven people, in 1206 the population can be estimated at 665,000. Elsewhere in the empire, however, the typical recruitment figure was one out of ten. While one may argue that this figure was mainly used in sedentary populations such as Iran or China, it seems odd that an army organized along decimal figures would use any method other than decimal recruiting in the early stages of the empire. Thus the population of Mongolia may be closer to 950,000 people, perhaps topping a million. H. D. Martin, in his classic study of the Mongol military, estimated that the Mongols possessed an army of roughly 138,000 on the eve of the Mongol invasion of the Jin Dynasty.[8] Thus if we use either one soldier per seven or one per ten, the population of Mongolia ranges from 966,000 to 1,380,000.

Perhaps 10 per cent of the population moved out of Mongolia and others died in combat, but Mongolia remained a troop reservoir. The Mongols incorporated other nomads into their military, which meant that they did not have to continually recruit from Mongolia. With the appropriate haircut, training and incorporation into the army, other nomads became Mongol too.[9] The majority of these were Turks, yet by being incorporated into the decimal units they assumed one of these tribal identities, such as the Kereit, Barulas, Jalayir and so on – those that submitted to the Mongols peacefully or, in the case of the Kereit, had been so important that they were not eradicated. While these Mongolian identities remained, they eventually became Turkicized outside Mongolia, as will be discussed below. But Mongolia itself appears to have maintained a stable population yet remained nomadic, despite the presence of the capital in the Orkhon River basin.

The major transition occurred after Khubilai moved the capital from Mongolia. Combined with rebellion and the threat from Qaidu, this eventually led to Mongolia, in this sense northern Mongolia (Mongolia north of the Gobi Desert), becoming a forgotten province of the Yuan Empire. As discussed previously, the Yuan emperors grew distant from Mongolia and the Mongols in Mongolia reciprocated. While they remained loyal for the most part, they preferred the emperor and the government to remain at a distance. Their attitude became more apparent with the collapse of the Yuan Empire.

Approximately 240,000 to 400,000 Mongol troops (40 *tümens*) were stationed in China during the Yuan Empire, where they played an important role in expanding China proper, as will be discussed below. With the collapse, only 60,000 returned to Mongolia. The rest remained in China and eventually were absorbed into the Ming armies. The 60,000 soldiers returned with their families. Using the numbers above, this could range from 300,000 (factor of 5), 420,000 (factor of 7) or 600,000 (factor of 10) refugees retreating to Mongolia. For any area at any time these numbers would cause considerable strain on society and resources. Pastoral nomadism can be a precarious lifestyle. Natural disasters such as *zhuds,* particularly nasty blizzards, can devastate a herd, twenty-first-century Mongolia *zhuds* have ended the nomadic lifestyle for many families.

The Mongolia Temür Toghon returned to include a dominant strata of Chinggisids (particularly from Ariq Böke) and officers. Some officer positions became hereditary and accumulated significant power. In western Mongolia the Oirats or western Mongols (non-Chinggisids) gained ascendency. They, too, had little interest in the imperial court moving to Mongolia, where it settled in northern Mongolia at the town of Bars Khoton (Tiger City) near the Kerülen River.[10] The migration caused a sudden increase of population that may or may not have brought back herds and flocks with them. If they did, this could strain the available pasture. If they did not, they needed food – which meant requisitioning the herds of the native Mongols. Either way, economic and political stresses emerged as local elites struggled to assert their own authority against imperial prestige. Added into the mix was warfare between the Northern Yuan (as the Mongol Empire became known) and the Ming.

The most damaging effect was that the newcomers, many of whom had never herded an animal in their life, decimated the herds of the native Mongols. The herd population could not overcome the losses. This affected everything else. If too many animals are killed, not only does it affect the reproduction and replacement of animals killed for food, but the nomads also lose those animal by-products that are so necessary to survival on the steppe, leading to human population decline. Economic collapse and political instability followed. The ability of the Oirats to challenge and even usurp Chinggisid prerogatives in the late fourteenth and fifteenth centuries demonstrates the instability of the end of the Yuan Empire; a trend not reversed until the late fifteenth century.

Artisans, Technicians and Entertainers

Though Mongol military units and their families left Mongolia, other groups moved to Mongolia – often against their will. While merchants and missionaries flocked to Mongolia in hopes of striking it rich or saving souls by converting the khan in Karakorum, others came as a workforce for the empire. When the Mongols defeated a city or kingdom if they found people with useful skills, such as artisans, craftsmen, engineers, and so on, these fortunate souls escaped possible massacre and were sent to designated sites to work for the Mongols. This could result in joining the Mongol army as an artillerist or engineer. Other artisans, however, were sent to manufacture goods for the Mongol court and military, perhaps the most famous being William Buchier, a Parisian gold and silversmith in Karakorum, who designed the famed silver drink fountain described by William of Rubruck.[11]

The most famous site besides Karakorum was Chinqai Balsaghun (Chinqai's City). Chinqai, a high-ranking minister in the Mongol court, established a city in west central Mongolia, first as a military colony, in 1212. This gradually expanded into a city that included a sizeable workforce of Chinese artisans, many of whom were allowed to return to China in 1265 where they worked around Dadu and Shangdu.[12] This move may have been a result of Khubilai's victory over Ariq Böke and to deny others, like Qaidu, technical resources. Another city, Bai Baliq (Rich Town), was established along the Selenge River in Mongolia. It became a centre of jewellery design and goldsmithing. While Mongolia was a logical choice to establish these production centres, it necessitated creating a logistical system to supply the inhabitants with food and work supplies. Of course, this also increased the traffic of people to Mongolia.

Yet Mongolia was not the only site of industrial production. The Mongols established a silk and brocade weaving centre along the reaches of the Upper Yenisei River.[13] Siberia has historically not been known as a producer of silk but it demonstrates the ability of the Mongols to not only relocate workers but also provide them with

Three Muslim prisoners being lead away by Mongol horsemen, Persian miniature from the Saray album of Rashid al-Din's *Jami' al-Tawarikh* (14th century). Although they are dressed in Mongol garb, the prisoners could be artisans that are being led to production centres in Mongolia, central Asia or northern China.

materials and thus control the production of luxury goods. The major product made here and at a number of other locations was the gold brocade so beloved by the Mongol court, known as *nasij*. The production of this cloth required copious amounts of silk and gold. The silk primarily came from China but locating the production centres in Mongolia and Siberia placed them relatively near gold deposits in the Altai Mountains in western Mongolia as well as those by the Yenisei River. This reduced the cost of *nasij* production. A single troy ounce of gold can be transformed into 80 km (50 miles) of wire and, wrapped around a substrate, that ounce can produce 1,600 km (1,000 miles) of thread.[14] Although very little gold was needed to produce *nasij* it made sense to have the *nasij* production centres near the gold as it was more valuable. Silk was also valuable (indeed, silk, rather than gold, backed the Yuan Empire's currency) but it was easier to keep track of a caravan of camels transporting bales of silk than a couple of camels transporting a few bags of gold, which disappeared more easily than silk cloth.

Of course, to get the gold one required skilled labour besides strong backs. After the Mongol victory at Liegnitz over a combined army of Poles, Teutonic Knights and others, a Mongol prince, Büri, took prisoners. Among them was a sizeable contingent of German gold miners. These prisoners of war spent the rest of their lives in central Asia, where they worked on behalf of Büri's court near Talas, approximately 270 km (170 miles) northeast of modern Tashkent.[15] The Mongol invasions of the Khwarazmian Empire yielded thousands of artisans with technical skills. Although we should not take for granted Rashid al-Din's assessment that the Mongols moved 100,000 artisans to the lands of the east (*bilad-i sharqi*), there is little doubt that thousands did move.[16]

Xunmalin was one such location, near modern Beijing. It received 3,000 weavers from Samarqand while Hangzhou, west of Beijing, received 3,000 households of weavers from central Asia in addition to 300 households of weavers from the Jin Empire. Indeed, considering the predicament of the German miners, it appears the Mongols moved whomever they had to where they needed them.[17] We know that in Karakorum the artisans' households were locked into occupations. As the Mongols also imposed this policy in China to ensure the continued production of goods and services it is likely that it applied to all of their industrial centres.[18]

Despite their propensity to move workers around their empire to further the needs of the Mongol court, the Mongols understood the adage 'all work and no play makes Chinggis a dull boy'. Indeed, as it is today, wrestling was a favourite source of entertainment for the Mongols. Although in the early days of Chinggis Khan local champions wrestled for entertainment and for political purposes,[19] in the days of the empire wrestling was a major spectacle for the amusement of the khan. Ögödei kept in his service a number of Mongolian wrestlers but also Kipchaks and Chinese.[20] Once Chormaqan conquered Iran and Transcaucasia, Ögödei added Iranian and Georgian wrestlers to his stable. Indeed so popular was wrestling that even on campaign the Chinggisid princes arranged intercontinental championships. Möngke sent his best wrestler (a Mongol) to find suitable competition in Hülegü's domain. Hülegü eventually found an Armenian who bested Möngke's champion.[21] As Thomas Allsen indicates, considering that the Mongolian wrestler had travelled 4,500 km (2,796 miles), the Chinggisid wrestling league, if we may call it that, may have produced the first 'truly international, if not quite world, championship sporting matches in history'.[22]

Other entertainers also moved through the empire. These included dancers, jesters, jugglers, actors and so on. Some came as tribute, others, like entertainers of any age, went where they could find employment. Peking opera, which introduced a seven-tone scale during the Yuan period, gained popularity over southern forms due to Mongol patronage.[23] Music served not only as a primary form of entertainment but also to provide background to public events at royal courts as well as those of the officers, as observed by several travellers throughout the time of the empire.[24] Musicians also played in the background for the khans during their drinking sessions. In the eastern empire one could find Persian performers and in the western empire one could listen to Chinese melodies. And in some areas one could find orchestras with a wide variety of musicians. Of course the incorporation of musicians and instruments from across the empire could lead to a potential cacophony; the musicians, however, found ways of adapting melodies[25] leading to an exchange of techniques and instruments.[26]

One must not exclude the acquisition of women. The Mongols, as evinced by Chinggis Khan's efforts to go forth and multiply, were not averse to sex.[27] They brought women back with them to serve as concubines and slaves. Some became menials or entered the service of aristocratic households. One such was Pascha or Paquette of Metz, who was captured in Hungary. Carried back to Karakorum, she entered the household service of a Mongol princess and was allowed to marry a Russian in a similar predicament.[28] Women were seen as part of the booty to be divided, with the khan naturally getting the

Mongolian wrestlers traditionally wore an open jacket, trunks and boots. The open jacket became official dress, according to legend, in order to prevent women from participating in the sport, after Qaidu's daughter, Khutulun, defeated all challengers. In addition, the Mongol khans scouted out talent and held competitions in their court, where wrestlers from other Mongol courts also came to compete.

Musicians and man dancing before Ghazan, illustration from Rashid al-Din's *Jami' al-Tawarikh*. Due to the Chinggis Exchange, the Mongol khans had access to performers from across Eurasia and perhaps even beyond.

most beautiful. As the Mongols established their rule women became part of the tribute. Allegedly, when the Mongols demanded the submission of Antioch the demands for tribute included 3,000 virgins.[29]

In the Yuan era the court's acquisition of women as tribute became more sophisticated, with screeners selecting the women who entered the harem of the khan.[30] Korean women appeared to be among the preferred in the later Yuan period. Yet not all of these women traversed the empire for the sexual pleasure of the Mongols or as labour. Marriage was key as well. Korean women not only entered the Mongol court as concubines but also as wives.[31] In addition, Mongol women became wives to various local rulers. If the woman was a Chinggisid, the husband then claimed the title of *güregen* or son-in-law. In effect the Chinggisid princess ruled or ensured the good behaviour of her husband's territory. The marriages also provided a modicum of safety for rulers who had not submitted, as evinced by the Byzantine princess Bayalun, Üzbek Khan's third wife.[32] Although the Byzantines never submitted to the Mongols, through the peculiar perspective of the Mongols Constantinople may have been a subject as the illegitimate Byzantine princess Maria Despina married the Ilkhan Abaqa. Of equal importance was that wives could exert influence on Mongol policy such as that pertaining to religious matters, but sometimes this included cultural influence, creating a greater diffusion of world culture.

With the great military conquests of the Mongols, one cannot ignore the diffusion of military expertise. Although the Turks often comprised the bulk of the Mongol army as well as the bulk of armies opposed to the Mongols, throughout the domains of the Mongol Empire there was a diffusion of military technology, which has already been discussed, and also ethnic groups. In addition to the Mongols and Turks, other ethnicities served in the Mongol military machine and found themselves distant from home. For instance, when 1,000 Chinese engineers accompanied Hülegü to the west, there is no indication that these individuals returned home. Central Asian and Middle Eastern engineers also found themselves serving in East Asia. In the *keshik* or bodyguard of the Yuan emperors we find Rus' and Alans,[33] while Oirats from western Mongolia fought in the Middle East and actually deserted to the Mamluks.[34] While not all individuals returned to their place of origin after the dissolution of the Mongol

Khubilai Khan hunting with lions, greyhounds and cheetahs, illustration from Marco Polo's *Livre de Merveilles*. The variety of animals in this image not only demonstrates that the khan had access to hunting creatures from across the globe, but also that he acquired people who knew how to handle and take care of them.

Empire, some did and brought with them a larger sense of the world.

Finally, one cannot overlook the place of intellectuals in the Mongol Empire. As discussed in chapter Seven, the movement of many religious scholars and Sufis assisted in the spread of Islam as well as the establishment of new centres of learning. This occurred with other religions, such as Nestorianism, with the journey of Rabban Sauma and Mar Yaballaha who left the Yuan Empire and settled in the Ilkhanate to serve as high-ranking officials in the Church of the East there.[35] In addition we see secular intellectuals traversing the Mongol Empire. The meritocracy of the Mongols permitted talented and ambitious fellows like Marco Polo to serve in government positions in East Asia along with central Asians, and Ibn Battuta to find employment throughout his journeys. Through the publication of their travels we know what kind of influence they extended beyond the empire, yet others also travelled across the empire and did not leave detailed records but certainly told stories that fired the imagination of others.

While forced movement and flight changed the demographics of Eurasia, others came willingly. These individuals had only a slight impact on the demographic situation but in the greater scheme it is they who probably had the most impact on the dispersal of culture, ideas and material goods.

China and Colonization

As the Mongol generals had no qualms about decimating the sedentary population the best way to avoid this fate was to join the Mongols. Although against the Jin Empire, many Han did, other Han resisted until the end. If we believe the Muslim sources thousands of Han virgins leapt to their death to avoid capture during the fall of Zhongdu.[36] The Song Empire also suffered tremendous losses, not terribly surprising considering that the Mongols and Song warred from 1234 until 1279. Some 65 years of warfare will do that to a country. What is surprising, though, is that a twelfth-century census places the Song population at more than 100 million, while a 1290 Yuan census shows the population to be less than 60 million.[37]

Certainly decades of war can result in an immense loss of life but even when considering the side-effects of war – famine (perhaps an early appearance of the plague?), disease, social disorder and so on – were 40 million lives lost through the Mongol conquest of the Song Empire? Even with the effectiveness and viciousness of the

Mongol army, 40 million seems excessive. Most scholars, however, believe that a more realistic post-conquest population ranges between 70 and 90 million. A 10 to 30 million drop in population is still remarkable considering that the fighting was much more visceral and personal than modern warfare, but other factors contributed to this drop in the census. The census takers noted that they knew the population was higher but could not register many households as they had become refugees or fugitives (depending on whose side you took) and avoided Yuan government functionaries by hiding in the forests.[38]

While warfare certainly contributed a high percentage in the demographic drop, we also know that thousands of Han were enslaved or enserfed. As always, the Mongols removed skilled artisans to other regions to work in government workshops. Furthermore, the loss of males through warfare could have slowed the reproduction of the population while the initial chaos of the conquest certainly hampered medical care. Even in the medieval world lack of medical care had tremendous consequences. In addition there was a simple matter of migration. We know hundreds if not thousands attempted to flee the Mongols by immigrating into Southeast Asia. This was partly responsible for the Mongol invasion of that region. In Northeast Asia it is estimated that 40,000 Mongol Yuan households fled to Koryo between 1359 and 1361 due to the violence of the Red Turban rebellion.[39] One can speculate that an equal or perhaps greater number of other refugees joined them or fled to other areas.

At the same time the Mongols also settled in China and surrounding areas. Afterwards some of these regions became part of China, although previously they had only been on the fringes of Chinese civilization and culture. As discussed earlier, 40 *tümens* of Mongols were stationed in China (China proper and not what are now Inner Mongolia, Tibet or Xinjiang Autonomous Region). In a sense, like empires throughout time, the Mongols began a process of colonization of their empire in part to tie it to the homeland. Some of the colonization was the assignment of appanages to members of the Altan Urugh (Golden Kin of Chinggis Khan) as well as Mongol military commanders, but also larger military colonies. In the other areas of the empire this was completed largely through other nomadic groups, primarily Turks. In China, while Turks were also used, it appears more Mongols were used, perhaps due to the extended war with both the Jin and the Song. While colonization failed to bind China to Mongolia, partly because of the move of the capital out of Mongolia, it did alter the territorial integrity of China.

Early in the campaign against the Jin, in 1211, the Mongols seized the pastures of the imperial stud in Yünnei.[40] This area and other pasturelands became staging grounds for the Mongols, colonies in effect, and were prized areas as much of the soil of China lacks the selenium vital to a horse's nutrition. The conquest of Da-Li in 1257, to the southwest of the Song Empire, provided the Mongols with additional pasturelands. This region, comprising much of the modern Yunnan province of China, historically had never been part of China and was populated by a variety of non-Han people. For the Mongols, the pastureland allowed them to use Yunnan as a military colony. It opened a southwestern front against the Song as well as permitting them to operate in Southeast Asia. Indeed, in 1257, Uriyangkhadai, the son of Sübedei, invaded Annam, briefly occupying Hanoi until the ruler agreed to pay tribute. From Da-Li the Mongols tightened their grip on neighbouring Tibet. Due to Yunnan's strategic importance a disproportionate number of Mongols were stationed there.[41]

Many of the Mongols who failed to return to Mongolia after the collapse of the Yuan state in 1368 were stranded in Yunnan. Initially, the Red Turban rebellion that raged from the 1340s to 1368 triggered much of the early Han migration into Yunnan. Although the rebellion keyed the collapse of the Yuan, it also motivated many Han with a desire to escape the chaos of that collapse. More Han entered Yunnan as the new Ming Dynasty sought to crush Red Turban groups who did not swear loyalty to it. Although Yunnan was not a centre of Red Turban activity it bordered Sichuan, which was a Red Turban stronghold. In the early 1370s Ming armies crushed the Red Turbans of Sichuan and the fighting sent many additional Han peasants fleeing to the safety of Yunnan.

Yunnan remained a Mongol stronghold even though cut off from Mongolia. Yunnan has suitable pastures and a diversity of microregions that allowed them to sustain their lifestyle. Although the Yuan Dynasty fell in 1368, the Ming did not deal with the Yunnan Mongols until 1381. The Ming desired not only to end any potential threat from the Mongols but also wanted to bring the region under its administrative authority. This decision sent a 300,000-man Ming army to Yunnan and marked the official beginning of Han Chinese migration to Yunnan. With the conquest of the region in 1382 Yunnan became part of the Ming Empire with an army permanently stationed there. Along

Shen Du (1357–1434), giraffe brought back from east Africa during the voyages of Admiral Zheng He, silk scroll. Although the Ming Dynasty supplanted the Yuan in China, Mongol influence still existed. The clothing of the giraffe wrangler indicates that he is a Mongol.

with the soldiers came their wives and children, forming a sizeable Han population, although they were still a minority within Yunnan. The majority of the population consisted of Yi, Tibetans and numerous Tai-speaking groups, although the Mongol population remained quite sizeable until the modern era.

TURKICIZATION

The Mongols greatly contributed to the Turkicization of many areas of central Eurasia. Although the Mongols remained the political and military elite, Turks constituted the majority of their armies. As the Mongols moved westward they incorporated more Turkic nomads into their army. Other Turks fled before the Mongols, which set off other waves of immigration, particularly among the Kipchak Turks. Yet this was not the first Turkic expansion. Waves of Turkic groups (and some proto-Mongolians) had moved out of Mongolia since the ancient period, with the arrival of the Oghuz Turks in the form of the Seljuks in the eleventh century perhaps being the most well known. The Mongol expansion perhaps accelerated the Turkicization of much of central Eurasia and beyond not only by enrolling Turkic nomads into its army but also due to waves of Turkic refugees who sought to avoid Mongol rule.

Kipchak Turks under Köten Khan fled into Hungary at the invitation of King Bela IV. Their flight triggered the Mongol invasion of Hungary or at least served as the official *casus belli*. The Kipchaks, already refugees from the steppes, found themselves unwelcome in Hungary as the nobility rightly saw the arrival of 40,000 Kipchak warriors, at the invitation of the king who was attempting to centralize his authority, as a threat to their prerogatives. In addition the sudden appearance of pastoral nomads in the midst of an agrarian sedentary population caused tension with the peasantry and manor-owners as sheep and horses could be found grazing in their fields. Soon the nobility executed Köten, leading to a Kipchak rampage south through Hungary, eventually settling in Bulgaria and parts of the Byzantine Empire where both kingdoms found use for their military skills.[42]

The Mongol expansion also helped solidify the creation of other Turkic states. Although the Sultanate of Delhi existed prior to the arrival of the Mongols, it was a nascent state that spun off from the Sultanate of Ghur in Afghanistan. Sultan Muhammad of Khwarazm conquered Ghur but did not attempt to conquer Ghurid domains across the Indus, thus allowing a Ghurid mamluk, Qutb al-Din Aybek, who ruled Delhi as its governor, to establish his own state in 1206, the year Temüjin became Chinggis Khan. Sultan Qutb al-Din Aybek expanded his empire to the Bay of Bengal and dominated northern India, but it was a tenuous existence as various Hindu states challenged its dominance. The Mongol conquest of the Khwarazm Empire did not help matters initially as the Mongols invaded India

THE MONGOL CONQUESTS IN WORLD HISTORY

only to withdraw because they found the climate not to their liking. Now the Sultanate of Delhi faced attacks from the Hindu states as well as frequent raids from the Mongols. Pretenders to the throne of Delhi also found refuge in the Mongol domains.[43]

Yet the Mongol presence also helped transform Delhi into a powerful state. The Sultanate of Delhi held its own against the Hindu kingdoms and gradually penetrated southward, but the looming Mongol threat forced the sultanate to remain vigilant and cultivate a potent military that served not only to fend off the Mongols but to expand its domain in India.[44] The court of Delhi blossomed with the arrival of many scholars, poets, musicians and members of the *ulama*. Although most of the intelligentsia who fled to Delhi were not Turks, their presence continued the trend of a Perso-Turkic Islamic court culture that existed throughout much of the eastern Islamic world. India also saw the arrival of Turkic immigrants. Turko-Mongol tribes even pastured near Delhi, adding manpower to Delhi's army and transforming the character of northern India in both religion and cultural identity.[45] Lahore had previously been the centre of Muslim power in India but with Mongols being so close to it, Delhi transformed into the major centre of authority.[46] It proved an astute choice of location as the Mongols sacked Lahore in 1241, although, as discussed below, not all the inhabitants were upset about it. Nonetheless princes in the Punjab and Sind had to come to an accommodation with the Mongols simply out of proximity.[47]

The slave trade in Turks cannot be overlooked either. As mentioned earlier the Mamluk Sultanate of Egypt experienced growth and sustainability due to the sale of Kipchak Turks from the Pontic and Caspian steppes (Dasht-i-Kipchak). Indeed the market was glutted with Kipchaks after the Mongol conquest of the steppe. The Jochid Khanate continued the trade, extending well beyond Egypt. Turkic slaves appeared in Tuscany. The Mamluk amirs purchased slaves suitable for military service. If they were not suitable for military service, they were not purchased. To have menial Kipchak Turk slaves ran the risk of undermining the ethnic superiority of the Kipchak Mamluks. Even in the medieval world keeping up appearances was important. Thus what was a Genoese slave merchant to do? Sell them in Italy.

'Tartar' slaves appeared in Italy, particularly Tuscany, until the fifteenth century. This part of the Chinggis Exchange was a result of the depopulation of Italy by the Black Plague. With a lack of domestic servants, the government of Florence issued a decree in 1363 permitting the importation of slaves. The sole caveat was that they had to be non-Christians.[48] The custom spread quickly throughout Italy. Brides bought them as part of their dowry, priests gave them as gifts, and thus the presence of Tartars, as they were called, in Italy became somewhat ubiquitous. Other ethnicities were also present, but the majority tended to be Tartars, meaning Kipchak Turks, although there were some Mongols, often children whose parents sold them into slavery due to poverty. On more than one bill of sale the slaves were overwhelmingly Tartars and female; the majority of the male slaves had probably been sold in the Mamluk Sultanate. When male slaves went to Italy they were under sixteen years of age. In the late fifteenth century, however, demand shifted to Russian or Circassian slaves for their looks and less barbarous behaviour.[49] These the Crimean Tatars, who sold slaves to the Genoese in Kaffa, could certainly supply.[50]

The Italians were not the only ones involved in the slave trade. Muslim merchants, known as *khwajas*, also actively engaged in the lucrative trade. In the Mongol Empire they obtained licences or patents to participate in the slave trade – a form of regulation. Although many of the merchants came from within the Mongol Empire, others originated from Egypt, Delhi and perhaps even included Italians. With the security of trade routes and the existence of long-range trade networks we see Kipchaks from the Pontic steppes not only appearing in Egypt and Italy but also in northern India. Indeed, when the Mongols took over the city of Lahore in 1241 the *khwajas* supported Mongol occupation.[51] As they already possessed letters of protection, perhaps even *gerege* from the Imperial court, they must have recognized the benefit of the extension of Mongol power and the profit that could be made.

The Turkiciziation of the Mongol Empire, at least the western part, manifested itself in other ways. With a vast Kipchak Turkic population it is not surprising that the Jochid Ulus was the first khanate to abandon Mongolian in favour of Turkic by the end of the thirteenth century. With the Mongol conquests the Turks were incorporated into the Mongol decimal military. The units often retained tribal names. As mentioned earlier, the Kereit retained an identity due to ties between Chinggis Khan and the Kereit aristocracy. As the Mongol Empire dissipated the Kereit and other now Turkicized Mongol tribes carried on in new forms. The Kereit appear as the Kirei not only among the Mongols but also the Kazakhs, Uzbeks and Bashkorts, as well as the Girays among the Crimean Tatars.[52] Other Turkicized groups included the Qiyat (Kiyat – Yesügei's clan) and the Mangghut (Manghit) among the Crimean Tatars.

The rise of the Mongols also created other identities. Just as troops were organized into *mingans* and *tümens* named after Mongol groups, new units assumed the name of the commander they served. This 'became a new model of social cohesion for survivors and later descendants who could not return to the old solidarities'.[53] Among the most significant were the Noghai or Nogay, named after the Jochid general Noghai. The Noghai remained an important part of steppe politics well into the eighteenth century. The Uzbeks assumed the name of Üzbek Khan, the ruler of the Jochid Khanate at its height.

Turkicization also occurred outside the Jochid Khanate. A similar process occurred in central Asia, albeit at a slower rate due to its proximity to Mongolia.[54] Nonetheless, evidence of the transition is clear by the fourteenth century. The Barulas *mingan* was stationed in Mawarannahr; with the large Turkic population in the region it too Turkicized and became known as the Barlas. From Moghulistan, the northeastern part of the former Chaghatayid Khanate, emerged the Moghuls, who were an intermediary between the Turkic and Mongol worlds. Although they still used Mongolian as a language, at least in correspondence with the Ming,[54] gradually they Turkicized as they were absorbed by the Kazakhs, Uzbeks and Kyrgyz in the fifteenth century. Internecine warfare along with the wars with Emir Timur in the late fourteenth century weakened them, opening the door for the new Turkic groups from the Jochid Khanate to dominate the region.[55] The Turkic language that evolved in the region became known as Chaghatai. In the Timurid realm and the Uzbek khanates it was not only spoken by the nomadic population but also became a literary language (written in an Arabic script). Although other dialects emerged in central Asia, Chaghatai Turk remained the written form until the twentieth century.

In the domains of the Ilkhanate the Mongols also gradually assimilated, although here some Mongols assumed a more Iranian identity. Those who remained primarily nomadic Turkicized. As with other groups a Mongol veneer remained, as evinced in the Jalayir polity around Baghdad. The Jalayirs were initially a Mongol clan, that of the general Muqali.[56] In the wake of the Ilkhanate they assumed a Perso-Turkic court culture and life. Other Turkic groups emerged, such as the Aq Qoyunlu and the Kara Qoyunlu (white and black sheep, respectively) Turkoman confederations. The Mongol presence also caused numerous Turkic tribes to flee east into Anatolia. Prior to the 1240s the Seljuk

Sultanate of Rum benefited from this, along with other refugees (including the Sufi and poet Rumi's family) in the same manner as the Sultanate of Delhi and the Mamluk Sultanate did. The Seljuks moved many of the more unruly nomads to their western frontier where they could raid the Byzantines as well as find pasturelands. From these evolved another Turkic group that assumed the name of its leader to become the Ottomans.

10

CULTURAL EXCHANGES

The Chinggis Exchange did more than facilitate trade and the spread of religions. It also led to the exchange of ideas and technology on a global scale. Technology included more than gunpowder and other military technology. In terms of cultural exchange the Mongols themselves were not always the agents of dissemination, although they certainly participated in both direct and indirect roles. The awesome might of the Mongol military secured the trade routes, yet these trade routes were the roads used by merchants, missionaries and mercenaries alike. Thus travellers witnessed and experienced new ideas, culture and technology and often brought them back to their homes. Thomas T. Allsen's work on the exchange of culture and knowledge between the Yuan and Ilkhanate provides the most detailed research in this area.[1] What follows is an exploration of the transfer of ideas, art, food and material goods through the Mongol Empire and beyond. Due to space limitations, as the topic could fill some books, I have tried to include items not only for their importance, but also some things that are underappreciated.

IDEAS

The Chinggis Exchange greatly altered the world by the simple transfer of ideas, particularly during the post-dissolution period. While scholars, scientists and other learned figures moved around the empire prior to the dissolution, ties between the Ilkhanate and the Yuan Empire led to an intensified, or at least better documented, exchange of scholarship. Scholarship in virtually every area benefited from the international forums that now assembled under Mongol patronage. Persian scholars solidified their language as not only a literary language but also one of scholarship in the court of the Ilkhans as well as in Central Asia, continuing a trend that began prior to the Mongol period, Persian being the language used by Turkic courts. Persian-influenced literature and art spread into Anatolia and India and became the dominant mode in both locations.

Mongol sponsorship of an observatory at Maragheh led to a consolidation of advances in Islamic and Chinese astronomy as scholars from throughout the empire took advantage of this scientific institute.[2] Here Nasir al-Din Tusi discovered that the solar system was heliocentric almost 200 years prior to Copernicus. While independent discovery is possible, one might wonder if Copernicus somehow came across a translation of Tusi's work. Other projects included developing conversion charts for Islamic and Chinese calendars. Curiously, while astronomy benefited from Mongol patronage, this was indirect as Hülegü ordered the building of the observatory to aid Tusi in casting astrological charts for him.[3] Ideas of this kind then had the opportunity to disseminate throughout the rest of the empire as demonstrated by Middle Eastern astronomical and mathematical principles entering Korea during the thirteenth and fourteenth centuries as East Asian practices entered the Middle East.

Medical knowledge became quite intermingled. Although many Mongol khans had short life spans, particularly during the plague years, others showed considerable longevity. Chinggis Khan lived approximately 65 years and Khubilai Khan almost 85 years. Both lived very active lives in a dangerous profession, with Chinggis Khan barely escaping death on more than one occasion. Their longevity is undoubtedly due, at least in part, to the best health care in the medieval world. By virtue of the geographic scope of the empire, the Mongol khans had access not only to traditional Mongol methods of healing, but also to Chinese medicine, Islamic medicine, which included Galenic practices, as well as Tibetan and Indian Ayurvedic treatments. When one system did not heal, they could switch to another, as did Ghazan when Muslim doctors failed to cure a disease. He brought in a Chinese doctor. Abaqa, Hülegü's son, also favoured Chinese doctors, although on his deathbed he also drank potions from Indian and Uighur Buddhist medical experts. Unfortunately these only seemed to hasten his demise.[4]

This intermingling of medical practitioners led to a syncretic medicine where new ideas and items entered other systems. For instance, traditional Chinese medicine experienced an explosion of new ingredients with the introduction of new foods into China and Mongolia. As a result Chinese scholars examined the uses of these ingredients in medicine and categorized them. From their records we not only have the recipes for cures for illnesses but also know what foods pregnant women should avoid.[5] The latter suggestion appears to have been based on the ideas of Ibn Sina (d. 1047), Avicenna in western tradition, the great central Asian scholar. Other categories existed as well. While Chinese medicine may have viewed many of the recipes as medicinal, the Mongols also viewed them as dinner, as will be discussed below. Rashid al-Din, a former doctor himself, included information about Chinese and other medical practices in his own work, making them available in translation and not just through practice.[6]

One should not overlook developments in history either. Rashid al-Din wrote one of the first attempts at a world history – *The Compendium of Chronicles* or *Jami' al-Tawarikh*. While it is tempting to believe that he wrote it himself while he also managed the affairs of state and various other projects, he followed a pattern that many modern political figures do – he worked with ghostwriters and research assistants. Even with unparalleled access to Mongol records and personalities Rashid al-Din needed assistance in order to draw upon the Mongolian, Chinese, Persian, Arabic, Tibetan, Uighur and other sources he used.[7] Although Rashid al-Din may not have written the work by himself it is nonetheless remarkable in terms of methodology and use of sources and informants, making it one of the most important sources for the study of the Mongol Empire. While the *Yuan Shi* and other Chinese sources equal or perhaps surpass the *Jami' al-Tawarikh* in importance, there is an important difference. Rashid al-Din's work was written for Ghazan Khan and thus reflects a sense of what was important to the Mongols and the government at that time, whereas the *Yuan Shi* was compiled during the Ming Dynasty according to Chinese historical practices. Thus while it contains much information it is filtered through another government and is tailored more towards Chinese interests than those of the Mongols.[8] Yet the Mongols also engaged in Chinese historical practices by compiling the *Song Shi* and *Jin Shi*, along with other historical sources, which lent themselves to Rashid al-Din's work. Thomas T. Allsen's groundbreaking study of the historiography of the *Jami' al-Tawarikh* reveals that the Yuan and Ilkhanate shared information – not only source material but also historical organization and methodology.[9] In some ways they were doing the thing for which the internet was originally conceived – sharing information between scholars and government institutions.

Geography and cartography were also greatly enhanced by the simple fact that the Pax Mongolica allowed travellers to traverse the empire more easily and securely. Each traveller's information built upon what was known. For instance, it is clear that Carpini did not know where India was, other than east of Jerusalem, much like many of his contemporaries. Yet Marco Polo travelled from China around India and into the Persia Gulf while returning to Venice. While the Islamic world was more knowledgeable, the information provided by others, whether by chroniclers like Juvaini or Rashid al-Din or travellers such as Ibn Battuta, helped fill in the lacunae on maps. Indeed, their works demonstrate an impressive knowledge of many areas in East Asia. Although it did not happen overnight, monsters and curiosities inhabited less and less of the world as travellers unveiled the truth behind some of the myths. William of Rubruck's scepticism about Prester John comes to mind in this regard – of course, considering that the Portuguese finally designated the Negus or ruler of Ethiopia as Prester John in the sixteenth century, it also demonstrates that some people refuse to let go of a good story.[10]

The Mongols certainly were not passive in geographical transformation. Through their military campaigns and the creation of postal stations to link the empire together, the Mongols directly contributed to improved knowledge of geography. Although Mongols probably created the initial postal stations without the aid of maps, as they extended out of Mongolia, they needed maps not only to plan the best routes but also so that the stations were placed at regular intervals. To achieve the latter engineers set markers to gauge the distance between each station, which provided a better sense of distance and the extent of the empire.

Concepts of kingship and authority changed through the crucible of the Mongol Empire. After the rise of the Mongols, for most of central Eurasia, and to a certain extent beyond, the only true and legitimate ruler had to be descended from Chinggis Khan as decreed by Heaven.[11] This was particularly true in nomadic areas as it was difficult to argue against the success and prestige of the Mongols. After the dissolution the Mongols did modify their ideas of legitimacy. The Yuan leader had to be both Mongol khan and Chinese emperor; the Ilkhans assumed some trappings of Persian kingship. Ghazan and his successors used the title of Padishah on occasion. After converting to Islam those khanates adapted some Islamic aspects as well, although the Mongol ideology of authority remained the most dominant element. In the Islamic world pre-Mongol models still existed but a Mongol shadow loomed. With the destruction of the Abbasid Caliphate, any claim to a universal Islamic empire ended.[12] For the Mamluks, their own rise to power through regicide gave them a shaky claim to rule. This was only bolstered by holding the Mongols at bay and a pro-gramme of patronage for members of the *ulama*. In the eyes of the Mongols, however, the Mamluks remained pretenders, even slaves.[13]

In the post-empire world Mongol ideology remained influential. The Ming did not have to establish their legitimacy in relation to the Mongols. They could use traditional Chinese methods by arguing that the Yuan lost the Mandate of Heaven. After the Ilkhanate collapsed and Mongol authority weakened in central Asia, the new emerging polities used aspects of Mongol authority. The most well-known example is Timur's placing three Chinggisid khans on his throne while he married Chinggisid princesses and used the title of *güregen* or son-in-law. Timur's primary title was Amir and on more grandiose occasions *sahib qiran* or Lord of the Favourable Planetary Conjunction. Other Turkic groups such as the Ottomans and Aq Qoyunlu retained the Mongol model but replaced Chinggis Khan with illustrious Turkic ancestors.[14] Muscovy also wrestled with a Mongol heritage as it tried to establish legitimacy in the steppe against sedentary neighbours.

The Mongols also influenced the role of women in politics and as patrons of art, sciences and religious architecture. The latter has been discussed in chapter Seven. The role of Mongolian women run-ning the state and participating in *quriltais* astonished many travellers who commented on it and Christian, Muslim and Confucian com-mentators were clearly uncomfortable with the idea of a woman openly issuing governmental orders. While female rulers who actively ruled occurred occasionally in sedentary realms, among the nomads this was not unusual. Chinggisid princesses had their own appanage and were involved in its administration. As *khatuns* or queens they openly gave advice to their husbands whereas in other Islamic states women who played a role in government did not do so in public but from the harem. Though the role of women explicitly involved in politics and government diminished at the end of the Mongol Empire until the twentieth century, in many areas of the for-mer Mongol Empire this legacy continued. Indeed the stronger the Mongol-influenced heritage, the more freedom women had. The Empire of Timur and his successors illustrates this nicely as women continued to participate in *quriltais*, leading public ceremonies as well as serving as regents.[15]

The relative equality of women in nomadic societies shaped how Mongol women had a greater and more open involvement in matters

The Mongol court, illustration from Rashid al-Din's *Jami' al-Tawarikh*, which shows the khan and his queen sitting together in typical dress along with various members of the court dressed in Mongol fashion.

of state from the dawn of the Mongol Empire.[16] Although not egalitarian, the division of work and lifestyle of nomads necessitated that women be able to do the same jobs as men and vice versa.[17] As a result Mongolian women regularly assumed positions of leadership in the absence of husbands or fathers. Although it was customary for widows to marry the brothers or relatives of their deceased husband, they could also refuse marriage offers. In the post-Mongol world the egalitarianism of nomadism was not the sole factor. Even as the courts and elites became more sedentary women continued to play a significant role in the court. This may have to do with their role in providing legitimacy to *güregen* rulers such as the Timurids.[18] An active role for the daughters (even if they were great-great-granddaughters) kept alive the perception of Chinggisid connection. Indeed, non-Chinggisid successors found the *güregen* role a convenient method of legitimacy.

A clear sign of a successor losing its status as a successor to the Mongol Empire and establishing its own separate identity was often connected to the status of the royal women. This was most apparent in the Safavid, Ottoman and Mughal empires. Royal women in the early Safavid Empire enjoyed greater freedom than in the later. The early Safavids followed nomadic tradition as well as the institutions of their Aq Qoyunlu, Timurid and Mongol predecessors. Women played public and diplomatic roles. Although Mongol and Timurid women rarely wore veils, Safavid women did, often of diaphanous material. Over time Mongol cultural influences ended as the empire became more sedentary. As the Kizilbash Turks' nomadic customs lost influence to Persian-style kingship and court life, the status of women became more restricted.[19]

The Mughal Empire, on the other hand, did not see a diminishment of female influence in the court. If anything it appears to have spread. With the dual legitimacy of Timurid and Chinggisid traditions, perhaps it became too entrenched to fade away before other influences, whether Persian or Indian. We see even Afghan or Pashtun wives now assuming the same stance that a Chinggisid princess had when she married a Mughal prince. In essence they became their tribe's ambassador or representative to the court.[20] Furthermore, although the Mongol rulers had concubines, their wives remained important to the state as only the children of the wives had a claim to the throne. At the same time the wives' purpose was not solely to produce heirs or sate sexual needs, unlike the harem concubines in the Islamic world.[21] Thus childless wives could play a role in court life. This tradition carried over into the Timurid and Mughal states.

A similar yet different situation occurred in the Ottoman Empire. Initially wives played a significant role. As with the Safavids, when the Mongol influence among the Ottomans declined the status of women in the Ottoman court altered. Although wives remained important for marriage alliances, they did not play a diplomatic role as in the Mongol or Mughal courts. Furthermore, concubines became the preferred

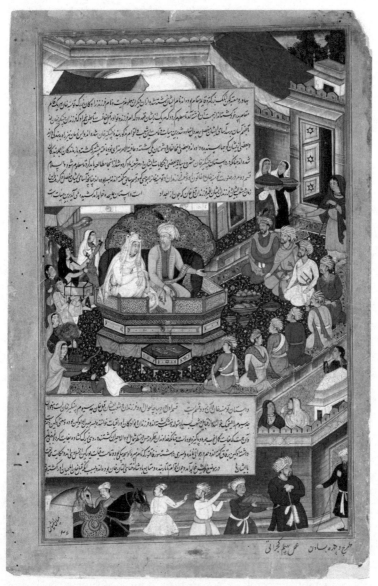

Chinggis Khan dividing his empire among his sons in 1219, on the eve of the Mongol invasion of Khwarazm, illustration by Basawan and Bhim for a Mughal Dynasty production of Rashid al-Din's *Jami' al-Tawarikh*, 16th century. The participants are dressed according to 16th-century Mughal fashion. Chinggis Khan is accompanied by one of his wives; in this case Yisui, a Tatar, who advised him to arrange for his successor before the campaign.

Xie Chufang, *Fascination of Nature*, Yuan Dynasty, 1321. The colophon on the left reveals the deeper meaning of the painting – underneath the beauty of nature is the disorder and chaos of the fight for survival. This idea was endemic among many of the Chinese during the Yuan – to work for the Mongols or remain loyal to the former Song Empire and starve while unemployed.

method of producing an heir, which became their *raison d'être* although they served other purposes as well. After producing an heir the woman's status was then tied to her son's position. While women continued to play a role in politics it was usually not in the public domain but behind the scenes.[22]

Political thought changed in other ways, too. Although Khubilai Khan had little use for Confucianism and even banned the Confucian exam system, preferring to recruit non-Confucians, Confucianism made a comeback. In 1313 the Yuan revived the civil service exams using the Neo-Confucianism of Zhu Xi as their interpretation in an effort to aid them in managing an increasingly Chinese-style state. While scholars in the Song Empire first developed Neo-Confucianism, the Yuan expanded its influence. In the cosmopolitan Yuan Empire Korean scholars and officials encountered Neo-Confucianism and brought it with them to the peninsula. Sustained contact with Chinese intellectuals as well as the patronage of the Mongol government during the Yuan Dynasty no doubt aided the process of Neo-Confucianism taking root in Korea and elsewhere. By way of example, during the Yuan Empire the government permitted foreigners to sit for the Chinese civil exams. As a result, Koreans studied and took exams in China. While some remained in the Yuan capital of Dadu, others returned to Korea. This caused many educated Koreans to re-examine their government, their society and even their personal behaviour. The reverberation of this transformation is still felt today as it 'led to a revolution that transformed Korean society and formed the basis of cultural norms, ethical standards, and conceptions about state and society that still influence Koreans in the twenty-first century'.[23]

Ideas manifested in numerous other ways. Above is just a sampling. What follows is an exploration of other ways that the Chinggis Exchange altered the perception of culture, food and material goods and how it impacted on the world.

THE ARTS

While the popular image of the Mongols often remains one of fur-clad barbarians burning and pillaging as they swept across Eurasia, this (while at times true) neglects the fact that they were instrumental in the spread of particular types of culture and also the reconceptualization of art. The Mongols instigated cultural change whether through invasion, refugees or patronage.

In Anatolia, today's Turkey, the transformation of a largely Greek culture into a Turkic one came largely during the Mongol period. The process of Turkicization began, of course, in 1071 with the Seljuk victory at Manzikirt over the Byzantines. Afterwards a steady influx of Turkic nomads and the loss of Byzantine influence led to a decline in the Greek presence. Nonetheless, the peasantry remained by and large Greek in ethnicity and culture. The courts of the Seljuk sultans had a distinct Persian influence as they mimicked their cousins in Iran in terms of systems of governance; nonetheless, Anatolia was still very provincial in terms of culture – at least until the 1220s.

It was at this time that the armies of Chinggis Khan truly played the role of fur-clad barbarians burning and pillaging as they rode into central Asia and northwestern Iran. For obvious reasons those who could do so decided that it would be better to flee than stay with the Mongols. Many poets, scholars and other intellectuals fled 1,800 or more miles to Konya, the capital of the Seljuks. Others found refuge at other courts, but Anatolia suddenly found itself the cultural recipient and benefactor of the refugees' knowledge and creative works. It would be as if the theatre, television and educational centres of New York City suddenly relocated to Tulsa, Oklahoma – a fine city in its own right, but not one that tops lists of 'leading cultural centres' in the United States. Although the Mongols conquered most of Anatolia twenty years later with the decisive victory at Köse Dagh in 1243 – proving that 1,800 miles was not far enough to escape the Mongols – the destruction was limited. Furthermore, the Mongols ruled the region with a relatively light hand, only interfering when local rulers rebelled. With the Mongols' own preference for Persian culture over Arab, the Persianization of high culture in Anatolia continued. The arrival of the Mongols also led to the appearance of more Turks in Anatolia, both as refugees and as members of the Mongol army, increasing the Turkicization and later the Islamization of the region, particularly after Islam became the state religion of the Ilkhanate.[24]

Art historians increasingly note that the Mongol period, specifically in the Ilkhanid region, was a high point for Islamic art. Much of this has to do with the arrival of new styles due to the combination of Western, Persian and Chinese traditions. As part of his efforts to illustrate the *Jami' al-Tawarikh*, which was to be produced in Persian and Arabic annually, Rashid al-Din brought a variety of artists to his workshops. They drew not only upon traditional Persian motifs but incorporated Chinese, central Asian Buddhist and Byzantine iconic artwork, as well as Siennese influences from Italy. The influences were brought about not only through imitation of material objects but also through techniques introduced by Chinese, Italian, Greek and other

Persian miniature of Chinggis Khan and two of his son, illustration from Rashid al-Din's *Jami' al-Tawarikh* (15th-century edition). The illustration also shows Chinese influences particularly in the landscape.

An illustration of a Mongol soldier galloping through mountainous terrain from the Saray album, 14th century. The landscape is clearly influenced by Chinese artistic sensibilities.

artists who lived in Tabriz, arriving there via the benefits of the Pax Mongolica. The most obvious evidence is the use of Chinese garden painting where the artwork is framed by rocks, folds in the terrain and other natural features.[25] Similar things happened in East Asia, where Middle Eastern influences entered Chinese art – most vividly in porcelain, which will be discussed below. The art of the period also benefited from cross-cultural views on what could be depicted in art. Neither Mongolian culture nor the Buddhist religion had any prohibitions of depicting people or sacred beings.[26] Thus even Muslim Mongols commissioned Persian miniatures featuring the Prophet Muhammad –

something that would never occur in the Mamluk Sultanate. In this fashion both Chinese and Persian art became more international; one can even view it as distinctive period in art history. This cross-pollination extended well beyond Iran and China as Armenia and others within the Ilkhanate emulated the new forms.[27]

At the same time, while Italian artists worked in Tabriz these styles reached Italy and infused Italian art with new energy.[28] Events from the Mongol Empire appeared in Italian art, such as the martyrdom of Franciscans at Tana in 1321. While one cannot credit the Mongols with creating the Italian Renaissance, it is clear that they influenced it through art and also the wealth that Italian merchants gained via trade with them. Italian merchants, who were the patrons of the Renaissance and provided much of the capital for projects, were active in the eastern Mediterranean and the Black Sea before the Mongols arrived but it is likely that the Renaissance would have looked different without the Chinggis Exchange.

On some levels the Mongol influence should not be surprising. As Roxann Prazniak noted, the Mongols imperial ideology 'explicitly proposed to move toward religious pluralism and locate its project in a contemporary social space not limited by place-based cultural geography. In so doing, Mongol-sponsored cultural projects placed emphasis on human agency in the making of history and naturalism in the representation of the phenomenological world.'[29] She also observed that Italian art increasingly included Asian faces, a fourteenth-century trend.[30] This, however, may not be completely accurate as the inclusion of Mongols or Tartars, to use the European label for any steppe nomad, in art may reflect the presence of the Tartar slaves in Italy.[31]

Italy and Persia were not the only regions to undergo a cultural transformation. The Mongol invasions may have also contributed to Korea's cultural consciousness.[32] Very little remains of pre-fourteenth-century literary or artistic works due to repeated Mongol invasions but in the Yuan period the invasions stopped, resulting in a sort of cultural renaissance. It is during this time that the legend of Tan'gun, the founding father of Korea, appeared in written form in the *Samguk Yusa* and in the historical verse *Chewang Un'gi* (Song of Emperors and Kings). Increased contact between Korean Buddhist monks and the larger Buddhist world also led to the Korean compilation and translation of the Buddhist canon, *Tripitaka Koreana*.[33] This is the most complete extant version of the *Tripitaka* (The Three Baskets). Originally completed in the eleventh century, the work was destroyed in the 1231 Mongol invasion. Between 1235 and 1251 the Koreans undertook a massive project to reproduce it at Kanghwa, resulting in 81,137 woodblocks – enough to print 160,000 pages.

In order to reach or leave Korea, however, new ideas and culture travelled through China. China has exchanged goods and ideas with Korea for centuries. The arts are no exception. The Yuan, unlike the Song, did not create a government-sponsored painting academy. The Hanlin Academy, established by the Tang Dynasty in the eighth century, continued with artists and scholars that the Mongols appointed to it, including Zhao Mengfu, one of the most important medieval Chinese artists. Other artists, however, refused to receive Mongol patronage yet nonetheless proved very productive and developed an 'amateur painting system that would dominate Chinese painting henceforth'.[34] As with the rest of the empire, artists outside of the Hanlin Academy also found Mongol patrons. Khubilai Khan's great-granddaughter Sengge was an art collector and patron of several artists. Other Mongol princesses followed suit and the Mongol aristocracy also supported artists who manufactured religious objects.

Mongol influence in Chinese art is similar to that of other foreign dynasties that ruled China – more non-Chinese animals. If you see a horse as a central component in a Chinese painting, odds are it is from a foreign (steppe-based) art, although the Han did have their tribute horse art. Central Asian art has had numerous animal motifs in its artistic expression; deer, eagles and horses are among the favourite themes. This continued not only in painting but particularly in metalwork, even on ubiquitous items such as saddle decorations, belt fittings and the *gerege* or *paiza*.[35]

The Yuan period also marked an innovative period for calligraphy and poetry, partly revitalized by the Zhu Xi school of Neo-Confucianism. One of the most influential figures in the Neo-Confucian artist movement was Guan Yunshi (1286–1324), a Uighur. He not only served in the bureaucracy after passing the civil service exams but was also a poet in the tradition of Chinese literature, yet was able to operate comfortably in Confucian scholarship as well as more popular lyric poetry.[36] He is also known as one of the greatest poets of the *qu* or *sanqu* form, which appeared during the Yuan period and developed from the arias of the Yuan dramas.

It is impossible to discuss all the artistic changes that occurred due to the Mongol Empire but the key component was that it allowed new

Ambrogio Lorenzetti, Mongols in Italy from the *Martyrdom of the Franciscans*, 14th century, fresco. This section of the fresco demonstrates the Chinggis Exchange's influence on Italian art as well as the prescence of Mongol/Tatar slaves in Italy.

syncretic styles to emerge as artists of all sorts could share ideas. Indeed, while it is easy to see the influences of China in Middle Eastern art and vice versa, we must not forget that the Mongol Empire unified north and south China for the first time in 300 years. As Frederick Mote noted, the cultural ambience of both regions was significantly different.[37] The influences derived from the unification of China thus rendered the north–south exchange equally as important as the east–west.

FOOD

Anyone who has travelled to another region or country knows that food can be very similar or greatly different, whether it is pizza in Chicago or New York or the spices used in cuisine in Henan and Sichuan provinces in China. The medieval period was no different and a major change prompted by the Mongol Empire affected culinary habits. With an empire spanning a continent and actively moving populations across the empire, new foods and tastes spread, commingled and evolved. While the Mongols never abandoned their meat and dairy diet (a forerunner to protein rich diet fads today) they did show interest in new cuisines. Although China had considerable contact with central Asian groups prior to the Mongols, it was during the period of the Mongol Empire that major culinary exchanges occurred. What is particularly notable is that many of the recipes appearing in Chinese sources, usually medical manuals, contain clear Middle Eastern influences.

For instance, the chickpea, a staple food of the Middle East, along with gluten-rich 'hard-wheat' or *Triticum durum* appears in China during the Mongol period and entered the Chinese culinary experience. The wheat is perhaps of greater importance as it is the key ingredient for leavening bread, and also in the production of thin sheets of dough for wrapping foods such as dumplings or use in layers such as filo, and of course noodles and pastas.[38]

While Marco Polo allegedly brought spaghetti to Italy, in essence it is the Mongol Empire that should be credited for giving noodles to the masses.[39] One should not overlook the spread of the chickpea either. In the *Yin-shan Cheng-yao* (Proper and Essential Things for the Emperor's Food and Drink), we find chickpeas in thirteen recipes.[40] This work is a marvellous insight not only into Chinese medicine but also into what was served at the court of the khans. Indeed, the translators of the *Yin-shan Cheng-yao* even sampled all of the dishes, although some substitutions had to be made as not all grocers had leg of wolf or badger in stock. Nonetheless, with an empire the size of the Mongols', a wide assortment of flavours and food, not to mention chefs, were available. The 'fusion' chefs of the late twentieth and early twenty-first centuries are clearly not a new phenomenon.

Significant contributors to the food ways of the Mongol Empire were the Turks. The Turks preceded the arrival of the Mongols in the Middle East by 200 years, if we discount earlier importation of Turkic mamluks, purchased as military slaves, who may have retained some of their cultural norms but did not actually bring their cultural milieu with them. With the Mongol irruption, not only did the Mongols come but more Turks. After the dust settled the Turks remained important interlocutors of cuisine. Not only did they incorporate Middle Eastern foods into their diet, they also introduced other foods to the Middle East.[41] For this reason perhaps it is not surprising that the author of the *Yin-shan Cheng-yao* was a sinicized Uighur named Hu Szu-hui. The Mongol conquest of China brought the Turkicization of Chinese and Mongolian cuisine, at least at the court level of society, as demonstrated in the *Yin-shan Cheng-yao*. Often basic Mongol recipes were Turkicized with the addition of chickpeas or other foods more clearly Turkic in origin, like *börek*, which appears for the first time in China in the early fourteenth century (Yuan era). Other foods included baklava, whose name may have been derived from a Mongolian word. The name for a standard Turkic food, *manty*, may have been derived from the Chinese *mantou* or steamed buns. *Manty* among the Turks usually has a meat filling, thus the connection may simply be a coincidence.[42]

One cannot dine without drink and the Mongols were no exception. The silver fountain designed by Buchier dispensed four different types of alcohol. The native drink of the Mongols was *airag* or, to use the Turkic word, *kumiss*, fermented mare's milk. After early autumn *airag* is difficult to come by, indeed, speaking from personal experience trying to find *airag* after September is truly a Herculean task. The khans, however, were apparently able to make arrangements to ensure their own personal supply.[43] Other alcoholic drinks were served from Buchier's fabulous silver tree and clearly represented the extent of the Mongol Empire: rice wine from China, grape wine from the Middle East and central Asia and mead made from honey from the forests of the Rus'. It should be noted that with each generation the potency of alcohol increased.[44] Chinggis Khan enjoyed his *airag* and sampled the other drinks he encountered but Ögödei enjoyed his wine perhaps too much. Later khans encountered distilled alcohol through Chinese and Middle Eastern influence. With the modern production of Chinggis Khan vodka, it is safe to say that the Mongols even incorporated Russian influence.

MATERIAL GOODS

Whether one is eating or drinking, a device to contain that substance is always useful. One of the major goods that spread through the Eurasian world due to the Mongol Empire was porcelain. Thirteenth-century porcelain from the Yuan Dynasty (1264–1370) has been found in archaeological sites near Damascus and in Egypt and almost everywhere between there and the centre of porcelain production, Jingdezhen, in the interior of Jiangxi province. A ready market emerged, particularly among elites. In Islamic areas prohibitions against the use of silver or gold dinner plates created a demand.[45] Similar demand appeared in medieval Europe. While porcelain may have been a desirable luxury item throughout the Eurasian world prior to the Mongols, Mongol influence made it much more available than before while also creating a distinctive style that shaped perceptions of porcelain for centuries to come.

The hallmark of Mongol-era porcelain was the blue dye used to decorate it. Prior to the Mongols Chinese porcelain tended to be undecorated. Around 1325 the porcelain factories at Jingdezhen began producing the distinctive blue and white porcelain, ranging from bowls to vases.[46] The white porcelain was glazed, then artists decorated the piece with the blue dye, which was then covered with another glaze, which was fired at such a high temperature that the surface became transparent yet hard.[47] The use of the blue dye is notable because blue was the sacred colour of the Mongols, since it was the colour of the Eternal Sky or *Möngke Tenggeri*, and because the dye was derived from cobalt dyes long used in Iranian ceramics. Through the trade in goods and expertise between Mongolian East Asia and the Mongolian Middle East new techniques were introduced to produce an aesthetically superior product. Many pieces were created specifically for Mongolian needs, such as *airag* or *kumiss* serving bowls. Furthermore, with the addition of the new cobalt blue dye, porcelain sales and production increased significantly compared to the Song period. In many ways this is not surprising as the pieces not only have aesthetic but also practical appeal. The glaze of the ceramics provided a sealant that prevented the liquid-based foods of the Mongols, such as *shülen* or soup, from penetrating or being absorbed by the container. Its creation was only possible due to the Chinggis Exchange. Persian ceramic artisans lacked the technique and white clay to make porcelain, while the Chinese lacked the cobalt dye. It should be noted, however, that this did not stop many a potter from attempting to make similar products, with ingenious methods to give the illusion of true porcelain.[48]

Its appeal continued for centuries. Although Europeans found the appropriate type of white clay in Austria, they still lacked the technique to make higher quality porcelain or the fine details of the design. The author's own experience with potsherds as an archaeology student confirms that pre-nineteenth century British, French and Dutch efforts paled in comparison to the finesse of Chinese ceramics. Yet it never stopped their elites from wanting them and, with the Industrial Revolution, didn't stop the middle class from wanting a close approximation to fine porcelain, or dinner china as it is often called today.

Other ceramics also criss-crossed the Mongol Empire. In addition to Chinese porcelain one might also find Iranian polychrome ceramics. Archaeological finds in the domains of the former Jochid Khanate reveal ceramics made to imitate porcelain. Craftsmen in Sarai used *kashin*, a silicate that creates a similar surface and white colour to Chinese porcelain.[49] The craftsmen also incorporated Iranian glazing techniques with not only the cobalt blue dye but a wide variety of colours on single pieces of ceramic. While a slight step below the Yuan porcelain, the *kashin* ceramics are of high quality. Those produced in the many workshops of the Golden Horde are equal to those produced in the Ilkhanate and the Mamluk Sultanate.[50] As this type of ceramic was not produced in the Jochid regions prior to the Mongol conquests it is certain some technological exchange occurred either during the pre-dissolution phase or perhaps through the Mongol–Mamluk alliance. In order to make *kashin* or porcelain ceramics high temperature kilns are a necessity. Archaeologists have uncovered highly advanced kilns with an intricate system of vertical ducts to distribute heat through the firing chamber.[51]

While porcelain was a luxury item, more mundane items also moved around Eurasia. One such was the wheelbarrow. Although it had existed in China since the Han dynasty the wheelbarrow did not appear in Europe until the thirteenth century, just a few years after the Mongols burst into Europe. Considering that it is unlikely that a wheelbarrow happened to fall off the saddle of a Mongol horse, it was most probably observed by some traveller in East Asia who then related how it was used.

Another item was the printing press, used in China and Korea since the tenth and eleventh centuries respectively. Printing with woodblocks or xylography had been in use prior to the printing press but the use of moveable type dramatically changed the publishing world. The Chinese commoner Bi Sheng created a moving type printing press in the 1040s during the Song Dynasty.[52] Initially it was made from earthenware and occasionally wood. Both types were in use in China during the Yuan era.[53] This technology had begun a westward transmission as the Tangut also used moveable wooden type, as did the Tibetans on occasion.[54]

With the Mongols, the printing press reached the Middle East. Persian and Arabic fonts did not develop. Rather the press was introduced when Geikhatu introduced *ch'ao* or paper money (*chaw* in Persian) in 1294, although block printing pre-dated the Mongols. Marco Polo mentions the use of paper money but did not describe how the printing press functions, thus one of its most important uses remained overlooked by Europeans until the seventeenth century, when Sweden issued notes in 1661.[55] In the Yuan Empire they initially used woodblocks but after 1275 switched to bronze. Playing cards were produced in a similar manner in the Yuan realm but currently there is no evidence that Geikhatu's printing press or any Ilkhanid printing press produced them.[56] Thus if they reached Europe it was from East Asia or perhaps the Jochid Khanate, although the latter is less likely.

The next major innovation was the development of moveable metal type. The first known moveable metal type produced 28 copies of the Korean book, *Sangjong Kogum Yemun* (Prescribed Ritual Texts of the Past and Present) in 1234.[57] Considering the number of woodblocks needed for the *Tripitaka Koreana*, perhaps the Korean invention of metal type occurred out of fear of running out of materials for woodblock production. Although travellers must have seen printed books, rather than copied, it is not clear if any were carried west to Europe or the Middle East. Rashid al-Din clearly saw the potential ramifications of the printing press just from Geikhatu's introduction of printed paper money.[58] Unfortunately, it did not catch on – possibly as a backlash to the printed money. As Thomas Allsen indicates, the Middle East rejected moveable type technology for centuries, accepting it only in the nineteenth century. Their rejection was based on social, religious and political rationales. Perhaps it was xenophobia but considering the acceptance of other items the rejection of the printing press seems out of place.[59] The difficulties in creating the frontal, median and final forms of Arabic letters seems more likely to be the cause. Imagine if Gutenberg had to tackle cursive rather than block printing for his first press.

Thus printing presses remained an East Asian phenomenon and did not make a lasting impression in the Middle East. Yet almost 150 years after Rashid al-Din wistfully dreamed of printing presses, Johannes Gutenberg constructed a modified version of the Korean moveable metal type press. Although independent inventiveness is always possible, the complexity of a printing press suggests that outside influences played a role. Considering that the Koreans had a printing press 300 years before Gutenberg and moveable metal type 200 years before he came along, it is likely that the idea reached him through Mongol agency, such as a now lost travel account by missionaries or merchants, although other aspects of his press were clearly borrowed from other technologies such as wine and olive presses.

Although in the popular imagination the Mongol sense of style is the leather and fur-clad barbarian, the Mongols were quite fashion conscious and indeed appear to have exerted considerable influence on medieval fashions. As mentioned previously, they loved the gold-threaded silk brocade known as *nasij*. This cloth could be plain or quite elaborate, combining Islamic, central Asian and Chinese motifs and patterns. Known as Tartar cloth in Europe, its exoticism and luxurious material soon prompted a fad. Although Mongolian models did not strut down the Karakorum catwalk, travellers saw it and received it as gifts. Indeed, Tatar clothes were even present in the papal inventory of 1295. King Phillip V in 1317 also had various Tatar clothes: *tartair, draps d'or applez naques,* or *nachis.*[60] Thus we see the introduction of *nasij* into European languages as a loan word. As with present day fashion, imitators soon geared up, somewhat ironically in Italy, with Arabian and Asian scripts or faux scripts in an attempt to mimic the Phagspa or so-called square script of the Mongol Empire.[61] Although some silk production occurred in Italy, Italian merchants also had access to silk from the east as Tabriz became a major centre of silk under the Mongols as well as Cilicia at Ayas. In addition the Genoese purchased Mongol silk from Acre for export to Europe, although that outlet ended in 1291 with Acre's fall to the Mamluks.

Silk was not the only medium in which the Mongols influenced fashion. Cotton too was a cloth for which the Mongols stimulated demand, although not as a luxury item. Cotton production came late to China in the thirteenth and fourteenth century. It grew in areas of eastern Turkestan (modern Xinjiang) and in Yunnan but both were beyond the control of the Jin and Song. Thus cotton came in only via trade, where it did not compete well with silk or hemp-based cloth.[62] This changed with the development of better cotton ginning technology but also with the arrival of the Mongols who demanded it for military uniforms in the Yuan Empire.[63] Five provinces paid a tax in cotton. No doubt the ever-pragmatic Mongols recognized the limitations of wearing felt or silk in the humidity of south China and Southeast Asia. Cotton also made a better garment for their military needs. Cotton, however, did not stop with the Mongol military. Cotton and cotton cloth-making became known to Koreans by virtue of a diplomatic mission in 1363. This mission included one Mun Ik-Chom, who witnessed the production of cotton. Procuring some cotton seeds, he gave them to his father-in-law, who successfully planted them.[64]

Just as the Italians started to imitate Mongol-influenced fashions, at the other end of the empire the Koreans did as well. With thousands of Koreans serving in the Mongol court, visiting it or marrying Mongol aristocrats, Mongol fashions gained prominence in Korea with many Koreans adopting Mongol clothing and hairstyles.[65] This included the Mongol style coat, the *deel*, which today remains essentially unchanged since the thirteenth century. A long, loose robe that comes down to somewhere between the knees and mid-shin level, the *deel* is fastened in the front with two buttons on strings with loops on the overlapping side, connecting on the upper right-hand side and then

Mongolian royal women, Yuan era, tapestry made from silk and metallic thread. The robes it depicts were the ubiquitous *deel* worn by all Mongols. The headgear also was standard among the Mongolian female nobility.

253

Mongolian re-enactor dressed as a Mongolian royal lady. Mongolian court fashions influenced the dress of the nobility from Korea to Europe.

at intervals on the right side. It is usually also fastened with a sash. Underneath, trousers are worn by men and women. It was the fact that the Mongols fastened their robes on the right that distinguished them from other nomads, who typically fastened them on the left.

Mongol headgear also influenced haberdashers in Europe. The ubiquitous princess crown, pointy with a veil or train attached, found inspiration in the hats worn by Mongolian princesses. Other tall conical hats also found inspiration in the Mongols. Most Mongol hats tended to have a folded brim and were made of felt, although leather and fur-lining were also common. As with European fashions, the crown of the hat gradually became taller. In Europe this would become the basis of the stereotypical wizard's or witch's hat. Considering the church's opinion on witchcraft, the fact that key garments were connected to the Mongols associated witchcraft with the Other more than anything else.

Conclusion

This has been but a sampling of the results of the Chinggis Exchange. While the Mongol Empire's impact in world history has really only been appreciated for a few decades beyond scholars who study the empire, others noted the Mongol impact much earlier:

> Many of these adventurers must have established themselves and died in the countries they went to visit. Others returned to their country as obscure as when they left it; but with their imaginations full of what they had seen, relating it all to their families and friends, and doubtless with exaggerations; but leaving around them, amidst ridiculous fables, a few useful recollections and traditions productive of advantage. Thus were sown in Germany, in Italy, in France, in the monasteries, among the nobility, and even in the lowest grade of society, precious seeds destined to bud at a later period. All these obscure travelers, carrying the arts of their native country to distant lands, brought back other information about these no less precious, and thus effected, unconsciously, exchanges more productive of good than all of those in commerce. By this means not merely the traffic in silks, in porcelains, in commodities from Hindostan, was made more extensive and more practicable, opening new routes to industry and commerce; but, that which was far more valuable, foreign manners and customs of before unknown nations, extraordinary productions, were presented to the European mind, confined, since the fall of the Roman empire, within too narrow a circle. Men began to have an idea that, after all, there was something worthy of notice in the finest, the most populous and most anciently civilized of the four quarters of the world. People began to think of studying the arts, the religions, the languages of the nations who inhabited it, and there was even a proposition to establish a professorship of the Tartar language in the University of Paris. Romantic narrative, reduced by discussion within reasonable proportions, diffused in all directions juster and more varied information: the world seemed opening towards the East. Geography made immense strides, and ardour of discovery became the new form assumed by the adventurous spirit of Europeans. The idea of another hemisphere ceased, as soon as our own became better known, to present itself to the mind as a paradox

destitute of all probability, and it was in going in search of the
Zipangri [Zipangu] of Marco-Polo that Christopher Columbus
discovered the New World.[66]

This chapter has been but an introduction to the cultural exchanges
that occurred during the Mongol period. An entire book could be written on it. At the beginning of the chapter I alluded to Thomas Allsen,
arguably the most significant scholar on the Mongol Empire from a
global perspective, whose *Culture and Conquest in Mongol Eurasia* examines this very issue. Yet even with seven chapters devoted to specific
topics such as medicine and printing, it is not enough. Undoubtedly
scholars will continue to study these exchanges and bring to light more
data and reveal more information about the diffusion of culture. Thus
far most of the work, including this chapter, has focused on an
east–west exchange. Perhaps in the future scholars will also give emphasis to a north–south exchange and indicate how the Mongol Empire
impacted the culture of Siberia and south and Southeast Asia in greater
detail, although as evinced with studies on the Delhi Sultanate this
process has begun.

GLOSSARY

Alba qubchiri	Tribute or tax, sometimes impromptu and sometimes scheduled, that took the form of service to the Mongol government. Usually it was military service but could come in other forms
Altan Orda	Literally the 'golden camp' or 'golden palace', meaning the imperial camp
Altan Urugh	The 'golden kin' or family of Chinggis Khan
Anda	A blood brother
Aq Orda	White Horde as opposed to the Golden Horde. The 'white camp' or palace referred to the part of the Jochid Khanate that dominated the Caspian steppes and extended into Kazakhstan
Bichegchi	A secretary within the Mongol civil administration
Dalai	State land within the empire. In essence the khan owned it and all revenues went to the state treasury and not to other princes
Darughachi	A civilian governor. The *darughachi*'s authority could extend over a village or town to an entire region. They had the authority to collect taxes and maintain order
Dinar	Currency in the Islamic world based on the Roman and Byzantine *denarius*. Typically it was coined in gold, but during Ghazan's reign it was switched to silver
Dirhem	Derived from Sasanian currency, the dirhem became the smaller currency denomination in the Islamic world. During the late Ilkhanid state, six silver dirhems comprised a dinar
Faqih	A jurist of Islamic law
Gerege	Official documentation or passport necessary to use the *yam*. The *gerege* or *paiza* was made from wood, bronze, silver or gold. The value of the material correlated with the importance and privileges of the bearer
Güregen	Son-in-law of Chinggis
Inje	The property belonging to a member of the Mongol aristocracy and sometimes other high ranking officials. This included not only landed property, but also slaves and free subjects

Inju	See *inje*
Iqta	In the Islamic world, a land grant that provides the salary or goods for a solider or bureaucrat. The individual does not necessarily rule over it, but rather collects the proceeds
Jarghuchi	A judge in the Mongol Empire. Also see *yeke jarghuchi*
Keshik	The bodyguard and household staff of the khan
Kizilbash	Literally the 'red hats'. Turkic nomads and followers of the Safaviyya sufi order. The *kizilbash* became the backbone of the later Shi'a Safavid state
Köke Orda	The Blue Horde or camp. Generally considered the orda of Shayban b. Jochi and part of the larger Jochid Khanate
Khamag Monggol Ulus	The All Mongol State – the original name of Chinggis Khan's kingdom before it changed to Yeke Monggol Ulus or Great Mongol State
Khwajas	Muslim merchants involved in long-distance trade
Madrasa	An Islamic school with the education focused on religion, but also history, Arabic and law
Nutag	Mongolian word for pasturelands
Orda	Camp or palace in Turkic and Mongolian. Also the origin of the word 'horde'. It also referred to the territory controlled by that particular camp
Ordu	See *orda*
Ortagh	Merchant–Mongol aristocracy partnerships. Often merchants operating in such as a partnership received tax-exempt status. In the 1240s, many *ortaghs* abused their privileges. Most of the merchants involved in the *ortagh* tended to be Muslims who dominated much of the Eurasian trade
Paiza	See *gerege*
Qadi	A judge in Islamic legal systems. Qadis were appointed by the state
Qarachi beys	The four high-ranking non-Chinggisid leaders within a khanate. Typically they led a clan or tribe and could balance the authority of a khan
Quriltai	A meeting or congress in which the princes and leading figures of the empire met to discuss important matters and/or select and enthrone a new khan
Sheng	A Chinese term for 'province' referring to the territorial divisions the Yuan Dynasty made
Tael	Chinese monetary unit of silver. It was the equivalent of 10,000 Ilkhanid silver dinars
Tamgha	A value added tax placed on goods carried by merchants. It ranged from 5 to 10 per cent and was paid on each transaction. The term means stamp or seal. The goods would receive a stamp to show that the *tamgha* had been paid
Tamma	A special military force placed on the borders of the Mongol Empire used to maintain control and extend

	Mongol influence and territory. The *tamma* moved forward as the borders did so that it was always on the frontier
Tammachin	Members of the *tamma*. The singular form is *tammachi*
Tian	The Chinese word for Heaven, tied to the concept of the Mandate of Heaven in which Heaven legitimizes a dynasty but may also revoke its legitimacy when the dynasty no longer fulfills its function
Timar	See *iqta*
Tögrög	Modern Mongolian currency
Tûmân	Mongolian loan-word in Persian for ten thousand
Tümen	A Mongol military and taxation unit of ten thousand men or households respectively
Ulama	A group of scholars, jurists, and other men of knowledge and religion in an Islamic community. Generally, the consensus of the *ulama* decided most matters of religion
Ulagh	A Mongolian word for horse. Usually used in reference to postal horses
Yam	The postal system of the Mongol Empire. Relay stations were posted at regular intervals allowing messengers to quickly exchange mounts and travel hundreds of miles a day. When the terrain limited travel by horse, runners were used
Yamchin	The personnel who manned the yam stations
Yarligh	A decree or order by the Mongol government
Yasa	The Mongol law code. We do not have a surviving copy of the *yasa* despite numerous references to it
Yasak	Tribute paid to the khan or other authority. It usually referred to the fur tribute paid by Siberian peoples to Kazan and Sibir, but then paid to Moscow after it conquered Kazan and Sibir
Yeke jarghuchi	Literally a 'great judge'. The *yeke jarghuchi* served in a capacity similar to that of a viceroy and had authority to collect tribute, resolve disputes, and had authority over the *darughachin*

Dynastic Tables

THE MONGOL EMPIRE

RULER	REIGN
Chinggis Khan (Temüjin)	1206–27
Tolui (as regent)	1227–9
Ögödei	1229–41
Töregene Khatun (as regent)	1242–6
Güyük	1246–8
Oghul-Qaimish Khatun (as regent)	1248–51
Möngke	1251–9
Ariq Böke/Khubilai (as opposing regents)	1260–4

THE YUAN EMPIRE

RULER	REIGN
Khubilai Khan	1264–94
Temür Öljeitü	1294–1307
Khaishan	1307–11
Ayurbarwada	1311–20
Shidebala	1320–3
Yisün-Temür	1323–8
Qoshila	1328–9
Tuq-Temür	1328, 1329–32
Irinchinbal	1332
Toghan Temür	1332–70

THE CHAGHATAYID KHANATE

RULER	REIGN
Chaghatai Khan	d. 1242
Qara-Hülegü	1242–6
Yisü-Möngke	1246–51
Ergene Khatun (regent)	1251–60
Alghu	1260–65/6
Mubarak-Shah	1265/6–66
Baraq	1266–71

Negübei	1271
Toqa-Temur	1272
Interregnum – domination by Qaidu	
Du'a	1282–1307
Könchek	1307–8
Nalighu	1308–9
Esen-Buqa	1309–18
Kebeg	1318–27
Eljigidei	1327–30
Töre-Temür	1330–1
Tarmashirin	1331–4
Buzan	1334–5
Changshi	1335–8
Yisün-Temür	1338–41
Ali Khalil	1341–3
Muhammad	1343
Qazan	1343–6/7
Danishmendji	1347–58
Buyan Quli	1358–9
Shah Temür	1359
Tughluq Temür	1359–63

THE ILKHANATE

RULER	REIGN
Hülegü	1260–5
Abaqa	1265–82
Tegüder	1282–4
Arghun	1284–91
Gaykhatu	1291–1295
Baidu	1295
Ghazan	1295–1304
Öljeitü	1304–16
Abu Said	1316–35

THE JOCHID KHANATE

RULER	REIGN
Jochi	d. 1225
Batu	1225–55
Sartaq	1256–7
Ulaghchi	1257
Berke	1257–66
Möngke-Temür	1267–80
Töde-Möngke	1280–7
Telebogha	1287–91
Toqta	1291–1312

Üzbek	1313–41
Tinibeg	1341–2
Janibeg	1342–57
Berdibeg	1357–9
Qulpa	1359–60
Nawroz	1360
Interregnum – civil war	1360–75
Urus (Khan of Aq Orda takes over)	1375–6
Toqtaqiya	1376–7
Temür Malik	1377
Toqtamysh	1377–95
Temür Qutlugh	1395–1401
Shadi Beg	1401–7
Pulad or Bolad	1407–10
Temür	1410–12
Jalal al-Din	1412
Karim Berdi	1412–14
Kebek	1414–17
Yeremferden	1417–19
Ulugh Muhammad (first reign)	1419–20
Dawlat Berdi	1420–2
Baraq	1422–7
Ulugh Muhammad (second reign)	1427–33
Sayyid Ahmad I	1433–5
Küchük Muhammad	1435–65
Sayyid Ahmad II	1465–81
Shaykh Ahmad	1481–1505

REFERENCES

Introduction

1 John A. Boyle, *The Mongol World Empire, 1206–1370* (London, 1977).
2 Owen Lattimore, 'Preface', in Boyle, *Mongol World Empire, 1206–1370*.
3 Arthur Waldron, 'Introduction', Bertold Spuler, *The Mongol Period*, trans. F.R.C. Bagley (Princeton, NJ, 1994), p. vii.
4 These basically fill the gap between the original publication of Morgan's book in 1986 and roughly 2007. Denis Sinor, 'Notes on Inner Asian Bibliography IV: History of the Mongols in the 13th Century', *Journal of Asian History*, XXIII/1 (1989), pp. 26–79; Peter Jackson, 'The State of Research: The Mongol Empire, 1986–1999', *Journal of Medieval History*, XXVI/2 (2000), pp. 189–210; David O. Morgan, 'The Mongols in Iran: A Reappraisal', *Iran*, XLII (2004), pp. 131–6; Paul D. Buell, *Historical Dictionary of the Mongol World Empire* (Lanham, MD, 2003), pp. 1–99; David O. Morgan, *The Mongols*, 2nd edn (2007), pp. 180–206.
5 Manuel Komroff, 'Afterword', in Marco Polo, *The Travels of Marco Polo*, trans. William Marsden (New York, 2001), p. 313.
6 Frances Wood, *Did Marco Polo Go to China?* (Boulder, CO, 1996); Stephen G. Haw, *Marco Polo's China* (London, 2009); Peter Jackson, 'Marco Polo and His "Travels"', *Bulletin of the School for Oriental and African Studies*, XLI/1 (1998), pp. 82–101; Igor de Rachewiltz, 'Marco Polo Went to China', *Zentralasiatishe Studien*, XXVII (1997), pp. 34–92; David Morgan, 'Marco Polo in China – or Not', *Journal of the Royal Asiatic Society*, 3rd ser., VI (1996), pp. 221–5.
7 Buell, *Historical Dictionary*, pp. 68–9.
8 Ibid., p. 69.
9 Paul D. Buell and Eugene N. Anderson, trans. and eds, *A Soup for the Qan* (London, 2000). An expanded second edition appeared in 2010.
10 Arthur Waley, trans., *The Travels of an Alchemist* (London, 2005).
11 James P. Delgado, *Khubilai Khan's Lost Fleet: In Search of a Legendary Armada* (Berkeley, CA, 2008).
12 This is best exemplified in Jack Weatherford, *Genghis Khan and the Making of the Modern World* (New York, 2004) and Richard Gabriel, *Genghis Khan's Greatest General: Subotai the Valiant* (Norman, OK, 2006).
13 Hidehiro Okada and Junko Miyawaki-Okada, 'Haslund's *Toregut Rarelro* in the Parallel Text in Ulaanbaatar', *Mongolian Studies*, XXIX (2007), p. 127.
14 Jeremy Page, 'Russians Who Get Drunk as a Warlord', *The Times* (19 January 2004).

15 'Eurovision Song Contest 1979', at www.eurovision.tv, accessed 12 August 2010. Their Mongol Empire-related songs appear on a variety of websites, see 'Dschinghis khan eurovision', at www.youtube.com; a later hit was 'The Rocking Son of Dschinggis Khan', which may explain the real reason for the ascension of Ögödei, see 'The Rocking Son of Dschinghis Khan', at www.youtube.com. The song 'Dschinggis Khan' has been remade by Japanese pop group Berryz Koubou (also spelled Berryz Kobo) and is transliterated as Jingisukan, see 'Berryz Koubou-Jingisukan (Dschinggis Khan)', at www.youtube.com.

1 THE FORMATION OF THE MONGOL EMPIRE

1 1162 is the date established by the government of Mongolia. Scholars have speculated that 1165 or 1167 are also plausible. In any case there is no absolute certainty as to the date of Temüjin's birth other than that it was in the 1160s. The conflicting dates make the creation of an early chronology for Chinggis Khan's life problematic.

2 Paul Ratchnevsky, *Genghis Khan: His Life and Legacy*, trans. Thomas Nivison Haining (Cambridge, MA, 1992), pp. 15–16.

3 Igor de Rachewiltz, trans. and ed., *The Secret History of the Mongols* (Leiden, 2004), p. 14. This and the dream may be apocryphal and added later to justify and explain Chinggis Khan's extraordinary success.

4 Ibid., p. 14.

5 Ibid., p. 20. Temüjin and Jochi-Kasar successfully caught a fish. This was a major accomplishment not only in terms of securing food but also because the Mongols typically do not catch or eat fish. Bekhter and Belgütei then took the fish from the children of Hö'elün. Despite their protestations, Hö'elün did not intervene, telling them essentially to learn to get along. For Temüjin this was the last straw as a few days before Temüjin and Jochi-Kasar had brought down a lark only to have Bekhter take it away. Thus the two conspired to kill Bekhter but allowed Belgütei (the younger of the two) to survive.

6 Ratchnevsky, *Genghis Khan*, pp. 24–8; Rachewiltz, *Secret History of the Mongols*, pp. 22–6. There are no clear dates for how long Temüjin was imprisoned, or exactly when, other than that it occurred after Bekhter's death. It is quite possible that Temüjin was captured several times as *The Secret History of the Mongols* indicates that in his youth he suffered at the hands of his relatives on multiple occasions.

7 Rachewiltz, *Secret History of the Mongols*, p. 30.

8 Ratchnevsky, *Genghis Khan*, pp. 34–7; Timothy May, 'The Mechanics of Conquest and Governance: The Rise and Expansion of the Mongol Empire, 1185–1265', PhD dissertation, University of Wisconsin-Madison (2004), pp. 169–76.

9 May, 'The Mechanics of Conquest and Governance', pp. 169–76; Timothy May, 'Jamuqa and the Education of Chinggis Khan', *Acta Mongolica*, VI (2006), pp. 273–86.

10 David Sneath, *The Headless State: Aristocratic Orders, Kinship Society, and*

Misrepresentations of Nomadic Inner Asia (New York, 2007).

11 Ratchnevsky, *Genghis Khan*, pp. 45–7, 49–50. Another possibility was that he fled to Xi Xia as portrayed in the film by Arif Aliyev and Sergey Bodrov, *Mongol* (2007). The latter scenario is less likely.

12 Rachewiltz, *The Secret History of the Mongols*, p. 76.

13 Ibid., pp. 84–6.

14 Ibid., pp. 111–12.

15 Rachewiltz, *Secret History of the Mongols*, p. 164; He Qiutao, *Sheng Wu Qin Zheng Lu (Bogda Bagatur Bey-e-Ber Tayilagsan Temdeglel)*, ed. Arasaltu (Qayilar, 1985), pp. 39–40; Rashid al-Din, *Jami' al-Tawarikh*, ed. Muhammad Rushn Mustafi Musavi (Tehran, 1995), pp. 422–3; Rashid al-Din, *Jami' al-Tawarikh*, ed. B. Karimi (Tehran, 1983), pp. 308–9; Rashid al-Din, *Jami'u't-tawarikh: Compendium of Chronicles*, trans. W. M. Thackston, (Cambridge, MA, 1998), vol. I, p. 204. Rashid al-Din noted that Quduqa-Beki submitted in 604 H./1208 while Chinggis Khan, after conquering Xi Xia, led his army to the Irtysh to deal with Güchülüg and Toqtoa Beki of the Merkit. It is possible that Jochi was acting as a wing of the army that defeated the Merkits and Naimans at the Irtysh.

16 Rachewiltz, *Secret History of the Mongols*, pp. 164–5. This included the Buriyat, Barqut, Ursut, Qabqanas, Tubas, Shibir, Kesdiyim, Tuqas, Bayid, Tenleg, Tö'eles, Tas and the Bajigid. The Buriyat dwelled on the eastern side of Lake Baikal with the Barqut to the north of them. The location of the Ursut and Qabqanas is uncertain but probably to the west of Baikal and the Tubas dwelt in the modern region of Tannu Tuva.

17 Rachewiltz, *Secret History of the Mongols*, p. 164; Rashid al-Din, *Jami'u't-tawarikh*, vol. I, p. 204; H. Desmond Martin, *The Rise of Chingis Khan and His Conquest of North China* (Baltimore, MD, 1950), p. 102. Rashid al-Din noted that the Kirgiz submitted to Chinggis Khan's envoys Altan and Bu'ura.

18 Ibid.

19 Martin, *Rise of Chinggis Khan*, p. 102.

20 Xi Xia consisted of a Tangut, Tibetan and Chinese population with a mixture of nomadic pastoralist and sedentary cultures.

21 David O. Morgan, *The Mongols* (Oxford, 1986), pp. 64–5. Like many scholars, Morgan viewed the attack on Xi Xia as a practice run on the Jin, 'against a state which was organised largely on Chinese lines, and if successful it would open a western route into China to add to the more direct northern path of invasion. No doubt the Mongols, always alive to the importance of commerce, were also interested in control of the major trade routes that passed through Xi-Xia.'

22 Isenbike Togan, *Flexibility and Limitation in Steppe Formations: The Kerait Khanate and Chinggis Khan* (Leiden, 1998), p. 70. Xi Xia always served as a refuge for the steppes. Toghril Ong-Qan's uncle, Gur Qan (not the Gur Qan of Kara Khitai), took refuge there after Toghril and Yisügei defeated him. There may have also been some clan relation between the Kerait Tübe'en and the Tangut T'o-pa clans.

23 Ruth Dunnell, 'The Hsi Hsia', in *The Cambridge History of China, Alien Regimes and Border States, 907–1368*, ed. Herbert Franke and Denis Twitchett

(Cambridge, 1994), vol. VI, p. 164. It is not clear whether he had actually found refuge in Xi Xia or simply attempted to establish himself there. In any case he then moved into northeastern Tibet before being driven into the Tarim Basin.

24 Martin, *Rise of Chingis Khan*, p. 112.

25 Rachewiltz, *Secret History of the Mongols*, pp. 177–8. See also Rashid al-Din, *Jami' al-Tawarikh*, ed. Musavi, p. 572; Rashid al-Din, *Jami' al-Tawarikh*, ed. Karimi, p. 427; Rashid al-Din, *Jami'u't-tawarikh*, vol. II, pp. 289–90. Martin, *Rise of Chingis Khan*, p. 119, sees the Tangut as vassals, whereas Rachewiltz, in *Secret History of the Mongols*, states that the Tangut king actually submitted and offered to serve as the right wing of the Mongol forces. The treaty that resulted from the negotiations stipulated that Chinggis Khan would receive Chaqa, a daughter of Li An-Chuan, a tribute of camels, woollen cloth and falcons, and the Tangut would be vassals of Chinggis Khan and contribute troops.

26 Paul D. Buell, 'Tribe, Qan, and Ulus in Early Mongol China, Some Prolegomena to Yüan History', PhD dissertation, University of Washington (1977), p. 47; Martin, *Rise of Chingis Khan*, pp. 101, 149; Thomas Allsen, 'The Rise of the Mongolian Empire and Mongolian Rule in North China', in *The Cambridge History of China, Alien Regimes and Border States, 907–1368*, ed. Herbert Franke and Denis Twitchett (Cambridge, 1994), vol. VI, pp. 348–9. The Önggüd tribes switched their loyalty to the Mongols. It is unclear if the Juyin also sought Mongol protection. Thomas Allsen describes the Juyins as an 'ethnically mixed people inhabiting the sensitive Jin-Tangut-Önggüd border regions, who frequently served the Jin as military auxiliaries'.

27 Rachewiltz, *Secret History of the Mongols*, pp. 177–8; *Sheng Wu Qin Zheng Lu*, p. 45. Chinggis Khan agreed to peace and accepted the Jin princess Gungju as a wife while the Jin emperor sent gold, silver, satin and other goods.

28 Muhammad al-Nasawi, *Sirah al-Sultan Jalal al-Din Mankubirti* (Cairo, 1953), pp. 44–5; Muhammad al-Nasawi, *Histoire du Sultan Djelal ed-din Mankobirti*, trans. O. Houdas (Paris, 1895), pp. 19–20.

29 Serge A. Zenkovsky, ed., *Medieval Russia's Epics, Chronicles, and Tales* (New York, 1974), p. 193.

30 For a fascinating study on Ögödei and his alcoholism, and indeed the progression of alcoholism among the Mongol elite, see Thomas Allsen, 'Ögedei and Alcohol', *Mongolian Studies*, XXIX (2007), pp. 3–12.

31 Greg S. Rogers, 'An Examination of Historians' Explanations for the Mongol Withdrawal from East Central Europe', *East European Quarterly*, XXX (1996), p. 8. In this article Rogers outlines the leading hypotheses: '(1) the political struggle for succession to the Mongol throne following the death of Ögödei, the Great Khan of the Mongols, in December 1241; (2) the inability of the Hungarian plain to provide pasture for a sufficient number of horse-mounted troops; (3) the weakness of the Mongol military after its numerous and unceasing campaigns in East Central Europe, Rus', and the Middle Volga region. It must be added at the outset that this particular explanation has been used by some historians to proffer irrational and biased statements regarding which nationality helped save Western and Central Europe from the Mongol

marauders; (4) the Mongol military tactic of "gradual conquest".' Ultimately he dismisses them as monocausal but suggests that all of them combined play a role in the Mongol withdrawal.

32 'Ala al-Din Ata Malik Juvaini, *The History of the World-Conqueror*, trans. J. A. Boyle (Seattle, WA, 1997), p. 240; 'Ala al-Din Ata Malik Juvaini, *Ta'rîkh-i-Jahân-Gusha*, ed. Mirza Muhammad Qazvini (Leiden, 1912, 1916, 1937), 3 vols, pp. 195–6.

33 Juvaini, *History of the World-Conqueror*, p. 240; Juvaini, *Ta'rîkh-i-Jahân-Gusha*, vol. II, pp. 195–6.

34 Juvaini, *History of the World-Conqueror*, p. 241; Juvaini, *Ta'rîkh-i-Jahân-Gusha*, vol. II, pp. 196–7.

35 Rene Grousset, *The Empire of the Steppes*, trans. Naomi Walford (New Brunswick, NJ, 1970), p. 268.

36 Ibid.

37 Juvaini, *History of the World-Conqueror*, pp. 507, 534; Juvaini, *Ta'rîkh-i-Jahân-Gusha*, vol. II, pp. 243–4, 270.

38 Juvaini, *History of the World-Conqueror*, p. 540; Juvaini, *Ta'rîkh-i-Jahân-Gusha*, vol. II, pp. 275–6.

39 Rashid al-Din, *Jami'u't-tawarikh*, vol. II, p. 305; Rashid al-Din, *Jami' al-Tawarikh*, p. 445.

40 Rachewiltz, *Secret History of the Mongols*, p. 207. Also Hodong Kim, 'A Reappraisal of Güyüg Khan', in *Mongols, Turks, and Others: Eurasian Nomads and the Sedentary World*, ed. Reuven Amitai and Michal Biran (Leiden, 2005), pp. 309–38. Kim suggests that Güyüg may have been more competent than *Secret History of the Mongols* implies.

41 Rashid al-Din, *Jami'u't-tawarikh*, vol. II, p. 393; Rashid al-Din, *Jami' al-Tawarikh*, ed. Karimi, p. 568.

42 Rashid al-Din, *Jami'u't-tawarikh*, vol. II, p. 305; Rashid al-Din, *Jami' al-Tawarikh*, ed. Karimi, p. 445.

43 Rashid al-Din, *Jami'u't-tawarikh*, vol. II, p. 391; Rashid al-Din, *Jami' al-Tawarikh*, ed. Karimi, p. 566.

44 Rashid al-Din, *Jami'u't-tawarikh*, vol. II, p. 391; Rashid al-Din, *Jami' al-Tawarikh*, ed. Karimi, p. 566.

45 Guillelmus de Rubruc, 'Itinerarium Willelmi de Rubruc', in *Sinica Franciscana: Itinera et Relationes Fratrum Minorum Saeculi XIII et XIV*, ed. P. Anastasius Van Den Vyngaert (Florence, 1929), p. 286; William of Rubruck, 'The Journey of William of Rubruck', in *The Mission to Asia*, trans. a nun from Stanbrook Abbey, ed. Christopher Dawson (Toronto, 1980), p. 184; William of Rubruck, *The Mission of Friar William of Rubruck: His Journey to the Court of the Great Khan Mongke, 1253–1255*, trans. Peter Jackson (London, 1990), p. 222.

46 Juvaini, *History of the World-Conqueror*, p. 725; Juvaini, *Ta'rîkh-i-Jahân-Gusha*, vol. III, p. 278.

47 Muhammad ibn Ahmad al-Dhahabi, *Kitab Duwal al-Islam*, trans. Arlette Negre (Damascus, 1979), pp. 266–7; Grigor of Akanc, 'The History of the Nation of the Archers', trans. R. P. Blake and R. N. Frye, *Harvard Journal of Asiatic Studies*, XII (1949), pp. 333–5; Minhaj Siraj Juzjani, *Tabaqat-i Nasiri*, ed.

'Abd al-Hayy Habibi (Kabul, 1964–5), vol. II, p. 708; Minhaj Siraj Juzjani,
Tabaqat-i Nasiri, trans. H. G. Raverty (New Delhi, 1970), pp. 1252–3. Grigor
of Akanc wrote that before the execution Hülegü berated the caliph for
hoarding his wealth rather than having spent it on the defence of Baghdad.
48 Juvaini, *History of the World-Conqueror*, p. 607; Juvaini, *Ta'rîkh-i-Jahân-Gusha*,
vol. III, p. 90.
49 Huang K'uan-chung, 'Mountain Fortress Defence: The Experience of the
Southern Sung and Korea in Resisting the Mongol Invasions', in *Warfare in
Chinese History*, ed. Hans Van de Ven (Leiden, 2000), p. 237; Morris Rossabi,
Khubilai Khan: His Life and Times (Berkeley, CA, 1988), p. 45.
50 Rashid al-Din, *Jami' al-Tawarikh*, ed. Musavi, pp. 851–2; Rashid al-Din, *Jami' al-
Tawarikh*, ed. Karimi, pp. 602–3; Rashid al-Din, *Jami'u't-tawarikh*, vol. II, p. 415.
51 Rashid al-Din, *Jami' al-Tawarikh*, ed. Musavi, pp. 851–2; Rashid al-Din, *Jami' al-
Tawarikh*, ed. Karimi, pp. 602–3; Rashid al-Din, *Jami'u't-tawarikh*, vol. II, p. 415.
52 K'uan-chung, 'Mountain Fortress Defence', p. 238.
53 Rashid al-Din, *Jami' al-Tawarikh*, ed. Musavi, p. 853; Rashid al-Din, *Jami' al-
Tawarikh*, ed. Karimi, p. 604; Rashid al-Din, *Jami'u't-tawarikh*, vol. II, p. 416.

2 Dissolution of the Empire

1 Morris Rossabi, 'The Vision in the Dream: Kublai Khan and the Conquest of
China', in *Genghis Khan and the Mongol Empire*, ed. William W. Fitzhugh,
Morris Rossabi and William Honeychurch (Bellingham, WA, 2009), p. 209.
2 Richard Christian Danus and Marc Reid Rubel, *Xanadu*, dir. Robert
Greenwald (1980).
3 Rossabi, 'The Vision in the Dream', p. 209.
4 Morris Rossabi, *Khubilai Khan: His Life and Times* (Berkeley, CA, 1988), p. 13.
5 Michal Biran, *The Empire of the Qara Khitai in Eurasian History: Between China
and the Islamic World* (Cambridge, 2005), pp. 202–11.
6 Rossabi, 'The Vision in the Dream', p. 209.
7 David Bade, *Khubilai Khan and the Beautiful Princess of Tumapel* (Ulaanbaatar,
2002).
8 James P. Delgado, *Khubilai Khan's Lost Fleet: In Search of a Legendary Armada*
(Berkeley, CA, 2008), pp. 154–64.
9 Rossabi, 'The Vision in the Dream', p. 213.
10 Delgado, *Khubilai Khan's Lost Fleet*, p. 155–6.
11 Paul D. Buell, *Historical Dictionary of the Mongol World Empire* (Lanham, MD,
2003), p. 66.
12 Henry G. Schwarz, 'Some Notes on the Mongols of Yunnan', *Central Asiatic
Journal*, XXVIII (1994), pp. 102–3. Mongol rule in Yunnan lasted until 1381,
thirteen years longer than their hold over China proper. Schwarz comments,
'Because of Yunnan's strategic importance, the Mongols stationed a
disproportionately large number of troops throughout the province.'
13 George Lane, *Genghis Khan and Mongol Rule* (Westport, CT, 2004), p. 56.
14 'Ala al-Din Ata Malik Juvaini, *Ta'rîkh-i-Jahân-Gusha*, ed. Mirza Muhammad
Qazvini (Leiden, 1912, 1916, 1937), 3 vols. p. 31; 'Ala al-Din Ata Malik Juvaini,
The History of the World-Conqueror, trans. J. A. Boyle (Seattle, WA, 1997), p. 42.

15 Peter Jackson, 'The Dissolution of the Mongol Empire', *Central Asiatic Journal*, XXII (1978), pp. 212–20.
16 George Lane, *Early Mongol Rule in Thirteenth-Century Iran*: Lane, *A Persian Renaissance* (London, 2003), pp. 39–40.
17 William of Rubruck, *The Mission of Friar William of Rubruck*, trans. Peter Jackson (Indianapolis, IN, 2009), p. 127.
18 Lane, *Early Mongol Rule*, p. 40.
19 Judith Kolbas, *The Mongols in Iran: Chingiz Khan to Uljaytu, 1220–1309* (London, 2009).
20 Lane, *Early Mongol Rule*, pp. 145–50; *Genghis Khan and Mongol Rule*, p. 71.
21 A. P. Martinez, 'Some notes on the Il-Xanid Army', *Archivum Eurasiae Medii Aevi*, VI (1986), pp. 143–5.
22 Reuven Amitai, 'Continuity and Change in the Mongol Army of the Ilkhanate', paper presented at the World Congress for Middle East Studies, Barcelona (23 July 2010).
23 Thomas T. Allsen, *Commodity and Exchange in the Mongol Empire: A Cultural History of Islamic Textiles* (Cambridge, 1997).
24 Anne Broadbridge, *Kingship and Ideology in the Islamic and Mongol Worlds*, (Cambridge, 2008), pp. 84–5.
25 Ibid., pp. 102–3.
26 Michal Biran, *Qaidu and the Rise of the Independent Mongol State in Central Asia* (Richmond, Surrey, 1997), pp. 22–3.
27 Biran, *Qaidu and the Rise of the Independent Mongol State*, pp. 26–9; Buell, *Historical Dictionary*, pp. 82–3.
28 Biran, *Qaidu and the Rise of the Independent Mongol State*, pp. 26–7.
29 Ibid., pp. 27–8.
30 Michal Biran, 'The Chaghadaids and Islam: The Conversion of Tarmashirin Khan (1331–34)', *Journal of the American Oriental Society*, CXXII/4 (2002), p. 748.
31 Devin DeWeese, 'The Eclipse of the Kubraviya in Central Asia,' *Iranian Studies*, XXI/1–2 (1988), pp. 48–9; Biran, 'The Chaghadaids and Islam', p. 751; John Woods, *The Timurid Dynasty* (Bloomington, IN, 1990), p. 12.
32 Biran, 'The Chaghadaids and Islam', pp. 749–50.
33 Broadbridge, *Kingship and Ideology*, p. 58. Broadbridge argues that Berke viewed his relations with the Mamluk Sultan Baybars as one of lord and vassal, whereas the Mamluk sources indicate one of equals. Considering the Mongol outlook and the status of the Chinggisid lineage, I must agree with Broadbridge. The Kipchak origin of many of the Mamluk sultans meant they were subjects of the Golden Horde, if not in reality in Egypt, then in the worldview of the Golden Horde khans.
34 J. J. Saunders, 'The Mongol Defeat at Ain Jalut and the Restoration of the Greek Empire', in *Muslims and Mongols: Essays in Medieval Asia* (Christchurch, 1977), pp. 71–6.
35 Ibn Battuta, *Rihala Ibn Battuta* (Beirut, 1995), pp. 255–7; Ross Dunn, *The Adventures of Ibn Battuta: A Muslim Traveler of the 14th Century* (Berkeley, CA, 2005), pp. 160–1.

3 The World of 1350: A Global World

1 William Shakespeare, *Much Ado About Nothing*, Act II, Scene II.
2 For the best discussion of this see David Sneath, *The Headless State: Aristocratic Orders, Kinship Society, and Misrepresentations of Nomadic Inner Asia* (New York, 2007).
3 Andre Wink, *Al-Hind: The Making of the Indo-Islamic World, vol. 2: The Slave Kings and the Islamic Conquest, 11th–13th Centuries* (Leiden, 1997), p. 16.
4 Ibid.
5 Charles Melville, 'The *Keshig* in Iran: The Survival of the Royal Mongol Household', in *Beyond the Legacy of Genghis Khan*, ed. Linda Komaroff (Leiden, 2004), p. 60.
6 Rudi Paul Lindner, *Explorations in Pre-Ottoman History* (Ann Arbor, MI, 2007), pp. 21–34.
7 Cemal Kafadar, *Between Two Worlds: The Construction of the Ottoman State* (Los Angeles, 1995), pp. 44–5; Colin Heywood, 'Filling the Black Hole: The Emergence of the Bithynian Atamanates', *The Great Ottoman–Turkish Civilization*, ed. K. Cicek *et al.* (Ankara, 2000), vol. I, pp. 109–10.
8 Rudi Paul Lindner, 'How Mongol were the Early Ottomans?', in *The Mongol Empire and its Legacy*, ed. Reuven Amitai-Preiss and David O. Morgan (Leiden, 2001), pp. 287–9.
9 Melville, 'The *Keshig* in Iran', p. 58.
10 J. Pelenski, 'The Contest between Lithuania-Rus' and the Golden Horde in the Fourteenth Century for Supremacy over Eastern Europe', *Archivum Eurasiae Medii Aevi*, II (1982), pp. 303–20.
11 For a more complete discussion on wars and diplomacy in the early modern western steppe, see Brian L. Davies, *Warfare, State and Society on the Black Sea Steppe, 1500–1700* (London, 2007).
12 Martha Brill Olcott, *The Kazakhs*, 2nd edn (Stanford, CA, 1995), p. 8.
13 Ibid., p. 9.
14 Chantal Lemercier-Quelquejay, 'The Kazakhs and the Kirghiz', in *Central Asia*, ed. Gavin Hambly (New York, 1969), p. 146.
15 David M. Robinson, *Empire's Twilight: Northeast Asia Under the Mongols* (Cambridge, MA, 2009), p. 64.
16 Michael J. Seth, *A Concise History of Korea: From the Neolithic Period through the Nineteenth Century* (Lanham, MD, 2006), pp. 109–10.
17 Peter C. Perdue, *China Marches West: The Qing Conquest of Central Eurasia* (Cambridge, MA, 2005), pp. 549–65.
18 Alexander Burnes, *Cabool*, 2nd edn (London, 1843), p. 168.
19 See Joshua Fogel, 'Chinggis on the Japanese Mind', *Mongolian Studies*, XXXI (2009), pp. 259–70 for an interesting discussion on the history of this idea.
20 Timothy May, *Culture and Customs of Mongolia* (Westport, CT, 2009), pp. 145–6.
21 Jack Weatherford, 'A Scholarly Quest to Understand Genghis Khan', *Chronicle of Higher Education*, XLVI/32 (2000).
22 Joshua Kucera, 'The Search for Genghis Khan: Genghis Khan's Legacy Being Reappraised in China, Russia', at www.eurasianet.org, accessed 23 January

2011. The number of visitors is probably inflated.
23 Charles Halperin, *The Tatar Yoke* (Columbus, OH, 1985).
24 Kucera, 'The Search for Genghis Khan'.
25 Ibid.
26 Ibid.
27 *Storm from the East: From Genghis Khan to Khubilai Khan* [TV series] (London, 1993).
28 Alan Zelentz, 'Runequest', *Thor*, 1/334 (1983), p. 60.
29 *Scooby-Doo and the Reluctant Werewolf*, dir. Ray Patterson (1968).
30 Christy Marx, *Spider-Man and His Amazing Friends*, episode 'The Fantastic Mr Frump', dir. Don Jurwich (26 September 1981).
31 John Milius and Kevin Reynolds, *Red Dawn*, dir. John Milius (1984).
32 Ruth Dunnell, *Chinggis Khan: World Conqueror* (Boston, MA, 2010), p. 93.
33 Araminta Wordsworth, 'Saddam Plays on Fears of Mongol Devastation: Genghis Khan's Warriors Destroyed 13th-century Iraq', *National Post* (22 January 2003), p. A15.
34 Michael Scott Doran, 'Somebody Else's Civil War', *Foreign Affairs*, LXXXI/1 (2002), pp. 31–2.
35 May, *Culture and Customs of Mongolia*, p. 141.
36 Fitzroy Raglan, *The Hero: A Study in Tradition, Myth, and Drama* (New York, 1937), pp. 41–2.
37 Paula Sabloff, 'Why Mongolia? The Political Culture of an Emerging Democracy', *Central Asian Survey*, XXI/1 (2002), pp. 19–36. Also see Andrew F. March, 'Citizen Genghis? On Explaining Mongolian Democracy through "Political Culture"', *Central Asian Survey*, XXII/1 (2003), pp. 61–6.
38 Richard Orange, 'Kazakhs striving to prove Genghis Khan descent', *Daily Telegraph* (4 October 2010), p. 20.
39 'Kazakhstan seeks identity on the big screen', *Christian Science Monitor* (8 May 2008), p. 20.

4 PAX MONGOLICA AND TRADE

1 Thomas T. Allsen, 'Mongolian Princes and Their Merchant Partners, 1200–1260', *Asia Major* (1989), 3rd ser., II/2, p. 86.
2 Hilda Ecsedy, 'Trade-and-War Relations between the Turks and China', *Acta Orientalia Hungaricae*, XXI (1968), p. 141.
3 Sechin Jagchid and Van Jay Symons, *Peace, War, and Trade Along the Great Wall: Nomadic-Chinese Interaction Through Two Millennia* (Bloomington, IN, 1989), pp. 13–14.
4 Janet Abu-Lughod, *Before European Hegemony: The World System AD 1250–1350* (New York, 1989), p. 182.
5 Igor de Rachewiltz, trans. and ed., *The Secret History of the Mongols* (Leiden, 2004), p. 104.
6 Ibid., p. 658.
7 'Ala al-Din Ata Malik Juvaini, *The History of the World-Conqueror*, trans. J. A. Boyle (Seattle, WA, 1997), p. 78; 'Ala al-Din Ata Malik Juvaini, *Ta'ríkh-i-Jahân-Gusha*, ed. Mirza Muhammad Qazvini (Leiden, 1912, 1916, 1937), 3 vols, p. 5.

THE MONGOL CONQUESTS IN WORLD HISTORY

8   Juvaini, *Ta'rīkh-i-Jahân-Gusha*, pp. 59–60; Juvaini, *History of the World-Conqueror*, p. 78.

9   Juvaini, *Ta'rīkh-i-Jahân-Gusha*, p. 60; Juvaini, *History of the World-Conqueror*, p. 79.

10 Juvaini, *Ta'rīkh-i-Jahân-Gusha*, p. 60; Juvaini, *History of the World-Conqueror*, p. 79. Most accounts indicated that Inalchuq, governor of Otrar, with the title Ghayir Khan, massacred the caravan because he thought they were spies, but Juvaini indicates that it may have been out of pride as one of the Indian merchants addressed the governor by his name, Inalchuq, rather than by his title.

11 Allsen, 'Mongolian Princes and Their Merchant Partners', p. 92.

12 Juvaini, *Ta'rīkh-i-Jahân-Gusha*, p. 60; Juvaini, *History of the World-Conqueror*, p. 79; Leslie Whitaker, *The Beardstown Ladies' Common-Sense Investment Guide: How We Beat the Stock Market – And How You Can, Too* (New York, 1996).

13 Allsen, 'Mongolian Princes and Their Merchant Partners', p. 93.

14 Larry W. Moses, 'A Theoretical Approach to the Process of Inner Asian Confederation', *Etudes Mongoles*, v (1974), pp. 115–16. One environmental reason was that the Orkhon, Tula and Selengge rivers offered well-watered pastures, ideal for any nomadic ruler. Other reasons were spiritual and traditional.

15 For more on Avarga see Noriyuki Shiraishi, 'The "Great Orda" of Genghis Khan', in *Beyond the Legacy of Genghis Khan*, ed. Linda Komaroff (Leiden, 2006), pp. 83–93.

16 William of Rubruck, 'The Journey of William of Rubruck', in *The Mission to Asia*, trans. a nun from Stanbrook Abbey, ed. Christopher Dawson (Toronto, 1980), p. 175; William of Rubruck, *The Mission of Friar William of Rubruck: His Journey to the Court of the Great Khan Mongke, 1253–1255*, trans. Peter Jackson (London, 1990), p. 209.

17 William of Rubruck, 'The Journey of William of Rubruck', p. 144; William of Rubruck, *Mission of Friar William of Rubruck*, p. 162.

18 William of Rubruck, 'The Journey of William of Rubruck', p. 144; William of Rubruck, *Mission of Friar William of Rubruck*, p. 162.

19 For more on the importance of *nasij* and the Mongol production centres see Thomas T. Allsen, *Commodity and Exchange in the Mongol Empire: A Cultural History of Islamic Textiles* (New York, 1997).

20 William of Rubruck, 'The Journey of William of Rubruck', p. 152; William of Rubruck, *Mission of Friar William of Rubruck*, pp. 175–6.

21 William of Rubruck, 'The Journey of William of Rubruck', p. 183; William of Rubruck, *Mission of Friar William of Rubruck*, p. 221.

22 Timothy May, 'Mongol Resistance to Christian Conversion', in *Christianity and Mongolia: Past and Present – Proceedings of the Antoon Mostaert Symposium on Christianity and Mongolia*, ed. Gaby Bamana, 13–16 August 2006 (Ulaanbaatar, 2006); Timothy May, 'Монголы и мировые религии в XII веке' ('The Mongols and World Religions in the Thirteenth Century'), in Монгольская Империя и Кочевой Мир *(Mongolian Imperial and Nomadic Worlds)* ed. N. N. Kradin and T. D. Skrynnikova (Ulan Ude, 2004), pp. 424–43; Timothy May, 'Attitudes Towards Conversion Among the Elite in the Mongol Empire', *E-ASPAC:*

The Electronic Journal of Asian Studies on the Pacific Coast (2002–3), at http://mcel.pacificu.edu/easpac/2003/may.php3, accessed 25 August 2011.

23 Rachewiltz, *Secret History of the Mongols*, p. 214.

24 Ibid.

25 Ibid., pp. 214–15.

26 Ibid., p. 217.

27 Juvaini, *History of the World-Conqueror*, p. 198; Juvaini, *Ta'rîkh-i-Jahân-Gusha*, p. 156.

28 Juvaini, *Ta'rîkh-i-Jahân-Gusha*, p. 169; Juvaini, *History of the World-Conqueror*, p. 212.

29 Juvaini, *History of the World-Conqueror*, pp. 213–14; Juvaini, *Ta'rîkh-i-Jahân-Gusha*, p. 170.

30 Juvaini, *Ta'rîkh-i-Jahân-Gusha*, pp. 173–6; Juvaini, *History of the World-Conqueror*, pp. 216–18.

31 Allsen, 'Mongolian Princes and Their Merchant Partners', pp. 94–6.

32 Ibid., p. 104.

33 Juvaini, *Ta'rîkh-i-Jahân-Gusha*, p. 76; Juvaini, *History of the World-Conqueror*, p. 598.

34 Juvaini, *History of the World-Conqueror*, pp. 598–9; Juvaini, *Ta'rîkh-i-Jahân-Gusha*, p. 76.

35 Juvaini, *History of the World-Conqueror*, p. 606. Juvaini, *Ta'rîkh-i-Jahân-Gusha*, pp. 87–8.

36 Juvaini, *History of the World-Conqueror*, p. 606; Juvaini, *Ta'rîkh-i-Jahân-Gusha*, p. 88; Thomas T. Allsen, *Mongol Imperialism: The Policies of the Grand Qan Möngke in China, Russia, and the Islamic Lands, 1251–1259* (Berkeley, CA, 1987), pp. 80–2.

37 Marco Polo, *The Travels of Marco Polo*, trans. William Marsden, ed. Manuel Komroff (New York, 2001), pp. 4–6.

38 James P. Delgado, *Khubilai Khan's Lost Fleet: In Search of a Legendary Armada* (Berkeley, CA, 2008), pp. 88–9.

39 Polo. *The Travels of Marco Polo*, pp. 224–5.

40 David M. Robinson, *Empire's Twilight: Northeast Asia Under the Mongols* (Philadelphia, PA, 2009), p. 260.

41 Ross Dunn, *The Adventures of Ibn Battuta: A Muslim Traveler of the 14th Century* (Berkeley, CA, 2005), p. 220

42 Ibn Battuta, *Rihala Ibn Battuta* (Beirut, 1995), pp. 247–8; Dunn, *Adventures of Ibn Battuta*, p. 163.

43 Simon Digby, *War-horse and Elephant in the Delhi Sultanate: A Study of Military Supplies* (Oxford, 1971), pp. 21–2.

44 Daniel Waugh, 'The Golden Horde and Russia', in *Genghis Khan and the Mongol Empire*, ed. William Fitzhugh, Morris Rossabi and William Honeychurch (Seattle, WA, 2009), pp. 178–9; Thomas S. Noonan, 'Medieval Russia, the Mongols, and the West: Novgorod's Relations with the Baltic, 1100–1350', *Medieval Studies*, XXXVII (1975), pp. 316–39; Mark G. Kramarovsky, 'Jochid Luxury Metalwork: Issues of Genesis and Development', in *Beyond the Legacy of Genghis Khan*, ed. Linda Komaroff (Leiden, 2006), pp. 43–50.

45 Matthew Paris, *English History*, trans. and ed. J. A. Giles (New York, 1968), 3 vols, vol. I, p. 131.
46 Ibn Battuta, *Rihala Ibn Battuta*, pp. 177–8; Dunn, *Adventures of Ibn Battuta*, p. 101.
47 Dunn, *Adventures of Ibn Battuta*, p. 49.
48 Bert G. Fragner, 'Ilkhanid Rule and Its Contributions to Iranian Political Culture', in *Beyond the Legacy of Genghis Khan*, ed. Linda Komaroff (Leiden, 2006), p. 76.
49 Ibid., pp. 76–7.
50 See Judith Kolbas, *The Mongols in Iran: Chingiz Khan to Uljaytu, 1220–1309* (London, 2009).
51 Fragner, 'Ilkhanid Rule and Its Contributions', p. 76.
52 Ibid., p. 77.

5 New Forms of Warfare

1 This initial section is a condensed version of my book *The Mongol Art of War* (Barnsley, Yorkshire, 2007).
2 John of Plano Carpini, 'History of the Mongols', in *The Mission to Asia*, trans. a nun from Stanbrook Abbey, ed. Christopher Dawson (Toronto, 1980), p. 46.
3 Marco Polo, *The Travels*, trans. Ronald Lathem (New York, 1958), pp. 206–8; Marco Polo, *The Travels of Marco Polo*, trans. Henry Yule (New York, 1992), pp. 158–60.
4 Oliver of Paderborn, 'The Capture of Damietta', trans. Joseph J. Gavigan, in *Christian Society and the Crusades, 1198–1229*, ed. Edward Peters (Philadelphia, PA, 1971), pp. 90, 123–4.
5 Ibid., p. 91.
6 Matthew Paris, *Chronica Majora* (London, 1873), vol. IV, pp. 337–44; Malcolm Barber and Keith Bate, *Letters from the East: Crusaders, Pilgrims and Settlers in the 12th–13th Centuries* (Aldershot, Surrey, 2010), pp. 143–6.
7 When discussing mamluks, scholars generally capitalize the 'M' when referring to the Mamluks of the Mamluk Sultanate – a state where the ruling element were mamluks. Mamluk with a lower case 'm' refers to a member of the military slave institution of mamluks, which was endemic throughout the Islamic world.
8 Peter Jackson, *The Mongols and the West* (Harlow, 2005), pp. 95–7, 103–5.
9 A. Rahman Zaky, 'Introduction to the Study of Islamic Arms and Armour', *Gladius*, I (1961), p. 17.
10 *Iqta* and *timars* were grants given to soldiers and bureaucrats. Unlike fiefs in Europe, the owner did not actually rule the *timar*, but received income from them. They could be villages, markets, orchards or virtually any other revenue-producing area.
11 For discussions on this see John Masson Smith Jr, 'Mongol Society and Military in the Middle East: Antecedents and Adaptations', in *War and Society in the Eastern Mediterranean, 7th and 15th Centuries*, ed. Yaacov Lev, *The Medieval Mediterranean Peoples, Economies, and Cultures, 400–1453*, vol. IX, ed.

Michael Whitby, Paul Magalino, Hugh Kennedy, *et al.* (Leiden, 1996); John Masson Smith Jr, 'Ayn Jalut: Mamluk Success or Mongol Failure?', *Harvard Journal of Asiatic Studies*, XLIV (1984), pp. 307–45; and A. P. Martinez, 'Some notes on the Il-Xanid Army', *Archivum Eurasiae Medii Aevi*, VI (1986), pp. 129–242.

12 Reuven Amitai, 'Continuity and Change in the Mongol Army of the Ilkhanate', paper presented at the World Congress for Middle Eastern Studies, Barcelona, 23 July 2010.

13 Peter Jackson, *The Delhi Sultanate, A Political and Military History* (Cambridge, 1999), p. 104.

14 Ibid., p. 39.

15 Ibid., p. 104.

16 Minhaj Siraj Juzjani, *Tabaqat-i Nasiri*, trans. H. G. Raverty (New Delhi, 1970), pp. 809–13.

17 Jackson, *The Delhi Sultanate*, p. 105. In 1241 Dayir and Mönggetu captured Lahore.

18 Simon Digby, *War-horse and Elephant in the Delhi Sultanate: A Study of Military Supplies* (Oxford, 1971), p. 22.

19 Ibid., p. 21.

20 Juzjani, *Tabaqat-i Nasiri*, trans. Raverty, p. 711.

21 Peter Golden, 'War and Warfare in the Pre-Cinggisid Western Steppes of Eurasia', in *Warfare in Inner Asian History, 500–1800*, ed. Nicola Di Cosmo (Leiden, 2002), p. 106.

22 George Perfecky, trans. and ed., *The Hypatian Codex II: The Galician–Volynian Chronicle* (Munich, 1973), pp. 61–2; George Vernadsky, *The Mongols and Russia* (New Haven, CT, 1953), p. 145.

23 Perfecky, *The Hypatian Codex II*, pp. 73–4; Francis Dvornik, *Origins of Intelligence Services: The Ancient Near East, Persia, Greece, Rome, Byzantium, the Arab Muslim Empires, the Mongol Empire, China, Muscovy* (New Brunswick, NJ, 1974), pp. 302–4.

24 For a very good analysis of what Muscovy adopted see Donald Ostrowski, *Muscovy and the Mongols: Cross Cultural Influences on the Steppe Frontier, 1304–1589* (New York, 1998). Ostrowski gives the Mongols credit where it is due, but also dispels some myths about other less favourable 'gifts' the Mongols allegedly gave the Russians.

25 Vernadsky, *The Mongols and Russia*, pp. 145.

26 A. E. Tsepkov, trans., *Ermolinskaia Letopis'*, (Riazan, 2000), p. 110–11; Robert Michell and Nevill Forbes, trans., *The Chronicle of Novgorod, 1016–1471* (London, 1914), p. 95.

27 Francis Gabriel, *Subotai the Valiant: Genghis Khan's Greatest General* (Westport, CT, 2004), pp. 128–9.

28 Peter A. Lorge, *The Asian Military Revolution: From Gunpowder to the Bomb* (Cambridge, 2008), pp. 24, 32–3.

29 Ibid., pp. 34–5.

30 Jack Weatherford, *Genghis Khan and the Making of the Modern World* (New York, 2004), p. 182; Iqtidar Alam Khan, *Gunpowder and Firearms: Warfare in Medieval India* (New Delhi, 2004).

31 'Ala al-Din Ata Malik Juvaini, *The History of the World-Conqueror*, trans. J. A. Boyle (Seattle, WA, 1997), pp. 630–1; 'Ala al-Din Ata Malik Juvaini, *Ta'rîkh-i-Jahân-Gusha*, ed. Mirza Muhammad Qazvini (Leiden, 1912, 1916, 1937), 3 vols, p. 128.

32 Takezaki Suenaga, 'Takezaki Suenaga's Scrolls of the Mongol Invasions of Japan', at www.bowdoin.edu/mongol-scrolls/, accessed 22 November 2010; Also see James P. Delgado, *Khubilai Khan's Lost Fleet: In Search of a Legendary Armada* (Berkeley, CA, 2008). Delgado summarizes the marine archaeological finds, including recovered bombs that are depicted in the scrolls.

33 Juvaini, *Ta'rîkh-i-Jahân-Gusha*, pp. 39–42; Juvaini, *History of the World-Conqueror*, pp. 574–6.

34 Paul Buell, personal communication, 11 November 2010. I also owe a debt of thanks to Dr Ulrike Unschuld for the characters and to Paul for his intelligence network that procured the information.

35 Juvaini, *Ta'rîkh-i-Jahân-Gusha*, p. 126; Juvaini, *History of the World-Conqueror*, p. 629. Against the Ismailis, the Mongols used local pine trees and constructed siege weapons on the spot, including the much feared *kaman-i-gav*, a ballista that had a range of 2,500 paces (more than a mile).

36 Lorge, *The Asian Military Revolution*, p. 69.

37 Michael W. Charney, *Southeast Asian Warfare, 1300–1900* (Leiden, 2004), pp. 43–4.

38 Kenneth Chase, *Firearms: A Global History to 1700* (Cambridge, 2003).

39 B. H. Liddell Hart, *Deterrence or Defense: A Fresh Look at the West's Military Position* (New York, 1960), p. 190.

40 B. H. Liddell Hart, *The Liddell Hart Memoirs*, vol. I (New York, 1965), pp. 75, 272.

41 B. H. Liddell Hart, *Great Captains Unveiled* (Freeport, NY, 1967), 11; Liddell Hart, *Deterrent or Defense*, p. 187.

42 Gabriel, *Subotai the Valiant*, p. 131.

43 Ibid.

44 Ibid., p. 132.

45 John Strawson, *Hitler as Military Commander* (New York, 1971), p. 37.

46 Ibid., p. 38.

47 Robert M. Citino, *The Evolution of Blitzkrieg Tactics: Germany Defends Itself Against Poland, 1918–1933* (New York, 1987), p. 41.

48 Ibid., pp. 71–2.

49 B. H. Liddell Hart, *The German Generals Talk* (New York, 1979), p. 91.

50 Strawson, *Hitler as Military Commander*, p. 31.

51 Colonel (retd) Keith Antonia, pers. comm. 2009.

52 Ibid.

53 Polo, *Travels of Marco Polo*, p. 260.

54 I owe a debt of thanks and a bottle of wine to Paul D. Buell for bringing this etymology to my attention.

6 THE MONGOL ADMINISTRATION

1 David O. Morgan, 'Who Ran the Mongol Empire?', *Journal of the Royal Asiatic Society* (1982), pp. 134–6; David O. Morgan, *The Mongols*, 1st edn (Oxford, 1986), p. 108.

2 David Morgan, 'Mongol or Persian: The Government of Ilkhanid Iran', *Harvard Middle Eastern and Islamic Review*, III (1996), pp. 62–76.

3 See Christopher P. Atwood, 'Inje', in *Encyclopedia of Mongolia and the Mongol Empire* (New York, 2004), p. 240 for an overview of the history of the *inje*.

4 See Thomas Allsen, 'Guard and Government in the Reign of the Grand Qan Mongke, 1251–1259', *Harvard Journal of Asiatic Studies*, XLVI/2 (1986), pp. 495–521; Charles Melville, 'The *Keshig* in Iran: The Survivial of the Royal Mongol Household', in *Beyond the Legacy of Genghis Khan*, ed. Linda Komaroff (Leiden, 2006), pp. 135–65.

5 Igor de Rachewiltz, trans. and ed., *The Secret History of the Mongols* (Leiden, 2004), pp. 113–14.

6 Ibid., pp. 152–8.

7 Thomas T. Allsen, *Mongol Imperialism: The Policies of the Grand Qan Möngke in China, Russia, and the Islamic Lands, 1251–1259* (Berkeley, CA, 1987), pp. 73–4.

8 Allsen, 'Guard and Government', pp. 517–18, 521; Allsen, *Mongol Imperialism*, p. 100.

9 Marco Polo, *The Travels of Marco Polo*, trans. Henry Yule (New York, 1992), p. 329.

10 Uli Schamiloglu, 'The Qaraci Beys of the Later Golden Horde: Notes on the Organization of the Mongol World Empire', *Archivum Eurasie Medii Aevi*, IV (1984), pp. 283–97.

11 Christopher P. Atwood, 'Keshig', in *Encyclopedia of Mongolia and the Mongol Empire* (New York, 2004), p. 298.

12 Paul D. Buell, 'Kalmyk Tanggaci People: Thoughts on the Mechanics and Impact of Mongol Expansion', *Mongolian Studies*, VI (1980), p. 47.

13 Ibid., p. 45.

14 Grigor of Akanc, 'The History of the Nation of the Archers', trans. R. P. Blake and R. N. Frye, *Harvard Journal of Asiatic Studies*, XII (1949), p. 337 (henceforth Grigor). The term Grigor uses is *t'emayc'ik'*. Clearly, it is a corruption of the *nomen actoris* term *tanmaghci* in the Mongolian language. Francis W. Cleaves also discusses this term in 'The Mongolian Names and Terms in *The History of the Nation of the Archers* by Grigor of Akanc', *Harvard Journal of Asiatic Studies*, XII (1949), pp. 439–42.

15 Buell, 'Kalmyk Tanggaci People', p. 45.

16 Ibid., p. 47.

17 'Ala al-Din Ata Malik Juvaini, *The History of the World-Conqueror*, trans. J. A. Boyle (Seattle, WA, 1997), pp. 349 and 351; 'Ala al-Din Ata Malik Juvaini, *Ta'rîkh-i-Jahân-Gusha*, ed. Mirza Muhammad Qazvini (Leiden, 1912, 1916, 1937), 3 vols, vol. II, pp. 81 and 83. On p. 349 *shahna* is used but on p. 351 Tört Aba is referred to as a *basqaq*.

18 Paul D. Buell, 'Tribe, Qan, and Ulus In Early Mongol China, Some
    Prolegomena to Yüan History', PhD dissertation, University of Washington
    (1977), p. 33.

19 Ibid., p. 87.

20 Iohannes de Plano Carpini, 'Ystoria Mongalorum', in *Sinica Franciscana:
    Itinera et Relationes Fratrum Minorum Saeculi XIII et XIV* (Florence, 1929), vol. I,
    p. 86; John of Plano Carpini, 'History of the Mongols', in *The Mission to
    Asia*, trans. a nun from Stanbrook Abbey, ed. Christopher Dawson (Toronto,
    1980), p. 40.

21 Charles J. Halperin, *Russia and the Golden Horde: The Mongol Impact on
    Medieval Russian History* (Bloomington, IN, 1985), pp. 33–5.

22 Buell, 'Tribe, Qan, and Ulus', pp. 32–3.

23 Thomas T. Allsen, 'Mongol Census Taking in Rus', 1245–1275', *Harvard
    Ukrainian Studies*, V/I (1981), pp. 47–8.

24 Halperin, *Russia and the Golden Horde*, p. 39; Donald Ostrowski, 'The *tamma*
    as the dual administrative structure of the Mongol Empire', *The Bulletin of
    the School of Oriental and African Studies*, LXI (1998), pp. 262, 275–6.

25 Istvan Vasary, 'The Golden Horde Term Daruga and Its Survival in Russia',
    Acta Orientale Hungarica, XXX (1976), p. 188; I. N. Berezin, *Tarchannye jarlyki
    Tochtamyka, Timur Kuluka i Saadet-Gireja* (Kazan, 1851), p. 45; Vasary, 'The
    Origin of the Institution of Basqaqs', *Acta Orientale Hungarica*, XXXII (1978),
    p. 201; Claude Cahen, *Pre-Ottoman Turkey*, trans. J. Jones-Williams (New York,
    1968), p. 41.

26 Thomas T. Allsen, 'Ever Closer Encounters: The Appropriation of Culture
    and the Apportionment of Peoples in the Mongol Empire', *Journal of Early
    Modern History*, I (1997), pp. 7–8.

27 Allsen, *Mongol Imperialism*, pp. 80–2, 85. See also Juvaini, *Ta'ríkh-i-Jahân-
    Gusha*, vol. III, pp. 75–8; Juvaini, *History of the World-Conqueror*, pp. 598–9.

28 Allsen, *Mongol Imperialism*, p. 85.

29 Paul D. Buell, 'Cinqai (*c.* 1169–1252)', in *In the Service of the Khan: Eminent
    Personalities of the Early Mongol-Yuan Period, 1200–1300*, ed. Igor de Rachewiltz
    et al. (Wiesbaden, 1993), p. 107.

30 Allsen, *Mongol Imperialism*, p. 104.

31 Matters of taxation have been discussed in detail elsewhere. For more than
    this overview, I refer the reader to the following studies: Allsen, *Mongol
    Imperialism*; Ann K. S. Lambton, *Continuity and Change in Medieval Persia:
    Aspects of Administrative, Economic and Social History, 11th–14th Century* (Albany,
    1988); I. P. Petrushevsky, 'Socio-Economic Conditions of Iran Under the
    Ilkhans', in *Cambridge History of Iran*, ed. J. A. Boyle (Cambridge, 1968); H. F.
    Schurmann, 'Mongolian Tributary Practices of the Thirteenth Century',
    Harvard Journal of Asiatic Studies, XIX (1956), pp. 304–89; H. F. Schurmann,
    Economic Structure of the Yuan Dynasty (Cambridge, 1956); John Masson Smith
    Jr, 'Mongol and Nomadic Taxation', *Harvard Journal of Asiatic Studies*, XXX
    (1970), pp. 46–85; John Masson Smith Jr, 'Mongol Manpower and Persian
    Population', *Journal of the Economic and Social History of the Orient*, XVIII/3
    (1975), pp. 271–99.

32 Schurmann, 'Mongolian Tributary Practices', pp. 311, 316. This formed the

basis for the later *alba*. Individuals who owed 'obligations of servitude to a superior were called albatu'.

33 Ibn Al-Athir, *al-Kamil fi al-Ta'rikh*, (Beirut, 1979), vol. XII, pp. 380–3, 502; Also see Smith Jr, 'Mongol and Nomadic Taxation', pp. 46–85. Ibn al-Athir provides numerous examples from the Khwarazmian campaign of Mongol commanders requisitioning cloth, food, mounts and money from cities that submitted to them.

34 Allsen, *Mongol Imperialism*, pp. 147–8; Morgan, *The Mongols*, p. 101; Bayarsaikhan Dashdondog, *The Mongols and the Armenians, 1220–1335* (Leiden, 2011), pp. 111–13.

7 Religion and the Mongol Empire

1 Michal Biran, *The Empire of the Qara Khitai in Eurasian History: Between China and the Islamic World* (Cambridge, 2005), p. 211; for a study of other empires see J. P. Roux, 'La tolerance religieuse dans l'empires Turco-Mongols', *Revue de l'Histoire des Religions*, CCIII (1986), pp. 131–68; Johan Elverskog, *Buddhism and Islam on the Silk Road* (Philadelphia, PA, 2010); Richard Foltz, *Religions of the Silk Road* (New York, 1999).

2 John of Plano Carpini, 'History of the Mongols', in *The Mission to Asia*, trans. a nun from Stanbrook Abbey, ed. Christopher Dawson (Toronto, 1980), p. 12.

3 Richard Foltz, 'Ecumenical Mischief under the Mongols', *Central Asiatic Journal*, XLIII (1999), p. 44.

4 Ibid., pp. 44–5.

5 Biran, *Empire of the Qara Khitai*, pp. 81–2, 194–6.

6 'Ala al-Din Ata Malik Juvaini, *Ta'rikh-i-Jahân-Gusha*, ed. Mîrzâ Muhammad Qazvini (Leiden, 1912, 1916, 1937), p. 50; 'Ala al-Din Ata Malik Juvaini, *The History of the World-Conqueror*, trans. J. A. Boyle (Seattle, WA, 1997), p. 67.

7 Anatoly Khazanov, 'Muhammad and Jenghiz Khan Compared: The Religious Factor in World Empire Building', *Comparative Studies in Society and History*, XXXV (1993), p. 468.

8 Sh. Bira, 'Mongolian Tenggerism and Modern Globalism: A Retrospective Outlook on Globalisation', *Journal of the Royal Asiatic Series*, XIV (2003), pp. 3–12.

9 William of Rubruck, 'The Journey of William of Rubruck', in *The Mission to Aisa*, pp. 117–19. By all appearances during William's visit, Sartaq seemed to be a Christian. This is further confirmed by the Persian author Juzjani. See Minhaj Siraj Juzjani, *Tabaqat-i Nasiri* (Lahore, 1975), vol. II, pp. 286–7; Minhaj Siraj Juzjani, *Tabaqat-i Nasiri*, trans. H. G. Raverty (New Delhi, 1970), vol. II, p. 1291.

10 Anatoly Khazanov, 'The Spread of World Religions in Medieval Nomadic Societies of the Eurasian Steppes', *Toronto Studies in Central and Inner Asia*, I (1994), p. 15.

11 Pope Innocent IV, 'Two Bulls of Pope Innocent IV Addressed to the Emperor of the Tartars', in William of Rubruck, *The Mission to Asia*, pp. 75–6.

12 James Muldoon, *Popes, Lawyers, and Infidels* (Philadelphia, PA, 1979), pp. 42–3.

13 Güyük Khan, 'Guyuk Khan's Letter to Pope Innocent IV (1246)', in William of Rubruck, *The Mission to Asia*, pp. 85–6.

14 Francis W. Cleaves, trans. and ed., *The Secret History of the Mongols* (Cambridge, 1980), p. 53.
15 Jean de Joinville, 'The Life of Saint Louis', in *Chronicles of the Crusades*, trans. and ed. M.R.B. Shaw (New York, 1963), pp. 287–8.
16 Muldoon, *Popes, Lawyers, and Infidels*, p. 50.
17 Ibid., p. 36. These irregularities often concerned marriage, such as degrees of affinity that might not coincide with those acceptable to the Catholic Church.
18 Güyük Khan, 'Guyuk Khan's Letter', p. 85. Güyük responds to the pope's request that the Mongols become Christians and cease their attacks on Christian lands: 'Though thou likewise sayest that I should become a trembling Nestorian Christian, worship God and be an ascetic, how knowest thou whom God absolves, in truth to whom He shows mercy?'
19 G. W. Houston, 'An Overview of Nestorians in Inner Asia', *Central Asiatic Journal*, xxiv (1980), pp. 64–5.
20 Khazanov, 'The Spread of World Religions', p. 24.
21 Cleaves, *Secret History of the Mongols*, pp. 181–2. It should be noted that there is some debate over whether or not Teb Tengri was a shaman. See Tatyana D. Skrynnikova, *Kharizma vlasti v epokhu Chingiskhana* (Moscow, 1997).
22 Samuel Hugh Moffet, *A History of Christianity in Asia, Vol. I, Beginnings to 1500* (New York, 1992), pp. 400–1. Also see J. M. Fiey, 'Chrétiens Syriaques sous les Mongols (Ilkhanat de Perse, xiiie–xive s.)', *Corpus Scriptorum Christianorum Orientalium*, vol. ccclxii, subsidia tomus 44 (Louvain, 1975).
23 James D. Ryan, 'Christian Wives of Mongol Khans: Tartar Queens and Missionary Expectations in Asia', *Journal of the Royal Asiatic Society*, 3rd ser., viii/3 (1998), p. 417.
24 Nestorian Christianity flourished in Asia for several centuries after a schism resulting from the Council of Ephesus in 431. See Moffet, *A History of Christianity in Asia*. Nestorianism was based on the school of thought of Theodore of Mopsuetia (350–428). He was a bishop of Mopsuetia, north of Antioch. He based his teachings on a literal reading of the Bible, with little interpretation and little emphasis on prophetic passages. He viewed sin as a weakness that could be overcome and not a disease or 'tainted will'. Nestorius was his pupil. In 428, Nestorius was elected Patriarch of Constantinople but many didn't like him because previously he was unknown. He launched a drive against the Arians as heretics and also other groups, but he too was accused of heresy by Cyril, Patriarch of Alexandria, partially for political reasons. Alexandria was the third-ranking city in Christianity behind Rome and Constantinople. And there was also rivalry between the schools of Alexandria and Antioch. Cyril accused Nestorius of 'denying the deity of Christ' (p. 174), and sent twelve anathemas. The Antiochenes sent twelve counter anathemas. Emperor Theodosius II called for a council at Ephesus in 431 to settle things. Before the Antiochene supporters of Nestorius arrived Cyril pushed forward the council and Nestorius boycotted the early start. As a result Cyril was able to get the council to excommunicate Nestorius in a vote of 200–0. Nestorius never really denied Christ's deity or unity. He just used the word 'prosopon' meaning appearance or presence while Cyril used 'hypostatis' meaning

substance or real being. Basically he recognized the humanity and deity of
Christ as being separate things.

25 Muldoon, *Popes, Lawyers, and Infidels*, pp. 59–60.
26 Ibid., p. 62.
27 Ibid.
28 Marco Polo, *Description of the World*, trans. A. C. Moule and P. Pelliot
(London, 1938), p. 79.
29 The Mongol prince Nicholas was the son of Hülegü and Qutui Khatun, a
Nestorian Christian. However, the sources are not clear when; Nicholas had
converted to Islam by the time he ascended the throne in 1282. As a Muslim
he used the name Ahmad and reigned from 1282–4. He was the first Muslim
ruler in the Ilkhanate and also the first to be deposed, possibly because he
sought a peaceful existence with his co-religionist in the Mamluk Sultanate.
For more on his conversion and the role it played, see Reuven Amitai, 'The
Conversion of Tegüder Ilkhan to Islam',' *Jerusalem Studies in Arabic and Islam*,
XXV (2001), pp. 15–43.
30 Muldoon, *Popes, Lawyers, and Infidels*, p. 67.
31 Leonard Lewisohn, 'Overview: Iranian Islam and Persianate Sufism', in *The
Legacy of Mediaeval Persian Sufism*, ed. Leonard Lewisohn (London, 1992),
p. 30; Leonard Lewisohn, *Beyond Faith and Infidelity: The Sufi Poetry and
Teachings of Mahmûd Shabistarî* (Aldershot, Surrey, 1995), pp. 57–8.
32 Istvan Vasary, 'History and Legend in Berke Khan's Conversion to Islam',
in *Aspects of Altai Civilization III* (Bloomington, IN, 1990), pp. 235–7. Also see
Minaj Siraj Juzjani, *Tabaqat-i Nasiri*, ed. 'Abd al-Hayy Habibi (Kabul, 1964–5),
pp. 284–8 and Juzjani, trans. Raverty, p. 1283.
33 Vasary, 'History and Legend in Berke Khan's Conversion to Islam', p. 238
34 Ibid., p. 256.
35 Devin DeWeese, *Islamization and Native Religion in the Golden Horde*
(University Park, PA, 1994), p. 89.
36 David Bundy, 'The Syriac and Armenian Christian Responses to the
Islamification of the Mongols', in *Medieval Christian Perceptions of Islam*, ed.
John Victor Tolan (New York, 1996), p. 35.
37 Devin DeWeese, 'Yasavina Legends on the Islamization of Turkistan', *Aspects
of Altaic Civilization III* (Bloomington, IN, 1990), pp. 108–9.
38 Johan Elverskog, *Buddhism and Islam on the Silk Road*, pp. 228–338; F. W. Cleaves,
'The Rescript of Qubilai Prohibiting the Slaughtering of Animals by Slitting
the Throat', *Journal of Turkish Studies*, XVI (1992), p. 69; numerous examples of
this exist in the sources, but Elverskog's summary is exemplary in gathering a
wide variety of sources.
39 Teresa Fitzherbert, 'Religious Diversity under Ilkhanid Rule *c.* 1300 as
Reflected in the Freer Bal'ami', in *Beyond the Legacy of Genghis Khan*,
ed. Linda Komaroff (Leiden, 2006), p. 397; also see Denise Aigle, 'The
Mongol Invasions of Bilâd al-Shâm by Ghâzân Khân and Ibn Taymîyah's
Three "Anti-Mongol" Fatwas', *Mamluk Studies Review*, XI/2 (2007),
pp. 89–119.
40 Aigle, 'The Mongol Invasions of Bilâd al-Shâm; Michal Scott Doran,
'Somebody Else's Civil War", *Foreign Affairs*, LXXXI/1 (2002), pp. 30–1.

41 Michal Biran, 'The Chaghataids and Islam: The Conversion of Tarmashirin Khan (1331–34)', *Journal of the American Oriental Society*, CXXII/4 (2002), pp. 742–52 goes into his conversion into detail. Also see Elverskog, *Buddhism and Islam on the Silk Road*, p. 189; Gyorgy Kara, 'Medieval Mongol Documents from Khara Khoto and East Turkestan in the St Petersburg Branch of the Institute of Oriental Studies,' *Manuscripta Orientalia*, IX/2 (2003), pp. 28–30.

42 Elverskog, *Buddhism and Islam on the Silk Road*, pp. 189–91.

43 Ross Dunn, *The Adventures of Ibn Battuta: A Muslim Traveler of the 14th Century* (Berkeley, CA, 2005), p. 41.

44 Ibid., p. 46.

45 Klaus Sagaster, 'The History of Buddhism among the Mongols', in *The Spread of Buddhism*, ed. Ann Heirmann and Stephan Peter Bumbacher (Leiden, 2007), pp. 381–2.

46 Ibid., p. 382.

47 Ibid., p. 384.

48 Ibid., p. 386–7.

49 Elverskog, *Buddhism and Islam on the Silk Road*, p. 134.

50 Ibid., p. 136.

51 Although the importance of the Uighurs in the Mongol government is well known, for an examination of the *longue duree*, see Michael C. Brose, *Subjects and Masters: Uyghurs in the Mongol Empire* (Bellingham, WA, 2007).

52 Biran, *The Empire of the Qara Khitai in Eurasian History*, p. 177 n. 53.

53 Luciano Petech, 'Tibetan Relations with Sung China and with the Mongols', in *China Among Equals*, ed. Morris Rossabi (Berkeley, CA, 1983), pp. 182–3.

54 Elverskog, *Buddhism and Islam on the Silk Road*, p. 150.

55 David M. Robinson, *Empire's Twilight: Northeast Asia Under the Mongols* (Philadelphia, PA, 2009), p. 260.

56 Morris Rossabi, *Khubilai: His Life and Times* (Berkeley, CA, 1988), p. 42.

57 Sagaster, 'The History of Buddhism among the Mongols', p. 387.

58 Ibid., p. 391.

59 Ibid., pp. 393–5.

60 Ibid., p. 388.

61 Sechin Jagchid, *Essays in Mongolian Studies* (Provo, UT, 1988), pp. 121–4.

62 Sh. Bira, 'Mongolian Tenggerism and Modern Globalism: A Retrospective Outlook on Globalisation', *Inner Asia*, V (2003), p. 110.

63 Igor de Rachelwiltz, trans. and ed., *The Secret History of the Mongols* (Leiden, 2004), pp. 52–3.

64 Carpini, 'History of the Mongols', p. 9. Plano Carpini wrote that the Mongols believed in one god who was the maker of all things and he gave good things and hardships. However, they did not worship this god with prayers or ceremonies.

65 Bira, 'Mongolian Tenggerism and Modern Globalism', p. 110.

66 Ibid., p. 111.

67 Khazanov, 'Muhammad and Jenghiz Khan', p. 466.

68 William of Rubruck, 'The Journey of William of Rubruck', p. 195.

69 There are several notices of mosques, churches and temples being looted and clergy beaten. Many of these activities took place during conquests but the

Mongols viewed all those who resisted as an enemy. After the conquest occasional raids upon clergy did occur; however these were more out of lust for plunder than a direct attack on a particular religion. Even in their plundering the Mongols did not favour one religion over the other.

70 William of Rubruck, 'The Journey of William of Rubruck', p. 111.

71 Ibid., p. 109.

72 Ibid., p. 212. Indeed, while at the camp of Baiju, the Mongol commander stationed in the Mughan plain near Tabriz, William was given wine but stated he would have preferred *kumiss* as it 'is a more satisfying drink for a hungry man'.

73 Khazanov, 'Spread of World Religions', p. 24.

74 Timothy May, 'The Relationship Between Sufis and Inner Asian Ruling Elites', *Southeast Review of Asian Studies*, xxx (2008), p. 88.

8 THE MONGOLS AND THE PLAGUE

1 Giles li Muisis, 'Receueil des Chroniques de Flander II', in *The Black Death*, trans. and ed. Rosemary Horrox (Manchester, 1994), p. 46.

2 The name Black Plague did not enter common parlance until the sixteenth century when the Danes and Swedes referred to the medieval plague as the Black Plague or Black Death, black signifying its terrible or dreadful nature rather than ascribing the colour black to any of the symptoms.

3 William H. McNeill, *Plagues and Peoples* (New York, 1998), pp. 140, 170; John Aberth, *The First Horseman: Disease in Human History* (Upper Saddle River, NJ, 2007), p. 12.

4 Susan Scott and Christopher J. Duncan, *Biology of Plagues: Evidence from Historical Populations* (Cambridge, 2001), pp. 51–2.

5 Ibid., pp. 57–8. There are 30 species of fleas that could carry it but evidence points to *Xenopsylla cheopis* being the culprit in the fourteenth century.

6 Ibid., p. 65. Other ways are possible but these are the two most likely methods of initial contact between the bacilli and humans out in the steppe.

7 Ibid., p. 53.

8 John of Plano Carpini, 'History of the Mongols', in William of Rubruck, *The Mission to Asia*, trans. a nun from Stanbrook Abbey, ed. Christopher Dawson (Toronto, 1980), pp. 16–17.

9 Scott and Duncan, *Biology of Plagues*, p. 59. The ideal temperature for a flea is between 50 and 80 degrees Fahrenheit.

10 Michael W. Dols, *The Black Death in the Middle East* (Princeton, NJ, 1977), p. 16.

11 Gabriele de Mussis, 'Historia de Morbo', in *The Black Death*, trans. and ed. Rosemary Horrox (Manchester, 1994), p. 17.

12 Ibid., p. 17. de Mussis wrote that the malady 'killed thousands upon thousands every day. It was as though arrows were raining down from heaven to strike and crush the Tartar's arrogance.'

13 Ibid.; Peter Jackson, *The Mongols and the West* (Harlow, 2005), p. 305, indicates that the Mongols hurled just the heads and not the entire bodies.

14 de Mussis, 'Historia de Morbo', p. 17.

15 Louis Sanctus, 'Letter April 27, 1348', in *The Black Death: The Great Mortality of 1348–1350*, ed. John Aberth (Boston, MA, 2005), p. 22.

16 Nicephorus Gregoras, 'Historias Byzantina', in *The Black Death: The Great Mortality of 1348–1350*, ed. John Aberth (Boston, MA, 2005), p. 15.

17 See David Herlihy, *The Black Death and the Transformation of the West* (Cambridge, MA, 1997); Norman Cantor, *In the Wake of the Plague: The Black Death and the World it Made* (New York, 2002). These are among the most well known but, like the Black Death, other works continue to spread.

18 Cantor, *In the Wake of the Plague*, p. 203.

19 Aberth, *The First Horseman*, pp. 19–20; Irwin W. Sherman, *The Power of Plagues* (Washington, DC, 2006), pp. 79–80.

20 Sherman, *Power of Plagues*, p. 78.

21 Cantor, *In the Wake of the Plague*, pp. 206–8.

22 Dols, *The Black Death in the Middle East*, pp. 10, 291–2.

23 Ross Dunn, *The Adventures of Ibn Battuta: A Muslim Traveler of the 14th Century* (Berkeley, CA, 2005), p. 270; Ibn Battuta, *Rihala Ibn Battuta*.

24 Abu Hafs Umar al-Wardi, 'Essay on the Report of the Pestilence', in *The Black Death: The Great Mortality of 1348–1350*, ed. John Aberth (Boston, MA, 2005), p. 17.

25 Imad al-Din Abu al-Fida Ismail ibn Umar Ibn Kathir, 'The Beginning and End: On History', in *The Black Death: The Great Mortality of 1348–1350*, ed. John Aberth (Boston, MA, 2005), p. 11.

26 Ahmad ibn Ali al-Maqrizi, 'A History of the Ayybids and Mamluks', in *The Black Death: The Great Mortality of 1348–1350*, ed. John Aberth (Boston, MA, 2005), pp. 84–5.

27 Ibid., p. 85.

28 Ibid., p. 86–7.

29 Dols, *The Black Death in the Middle East*, p. 294.

30 Uli Schamiloglu, 'The Rise of the Ottoman Empire: The Black Death in Medieval Anatolia and its Impact on Turkish Civilization', in *Views From the Edge: Essays in Honor of Richard W. Bulliet*, ed. Neguin Yavari, Lawrence G. Potter and Jean-Marc Ran Oppenheim (New York, 2004), pp. 270–3.

31 Nicephorus, *Historias Byzantina*, p. 15.

32 Sherman, *Power of Plagues*, pp. 68–9.

33 Uli Schamiloglu, 'Preliminary Remarks on the Role of the Disease in the History of the Golden Horde', *Central Asian Survey*, XII/4 (1993), p. 449.

34 Ibid., p. 450.

35 Ibid., p. 449.

36 Dols, *The Black Death in the Middle East*, p. 41; J. W. Dardess, *Conquerors and Confucians: Aspects of Political Change in Late Yuan China* (New York, 1973), p. 55.

9 Migrations and Demographic Trends

1 Minhaj Siraj Juzjani, *Tabaqat-i Nasiri*, trans. H. G. Raverty (New Delhi, 1970), pp. 1041–2. The Muhammad to whom Chinggis Khan refers is Muhammad Khwarazmshah.

2 'Ala al-Din Ata Malik Juvaini, *The History of the World-Conqueror*, trans.

J. A. Boyle (Seattle, WA, 1997), pp. 608–9; 'Ala al-Din Ata Malik Juvaini, *Ta'rîkh-i-Jahân-Gusha*, ed. Mirza Muhammad Qazvini (Leiden, 1912, 1916, 1937), 3 vols, p. 93. For more on Hülegü's march see John Masson Smith Jr, 'Hülegü Moves West: High Living and Heartbreak on the Road to Baghdad', in *Beyond the Legacy of Genghis Khan*, ed. Linda Komaroff (Leiden, 2006), pp. 111–34.

3 For more on tribal dynamics and identity see Rudi Paul Lindner, 'What Was a Nomadic Tribe?', *Comparative Studies in Society and History*, XXIV / 4 (1982), pp. 689–711.

4 Gareth Jenkins, 'A Note on Climatic Cycles and the Rise of Chingis Khan', *Central Asiatic Journal*, XVIII (1974), pp. 217–26.

5 Igor de Rachewiltz, trans. and ed., *The Secret History of the Mongols* (Leiden, 2004), p. 134.

6 John Masson Smith Jr, 'Mongol Society and Military in the Middle East: Antecedents and Adaptations', in *War and Society in the Eastern Mediterranean, 7th and 15th Centuries*, ed. Yaacov Lev (Leiden, 1996), p. 249; Valery Alexeev, 'Some Aspects of the Study of Productive Forces in the Empire of Chenghiz Khan', in *The Rulers From the Steppe: State Formation on the Eurasian Periphery*, ed. Gary Seaman and Daniel Marks (Los Angeles, CA, 1991), pp. 189–90. The most commonly accepted figure is that provided by Ts. Munkeyev at 700,000. E. I. Kychanov estimated it a bit higher at one million, while Alexeev considered it to be less than Munkeyev's approximation, at 500,000, while J. M. Smith Jr, put it at 850,000. A Mongolian scholar, Ch. Dalai, disagrees and estimates it to be between 2 and 2.5 million.

7 Ch'i-ch'ing Hsiao, trans., chapters 98 and 99 of the 'Yuan Shih', in *The Military Establishment of the Yuan Dynasty* (Cambridge, 1978), pp. 72–91; 92–124.

8 H. D. Martin, *The Rise of Chinggis Khan and his Conquest of North China* (Baltimore, MD, 1950), p. 15.

9 Timothy May, *The Mongol Art of War* (Barnsley, 2007), pp. 30–1.

10 Udo B. Barkmann, 'Some Comments on the Consequences of the Decline of the Mongol Empire on Social Development of the Mongols', in *The Mongol Empire and its Legacy*, ed. Reuven Amitai-Preiss and David O. Morgan (Leiden, 2001), p. 277.

11 William of Rubruck, *The Mission of Friar William of Rubruck: His Journey to the Court of the Great Khan Mongke, 1253–1255,* trans. Peter Jackson (London, 1990), pp. 183–6; William of Rubruck, 'The Journey of William of Rubruck', in *The Mission to Asia*, trans. a nun from Stanbrook Abbey, ed. Christopher Dawson (Toronto, 1980), pp. 157, 177–8.

12 Thomas T. Allsen, *Commodity and Exchange in the Mongol Empire: A Cultural History of Islamic Textiles* (Cambridge, 2002), p. 35.

13 Li Chih-Chang, *The Travels of an Alchemist* (London, 2005), pp. 85–7.

14 Allsen, *Commodity and Exchange*, p. 38.

15 William of Rubruck, *Mission of Friar William of Rubruck*, pp. 144–5; William of Rubruck, 'The Journey of William of Rubruck', p. 135.

16 Rashid al-Din, *Jami' al-Tawarikh*, ed. B. Karimi (Tehran, 1983), vol. I, p. 216; Juzjani, *Tabaqat-i Nasiri*, trans. Raverty, p. 1158.

17 The best detailed account of the movement of technicians through the Mongol Empire is Thomas T. Allsen, 'Technician Transfers in the Mongolian

Empire', *Central Eurasian Lectures*, II (Bloomington, IN, 2002). Also see James C. Y. Watt, 'A Note on Artistic Exchanges in the Mongol Empire', in *The Legacy of Genghis Khan*, ed. Linda Komaroff and Stefano Carboni (New Haven, CT, 2002).

18 William of Rubruck, *Mission of Friar William of Rubruck*, p. 162; William of Rubruck, 'The Journey of William of Rubruck', p. 144; Timothy Brook, *The Troubled Empire: China in the Yuan and Ming Dynasties* (Cambridge, MA, 2010), pp. 146–7.

19 Rachewiltz, *Secret History of the Mongols*, pp. 55, 61–2. The great Jurchen wrestler Büri-Bökö had his back broken by Chinggis Khan's half-brother Belgütei as a demonstration that the Jürkin's independence had ended. Büri-Bökö was a superior wrestler to Belgütei.

20 Thomas T. Allsen, 'Command Performances: Entertainers in the Mongolian Empire', *Russian History*, XXVIII (2001), p. 40; Juvaini, *Ta'ríkh-i-Jahân-Gusha*, pp. 183–4; Juvaini, *History of the World-Conqueror*, pp. 227–8.

21 Grigor of Akanc, 'The History of the Nation of Archers', trans. Robert P. Blake and Richard N. Frye, *Harvard Journal of Asiatic Studies*, XII (1949), pp. 345–9.

22 Allsen, 'Command Performances', p. 41.

23 Dolores Menstell Hu, 'Musical Elements of Chinese Opera', *Musical Quarterly*, L/4 (1964), p. 447.

24 John of Plano Carpini, 'History of the Mongols', in *The Mission to Asia*, trans. a nun from Stanbrook Abbey, ed. Christopher Dawson, (Toronto, 1980), pp. 57; William of Rubruck, *Mission of Friar William of Rubruck*, pp. 76–8; William of Rubruck, 'The Journey of William of Rubruck', pp. 96–7.

25 Allsen, 'Command Performances', p. 43.

26 Ibid., pp. 44, 45.

27 Tatiana Zerjal, Yali Xue, *et al.*, 'The Genetic Legacy of the Mongols', *American Journal of Human Genetics*, LXXII (2003), pp. 717–21.

28 William of Rubruck, *Mission of Friar William of Rubruck*, p. 182; William of Rubruck, 'The Journey of William of Rubruck', p. 157; Simon de Saint-Quentin, *Histoire des Tartares*, ed. Jean Richard (Paris, 1965), pp. 48, 75; Gregory G. Guzman, 'European Captives and Craftsmen among the Mongols, 1231–1255', *The Historian*, LXXII/1 (2010), p. 136.

29 Matthew Paris, *English History*, trans. and ed. J. A. Giles (New York, 1968), vol. II, p. 31.

30 Marco Polo, *The Travels of Marco Polo*, ed. Manuel Komroff (New York, 1953), pp. 107–9; Marco Polo, *The Travels of Marco Polo*, trans. Ronald Lathem (New York, 1958), pp. 122–3.

31 David M. Robinson, *Empire's Twilight: Northeast Asia Under the Mongols* (Philadelphia, PA, 2009), p. 142.

32 Ibn Battuta, *Rihala Ibn Battuta* (Beirut, 1995), p. 277.

33 Richard Paul Currie, 'An Annotated Translation of the Biography of Toghto Temur from the Yuan Shih', MA thesis, Indiana University, Bloomington, 1984.

34 Reuven Amitai-Preiss, *Mongols and Mamluks: The Mamluk–Ilkhanid War, 1260–1281* (Cambridge, 1995), p. 195.

35 Morris Rossabi, *Voyager from Xanadu: Rabban Sauma and the First Journey from China to the West* (Berkeley, CA, 2010).

36 Juzjani, *Tabaqat-i Nasiri*, trans. Raverty, pp. 964–5.

37 Timothy Brook, *Troubled Empire*, trans. Raverty, pp. 42–3.

38 Ibid., p. 43.

39 Robinson, *Empire's Twilight*, p. 142.

40 He Qiutao, *Sheng Wu Qin Zheng Lu (Bogda Bagatur Bey-e-Ber Tayilagsan Temdeglel)*, ed. Arasaltu (Qayilar, 1985), p. 42; Martin, *The Rise of Chingis Khan*, pp. 146–7.

41 Henry G. Schwarz, 'Some Notes on the Mongols of Yunnan', *Central Asiatic Journal*, xxviii (1994), p. 103.

42 For a detailed discussion on Kipchak activity and impact in the Balkans see Istvan Vasary, *Cumans and Tatars: Oriental Military in the Pre-Ottoman Balkans, 1185–1365* (Cambridge, 2005).

43 Aziz Ahmad, 'Mongol Pressure in an Alien Land', *Central Asiatic Journal*, vi (1961), pp. 183–4; Peter Jackson, *The Delhi Sultanate, A Political and Military History* (Cambridge, 1999), pp. 49; Andre Wink, *Al-Hind: The Making of the Indo-Islamic World, Vol. 2: The Slave Kings and the Islamic Conquest, 11th–13th Centuries* (Leiden, 1997), p. 202–11.

44 Ahmad, 'Mongol Pressure in an Alien Land', p. 182.

45 Jackson, *Delhi Sultanate*, p. 26.

46 Simon Digby, *War-horse and Elephant in the Delhi Sultanate: A Study of Military Supplies* (Oxford, 1971), pp. 34–5.

47 Wink, *Al-Hind*, pp. 204–6.

48 Iris Origo, 'The Domestic Enemy: The Eastern Slaves in Tuscany in the Fourteenth and Fifteenth Centuries', *Speculum*, xxx/3 (1955), p. 324.

49 Ibid., pp. 336–337.

50 Michael Khodarkovsky, *Russia's Steppe Frontier: The Making of a Colonial Empire, 1500–1800* (Bloomington, in, 2002), p. 19.

51 Wink, *Al-Hind*, p. 199.

52 Carter Vaughn Findley, *The Turks in World History* (Oxford, 2005) p. 87.

53 Paul D. Buell, 'Mongol Empire and Turkicization: The Evidence of Food and Foodways', in *The Mongol Empire and Its Legacy*, ed. Reuven Amitai-Preiss and David O. Morgan (Leiden, 2001), p. 201; Hodong Kim, 'The Early History of the Moghul Nomads: The Legacy of the Chaghatai Khanate', in *The Mongol Empire and Its Legacy*, pp. 292–3.

54 Kim, 'The Early History of the Moghul Nomads', p. 313–16.

55 Ibid., p. 313.

56 Rachewiltz, *Secret History of the Mongols*, p. 59.

10 CULTURAL EXCHANGES

1 Thomas T. Allsen, *Culture and Conquest in Mongol Eurasia* (New York, 1997).

2 'Ala al-Din Ata Malik Juvaini, *Ta'ríkh-i-Jahân-Gusha*, ed. Mirza Muhammad Qazvini (Leiden, 1912, 1916, 1937), 3 vols, vol. i, p. 116; 'Ala al-Din Ata Malik Juvaini, *The History of the World-Conqueror*, trans. J. A. Boyle (Seattle, wa, 1997), p. 148; Rashid al-Din, *Jami' al-Tawarikh*, ed. B. Karimi (Tehran, 1983), vol. ii, p. 734.

3 See George Saliba, 'Horoscopes and Planetary Theory: Ilkhanid Patronage of Astronomers', in *Beyond the Legacy of Genghis Khan*, ed. Linda Komaroff

(Leiden, 2006), pp. 257–368; John A. Boyle, trans., 'The Longer Introduction to the *Zij-i Ilkhani* of Nasir-ad-din Tusi', *Journal of Semitic Studies*, VIII (1963), pp. 246–7.

4 Allsen, *Culture and Conquest*, pp. 142–3.

5 See Paul D. Buell and Eugene N. Anderson, trans. and eds, *A Soup for the Qan* (London, 2000), pp. 6–7. The recipes are categorized by use and medicinal function.

6 Abdulhak Adnan, 'Sur le Tanksukname-i-Ilhani dar Ulum-u-Funan-i-khatai', *Isis*, XXXII (1940), pp. 44–7.

7 Allsen, *Culture and Conquest*, pp. 84–90. See chapter 12 for a complete study of Rashid al-Din's methodology.

8 Ibid., p. 93.

9 Ibid., p. 101.

10 William of Rubruck, *The Mission of Friar William of Rubruck*, trans. Peter Jackson (Indianapolis, IN, 2009), p. 122..

11 Igor de Rachewiltz, 'Some Remarks on the Ideological Foundations of Chingis Khan's Empire', *Papers in Far Eastern History*, VII (1973), pp. 21–36; Anatoly Khazanov, 'Muhammad and Jenghiz Khan Compared: The Religious Factor in World Empire Building', *Comparative Studies in Society and History*, XXXV (1993), pp. 464–6.

12 Anne F. Broadbridge, *Kingship and Ideology in the Islamic and Mongol Worlds* (Cambridge, 2008), p. 9.

13 For an extended discussion see Charles Halperin, 'The Kipchak Connection: The Ilkhans, the Mamluks and Ayn Jalut', *Bulletin of the School of Oriental and African Studies*, LXIII (2000), pp. 229–45.

14 Broadbridge, *Kingship and Ideology*, pp. 9–10.

15 Lisa Balabanlilar, 'The Begims of the Mystic Feast: Turco-Mongol Tradition in the Mughal Harem', *Journal of Asian Studies*, LXIX/1 (2010), p. 126.

16 This is a topic that deserves more attention. At the time of writing there is only one book in English on the Mongol queens: Jack Weatherford, *The Secret History of the Mongol Queens: How the Daughters of Genghis Khan Rescued His Empire* (New York, 2010). Otherwise the topic is discussed here and there through virtually all of the books on the Mongols but few specific studies exist. It is to be hoped this will change in the near future.

17 Timothy May, *Culture and Customs of Mongolia* (Westport, CT, 2009), pp. 37–9, 103–15.

18 Balabanlilar, 'The Begims of the Mystic Feast', p. 126.

19 Maria Szuppe, 'Women in Sixteenth Century Safavid Iran', in *Women in Iran from the Rise of Islam to 1800*, ed. Guity Nashat and Lois Beck (Urbana, IL, 2003), p. 162. Balabanlilar, 'The Begims of the Mystic Feast', p. 127; John Woods, *The Aqquyunlu: Clan, Confederation, Empire* (Salt Lake City, UT, 1999), p. 95.

20 Ruby Lal, *Domesticity and Power in the Early Mughal World* (New York, 2005), p. 176.

21 Leslie P. Pierce, *The Imperial Harem: Women and Sovereignty in the Ottoman Empire* (Oxford, 1993). This remains the best study of the harem, not only in the Ottoman world but as an institution.

22 Balabanlilar, 'The Begims of the Mystic Feast', p. 129.

23 Michael J. Seth, *A Concise History of Korea: From the Neolithic Period through the Nineteenth Century* (Lanham, MD, 2006), p. 117.

24 See Speros Vyronis, *The Decline of Medieval Hellenism in Asia Minor and the Process of Islamization from the Eleventh through the Fifteenth Century* (Berkeley, CA, 1971).

25 Oleg Grabar, *The Illustrations of the Maqamat* (Chicago, IL, 1983), p. 150.

26 Robert Hillenbrand, 'The Arts of the Book in Ilkhanid Iran', in *The Legacy of Genghis Khan*, ed. Linda Komaroff and Stefano Carboni (New Haven, CT, 2002), p. 150; Johan Elverskog, *Buddhism and Islam on the Silk Road* (Philadelphia, 2010), p. 167.

27 See Dickran Kouymjian, 'Chinese Motifs in Thirteenth-Century Armenian Art: The Mongol Connection', in *Beyond the Legacy of Genghis Khan*, ed. Linda Komaroff (Leiden, 2006), pp. 303–24 for more on the transformation of Armenian art.

28 Roxann Prazniak, 'Siena on the Silk Roads: Ambrogio Lorenzetti and the Mongol Global Century, 1250–1350', *Journal of World History*, XXI (2010), p. 216.

29 Ibid., pp. 215–16.

30 Ibid., p. 209.

31 Iris Origio, 'The Domestic Enemy: The Eastern Slaves in Tuscany in the Fourteenth and Fifteenth Centuries', *Speculum*, XXX/3 (1958), pp. 321–366.

32 Seth, *A Concise History of Korea*, p. 109.

33 Ibid.

34 Morris Rossabi, 'The Mongols and Their Legacy', in *The Legacy of Genghis Khan*, ed. Linda Komaroff and Stefano Carboni (New Haven, CT, 2002), p. 29.

35 James C. Y. Watt, 'A Note on Artistic Exchanges in the Mongol Empire', in *The Legacy of Genghis Khan*, ed. Linda Komaroff and Stefano Carboni (New Haven, CT, 2002), pp. 66–8.

36 F. W. Mote, *Imperial China 900–1800* (Cambridge, MA, 1999), pp. 508–9.

37 Ibid., pp. 511–12.

38 Buell and Anderson, *A Soup for the Qan*, pp. 65–7.

39 As with everything related to Marco Polo, there is doubt on when spaghetti actually appeared in Italy. Of course, Italians had to wait for the Columbian exchange to have tomatoes and tomato sauce did not come into use until the nineteenth century.

40 Buell and Anderson, *A Soup for the Qan*, pp. 275, 278–9, 281–2, 284–6, 288–9, 302, 517–18.

41 Paul D. Buell, 'Mongol Empire and Turkicization: The Evidence of Food and Foodways', in *The Mongol Empire and Its Legacy*, ed. Reuven Amitai-Preiss and David O. Morgan (Leiden, 2001), pp. 204–5.

42 Buell, 'Mongol Empire and Turkicization', pp. 216–17, n. 69.

43 William of Rubruck, *The Mission of Friar William of Rubruck: His Journey to the Court of the Great Khan Mongke, 1253–1255*, trans. Peter Jackson (London, 1990), p. 82.

44 Thomas T. Allsen, 'Ögedei and Alcohol', *Mongolian Studies*, XXIX (2007), pp. 3–12.

45 Timothy Brook, *The Troubled Empire: China in the Yuan and Ming Dynasties* (Cambridge, MA, 2010), p. 206.

46 Carswell, 'More about the Mongols: Chinese Porcelain from Asia to Europe',

Asian Affairs, xxxvi/ 11 (2005), p. 158.

47 Brook, *The Troubled Empire*, p. 206.

48 For all of the methods see Oliver Watson, 'Pottery under the Mongols', in *Beyond the Legacy of Genghis Khan*, ed. Linda Komaroff (Leiden, 2006), pp. 325–45.

49 Carswell, 'More About the Mongols', p. 160.

50 Mark G. Kramarovsky, 'Conquerors and Craftsmen: Archaeology of the Golden Horde', *Genghis Khan and the Mongol Empire* (Seattle, WA, 2009), pp. 187–8.

51 Ibid., p. 188.

52 Mote, *Imperial China*, p. 326.

53 Allsen, *Conquest and Culture*, p. 176.

54 L. Carrington Goodrich, 'Movable Type Printing: Two Notes', *Journal of the American Oriental Society*, xcix (1974), pp. 476–7; Richard P. Palmieri, 'Tibetan Xylography and the Question of Movable Type', *Technology and Culture*, xxxii (1991), pp. 82–90; Allsen, *Culture and Conquest*, p. 177.

55 Marco Polo, *The Travels of Marco Polo*, p. 134.

56 Allsen, *Conquest and Culture*, p. 181.

57 Seth, *A Concise History of Korea*, p. 114.

58 Allsen, *Conquest and Culture*, p. 184–5.

59 Ibid., p. 185.

60 David Jacoby, 'Silk Economies and Cross-Cultural Artistic Interaction: Byzantium, the Muslim World, and the Christian West', *Dumbarton Oaks Papers*, lviii (2004), p. 233.

61 Ibid., p. 235.

62 Stephen F. Dale, 'Silk Road, Cotton Road, or . . . Indo-Chinese Trade in Pre-European Times', *Modern Asian Studies*, xliii/ 1 (2009), p. 83.

63 Ibid.

64 Seth, *A Concise History of Korea*, p. 110.

65 Evariste-Regis Huc and Joseph Gabet, *Travels in Tartary, Thibet and China, 1844–1846* (New York, 1987) vol. i, pp. 315–16.

66 Seth, *A Concise History of Korea*, p. 110.

BIBLIOGRAPHY

Aberth, John, *The Black Death: The Great Mortality of 1348–1350, A Brief History with Documents* (Boston, MA, 2005)

——, *The First Horsemen: Disease in Human History* (Upper Saddle River, NJ, 2007)

Abu Hafs Umar ibn al-Wardi, 'Essay on the Report of the Pestilence', in John Aberth, *The Black Death: The Great Mortality of 1348–1350* (Boston, MA, 2005)

Abu-Lughod, Janet, *Before European Hegemony: The World System AD 1250–1350* (New York, 1989)

Ahmad, Aziz, 'Mongol Pressure in an Alien Land', *Central Asiatic Journal*, VI (1961), pp. 182–93

Aigle, Denise, 'The Mongol Invasions of Bilâd al-Shâm by Ghâzân Khân and Ibn Taymîyah's Three "Anti-Mongol" Fatwas', *Mamluk Studies Review*, XI/2 (2007), pp. 89–119

Alexeev, Valery, 'Some Aspects of the Study of Productive Forces in the Empire of Chenghiz Khan', in *The Rulers From the Steppe: State Formation on the Eurasian Periphery*, ed. Gary Seaman and Daniel Marks (Los Angeles, CA, 1991), pp. 186–7

Allsen, Thomas T., 'Mongol Census Taking in Rus', 1245–1275', *Harvard Ukrainian Studies*, V/1 (1981) pp. 32–53

——, 'The Yüan Dynasty and the Uighurs of Turfan in the 13th Century,' in *China Among Equals*, ed. Morris Rossabi (Berkeley, CA, 1983)

——, 'Guard and Government in the Reign of the Grand Qan Mongke, 1251–1259', *Harvard Journal of Asiatic Studies*, XLVI/2 (1986), pp. 495–521

——, *Mongol Imperialism: The Policies of the Grand Qan Möngke in China, Russia, and the Islamic Lands, 1251–1259* (Berkeley, CA, 1987)

——, 'Mongolian Princes and Their Merchant Partners, 1200–1260', *Asia Major*, II (1989), pp. 83–126

——, 'The Rise of the Mongolian Empire and Mongolian Rule in North China', in *The Cambridge History of China, Vol. 6: Alien Regimes and Border States, 907–1368*, ed. Herbert Franke and Denis Twitchett (Cambridge, 1994)

——, *Commodity and Exchange in the Mongol Empire: A Cultural History of Islamic Textiles* (New York, 1997)

——, 'Ever Closer Encounters: The Appropriation of Culture and the Apportionment of Peoples in the Mongol Empire', *Journal of Early Modern History*, I (1997), pp. 2–23

——, 'Command Performances: Entertainers in the Mongolian Empire', *Russian History*, XXVIII (2001), pp. 37–46

——, *Culture and Conquest in Mongol Eurasia* (New York, 2001)

——, 'Technician Transfers in the Mongolian Empire', *Central Eurasian Studies Lectures*, II (Bloomington, IN, 2002)

——, *The Royal Hunt in Eurasian History* (Philadelphia, PA, 2006)

——, 'Technologies of Governance in the Mongolian Empire: A Geographic Overview', in *Imperial Statecraft: Political Forms and Techniques of Governance in Inner Asia, Sixth–Twentieth Centuries*, ed. David Sneath (Bellingham, WA, 2006)

——, 'Ögedei and Alcohol', *Mongolian Studies*, XXIX (2007), pp. 3–12

Amitai, Reuven, 'The Conversion of Tegüder Ilkhan to Islam', *Jerusalem Studies in Arabic and Islam*, XXV (2001), pp. 15–43

——, 'Continuity and Change in the Mongol Army of the Ilkhanate', paper presented at the World Congress for Middle Eastern Studies, Barcelona, 23 July 2010

Amitai, Reuven and Michal Biran, eds, *Mongols, Turks, and Others: Eurasian Nomads and the Sedentary World* (Leiden, 2005)

Amitai-Preiss, Reuven, *Mongols and Mamluks: The Mamluk–Ilkhanid War, 1260–1281* (Cambridge, 1995)

Amitai-Preiss, Reuven and David O. Morgan, eds, *The Mongol Empire and Its Legacy* (Leiden, 2001)

Atwood, Christopher P., *Encyclopedia of Mongolia and the Mongol Empire* (New York, 2004)

——, '*Ulus* Emirs, Keshig Elders, Signatures and Marriage Partners; The Evolution of a Mongol Institution', in *Imperial Statecraft: Political Forms and Techniques of Governance in Inner Asia, Sixth–Twentieth Centuries*, ed. David Sneath (Bellingham, WA, 2006)

——, 'Informants and Sources for the *Secret History of the Mongols*', *Mongolian Studies*, XXIX (2007), pp. 27–40

——, 'The Sacrificed Brother in the *Secret History of the Mongols*', *Mongolian Studies*, XXXI (2009), pp. 189–206

Bade, David, *Khubilai Khan and the Beautiful Princess of Tumapel* (Ulaanbaatar, 2002)

Balabanlilar, Lisa, 'The Begims of the Mystic Feast: Turco-Mongol Tradition in the Mughal Harem', *Journal of Asian Studies*, LXIX/1 (2010), pp. 123–47

Barber, Malcolm and Keith Bate, *Letters from the East: Crusaders, Pilgrims and Settlers in the 12th–13th Centuries* (Aldershot, Surrey, 2010)

Barfield, Thomas J., *The Perilous Frontier: Nomadic Empires and China, 221 BC to AD 1757* (Malden, MA, 1989)

Barkmann, Udo B., 'Some Comments on the Consequences of the Decline of the Mongol Empire on the Social Development of the Mongols', in *The Mongol Empire and its Legacy*, ed. Reuven Amitai-Preiss and David O. Morgan (Leiden, 2001)

Berezin, I. N., *Tarchannye jarlyki Tochtamyka, Timur Kuluka i Saadet-Gireja* (Kazan', 1851)

Bergreen, Laurence, *Marco Polo: From Venice to Xanadu* (New York, 2007)

Bira, Sh., 'Mongolian Tenggerism and Modern Globalism: A Retrospective
    Outlook on Globalisation', *Journal of the Royal Asiatic Series*, XIV (2003), pp. 3–12
Biran, Michal, *Qaidu and the Rise of the Independent Mongol State in Central Asia*
    (Richmond, Surrey, 1997)
——, 'The Chaghadaids and Islam: The Conversion of Tarmashirin Khan
    (1331–34)', *Journal of the American Oriental Society*, CXXII/4 (2002), pp. 742–52
——, *The Empire of the Qara Khitai in Eurasian History: Between China and the
    Islamic World* (Cambridge, 2005)
——, *Chinggis Khan* (London, 2007)
Blair, Sheila S., 'Calligraphers, Illuminators, and Painters in the Ilkhanid
    Scriptorium', in *Beyond the Legacy of Genghis Khan*, ed. Linda Komaroff
    (Leiden, 2006)
Bloom, Jonathan M., 'Paper: The Transformative Medium in Ilkhanid Art', in
    Beyond the Legacy of Genghis Khan, ed. Linda Komaroff (Leiden, 2006)
Bold, Bat-Ochir, *Mongolian Nomadic Society: A Reconstruction of the 'Medieval'
    History of Mongolia* (New York, 1999)
Borsch, Stuart J., *The Black Death in Egypt and England: A Comparative Study*
    (Austin, TX, 2005)
Boyle, John A., trans., 'The Longer Introduction to the *Zij-i Ilkhani* of Nasir-ad-
    din Tusi', *Journal of Semitic Studies*, VIII (1963), pp. 244–54
——, *The Mongol World Empire, 1206–1370* (London, 1977)
Broadbridge, Anne F., *Kingship and Ideology in the Islamic and Mongol Worlds*
    (Cambridge, 2008)
Brook, Timothy, *The Troubled Empire: China in the Yuan and Ming Dynasties*
    (Cambridge, MA, 2010)
Brose, Michael C., *Subjects and Masters: Uyghurs in the Mongol Empire* (Bellingham,
    WA, 2007)
Buell, Paul D., 'Kalmyk Tanggaci People: Thoughts on the Mechanics and
    Impact of Mongol Expansion', *Mongolian Studies*, VI (1980), pp. 41–59
——, 'Cinqai (c. 1169–1252)', in *In the Service of the Khan: Eminent Personalities of
    the Early Mongol–Yuan Period*, ed. Igor de Rachewiltz et al., 1200–1300
    (Wiesbaden, 1993)
——, 'Mongol Empire and Turkicization: The Evidence of Food and Foodways',
    in *The Mongol Empire and Its Legacy*, ed. Reuven Amitai-Preiss and David O.
    Morgan (Leiden, 2001)
——, *Historical Dictionary of the Mongol World Empire* (Lanham, MD, 2003)
——, 'Cinggis-qan as the Third Man', *Mongolian Studies*, XXIX (2007), pp. 57–68
Buell, Paul D. and Eugene N. Anderson, trans. and eds, *A Soup for the Qan*
    (London, 2000)
Bundy, David, 'The Syriac and Armenian Christian Responses to the
    Islamification of the Mongols', in *Medieval Christian Perceptions of Islam*, ed.
    John Victor Tolan (New York, 1996)
Burnes, Alexander, *Cabool*, 2nd edn (London, 1843)
Cantor, Norman, *In the Wake of the Plague: The Black Death and the World it Made*
    (New York, 2002)
Carswell, John, 'More About the Mongols: Chinese Porcelain from Asia to
    Europe', *Asian Affairs*, XXXVI/II (2005), pp. 158–68

Charleux, Isabelle, 'Chinggis Khan: Ancestor Buddha, or Shaman? On the Uses and Abuses of the Portrait of Chinggis Khan', *Mongolian Studies*, XXXI (2009), pp. 207–58

Charney, Michael W., *Southeast Asian Warfare, 1300–1900* (Leiden, 2004)

Chase, Kenneth, *Firearms: A Global History to 1700* (Cambridge, 2003)

Cherniavsky, Michael, 'Khan or Basileus?: An Aspect of Russian Mediaeval Political Theory', in *The Structure of Russian History. Interpretive Essays*, ed. Michael Cherniavsky (New York, 1970)

Chih-Chang, Li, *The Travels of an Alchemist: Journey of the Taoist Ch'ang Ch'un*, trans. Arthur Waley (London, 2005)

Citino, Robert M., *The Evolution of Blitzkrieg Tactics: Germany Defends Itself Against Poland, 1918–1933* (New York, 1987)

Cleaves, Francis W., trans., *The Secret History of the Mongols* (Cambridge, MA, 1980)

Currie, Richard Paul, 'An Annotated Translation of the Biography of Toghto Temur from the Yuan Shih', MA thesis, Indiana University, Bloomington, 1984.

Dale, Stephen F., 'Silk Road, Cotton Road, or . . . Indo-Chinese Trade in Pre–European Times', *Modern Asian Studies*, XLIII/1 (2009), pp. 79–88

Danus, Richard Christian and Marc Reid Rubel, *Xanadu*, dir. Robert Greenwald (Universal Pictures, 1980)

Dardess, J. W., *Conquerors and Confucians: Aspects of Political Change in Late Yuan China* (New York, 1973)

Dashdondog, Bayarsaikhan, *The Mongols and the Armenians, 1220–1335* (Leiden, 2011)

Davies, Brian L., *Warfare, State and Society on the Black Sea Steppe, 1500–1700* (London, 2007)

Delgado, James P., *Khubilai Khan's Lost Fleet: In Search of a Legendary Armada* (Berkeley, CA, 2008)

DeWeese, Devin, 'The Eclipse of the Kubraviya in Central Asia', *Iranian Studies*, XXI/1–2 (1988), pp. 58–94

——, *Islamization and Native Religion in the Golden Horde* (University Park, PA, 1994)

——, 'Cultural Transmission and Exchange in the Mongol Empire: Notes from the Biographical Dicitonary of Ibn al-Fuwati' in *Beyond the Legacy of Genghis Khan*, ed. Linda Komaroff (Leiden, 2006)

——, '"Stuck in the Throat of Chingiz Khan": Envisioning the Mongol Conquests in Some Sufi Accounts from the 14th to 17th Centuries', in *History and Historiography of Post-Mongol Central Asia and the Middle East: Studies in Honor of John E. Woods*, ed. Judith Pfeiffer and Sholeh A. Quinn (Wiesbaden, 2006)

Digby, Simon, *War-horse and Elephant in the Delhi Sultanate: A Study of Military Supplies* (Oxford, 1971)

Dols, Michael W., 'Plague in Early Islamic History', *Journal of the American Oriental Society*, XCIV/3 (1974), pp. 371–83

——, *The Black Death in the Middle East* (Princeton, NJ, 1977)

Doran, Michael Scott, 'Somebody Else's Civil War', *Foreign Affairs*, LXXXI/1 (2002), pp. 22–42

Dunn, Ross, *The Adventures of Ibn Battuta: A Muslim Traveler of the 14th Century* (Berkeley, CA, 2005)

Dunnell, Ruth W., 'The Hsi Hsia', in *The Cambridge History of China, Vol. 6: Alien Regimes and Border States, 907–1368*, ed. Herbert Franke and Denis Twitchett (Cambridge, 1994)

——, *Chinggis Khan: World Conqueror* (Boston, MA, 2010)

Dvornik, Francis, *Origins of Intelligence Services: The Ancient Near East, Persia, Greece, Rome, Byzantium, the Arab Muslim Empires, the Mongol Empire, China, Muscovy* (New Brunswick, NJ, 1974)

Ecsedy, Hilda, 'Trade-and-War Relations between the Turks and China', *Acta Orientalia Hungaricae*, XXI (1968), pp. 131–80

Elverskog, Johan, *Buddhism and Islam on the Silk Road* (Philadelphia, PA, 2010)

Eurovision, 'Eurovision Song Contest 1979', at www.eurovision.tv, accessed 12 August 2010

Fiey, J. M, 'Chrétiens Syriaques sous les Mongols (Ilkhanat de Perse, XIIIE–XIVE s.)', *Corpus Scriptorum Christianorum Orientalium*, vol. CCCLXII, subsidia 44 (Louvain, 1975)

Findley, Carter Vaughn, *The Turks in World History* (Oxford, 2005)

Fisher, Alan W., 'The Ottoman Crimea in the Mid-Seventeenth Century: Some Problems and Preliminary Considerations', *Harvard Ukrainian Studies*, XXXIV/1 (1979–80), pp. 215–26

——, 'The Ottoman Crimea in the Sixteenth Century', *Harvard Ukrainian Studies*, V (1981–2), pp. 135–70

Fitzherbert, Teresa, 'Religious Diversity under Ilkhanid Rule c. 1300 as Reflected in the Freer Bal'ami', in *Beyond the Legacy of Genghis Khan*, ed. Linda Komaroff (Leiden, 2006)

Fitzhugh, William, Morris Rossabi and William Honeychurch, eds, *Genghis Khan and the Mongol Empire* (Seattle, WA, 2009)

Fogel, Joshua, 'Chinggis on the Japanese Mind', *Mongolian Studies*, XXXI (2009), pp. 259–70

Fragner, Bert G., 'Ilkhanid Rule and Its Contributions to Iranian Political Culture', in *Beyond the Legacy of Genghis Khan*, ed. Linda Komaroff (Leiden, 2006)

Gabriel, Richard, *Genghis Khan's Greatest General: Subotai the Valiant* (Norman, OK, 2006)

Golden, Peter, 'War and Warfare in the Pre-Cinggisid Western Steppes of Eurasia', in *Warfare in Inner Asian History, 500–1800*, ed. Nicola Di Cosmo (Leiden, 2002),

Goodrich, L. Carrington, 'Movable Type Printing: Two Notes', *Journal of the American Oriental Society*, XCIX (1974), pp. 476–7

Grabar, Oleg, *The Illustrations of the Maqamat* (Chicago, IL, 1983)

Gregoras, Nicephorus, *Historias Byzantina*, in *The Black Death: The Great Mortality of 1348–1350*, ed. John Aberth (Boston, MA, 2005)

Grigor of Akanc, 'The History of the Nation of the Archers', trans. Robert P. Blake and Richard N. Frye, *Harvard Journal of Asiatic Studies*, XII (1949), pp. 269–399

Grousset, Rene, *The Empire of the Steppes*, trans. Naomi Walford (New Brunswick, NJ, 1970)

Güyük Khan, 'Guyuk Khan's Letter to Pope Innocent IV (1246)', in *The Mission to Asia*, trans. a nun from Stanbrook Abbey, ed. Christopher Dawson (Toronto, 1980)

Guzman, Gregory G., 'European Captives and Craftsmen among the Mongols, 1231–1255', *The Historian*, LXXII/1 (2010), pp. 122–50

Halperin, Charles J., *Russia and the Golden Horde: The Mongol Impact on Medieval Russian History* (Bloomington, IN, 1985)

——, *The Tatar Yoke* (Columbus, OH, 1985)

——, 'The Kipchak Connection: The Ilkhans, the Mamluks and Ayn Jalut', *Bulletin of the School of Oriental and Asian Studies*, LXIII (2000), pp. 229–45

Hambly, Gavin, ed., *Central Asia* (New York, 1969)

Hartog, Leo de, *Genghis Khan: Conqueror of the World* (New York, 1989)

Haw, Stephen G., *Marco Polo's China: A Venetian in the Realm of Khubilai Khan* (London, 2009)

He Qiutao, *Sheng Wu Qin Zheng Lu (Bogda Bagatur Bey-e-Ber Tayilagsan Temdeglel)* ed. Arasaltu (Qayilar, 1985)

Herlihy, David, *The Black Death and the Transformation of the West* (Cambridge, MA, 1997)

Heywood, Colin, 'Filling the Black Hole: The Emergence of the Bithynian Atamanates', in *The Great Ottoman–Turkish Civilization*, vol. I, ed. K. Cicek *et al.*, (Ankara, 2000)

Hillenbrand, Robert, 'The Arts of the Book in Ilkhanid Iran', in *The Legacy of Genghis Khan*, ed. Linda Komaroff and Stefano Carboni (New Haven, CT, 2002)

Holmgren, Jennifer, 'Observations on Marriage and Inheritance Practices in Early Mongol and Yüan Society, with Particular Reference to the Levirate', *Journal of Asian History*, XVI (1986), pp. 127–92

Horrox, Rosemary, trans. and ed., *The Black Death* (Manchester, 1994)

Hsiao, Chi'i-ch'ing, trans., *The Military Establishment of the Yuan Dynasty* (Cambridge, MA, 1978), chs 98, 99

Hu, Dolores Menstell, 'Musical Elements of Chinese Opera', *Musical Quarterly*, L/4 (1964), pp. 439–51

Huc, Evariste-Regis and Joseph Gabet, *Travels in Tartary, Thibet and China, 1844–1846* (New York, 1987)

Ibn al-Athir, *al-Kamil fi al-Tarikh (The Complete History)* (Beirut, 1979)

Ibn Battuta, *Rihala Ibn Battuta* (Beirut, 1995)

Inalcik, H., 'The Khan and the Tribal Aristocracy: The Crimean Khanate under Sahib Giray I', *Harvard Ukrainian Studies*, III–IV/1 (1979–80), pp. 445–66

Innocent IV, Pope, 'Two Bulls of Pope Innocent IV Addressed to the Emperor of the Tartars' in *The Mission to Asia*, trans. a nun from Stanbrook Abbey, ed. Christopher Dawson (Toronto, 1980)

Jackson, Peter, 'The Dissolution of the Mongol Empire', *Central Asiatic Journal*, XXII (1978), pp. 186–244

——, 'Marco Polo and his "Travels"', *Bulletin of the School of Oriental and African Studies*, LXI/1 (1998), pp. 82–101

——, *The Delhi Sultanate, A Political and Military History* (Cambridge, 1999)

——, 'The State of Research: The Mongol Empire, 1986–1999', *Journal of Medieval History*, XXVI/2 (2000), pp. 189–210

——, *The Mongols and the West* (Harlow, 2005)

——, 'World Conquest and Local Accomodation: Threat and Blandishment in Mongol Diplomacy', in *History and Historiography of Post-Mongol Central Asia and the Middle East: Studies in Honor of John E. Woods*, ed. Judith Pfeiffer and Sholeh A. Quinn (Wiesbaden, 2006)

Jacoby, David, 'Silk Economies and Cross-Cultural Artistic Interaction: Byzantium, the Muslim World, and the Christian West', *Dumbarton Oaks Papers*, LVIII (2004), pp. 197–240

Jagchid, Sechin and Van Jay Symons, *Peace, War, and Trade Along the Great Wall: Nomadic-Chinese Interaction Through Two Millennia* (Bloomington, IN, 1989)

Jenkins, Gareth, 'A Note on Climatic Cycles and the Rise of Chingis Khan', *Central Asiatic Journal*, XVIII (1974), pp. 217–26

John of Plano Carpini, 'History of the Mongols', in *The Mission to Asia*, trans. a nun from Stanbrook Abbey, ed. Christopher Dawson (Toronto, 1980)

Joinville, Jean de, 'The Life of Saint Louis', in *Chronicles of the Crusades*, trans. and ed. M.R.B. Shaw (New York, 1963)

Juvaini, 'Ala al-Din Ata Malik, *Ta'rîkh-i-Jahân-Gusha (The History of the World-Conqueror)*, ed. Mîrza Muhammad Qazvini, 3 vols (Leiden, 1912, 1916, 1937)

——, *The History of the World-Conqueror*, trans. John A. Boyle (Seattle, WA, 1997)

Juzjani, Minhaj Siraj, *Tabaqat-i Nasiri*, vol. II, ed. 'Abd al-Hayy Habibi (Kabul, 1964–5)

——, *Tabakat-I Nasiri*, trans. H. G. Raverty (New Delhi, 1970)

Kadoi, Yuka, *Islamic Chinoiserie: The Art of Mongol Iran* (Edinburgh, 2009)

Kafadar, Cemal, *Between Two Worlds: The Construction of the Ottoman State* (Los Angeles, CA, 1995)

Kara, Gyorgy, 'Medieval Mongol Documents from Khara Khoto and East Turkestan in the St Petersburg Branch of the Institute of Oriental Studies', *Manuscripta Orientalia*, IX/2 (2003), pp. 28–30

Kauz, Ralph, 'The Maritime Trade of Kish During the Mongol Period', in *Beyond the Legacy of Genghis Khan*, ed. Linda Komaroff (Leiden, 2006)

Khan, Iqtidar Alam, *Gunpowder and Firearms: Warfare in Medieval India* (New Delhi, 2004)

Khazanov, Anatoly, 'Muhammad and Jenghis Khan Compared: The Religious Factor in World Empire Building', *Comparative Studies in Society and History*, XXXV (1993), pp. 461–79

——, 'The Spread of World Religions in Medieval Nomadic Societies of the Eurasian Steppes', *Toronto Studies in Central and Inner Asia*, I (1994), pp. 11–33

Khodarkovsky, Michael, *Russia's Steppe Frontier: The Making of a Colonial Empire, 1500–1800* (Bloomington, IN, 2002)

Kim, Hodong, 'The Early History of the Moghul Nomads: The Legacy of the Chaghatai Khanate', in *The Mongol Empire and Its Legacy*, ed. Reuven Amitai-Preiss and David O. Morgan (Leiden, 2001)

——, 'A Reappraisal of Güyüg Khan', in *Mongols, Turks, and Others: Eurasian Nomads and the Sedentary World*, ed. Reuven Amitai and Michal Biran (Leiden, 2005)

Kolbas, Judith, *The Mongols in Iran: Chingiz Khan to Uljaytu, 1220–1309* (London, 2009)

Komaroff, Linda, ed., *Beyond the Legacy of Genghis Khan* (Leiden, 2006).

Komaroff, Linda and Stefano Carboni, eds, *The Legacy of Genghis Khan: Courtly Art and Culture in Western Asia, 1256–1353* (New Haven, CT, 2002)

Komroff, Manuel, 'Afterword', in *The Travels of Marco Polo*, trans. William
    Marsden (New York, 2001)
Kouymjian, Dickran, 'Chinese Motifs in Thirteenth-Century Armenian Art:
    The Mongol Connection', in *Beyond the Legacy of Genghis Khan*, ed. Linda
    Komaroff (Leiden, 2006)
Kramarovsky, Mark G., 'Jochid Luxury Metalwork: Issues of Genesis and
    Development', in *Beyond the Legacy of Genghis Khan*, ed. Linda Komaroff
    (Leiden, 2006)
——, 'Conquerors and Craftsmen: Archaeology of the Golden Horde', in
    Genghis Khan and the Mongol Empire, ed. William Fitzhugh, Morris Rossabi
    and William Honeychurch (Seattle, WA, 2009)
K'uan-chung, Huang, 'Mountain Fortress Defence: The Experience of the
    Southern Sung and Korea in Resisting the Mongol Invasions', in *Warfare in
    Chinese History*, ed. Hans Van de Ven (Leiden, 2000)
Kucera, Joshua, 'The Search for Genghis Khan: Genghis Khan's Legacy Being
    Reappraised in China, Russia', *EurasiaNet.Org* (10 November 2009) at
    www.eurasianet.org, accessed 13 January 2011
Kumar, Sunil, 'The Ignored Elites: Turks, Mongols and a Persian Secretariat Class
    in the Early Delhi Sultanate', *Modern Asian Studies*, XLIII/1 (2009), pp. 45–77
Lal, Ruby, *Domesticity and Power in the Early Mughal World* (New York, 2005)
Lamb, Harold, *Genghis Khan: Emperor of All Men* (New York, 1927)
Lambton, Ann K. S., *Continuity and Change in Medieval Persia: Aspects of
    Administrative, Economic and Social History, 11th–14th Century* (Albany, NY, 1988)
Lane, George, *Early Mongol Rule in Thirteenth-Century Iran: A Persian Renaissance*
    (London, 2003)
——, *Genghis Khan and Mongol Rule* (Westport, CT, 2004)
Lattimore, Owen, 'Preface', in John. A. Boyle, *The Mongol World Empire, 1206–1370*
    (London, 1977)
Lemercier-Quelquejay, Chantal, 'The Kazakhs and the Kirghiz', in *Central Asia*,
    ed. Gavin Hambly (New York, 1969)
Lewisohn, Leonard, ed., *The Legacy of Mediaeval Persian Sufism* (London, 1992)
——, *Beyond Faith and Infidelity: The Sufi Poetry and Teachings of Mahmûd
    Shabistarî* (London, 1995)
Li Chih-Chang, *The Travels of an Alchemist* (London, 2005)
Liddell Hart, B. H., *Deterrent or Defense: A Fresh Look at the West's Military Position*
    (New York, 1960)
——, *The Liddell Hart Memoirs*, vol. 1 (New York, 1965)
——, *Great Captains Unveiled* (Freeport, NY, 1967)
——, *The German Generals Talk* (New York, 1979)
Lindner, Rudi Paul, 'What Was A Nomadic Tribe?', *Comparative Studies in Society
    and History*, XXIV/4 (1982), pp. 689–711
——, 'How Mongol were the Early Ottomans?', in *The Mongol Empire and Its
    Legacy*, ed. Reuven Amitai-Preiss and David O. Morgan (Leiden, 2001)
——, *Explorations in Pre-Ottoman History* (Ann Arbor, MI, 2007)
Little, Donald P., 'Diplomatic Missions and Gifts Exchanged by the Mamluks
    and Ilkhans', in *Beyond the Legacy of Genghis Khan*, ed. Linda Komaroff
    (Leiden, 2006)

Lorge, Peter A., *The Asian Military Revolution: From Gunpowder to the Bomb* (Cambridge, 2008)

McCleary, Rachel M. and Leonard W. J. Van der Kuijp, 'The Market Approach to the Rise of the Geluk School, 1419–1642', *Journal of Asian Studies*, LXIX/1 (2010), pp. 149–80

McNeill, William H., *Plagues and Peoples* (New York, 1998)

Manz, Beatrice Forbes, 'The Clans of the Crimean Khanate, 1466–1532', *Harvard Ukrainian Studies*, II (1978–9), pp. 282–309

——, *The Rise and Rule of Tamerlane* (Cambridge, 1989)

——, *Power, Politics, and Religion in Timurid Iran* (Cambridge, 2007)

al-Maqrizi, Ahmad ibn 'Ali, *Kitab al-Suluk li-M'arifat fi Dul al-Muluk* (Cairo, 1956)

Martin, Henry D., *The Rise of Chingis Khan and his Conquest of North China* (Baltimore, MD, 1950)

Martin, Janet, 'The Land of Darkness and the Golden Horde: The Fur Trade under the Mongols, XIII–XIV Centuries', *Cahiers du Monde Russe et Soviétique*, XIX (1978), pp. 401–22

Martinez, A. P., 'Some notes on the Il-Xanid Army', *Archivum Eurasiae Medii Aevi*, VI (1986), pp. 129–242

Marx, Christy, 'The Fantastic Mr Frump', *Spider-Man and His Amazing Friends*, dir. Don Jurwich, Season 1, Episode 3 (NBC, 26 September 1981)

May, Timothy, 'Attitudes towards Conversion among the Elite in the Mongol Empire', *E-ASPAC: The Electronic Journal of Asian Studies on the Pacific Coast* (2002–3), at http://mcel.pacificu.edu/easpac/2003/may.php3, accessed 27 August 2011

——, 'The Mechanics of Conquest and Governance: The Rise and Expansion of the Mongol Empire, 1185–1265', PhD dissertation, University of Wisconsin-Madison, 2004

——, 'Монголы и мировые религии в XIII веке' (The Mongols and World Religions in the 13th Century), in Монголъская Империя и Кочевой Мир (Mongolian Imperial and Nomadic Worlds), ed. N. N. Kradi and T. D. Skrynnikova (Ulan Ude, 2004)

——, 'Jamuqa and the Education of Chinggis Khan', *Acta Mongolica*, VI (2006), pp. 273–86

——, 'Mongol Resistance to Christian Conversion', in *Christianity and Mongolia: Past and Present – Proceedings of the Antoon Mostaert Symposium on Christianity and Mongolia*, ed. Gaby Bamana, 13–16 August 2006 (Ulaanbaatar, 2006)

——, *The Mongol Art of War* (Barnsley, 2007)

——, 'The Mongol Empire in World History', *World History Connected*, V/2 (2008), at http://worldhistoryconnected.press.uiuc.edu/5.2, accessed 11 June 2010

——, 'The Relationship Between Sufis and Inner Asian Ruling Elites', *Southeast Review of Asian Studies*, XXX (2008), pp. 84–101

——, *Culture and Customs of Mongolia* (Westport, CT, 2009)

Melville, Charles, 'The Mongols in Iran', in *Legacy of Genghis Khan*, ed. Linda Komaroff and Stefano Carboni (New Haven, CT, 2002)

——, 'The *Keshig* in Iran: The Survival of the Royal Mongol Household', in *Beyond the Legacy of Genghis Khan*, ed. Linda Komaroff (Leiden, 2006)

Michell, Robert and Nevill Forbes, trans., *The Chronicle of Novgorod, 1016–1471* (London, 1914)

Milius, John and Kevin Reynolds, *Red Dawn*, dir. John Milus (1984)

Moffet, Samuel Hugh, *A History of Christianity in Asia, Vol. 1: Beginnings to 1500* (New York, 1992)

Morgan, David O., 'Who Ran the Mongol Empire?', *Journal of the Royal Asiatic Society* (1982), pp. 124–36

——, 'Marco Polo in China – or Not', *Journal of the Royal Asiatic Society*, 3rd ser., VI (1996), pp. 221–5

——, 'Mongol or Persian: The Government of Ilkhanid Iran', *Harvard Middle Eastern and Islamic Review*, III (1996), pp. 62–76

——, 'The Mongols in Iran: A Reappraisal', *Iran*, XLII (2004), pp. 131–6

——, 'The Mongol Empire in World History', in *Beyond the Legacy of Genghis Khan*, ed. Linda Komaroff (Leiden, 2006)

——, *The Mongols*, 2nd edn (Oxford, 2007)

Moses, Larry W., 'A Theoretical Approach to the Process of Inner Asian Confederation', *Etudes Mongoles*, V (1974), pp. 113–22

Mote, Frederick W., *Imperial China, 900–1800* (Cambridge, MA, 2003)

Muhammad al-Nasawi, *Histoire du Sultan Djelal ed-din Mankobirti*, trans. Octave Houdas (Paris, 1895)

——, *Sirat al-Sultan Jalal al-Din Mankubirti* (Cairo, 1953)

Muhammad ibn Ahmad al-Dhahabi, *Kitab Duwal al-Islam*, trans. Arlette Negre (Damascus, 1979)

Muldoon, James, *Popes, Lawyers, and Infidels* (Philadelphia, PA, 1979)

Mussis, Gabriele de, 'Historia de Morbo', in *The Black Death*, trans. and ed. Rosemary Horrox (Manchester, 1994)

Nasonov, A. N., *Mongoly i Rus': Istoriia tatarskoi politiki na Rusi* (Moscow, 1940)

Naumov, Igor V., *The History of Siberia*, ed. David N. Collins (London, 2006)

Noonan, Thomas S., 'Medieval Russia, the Mongols, and the West: Novgorod's Relations with the Baltic, 1100–1350', *Medieval Studies*, XXXVII (1975), pp. 316–39

——, 'Russia's Eastern Trade, 1150–1350: The Archaeological Evidence', *Archivum Eurasiae Medii Aevi*, III (1983), pp. 201–64

al-Nuwayri, Ahmad ibn 'Abd al-Wahhab, *Nihayat al-Arab fi Funun al-Adabi* (Cairo, 1975)

O'Brien, Patrick, 'Historiographical Traditions and Modern Imperatives for the Restoration of Global History', *Journal of Global History*, I (2006), pp. 3–39

Okada, Hidehiro and Junko Miyawaki-Okada, 'Haslund's *Toregut Rarelro* in the Parallel Text in Ulaanbaatar', *Mongolian Studies*, XXIX (2007), pp. 123–40

Olcott, Martha Brill, *The Kazakhs*, 2nd edn (Stanford, CA, 1995)

Oliver of Paderborn, 'The Capture of Damietta', trans. Joseph J. Gavigan, in *Christian Society and the Crusades, 1198–1229*, ed. Edward Peters (Philadelphia, PA, 1971), pp. 49–140

Onon, Urgunge, trans., *The Secret History of the Mongols: The Life and Times of Chinggis Khan* (London, 2001)

Origo, Iris, 'The Domestic Enemy: The Eastern Slaves in Tuscany in the Fourteenth and Fifteenth Centuries', *Speculum*, XXX/3 (1955), pp. 321–66

Ostrowski, Donald, *Muscovy and the Mongols: Cross Cultural Influences on the Steppe Frontier, 1304–1589* (New York, 1998)

Page, Jeremy, 'Russians Who Get Drunk as a Warlord', *The Times* (19 January 2004)

Palmieri, Richard P., 'Tibetan Xylography and the Question of Movable Type', *Technology and Culture*, XXXII (1991), pp. 82–90

Paris, Matthew, *English History*, trans. and ed. J. A. Giles, 3 vols (New York, 1968)

Patterson, Ray, dir., *Scooby-Doo and the Reluctant Werewolf* (1988)

Pelenski, J. 'The Contest between Lithuania-Rus' and the Golden Horde in the Fourteenth Century for Supremacy over Eastern Europe', *Archivum Eurasiae Medii Aevi*, II (1982), pp. 303–20

Perdue, Peter C., *China Marches West: The Qing Conquest of Central Eurasia* (Cambridge, MA, 2005)

Perfecky, George, trans and ed., *The Hypatian Codex II: The Galician-Volynian Chronicle* (Munich, 1973)

Petech, Luciano, 'Tibetan Relations with Sung China and with the Mongols', in *China Among Equals*, ed. Morris Rossabi (Berkeley, CA, 1983)

Petrushevsky, I. P., 'Socio-Economic Conditions of Iran under the Ilkhans', in *Cambridge History of Iran*, ed. J. A. Boyle (Cambridge, 1968)

Pfeiffer, Judith, 'Ahmad Teguder's Second Letter to Qala'un (682/1283)', in *History and Historiography of Post-Mongol Central Asia and the Middle East: Studies in Honor of John E. Woods*, ed. Judith Pfeiffer and Sholeh A. Quinn (Wiesbaden, 2006)

——, 'Reflections on a "Double Rapprochement": Conversion to Islam among the Mongol Elite during the Early Ilkhanate', in *Beyond the Legacy of Genghis Khan*, ed. Linda Komaroff (Leiden, 2006)

Pfeiffer, Judith, and Sholeh A. Quinn, eds, *History and Historiography of Post-Mongol Central Asia and the Middle East: Studies in Honor of John E. Woods* (Wiesbaden, 2006)

Pierce, Leslie P., *The Imperial Harem: Women and Sovereignty in the Ottoman Empire* (Oxford, 1993)

Polo, Marco, *Description of the World*, trans. A. C. Moule and P. Pelliot (London, 1938)

——, *The Travels*, trans. Ronald Latham (New York, 1958)

——, *The Travels of Marco Polo*, trans. Henry Yule (New York, 1992)

——, *The Travels of Marco Polo*, trans. William Marsden, ed. Manuel Komroff (New York, 2001)

Porter, Patrick, *Military Orientalism: Eastern War through Western Eyes* (New York, 2009)

Prazniak, Roxann, 'Siena on the Silk Roads: Ambrogio Lorenzetti and the Mongol Global Century, 1250–1350', *Journal of World History*, XXI (2010), pp. 177–218

Rachewiltz, Igor de, 'Some Remarks on the Ideological Foundations of Chingis Khan's Empire', *Papers on Far Eastern History*, VII (1973), pp. 21–36

——, 'Marco Polo Went to China', *Zentralasiatishe Studien*, XXVII (1997), pp. 34–92

——, trans. and ed., *The Secret History of the Mongols* (Leiden, 2004)

Raglan, Fitzroy, *The Hero: A Study in Tradition, Myth, and Drama* (New York, 1937)

Rashid al-Din, *Jami' al-Tawarikh*, ed. B. Karimi (Tehran, 1983)

——, *Jami' al-Tawarikh*, ed. Muhammad Rushn Mustafi Musavi (Tehran, 1995)

——, *Jami'u't-tawarikh: Compendium of Chronicles*, trans. W. M. Thackston (Cambridge, MA, 1998)

Ratchnevsky, Paul, *Genghis Khan: His Life and Legacy*, trans. Thomas Nivison Haining (Cambridge, MA, 1992)

Rehm, Peter, 'Ventures into the Reign of Osman: A New Consensus on Early Ottoman Historiography', *Études Historiques*, II/1 (2010), at www.etudeshis-toriques.org, accessed 1 September 2011

Robinson, David M., *Empire's Twilight: Northeast Asia Under the Mongols* (Philadelphia, PA, 2009)

Rogers, Greg S., 'An Examination of Historians' Explanations for the Mongol Withdrawal from East Central Europe', *East European Quarterly*, XXX (1996), pp. 3–27

Rossabi, Morris, *China and Inner Asia: From 1368 to the Present Day* (New York, 1975)

——, *Khubilai Khan: His Life and Times* (Berkeley, CA, 1988)

——, 'The Mongols and Their Legacy', in *The Legacy of Genghis Khan*, ed. Linda Komaroff and Stefano Carboni (New Haven, CT, 2002)

——, 'The Vision in the Dream: Kublai Khan and the Conquest of China', in *Genghis Khan and the Mongol Empire*, ed. William Fitzhugh, Morris Rossabi and William Honeychurch (Bellingham, WA, 2009)

——, *Voyager from Xanadu: Rabban Sauma and the First Journey from China to the West* (Berkeley, CA, 2010)

Roux, J. P., 'La tolérance religieuse dans l'empires Turco-Mongols', *Revue de l'Histoire des Religions*, CCIII (1986), pp. 131–68

Ruotsala, Antti, *Europeans and Mongols in the Middle of the Thirteenth Century: Encountering the Other* (Helsinki, 2001)

Ryan, James D., 'Christian Wives of Mongol Khans: Tartar Queens and Missionary Expectations in Asia', *Journal of the Royal Asiatic Society*, 3rd ser., VIII/3 (1998), pp. 411–21

Sabloff, Paula, 'Why Mongolia? The Political Culture of an Emerging Democracy', *Central Asian Survey*, XXI/1 (2002), pp. 19–36

Sagaster, Klaus, 'The History of Buddhism among the Mongols', in *The Spread of Buddhism*, ed. Ann Heirmann and Stephan Peter Bumbacher (Leiden, 2007), pp. 379–432.

Saliba, George, 'Horoscopes and Planetary Theory: Ilkhanid Patronage of Astronomers', in *Beyond the Legacy of Genghis Khan*, ed. Linda Komaroff (Leiden, 2006)

Sanctus, Louis, 'Letter April 27, 1348', in John Aberth, *The Black Death: The Great Mortality of 1348–1350* (Boston, MA, 2005), pp. 21–22

Saunders, J. J., 'The Mongol Defeat at Ain Jalut and the Restoration of the Greek Empire', *Muslims and Mongols: Essays on Medieval Asia*, ed. Geoffrey Rice (Christchurch, 1977)

——, *The History of the Mongol Conquests* (Philadelphia, PA, 2001)

Schamiloglu, Uli, 'The Qaraci Beyes of the Later Golden Horde: Notes on the Organization of the Mongol World Empire', *Archivum Eurasie Medii Aevi*, IV (1984), pp. 283–97

——, 'Preliminary Remarks on the Role of Disease in the History of the Golden Horde', *Central Asian Survey*, XII/4 (1993), pp. 447–57

——, 'The Rise of the Ottoman Empire: The Black Death in Medieval Anatolia and Its Impact on Turkish Civilization', in *Views from the Edge: Essays in Honor of Richard W. Bulliet*, ed. Nguin Yavari, Lawrence G. Potter and Jean-Marc Ran Oppenheim (New York, 2004)

Schurmann, H. F., *Economic Structure of the Yuan Dynasty* (Cambridge, 1956)

——, 'Mongolian Tributary Practices of the Thirteenth Century', *Harvard Journal of Asiatic Studies*, XIX (1956), pp. 304–89

Schwarz, Henry G., 'Some Notes on the Mongols of Yunnan', *Central Asiatic Journal*, XXVIII (1994), pp. 100–18

Scott, Susan and Christopher J. Duncan, *Biology of Plagues: Evidence from Historical Populations* (Cambridge, 2001)

Seth, Michael J., *A Concise History of Korea: From the Neolithic Period through the Nineteenth Century* (Lanham, MD, 2006)

Shakespeare, William, *Much Ado About Nothing*, Act II, Scene II

Sherman, Irwin W., *The Power of Plagues,* (Washington, DC, 2006)

Shiraishi, Noriyuki, 'Avarga Site: The "Great Ordu" of Genghis Khan', in *Beyond the Legacy of Genghis Khan*, ed. Linda Komaroff (Leiden, 2006)

Simon de Saint-Quentin, *Histoire des Tartares*, ed. Jean Richard (Paris, 1965)

Sinor, Denis, ed., *The Cambridge History of Early Inner Asia* (Cambridge, 1987)

——, 'Notes on Inner Asian Bibliography IV: History of the Mongols in the 13th Century', *Journal of Asian History*, XXIII/1 (1989), pp. 26–79

Skrynnikova, Tatyana D., *Kharizma vlasti v epokhu Chingiskhana* (Moscow, 1997)

——, 'Relations of Domination and Submission: Political Practice in the Mongol Empire of Chinggis Khan', in *Imperial Statecraft: Political Forms and Techniques of Governance in Inner Asia, Sixth–Twentieth Centuries*, ed. David Sneath (Bellingham, WA, 2006)

Smith Jr, John Masson, 'Mongol and Nomadic Taxation', *Harvard Journal of Asiatic Studies*, XXX (1970), pp. 46–85

——, 'Mongol Manpower and Persian Population', *Journal of the Economic and Social History of the Orient*, XVIII/3 (1975), pp. 271–99

——, 'Ayn Jalut: Mamluk Success or Mongol Failure?', *Harvard Journal of Asiatic Studies*, XLIV (1984), pp. 307–45

——, 'Mongol Society and Military in the Middle East: Antecedents and Adaptations', in *War and Society in the Eastern Mediterranean, 7th and 15th Centuries*, ed. Yaacov Lev (Leiden, 1996)

——, 'Hülegü Moves West: High Living and Heartbreak on the Road to Baghdad', in *Beyond the Legacy of Genghis Khan*, ed. Linda Komaroff (Leiden, 2006)

Sneath, David, *The Headless State: Aristocratic Orders, Kinship Society, and Misrepresentations of Nomadic Inner Asia* (New York, 2007)

——, ed., *Imperial Statecraft: Political Forms and Techniques of Governance in Inner Asia, Sixth–Twentieth Centuries* (Bellingham, WA, 2006)

Soudavar, Abol al a, 'The Mongol Legacy of Persian *Farmans*', in *Beyond the Legacy of Genghis Khan*, ed. Linda Komaroff (Leiden, 2006)

Spuler, Bertold, *The Mongol Period*, trans. F.R.C. Bagley (Princeton, NJ, 1969)

Stewart, Angus, 'The Assassination of King Het'um II: The Conversion of the
    Ilkhans and the Armenians', *Journal of the Royal Asiatic Society*, 3rd ser., xv/1
    (2005), pp. 45–61
Storm from the East: From Genghis Khan to Khubilai Khan [TV series] (London, 1993)
Strawson, Jack, *Hitler as Military Commander* (New York, 1971)
Stuart, Kevin, *Mongols in Western/American Consciousness* (Lewiston, NY, 1997)
Subtelny, Maria E. *Timurids in Transition: Turko-Persian Politics and Acculturation
    in Medieval Iran* (Leiden, 2007)
Suenaga, Takezaki, 'Takezaki Suenaga's Scrolls of the Mongol Invasions of
    Japan', at www.bowdoin.edu/mongol-scrolls, accessed 22 November 2010
Sun, Guang-Zhen, 'Nasir al-Din Tusi on Social Cooperation and the Division of
    Labor: Fragment from the Nasirean Ethics', *Journal of Institutional
    Economics*, iv/3 (2008), pp. 403–13
Szuppe, Maria, 'Women in Sixteenth Century Safavid Iran', in *Women In Iran from
    the Rise of Islam to 1800*, ed. Guity Nashat and Lois Beck (Urbana, IL, 2003)
Togan, Isenbike, *Flexibility and Limitation in Steppe Formations: The Kerait Khanate
    and Chinggis Khan* (Leiden, 1998)
Tsepkov, A. E., trans., *Ermolinskaia Letopis'* (Riazan, 2000)
Turchin, Peter, 'A Theory for Formation of Large Empires', *Journal of Global
    History*, IV (2009), pp. 191–217
Vasary, Istvan, 'The Golden Horde Term Daruga and Its Survival in Russia', *Acte
    Orientale Hungarica*, xxx (1976), pp. 187–97
——, 'The Origin of the Institution of Basqaqs', *Acte Orientale Hungarica*, xxxii
    (1978), pp. 201–6
——, 'History and Legend in Berke Khan's Conversion to Islam', in *Aspects of
    Altaic Civilization III*, ed. Denis Sinor (Bloomington, IN, 1990)
——, *Cumans and Tatars: Oriental Military in the Pre-Ottoman Balkans, 1185–1365*
    (Cambridge, 2005)
Vernadsky, George, *The Mongols and Russia* (New Haven, CT, 1953)
Vyronis, Speros, *The Decline of Medieval Hellenism in Asia Minor and the Process of
    Islamization from the Eleventh through the Fifteenth Century* (Berkeley, CA, 1971)
Wade, Geoff, 'An Early Age of Commerce in Southeast Asia, 900–1300 CE',
    Journal of Southeast Asian Studies, XL/2 (2009), pp. 221–65
Waldron, Arthur. 'Introduction', in Bertold Spuler, *The Mongol Period*, trans.
    F.R.C. Bagley (Princeton, NJ, 1994)
Watson, Oliver, 'Pottery under the Mongols', in *Beyond the Legacy of Genghis
    Khan*, ed. Linda Komaroff (Leiden, 2006)
Watt, James C. Y., 'A Note on Artistic Exchanges in the Mongol Empire', in *The
    Legacy of Genghis Khan*, ed. Linda Komaroff and Stefano Carboni (New
    Haven, CT, 2002)
Waugh, Daniel, 'The Golden Horde and Russia', in *Genghis Khan and the Mongol
    Empire*, ed. William Fitzhugh, Morris Rossabi and William Honeychurch
    (Seattle, WA, 2009)
Weatherford, Jack, 'A Scholarly Quest to Understand Genghis Khan', *Chronicle of
    Higher Education*, XLVI/32 (14 April 2000)
——, *Genghis Khan and the Making of the Modern World* (New York, 2004)
——, *The Secret History of the Mongol Queens: How the Daughters of Genghis Khan*

Rescued His Empire (New York, 2010)

Whitaker, Leslie, *The Beardstown Ladies' Common-Sense Investment Guide: How We Beat the Stock Market – And How You Can, Too* (New York, 1996)

William of Rubruck, 'The Journey of William of Rubruck', in *The Mission to Asia*, trans. a nun from Stanbrook Abbey, ed. Christopher Dawson (Toronto, 1980)

——, 'Itinerarium Willelmi de Rubruc', in *Sinica Franciscana: Itinera et Relationes Fratrum Minorum Saeculi XIII et XIV*, ed. P. Anastasius Van Den Vyngaert (Florence, 1929)

Wing, Patrick, 'The Decline of the Ilkhanate and the Mamluk Sultanate's Eastern Frontier', *Mamluk Studies Review*, XI/2 (2007), pp. 77–88

Wink, Andre, *Al-Hind: The Making of the Indo-Islamic World, Vol. 2: The Slave Kings and Islamic Conquest, 11th–13th Centuries* (Leiden, 1997)

Wood, Frances, *Did Marco Polo Go to China?* (Boulder, CO, 1996)

Woods, John, *The Timurid Dynasty* (Bloomington, IN, 1990)

——, *The Aqquyunlu: Clan, Confederation, Empire* (Salt Lake City, UT, 1999)

Wordsworth, Araminta, 'Saddam Plays on Fears of Mongol Devastation: Genghis Khan's Warriors Destroyed 13th-century Iraq', *National Post* (22 January 2003), p. A15

Wright, David C., 'Navies in the Mongol Yuan Conquest of Southern Song China, 1274–1279', *Mongolian Studies*, XXIX (2007), pp. 207–16

Wyatt, James C. Y., 'A Note on Artistic Exchanges in the Mongol Empire', in *Legacy of Genghis Khan*, ed. Linda Komaroff and Stefano Carboni (New Haven, CT, 2002)

Zaky, A. Rahman, 'Introduction to the Study of Islamic Arms and Armour', *Gladius*, I (1961), pp. 17–29

Zelentz, Alan, *Thor*, 1/334 (1983)

Zenkovsky, Serge A., ed., *Medieval Russia's Epics, Chronicles, and Tales* (New York, 1974)

Zerjal, Tatiana, Yali Xue, *et al.*, 'The Genetic Legacy of the Mongols', *American Journal of Human Genetics*, LXXII (2003), pp. 717–21

Zhao, George Qingzhai, *Marriage as Political Strategy and Cultural Expression: Mongolian Royal Marriages from World Empire to Yuan Dynasty* (New York, 2008)

Ziegler, Philip, *The Black Death* (New York, 1969)

ACKNOWLEDGEMENTS

As with all books, it is rarely a solo effort. I owe a great deal of gratitude to a number of people. The first is Jeremy Black, editor of the Globalities series, who invited me to write the book in the first place. A number of people also suffered through the initial drafts. Their comments undoubtedly made my writing better, although any mistakes, alas, remain my own despite the best efforts of Anne Broadbridge of the University of Massachussetts, Amherst, who gave valuable input on the first chapters; Paul Buell of Charité – Universitätsmedizin Berlin who read and commented on all chapters as well as providing his usual assistance with Chinese sources, transliterations and the odd word in Tibetan, and a second opinion on Mongolian; David Morgan of the University of Wisconsin; and my research assistant Holly Hansen, who probably learned more about the Mongols than she had planned in the course of a semester. She also lent tremendous aid in the selection of illustrations. The comments of my editors and the anonymous reader were thoughtful and reasonable and greatly improved this book. The patience of my editors, Michael Leaman and John O'Donovan, at Reaktion Books is also to be commended. I believe both have a chance at sainthood. My students at North Georgia College & State University through the years in all classes have inevitably been lectured on the Mongols in world history. Those lectures are the basis of much of this book. Jim Feken is also thanked not only for the random cultural-media references but also for having to put up with a number of 'It's Chinggis, dammit!' rants through the years. My department at North Georgia College & State University kindly respected my 'writing time' and only asked me to act as department head during that time when absolutely necessary. Finally, thanks to my wife and children who tiptoed around me while I wrote and edited from home during the Georgia Blizzard of 2011 and made revisions while housebound after surgery during summer 2011, and who also made sure I went sledding or raced in Mario Carts every so often.

PHOTO ACKNOWLEDGEMENTS

Art Resource: pp. 41 (Bibliothèque Nationale, Paris: Snark / Art Resource, NY), 58 (Library, Golestan Palace, Tehran, Iran: Werner Forman / Art Resource, NY), 65 (Victoria and Albert Museum, London: Art Resource, NY), 68 (Bibliothèque Nationale, Paris: Bridgeman-Giraudon / Art Resource, NY), 84 (bpk, Berlin / Staatsbibliothek zu Berlin – Preussischer Kulturbesitz / Art Resource, NY), 114 (Bibliothèque Nationale, Paris: Scala / White Images / Art Resource, NY), 134 (Bibliothèque Nationale, Paris: Art Resource, NY), 135 (bpk, Berlin / Staatsbibliothek zu Berlin – Preussischer Kulturbesitz / Ruth Schacht / Art Resource, NY), 160 (bpk, Berlin / British Library London / Lutz Braun / Art Resource, NY), 181 (British Museum, London: Snark / Art Resource, NY), 184 (bpk, Berlin / Staatsbibliothek zu Berlin – Preussischer Kulturbesitz / Ellwardt. / Art Resource, NY), 218 (bpk, Berlin / Staatsbibliothek zu Berlin – Preussischer Kulturbesitz / Ruth Schacht / Art Resource, NY), 221 (Bibliothèque Nationale, Paris: Scala / White Images / Art Resource, NY), 226 (The Philadelphia Museum of Art / Art Resource, NY), 237 (bpk, Berlin / Staatsbibliothek zu Berlin – Preussischer Kulturbesitz / Ellwardt. / Art Resource, NY), 239 (image © The Metropolitan Museum of Art. Image source: Art Resource, NY), 240 (British Museum London: Erich Lessing / Art Resource, NY), 242 (Bibliothèque Nationale, Paris: Scala / White Images / Art Resource, NY), 243 (bpk, Berlin / Staatsbibliothek zu Berlin – Preussischer Kulturbesitz / Ruth Schacht / Art Resource, NY), 246 (S. Francesco, Siena: Scala / Art Resource, NY), 253 (image © The Metropolitan Museum of Art. Image source: Art Resource, NY); courtesy of the author: pp. 26, 56, 108, 116, 117, 120, 193, 220, 254; The Granger Collection: pp. 19 (The Granger Collection, NY – all rights reserved), 36 (Rue des Archives / The Granger Collection, NY – all rights reserved), 44 (The Granger Collection, NY – all rights reserved), 45 (The Granger Collection, NY – all rights reserved), 46 (Rue des Archives / The Granger Collection, NY – all rights reserved), 61 (The Granger Collection, NY – all rights reserved), 123 (The Granger Collection, NY – all rights reserved), 222 (The Granger Collection, NY – all rights reserved).

INDEX